THE COMING OF WAR

THE COMING OF WAR

*An Account of the Remarkable Events
Leading to the War of 1812*

BY ALBERT Z. CARR

Doubleday & Company, Inc., Garden City, New York
1960

FOR ANNE

Contents

(continued)

CONTENTS

CONCLUSION: ON THE COMING OF WAR

Introduction

For decades prior to 1812, England and America carried on a bitter diplomatic contest marked by sporadic violence, but they managed to avoid open warfare. Although they were on the brink of war in 1794, and again in 1807, 1809, and 1810, each time the danger was met by negotiation, and was followed by revived hopes of peace. Then all at once, in a crisis no more serious than those which had gone before, a new combination of circumstances pushed President James Madison to his reluctant decision that the war must be fought.

In many respects the forces that generated the War of 1812 were a rudimentary anticipation of the pressures of our own era. Then as now, the minds of men were focused on the personalities and transient crises of high politics, while the world below was in the grip of a vast social upheaval. Then as now, a swelling surge in the populations of the great powers was dislocating established ways of life; new inventions and techniques were breaking familiar economic and military patterns; comfortable ideas about the proper organization of society were being challenged by startling doctrines of radical change. Then, as in the years prior to 1917 and 1941, America, in spite of fancied isolation, was gradually sucked into the vortex of a foreign struggle for world dominion.

Professor Herbert Butterfield of Cambridge University, in his *History and Human Relations*, expresses the arresting thought that the function of history is to help us realize the problems of the past as problems of the present, or even of the future.

> "As the historiography of a given episode comes to be further removed from the passions of those who were active in the drama, it uncovers at the basis of the story a fundamental human predicament . . . Contemporaries fail to see the predicament or refuse to recognize its genuineness . . . [It] is only with the progress of historical science that men come really to recognize that there was a terrible knot almost beyond the ingenuity of man to untie."

Time has given us enough perspective so that we can now trace with some assurance the main strands of "the terrible knot" as it took shape in the years before 1812. We can see that the pressures toward war stemmed not merely from political events, but from the passionate attachment of men to their established ways, from their desperate reluctance to discard outworn ideas and modify laggard institutions in the face of a changing distribution of world power. There were of course continuous provocations on both sides, bursts of indignation, mutual threats and abuse, but beneath this emotional effervescence was the driving urge of the two nations to escape from a sense of profound frustration. Most Englishmen and Americans at the time, even those who did not want war, felt a sense of relief when it came. Nerve tissue had worn thin; whatever its perils, the war put an end to tensions and uncertainties which had been too long endured.

The coming of the War of 1812 exemplifies an obvious but often neglected fact: that a nation challenges another in the fatally provocative terms preliminary to war only because its leaders have chosen to use such terms. The passions of the ordinary citizen may be whipped into a frenzy by actual events or by artificial propaganda, but his passions in themselves do not produce the war unless the country's leaders yield to them. War expresses limitations of the leaders in at least one of the combatant countries—their mental limitations, which prevent them from seeing possible values in diplomatic negotiation without war; their moral limitations, which make them callous to human interests other than their own; and their physical limitations, which may result in a flagging of energy and a consequent deadening of the imaginative faculties necessary to preserve peace.

The "causes" which historians often assign for wars—desire for territory, economic competition, religious antagonism, and the like—are not truly causes. They are only motives for conflict which persist in peacetime as well as in war. Where leaders on both sides are competent men dedicated to peace, these pressures are adjusted without war. But for the firmness of George Washington the United States in 1794 would have fought England. Most Americans in 1797 wanted war with France, but John Adams insisted on continued diplomatic relations. In 1807 Thomas Jefferson resisted popular pressure for war after England had repeatedly outraged American patriotic feelings. Regardless of motive, a war usually does not occur until the leaders of a nation—the small group of personalities who control the government's official actions—issue the irrevocable order to commence firing.

For that reason a considerable amount of attention has been given in these pages to the individuals who held the historical stage as the eighteenth century ended and the nineteenth began. The ways in which they obtained and exercised power, their motives, attitudes, beliefs, and idiosyncracies are not only a valid part of the narrative; they touch its very heart. One might as well try to explain the human body without reference to its bloodstream as to describe a passage of history without recognizing the constant interaction between social forces and personality. There is no way of disentangling the event from the man, and in the fusion of the two lies much of the fascination of the past.

This is not to suggest that the individual, while he may move and shake the age, actually sets its course. On the contrary, it often seems as if the larger decisions of leaders are compelled rather than willed—as if their choice is actually quite narrow, despite a superficial appearance of self-assertion. The telling stroke of politics may turn out, under close analysis, to be something which its author did only with much reluctance. A keen ear for the whispers of necessity is the great man's final reliance. His fortune is made or broken not so much by his plans as by the quality of his instinctive response to events coming out of the blue. Of course, few statesmen care to admit the extent to which they are prodded by the unexpected and dependent on the unpredictable. In retrospect, they will not infrequently let it be understood that they controlled or dominated situations to which, in fact, they had only reacted. As Kipling says, "Men who stand or fall by the errors of their opponents may be forgiven if they turn Chance into Design."

A degree of skepticism especially needs to be brought to the personal statements and memoirs in which many national heroes have presented themselves to posterity. For example, Napoleon Bonaparte, in his rueful, boastful, reminiscent days on St. Helena, told his biographer, Las Cases, that it was he who had "developed the measures which compelled America to fight England in 1812." This was a characteristic overstatement. His power to manipulate events had never been so godlike as he wished the world to believe. He, too, was a creature of circumstance. To be sure, he had an extraordinary intuition of political reality, and like a skillful surgeon was from time to time able to touch diplomatic nerves to which the American government responded, almost by reflex. Three times, unmistakably, he turned American bellicosity away from France and toward England. But this is far from saying that he brought about the war.

The large impersonal forces and odd chances that led to the conflict expressed themselves through many major personalities of the period, besides Napoleon. His special role lay in the fact that he knew more clearly than the rest what he was doing. For in his time, as in our own, the coil of war was wound up largely by men who were convinced that they were working for peace. There was Lord Shelburne, who hoped for lasting amity between England and America; John Jay and Alexander Hamilton, who sought to conciliate British opinion; William Pitt, who tried to avoid the American war; John Adams, who wished no part in European embroilments; George Canning, who relied for peace on the techniques of diplomacy; Thomas Jefferson, who considered war a menace to democracy; Tecumseh, who wished only to protect his people; and many another. These men tried to restrain the haughty British sea captains, the arrogant West Indian planters, the sharp New England manufacturers, the Canadian fur traders, the firebrand Ohio editors, the intriguing French diplomats, the embittered Irish *émigrés*, the fanatical Indians, and the southern planters who saw war as a solution for their special problems. The advocates of peace were powerful, they were ardent, but again and again their well-intended actions merely provided new grounds of hostility, again and again their hopes were dashed as some spectacular coincidence played into the hands of the war parties. In the end, chance, as always, proved to be the master of politics.

While the political pattern of the period with which this story deals has much in common with our own era, in spirit we are almost as far away from it as we are from ancient Greece. Its optimistic faith in the power of reason, its respect for form and tradition, its slow communications and puny instruments of destruction created a political atmosphere as different from the one we breathe (with its charge of strontium 90) as a stately minuet is different from the mutating rhythms of jazz. Even the greatest poets of that time could not in their wildest flights of imagination guess at the colossal forces which science was preparing to release, and which would test as never before the adaptability of the human species.

Yet although men then had only a few technical contrivances, such as guns and telescopes, with which to shrink distance, their thoughts roamed high and far. Intelligence of an extraordinary richness and complexity marked the period, especially in the field of statesmanship. And perhaps this was in part because statesmen then did not have to stuff their minds with so many facts and statistics, file so many reports, give so many interviews, make so many speeches, and had time to concentrate on concepts, principles, and personalities. Their techniques of communication were pitifully inferior to our own, but the men concerned seem to have had more of substance to communicate. Unable to pick up a telephone, compelled to write numerous and lengthy letters for the careful scrutiny of critical minds, they had to think deeply and argue closely. Whatever the reason, the game of international diplomacy was never played more skillfully than in the world's chancelleries a century and more ago. At no other period of history were the wagers made and the dice tossed by gamblers so absorbed in the play, and at the same time so well-developed as human beings. There was an abundance then, or so it seems by comparison with our own time, of men of universal outlook, profound understanding of human nature, and power of expression—men of talent, of learning, of discriminating taste, and of open mind. A Winston Churchill would not have been quite so unique in the age which produced Franklin, Washington, Jefferson, Hamilton, Fox, Pitt, and Napoleon. It is true that the statesmen of that age did not succeed, any more than those of our own time, in mastering the "fundamental human predicament." But perhaps they came closer to an understanding of the nature of that predicament than most contemporary men of power, and perhaps we can learn something from their experience.

A comprehensive description of the historical road to any important war would of course fill many volumes. This book certainly does not pretend to be the whole story, but it may approximate the essential story. So as not to impede its flow, some thousands of references notes which once threatened to clot these pages have been omitted. It will be recognized that the book is essentially an informal narrative. At some points, in reconstructing the motives of individual statesmen where the documentary evidence is not conclusive, reasoned estimates of the information known to them and impressionistic appraisals of their states of mind have been allowed to supplement the factual record.

I am deeply grateful to Dr. Lawrence S. Finkelstein of the Carnegie Endowment for International Peace for his kindness in providing an invaluable general critique of the manuscript, and for perceptive and helpful readings from the standpoint of the specialized historian by Dr. Roger H. Brown of Harvard University, and Dr. David L. Jacobson of Princeton University. (It is hardly necessary to add that responsibility for all statements made and views expressed in the book is wholly mine.) Warm thanks go also to Mrs. Elizabeth Bartlett Gordon for the high competence with which she prepared the manuscript for publicaton. The Bibliography suggests the extent of my obligation to the many eminent historians and biographers on whose work I have drawn.

A.Z.C.

Truro, Mass.

PART ONE

THE PEACEMAKERS
1782–1783

CHAPTER ONE

The Shelburne Way

1. *Stocks Fall in London*

The stream of events leading to the War of 1812 can conveniently be entered a generation earlier, in 1782. The choice of this year is by no means arbitrary. The diplomatic adventures of 1782 were largely responsible for the character of the treaty of peace signed a few months later by England and the United States, and which contained the seeds of future violent dispute. As is often the way, the ending of the last war marked the beginning of the troubles that led to the next. Thirty years before the dilemma of 1812 presented itself to President Madison, it had begun to evolve.

Seventeen eighty-two, it will be recalled, found western Europe in a state of bubbling ferment. The main topic of the time was the exhausting sea struggle which France, Spain, and Holland were waging against weary England in the hope of pulling her down from her high place, under the guise of aid to the American revolutionists. But beneath the surface of the war, issues greater than naval power and colonial empire were asserting themselves. Change was in the air. New ideas agitated the minds of men; new movements shook their politics; new discoveries excited their imaginations. The almost Punic commerce that had ruled the world was yielding ground as the industrial revolution gnawed at the established organizations and ways of society. A far higher proportion of available money than ever before was coming into the tills of manufacturers and tradesmen; and their political influence rose with their wealth, threatening the age-long hold of the landed gentry on the governments of the great nations. At the same time, soaring birth rates were pressing hard on available supplies of food and housing, and the degraded condition of urban labor sent waves of unrest through the slums of the great cities.

England especially seethed with potentiality and frustration. The British had swallowed the humiliation of defeat at the hands of Washington's hodgepodge army; they had glumly put up with food scarcity and high prices; but with each day they became increasingly outraged by the war's futility. Military victories might justify hard times and shrinking profits, but where were the victories? Members of Parliament wrung their hands over the government's folly in not having accepted a proposal by the French a year earlier for a negotiated peace, which would have allowed the British to retain many of their American colonies. But at that time England's hopes had been high: General Benedict Arnold had just deserted from Washington's army, and there were rumors of dissension between France and America. In the resulting burst of false confidence, stubborn King George III had refused even to consider the French offer. Then came the shocking news of Cornwallis's surrender at Yorktown. The effect on public opinion was shown by a panic in stock prices on the Royal Exchange. British Consolidated Funds, the mirror of the government's credit, fell by over 50 per cent. Once the men of money had reappraised the outlook and found it bleak, the will to fight of the politicians thinned rapidly away. A powerful attack was promptly launched in Parliament on the war-to-the-end Tory government of Lord North, and late in February 1782, his imminent fall was widely rumored.

2.   *Dr. Franklin Writes a Letter*

London newspapers foretelling a change in the government were carried across the Channel to Paris, where they were read with enthusiasm, as presaging the end of the war. Among the diplomats stimulated by the news was the man generally recognized as one of the two greatest living Americans, Benjamin Franklin, then the envoy of the Continental Congress to the court of France. He was especially interested in learning that one of the leaders of the opposition to North was an old friend of his, the Earl of Shelburne, who was profoundly sympathetic to American aspirations. If Shelburne were to have a place in the next British government, could their personal friendship help to speed the anticipated peace? It was a question of great moment to Franklin. The survival of the rickety confederation of American states might depend on days gained or lost in ending the war. Lacking executive powers, disorganized, disastrously short of money, the Congress could barely maintain a pretense of influence over the contentious, suspicious, and jealously sovereign states. There was a sense of desperation in Philadelphia. The Secretary of Foreign Affairs to the Congress, Robert Livingston, had written to Franklin that "the treasury is empty . . . The people pant for peace." George Washington himself summed up the military position: "The long sufferance of the army is almost exhausted. It is high time for peace." Recruits for his weary forces were so few that he even advocated the enrollment of Hessian prisoners in the army. A little more war, regardless of how the battles went, and the flimsy federal structure might easily disintegrate, and the chief gains of the revolution be lost. No man who had dedicated his life to American unity and independence could contemplate this possibility without anguish.

To communicate secretly with Shelburne was Franklin's immediate thought—but how? After the outbreak of the revolution they had managed to maintain a private correspondence until some of Franklin's letters were intercepted and read by Lord North's agents. In spite of the false names with which the doctor had been careful to sign these missives, his identity was suspected; and in 1780 a Tory member of Parliament, Colonel Fullarton, openly accused Shelburne of corresponding "with an enemy of his country." It was a charge difficult to evade. To protect his reputation the Earl felt it necessary to turn to the dueling pistol. Early one morning he and Fullarton met in Hyde Park and exchanged shots. Shelburne missed, and he came away from the field slightly wounded in the groin, and without the apology he had sought. But the ensuing uproar brought him a burst of popular approval as a brave British gentleman, and by retiring to his country estate he was able to avoid further attacks on his loyalty. Now, as he re-emerged into the public view, he would have to be especially cautious. Although diplomatic couriers and underground agents moved without much difficulty back and forth between the enemy countries, Franklin could not risk putting a letter to the Earl into uncertain hands.

Winter, that year, was uncommonly harsh in Paris, and the aging philosopher stayed close to his warm house in Passy, on the outskirts of Paris. His thoughts turned often to the south, where several of his friends were seeking the sun, and especially he missed his favorite young Frenchwoman, Mme. Brillon—a charming and intelligent lady, his neighbor in Passy, who knew how to make him feel that his seventy-six years were a mere error in arithmetic. In the middle of March, he was delighted to receive a letter from her, full of solicitude and affection. Among other matters, she wrote that an amiable Englishman, Lord Cholmondeley, had been in Nice and was on his way to Paris, where he hoped to call on Dr. Franklin.

While private gentlemen traveling for their pleasure through enemy countries under diplomatic protection were then taken for granted, it had been a long time since Franklin received a visit from a British nobleman, and he awaited this one with curiosity. A week later Cholmondeley arrived at his house. Franklin later wrote of their talk in his *Journal of Negotiations for Peace with Great Britain*: "Great affairs sometimes take their rise from small circumstances . . . He [Cholmondeley] told me that he knew Lord Shelburne had a great regard for me, that he was sure his lordship would be pleased to hear from me, and that if I should write a line, he would have a pleasure in carrying it." The doctor did not waste time in wondering about the coincidence, if it was a coincidence, that brought the man to him at so appropriate a moment. The main thing was that a letter in Cholmondeley's hands would be safe. Taking paper and quill, he composed a careful note to Shelburne: "I embrace the opportunity of assuring you of my ancient respect . . . and of congratulating you on the returning good disposition of your country in favour of America . . . I hope it will tend to produce a general peace to which I shall with infinite pleasure contribute everything in my power." The doctor underlined the words "*a general peace*." It would do no harm to remind Shelburne that America stood staunchly by the alliance with France, and would make no peace without her.

Franklin had not yet heard, when he wrote this letter, that the North government had fallen. A new ministry had been formed, headed by the Marquis of Rockingham, and with Shelburne as one of its major figures.

3. "A Prodigious Deal of Ambiguity"

William Petty-Fitzmaurice, Lord Shelburne, was then forty-five years old, somewhat stout, a little gouty, but at the peak of his powers. Cholmondeley's arrival in London was providentially timed to fit his political needs. His position was exceedingly delicate. A few days earlier King George had offered to make him the head of the new government, instead of Rocking-ham, and he had felt compelled to refuse, on the ground that he lacked the required Parliamentary support. He was not a popular man, and he knew it. But the fact that the King had turned to him was proof of his unique place in the politics of the period. All London knew that George distrusted Shel-burne, and had dubbed him "the Jesuit of Berkeley Square"—a reference to the Earl's notorious predilection for the *sub rosa* stratagem and the art-ful dodge. Not only had Shelburne opposed the North government at every turn, but at one time he had even been accused of a plot to assassinate the King. Although the charge was baseless, it reflected the popular notion of their mutual feeling.

Shelburne was aware that the King's sudden friendliness did not signify a genuine change in the royal attitude. To George, he could be no more than a disagreeable necessity. It was not that the King hated him less, but that he hated Rockingham more. The Marquis, an out-and-out Whig, was determined to cut away the remaining powers of the throne, to reduce the King to a mere figurehead. His avowed advocacy of American independence challenged the royal policy at its root. The only good thing about Rocking-ham, in George's view, was his failing health—due it was gossiped, to his too great passion for an Italian mistress. George had sworn never to speak to Rockingham; to have him again close to the throne would be an un-bearable humiliation.

Although the King's bursts of paranoid irrationality had been openly dis-cussed in Parliament, he was still far from obvious insanity, and his narrow, opinionated mind functioned shrewdly in the subtle play of politics. Unlike Rockingham, Shelburne had never spoken outright for American independ-ence. During previous cabinet service he had advocated a species of home rule for the colonies, under a British viceroy, and he was still identified with this proposal—which, if conceded earlier, might have prevented the Revo-lution. George saw, or thought he saw, in Shelburne a man who, however devious his ways, might spare the Crown the indignity of a virtual surrender to America. The Earl preferred not to disabuse him of this idea. When he declined the post of First Lord of the Treasury, which normally meant primacy in the Cabinet, the King quickly put forward another proposal. He would accept Rockingham in the Treasury, he said, if he did not have to endure him in the flesh—if all negotiation with him were carried on through another—Shelburne, for example.

Nothing could have suited Shelburne better, and he undertook to persuade Rockingham to accept the unprecedented and insulting arrangement. The Marquis, a large-spirited man, shrugged; he would agree, he said, if the King would "place no veto on American independence." He insisted, too, that the post of Secretary for Foreign Affairs go to his foremost supporter, the gifted Charles James Fox, professional politician, much-quoted wit, gambler, philanderer, and the most brilliant orator of his day—who also stood high on the King's long list of hates. George boggled only briefly at these stipulations; Shelburne was his hope.

It was Fox's assumption, and Rockingham's, that peace with the allies, including America, would be negotiated by the Foreign Office. They were uneasy when Shelburne asked to be made Secretary of State for Home, Irish, and Colonial affairs. While they felt obliged to agree, the possibility was obvious that he had conspired with the King to keep the American peace in his own hands. For so long as England did not recognize the independence of the colonies, how could they be dealt with as a foreign power?

It was precisely this kind of maneuver that caused Shelburne's enemies to say of him that "falsehood is his profession," and that tempted cartoonists to portray him as Janus, showing two faces to the world at the same time. Even his friend Jeremy Bentham had to admit that there was "a prodigious deal of ambiguity about him." But Shelburne saw nothing unprincipled in his behavior. He regarded himself as an advanced liberal, carrying the torch of progress side by side with Franklin, Bentham, and Adam Smith. What if he flattered the reactionary King and lent himself to royal intrigues? In his view, these were no more than practical means justified by worthy ends. It was his hope to remake British economic policy in Adam Smith's image —to bring it into harmony with the requirements of a world of ever increasing population and productivity—to go down in history as the minister who established freedom of trade between England and other nations. He was a modern man, in the sense that the modern man in any age has a feeling for change, distrusts orthodoxy, and seeks to shake off the clutch of outworn tradition.

Intellectual enthusiasms were so closely blended in him with a passion for personal power that it was difficult to tell where one left off and the other began. He could subordinate himself to Rockingham, associate himself with Fox and pledge solidarity to the Cabinet, while scheming to get the threads of the American negotiation into his own hands, in the genuine belief that he was better fitted than anyone else to settle the terms of peace. When Fox challenged him, saying, "I perceive that the administration is to consist of two parts, one belonging to the King, the other to the public," Shelburne merely smiled. They were in open competition. As experienced politicians, both knew the importance of the initiative—that the first to establish contact with the Americans would have the advantage. From the moment that the Rockingham ministry was formed, each looked for suitable ways of communicating with Paris.

It was at this juncture that Lord Cholmondeley handed Shelburne Franklin's letter. Instantly he brought it to Rockingham. Here, tangibly, was proof of Franklin's regard, and a way to open informal and personal talks with the American without appearing to be overly anxious. If Rockingham would agree to let him send a private emissary to Franklin, he would keep him apprised of every development. To this the Prime Minister could not reasonably demur, nor could Fox, when he heard of the matter.

4. The Urge to Peace

For many years, Shelburne had known a Scottish merchant, Richard Oswald, who had made a fortune as an army contractor (and some say in the slave trade) before retiring to become an ardent humanitarian. Having lived in America, and thrived there, Oswald was regarded as something of an authority on transatlantic affairs, and had sometimes been consulted by the Colonial Office. His selection for the Paris assignment struck Fox as bizarre, for the man was untrained in the art of diplomatic bargaining; how could he stand up to an old hand like Franklin? Shelburne disposed of the objection at a cabinet meeting: "Some people . . . have been pleased to circulate an opinion that Dr. Franklin is a very cunning man . . . I have remarked to Mr. Oswald, 'Dr. Franklin knows very well how to manage a cunning man, but when the Doctor converses or treats with a man of candor, there is no man more candid than himself.'" Oswald's openness, sincerity, and personal warmth, Shelburne asserted, were in this instance likely to be more valuable than any amount of professional subtlety. Early in April, the Scot went off to Paris with a personal letter from his lordship to Franklin. The last sentence of this letter was its nub: "I wish to retain the same simplicity and good faith which subsisted between us in transactions of less importance." There is no reason to doubt that Shelburne meant it.

In their first talk, Oswald enchanted Franklin with a totally indiscreet remark: "Peace is absolutely necessary for England . . . Our enemies may now do what they please with us." Later, it is true, he added that if France "should insist on terms too humiliating" England could still continue the war, "having yet great strength and many resources left." But the earlier statement bore out Franklin's own estimate of the prevailing British state of mind. He sensed that the middle class of manufacturers and merchants, alarmed by the steady fall of trade, was leading the clamor in England for an early end of the war. It was well-known that the powerful textile industry in particular was in trouble. Prior to the Revolution, the American colonies had been its best export market, and since then mechanical improvements in spinning and looming had sharply increased the productive capacity of the Midlands' mills. Greatly expanded markets for calico woven from Indian cotton and for woolen fabrics had become business necessities. Whether America traded as a colony or as an independent republic was a matter of minor consequence to the textile interests so long as the traffic flowed briskly across the Atlantic. So, too, felt England's coal, metal, and hardware producers, whose potential output was expanding as Watt's new steam engines came into use.

Progressive British business men were pointing out that loss of American trade jeopardized the economy not only of England, but of her valuable West Indian possessions. These had formerly made handsome profits by exchanging sugar and rum for the mainland's lumber and foodstuffs. Why let France reap the benefit of America's low prices and growing needs? Postwar French competition in the transatlantic market was greatly feared. The London press had reported with foreboding that French merchants were again extending credit to American firms, and that the American alliance was expected to "give France the dominion and commerce" of the new country. The conclusion reached by many British businessmen like Oswald was that no time must be lost in re-establishing peaceful contact with American customers.

There were other reasons why, from England's standpoint, the war needed to be ended promptly. Until this period, thrifty owners of property had looked with pleasure on the climb of England's birth rate, with the resulting glut of the labor market, and its concomitant low wages and high profits. But as wartime unemployment and prices rose together, the distress of the poor had begun to generate explosive emotions. The destructive anti-Catholic riots of 1780, led by the deranged Lord George Gordon, were rooted more in the economic agony of London's unemployed than in religious bigotry. Practical men of wealth, whether Whig or Tory, could not fail to see that if the war lasted much longer a hurricane of reform would blow against them. Until this time, they had felt secure in their control of Parliament. Now England's Parliamentary pillar of wisdom, Edmund Burke, had begun a sustained attack on the ancient system of pensions and sinecures through which vast sums of public money were annually squandered. Moves were under way to improve the Poor Laws which attempted to prevent the actual starvation of the indigent, to broaden education and religious instruction, and to remove the property qualification for British voters. The slave trade, on which many a British fortune had been founded, was under heavy attack. There were even murmurs against the use of child labor in the factories, although this did not prevent the practice from expanding.

British authors were evincing a dangerous iconoclasm, borrowing doctrines of "natural equality" and "the rights of man" from French philosophers and American revolutionaries. William Ogilvie's *Essay on the Right of Property in Land,* which had just been published, challenged the entire social structure; while a friend of Franklin's, Dr. Joseph Priestley, the scientist, went so far in his attack on established institutions that copies of his *History of the Corruptions of Christianity* were officially burned. The passionate indignation of such kindly gentlemen over the miserable condition of British laboring families found sinister echoes in the slums of London, Manchester, and Liverpool. England, it was true, gave the appearance of being invincibly conservative, but who knew how far the preachments of soft-hearted reformers could drive popular resentment if wartime troubles were allowed to persist? Property owners of whatever political party had reason to press for a peace that would restore prosperity and bring a halt to incendiary working-class movements.

5. *The Vision*

No better time would ever come, Franklin saw, to state his terms of peace, for the defeated British had not yet realized the depth of America's own war-weariness. When it came to formulating the terms, however, he found himself in a quandary. The Continental Congress had announced that before peace could be negotiated England must recognize the independence of the United States. This was precisely what Shelburne wished to avoid, since recognition would mean the transfer of the talks to the authority of the Foreign Office. Having no doubt that there was everything to be gained by keeping the impressionable Oswald as England's representative, Franklin consented, finally, to advance some suggestions. But he could not proceed very far by himself, for he was only one of the five commissioners appointed by the Congress to serve in the event of a peace conference. Of the others, Thomas Jefferson, of Virginia, had decided to remain in America, John Jay, of New York, was on a mission to Madrid, John Adams, of Massachusetts, was trying to arrange a loan in Holland, and Henry Laurens, of South Carolina, had been captured by the British at sea, and was a prisoner in the Tower of London. Weeks were sure to elapse before Jay and Adams arrived in Paris. All that Franklin could do meanwhile was to make it plain to the British that the peace could not be cheaply bought, and at the same time to help Shelburne in his contest for power.

He began by summarizing the chief points on which the Congress had expressed positive views: a just settlement of boundaries, withdrawal of all British troops from American territory, the right to fish in the waters off Newfoundland. From that point, he went off on his own, urging that England cede all of Canada and Nova Scotia. This bold demand he buttressed with so many facts and arguments, set down in the form of a long memorandum, that Oswald was deeply impressed. If the border between Canada and the United States were allowed to remain, argued Franklin, it would be a constant invitation to strife. Would it not be better to eliminate it, rather than to jeopardize the great commercial advantages which would otherwise accrue to England from American friendship? In the long run, England would profit far more from trade across the Atlantic than from mere territorial possessions there. "To make future peace desirable," Franklin wrote, "what may give occasion for future wars should be removed."

As a patriot and statesman he was of course intent on obtaining the tangible rewards of victory for his country, but it was enduring peace above all that illuminated the old man's heart and mind as he spoke to Oswald. And he saw such a peace as being achieved only through courageous and inspired action on the part of great England. The world situation had been sharply altered by the development of a considerable new source of productive human energy on America's Atlantic coast. It was essential to peace that England recognize the altered balance of world power, and this she could do only by voluntary modification of her own established patterns and ways. If she were willing to give up territory and bases at points of potential conflict, abate her claim to rule all the seas, including American waters, and trade with the new republic as an equal, then there need be no bounds to their secure friendship, mutual support, and lasting advantage. British foresight and generosity at this point in history might cement the two nations forever in alliance to the benefit of all the world.

This was Franklin's vision, and Oswald caught fire from it, and made it his own. The need, he saw, was for imaginative and creative statesmanship which would link the interests of the two countries and weaken phobic prejudices in both. He asked if he could show Franklin's memorandum on Canada to Shelburne, rather than try to retain it all in his memory. After some hesitation, the doctor agreed, on condition that the memorandum go no farther than Shelburne, and that it be returned to him. Oswald had scarcely gone off to Calais and a channel boat when Franklin began to regret having let the document out of his hands on any terms. At its very end was a sentence capable of serious misunderstanding—a suggestion that, if Canada were ceded, land there might be sold "to indemnify the Royalists for the confiscation of their estates"—that is, compensate Americans who had fought on the British side for their economic losses. This idea not only ran counter to the temper of the Congress and the American people, but to Franklin's own feelings. He had added the clause on an impulse, as an additional inducement for the cession of Canada. If Shelburne were to pick up this line of thought, the result might be embarrassing. One of the most prominent of the Royalists (whom the British preferred to call Loyalists, and the embittered Americans called Tories) was Franklin's illegitimate son William—a refugee in England from the wrath of patriots. In his long political life the doctor had made his fair share of enemies, and if the memorandum were ever made public, there would be some, inevitably, to accuse him of seeking a benefit for William at the expense of his country, regardless of his long record of patient sacrifice for the Revolution.

6. Moment of Decision

Oswald, arriving in London, reported first to a meeting of the full Cabinet, for Shelburne wanted no one to accuse him of withholding information from his colleagues. Keeping his promise to Franklin, the Scot said nothing to the cabinet of the memorandum. In all other respects, however, he gave a complete exposition of the doctor's views, including his hope for the cession of Canada. This Oswald urged upon the ministers with unexpected eloquence. When Shelburne and Rockingham showed themselves inclined to consider the proposal seriously, Fox voiced surprise and alarm; it was folly, he thought, to encourage the Americans to expect large concessions at this early stage of negotiation. The ministers decided finally to authorize Shelburne to prepare a reply to Franklin for cabinet approval.

After the meeting, Oswald called privately on Shelburne at his office and handed over Franklin's memorandum. Shelburne read it with great care. Might he be permitted, he asked, to keep it overnight? Reluctantly Oswald consented, and the minister locked the paper into his personal file. Even if Oswald had not pledged his word to Franklin for secrecy, Shelburne would hardly have wished to share so challenging a document with Fox, who would certainly have regarded any note from the enemy as coming under his authority. But at the moment when Shelburne took the memorandum from Oswald's hands, he became vulnerable, and from the situation thus created, large historical consequences were shortly to flow.

Hearing Oswald's report, and reading the memorandum, Shelburne sensed that a moment of great decision was upon England. The minister, together with Franklin, belonged to a small historical group of statesmen to whom the name "idealist," with its connotation of impracticality, does not quite apply (for they were exceedingly capable in practical affairs, and had few illusions about the world and man)—whose eupeptic insistence on looking eagerly for new solutions entitles them, for want of a better word, to be called innovators, as distinguished from the large majority of conformists who generally dominate international affairs. When such men succeed, they are regarded as bold and shrewd; when they fail, as rash and naïve. Shelburne was psychologically prepared through experience, study, and reflection, as well as by ambition, to make an original peace, one that looked to the future rather than to the past. He was ready to take immense political risks to persuade the conservative Briton, to whom the voluntary giving up of any jot of national power was inconceivable, that he had no choice—that England, fairly defeated in war, would have to yield Canada, and make other important concessions—a point of view that the people, the Parliament, and the King would understand, however reluctantly they acceded. The Earl's thinking, like Franklin's, was centered on securing a quick peace that would withstand the tests of time. He was not disposed to haggle, certainly not with Franklin, in whose wisdom and fairness he had entire faith.

Shelburne's letters and speeches suggest that for all his personal limitations, for all his romantic and conspiratorial style in politics, he grasped better than most statesmen of his age (or of ours, for that matter) the process by which wars are generated. He perceived that at one root of war is man's reluctance to face and adjust to reality—the human tendency to shut the eyes to unpleasant change and to cling blindly to the familiar. It was clear to him that when the institutions of nations lag too far behind the requirements of a changing world environment—as he considered England's trade policies to be lagging—peoples seeking to maintain the old ways must hate and be hated by peoples seeking for change. He knew, too, that when such situations of stress are allowed to extend themselves in time, war becomes ever more and more likely, that mutual resentment prolonged between nations finally produces resignation to war and even impatience for it—that hate, multiplied by greed, equals calamity. Although the workings of men's glandular and nervous systems and the conception of neurosis were unknown to Shelburne's time, it was all too familiar with the effects on the human mind of sustained hostility. Thanks to Franklin, the nature of lightning had then been understood for thirty years, and it was easy to conceive that when die-hard conservatism stands continuously charged in polar opposition to hungry radicalism, the probability of a blasting spark is very great. Shelburne heartily shared Franklin's view that if an effective peace were to be made, its terms had to be put forth boldly and cogently to compel acceptance while the British people were still dazed by defeat and ready to pay almost any price to end the war.

He was only one minister among several, however; whatever official reply he made to Franklin had to be shaped to the views of men who thought very differently from himself and from each other—Fox, Rockingham, the King. When a few days later Oswald returned to Paris with a reply from Shelburne, he was far from happy with what he had been told to say. "Lord Shelburne will never give up the Loyalists"; there could be no treaty unless America agreed to compensate them. This position Franklin found disturbing and dangerous, and he refused to take it as final. As to Canada and the prevention of future wars, Shelburne wrote, "It is to be hoped that some more friendly method will be found." Franklin gathered that the Earl would go far to meet the American terms, but that he felt compelled, at this stage, to speak for Fox as well as for himself.

7. *Point Counterpoint*

Neither Oswald nor Franklin realized that Fox had made his first move to shake the American negotiation out of Shelburne's hands. It came as a shock to them both when an imperious British diplomat named Thomas Grenville appeared in Paris, hard on Oswald's heels, and announced that the Foreign Office had delegated him to open talks for peace with both France and America. The move was especially disturbing because no American was likely to forget that Grenville was the son of the man who two decades before had imposed the provocative Stamp Act on the colonies. When he called at the house in Passy, Franklin received him, but pointed out that they could not very well enter into serious discussion until the British Government formally clarified the situation. Seeing that Franklin was not to be hurried, Grenville sought out Oswald. Here he had better luck; he convinced the susceptible merchant that Shelburne had given up the struggle, and that Fox was in control. It seemed to Oswald that under the circumstances he had no right to withhold any information from his presumptive successor; and in confiding to Grenville the story of his negotiation with Franklin, he mentioned the secret memorandum on Canada. Avidly Grenville seized on this tidbit. A long letter went off to Fox, implying that Shelburne had violated his ministerial obligation by concealing important documents from the cabinet. This was all that was needed to release Fox's pent-up hostility toward Shelburne. Showing Grenville's letter to Rockingham, he charged that Shelburne had been guilty of "duplicity of conduct" intolerable in a minister of the government.

Shelburne, confronted with this accusation, expressed surprise that so much importance should be attached to "a mere paper of notes." Rockingham realized that disciplinary action against him would bring the entire ministry toppling down; so he attempted to reconcile him with Fox, but without success. Angered by Rockingham's caution, Fox then shifted his attack. It seemed to him that Franklin's attitude was the crux of his problem. If he could be separated from Shelburne, the issue would be decided. On this assumption, Fox wrote to Grenville, authorizing him to offer America the full and unconditional independence which Shelburne had withheld. But when Grenville returned to Franklin, expecting gratitude for so much magnanimity, he found to his disgust that the old man was in no way softened. It was evident to Franklin that independence would presently come, regardless of its ministerial source—and in all other respects Shelburne and Oswald were likely to be far more generous than Fox and Grenville. Because he was expecting the arrival in Paris of Jay and Adams, he had a good excuse to temporize. Grenville raged, Fox gritted his teeth, Shelburne and Oswald waited, and the peace negotiation marked time.

Crisis came late in June, with the not unexpected death of the ailing Lord Rockingham. Fox launched a drive to put himself or a dependable Whig puppet at the head of the ministry, but before he could organize his Parliamentary forces the King nominated Shelburne. A message promptly went to the Earl—if he accepted, Fox would resign from the government—a warning that his Whig followers in the Commons would be opposed to the new administration. This was a move so fraught with danger to Shelburne that he asked young William Pitt, then moving rapidly to political prominence and a friend of both men, to call privately on Fox, and urge him to remain in the Cabinet. Pitt found Fox implacable. (That night Fox celebrated his declaration of war on the Earl by staying up all night in a historic drinking bout with his roistering friend, the Prince of Wales, who hated the King as much as Fox hated Shelburne.)

Gloomily Pitt reported to Shelburne that the Whig leaders were planning a tremendous Parliamentary effort to prevent confirmation of his appointment as Prime Minister. But Shelburne was not without strong resources; the King was for him, and behind the King, Lord North's Tories. The ensuing debate in the House of Commons rocked not only the nation but the hemisphere, for the speeches were widely reprinted and closely read in Europe and America. Fox, in a spate of bitterness lasting for hours, accused Shelburne of denying independence to America and peace to England; he denounced him as a hypocrite without "principles of honour," one of those men who "would forget fifty promises when they were no longer necessary to their ends." Edmund Burke, always more effective at his desk than on his feet, supported Fox in a long oration that appalled even his friends, comparing Shelburne with Sulla, Catiline, Borgia, and Machiavelli. To all this Shelburne replied with restraint and dignity, confident that when the time came the North party and his own few followers would manage to squeeze out a vote of confidence for him. "Minister, attacked by Reynard, would be saved by Boreas," predicted the knowing wits. So the event proved. When the Commons adjourned, complete authority to conduct the peace negotiation was his. But for how long, none could predict.

CHAPTER TWO

Anxieties of a Patriot

1. *Escape to France*

No one could have been more relieved than John Jay to hear of the change in the British Government—relieved not only for his country's sake, but for his own and his wife's. Madrid had proved the most inhospitable of capitals. It was Jay's unfortunate assignment to apply to the Spanish court for a loan to his necessitous government, and he had found himself facing a wall of cold indifference. Although Spain was allied with France against England, she felt no obligation whatever toward America. Disdain was the core of her attitude toward the brash colonials who had dared to rebel against their royal master. The danger of the example which they had set for the peoples of South America was all too plain; and the Spanish foreign minister, Count Floridablanca, had declined to receive Jay officially as the envoy of an independent power. Unofficially, he barely condescended to exchange a word. Even the minimal diplomatic courtesies were withheld. The Jays were never invited to his receptions; his spies watched their movements and read their mail. When a letter of credit which had been sent to Jay failed to arrive on time, and he ran short of funds, he was compelled to ask Floridablanca for some minor assistance, and even this was refused. His house was chilly, Sarah Jay was ill, the children were unhappy, and his mission was a failure. To all this was added a further humiliation when the floundering Congress instructed him to tell Floridablanca that in exchange for a loan and a treaty of alliance it would give up its claim to free navigation of the Mississippi River. Although at this time Spain had clear title to the west bank of the river, as part of Louisiana, transferred to her by France some years earlier, ownership of lands to the east was in dispute among Americans, British, Spaniards, and Indians, so that the offer of the Congress represented a major concession. Jay profoundly disliked his role in this weak tactic. Carrying the message to the Count, he prepared himself to be contemptuously rebuffed, and he was. How, Floridablanca demanded, could the Congress give away a right which it did not possess?

It was a letter from Benjamin Franklin, received in May, that told Jay of England's sudden inclination toward peace, and urged him to come to Paris for the anticipated parleys. He did not have to reflect before beginning preparations for departure. When he called at the Foreign Ministry for a

formal leave-taking he was surprised to be greeted almost amiably by Floridablanca. For this change in tone, he realized, the news from England,
greatly enhancing America's position as a speculative risk, was responsible.
Spain, conveyed the Count, politely if vaguely, would continue to support
the common effort against the British, and even a future loan was not
impossible. Details, he said, would be worked out by the Spanish ambassador in Paris, Count d'Aranda.

The long trip northward by jolting carriage, by boat across the stormy
Bay of Biscay, by carriage again from Bordeaux to Paris, was one long discomfort, but the Jays were in high spirits. His wife's pleasure in this, her first
trip to France, was especially satisfying to Jay. Everything she saw delighted
her, and he reveled in her running commentary. She was an attractive
woman, with delicate features and a fine complexion; more than this, she
had a quick mind and a lively wit; more even than this, she was a Livingston,
born to large wealth and influence. Uncomprehending Spaniards, observing
his devotion to her, had set him down as an absurdly uxorious man. One
diplomat wrote of the Jays, "This woman, whom he blindly loves, dom-
inates him"—an exaggeration; he was sufficiently endowed by inheritance,
education, and talent to stand on his own feet. It had not been his marriage
alone that had made him, in his thirties, a successful lawyer, President of
the Continental Congress, and Chief Justice of New York, before being sent
abroad. Cool and careful calculation was one of his strengths; he was one
of the few important Revolutionary figures who was not yet ready, at the
time of the Declaration of Independence, to break with the British and
throw in his lot with Washington.

They arrived in Paris on June 23, and after he had deposited Sarah and
the children at an apartment which Franklin had reserved for them, Jay
drove eagerly to the doctor's house in Passy.

2. Franklin Explains

The briefing that Franklin gave Jay took up most of three days, and in
addition to a detailed account of his talks with Oswald and Grenville
included a review of France's precarious financial position. Franklin realized,
as few Americans then did, that in spite of imminent victory in the war,
the French Government was far from sanguine about the future. Under
the weight of a vast military budget and loans to the American revolutionists, the economy of the nation was visibly crumbling. The tragedy of the
situation was that although the French nobility and bourgeoisie held half
the cash in Europe, they paid so small a share of the nation's taxes that
the government had to rely primarily on precarious monies squeezed somehow from flattened peasantry and petty tradesmen.

Long before 1782, a former minister of finance, Turgot, had warned Louis XVI that the first shot of a French cannon in the American war would bankrupt the government. This prediction had been amply fulfilled. King Louis was confronted with debts which remained obdurately enormous in spite of the most frenzied efforts of his finance ministers. Except for prospering manufacturers and merchants, the economic condition of the people was steadily deteriorating. With the rapidly growing population approaching twenty-five millions, three times that of England, the distribution of goods was so lopsided that in most parts of the country typical living standards barely permitted survival.

As new factories, mills, and blast furnaces were erected, great numbers of ill-paid or unemployed laborers had concentrated in Paris; and to see a Paris of nearly 700,000 people, most of them living in harsh poverty, caused alarm even in the Cloud-Cuckoo-Land of Versailles. It was primarily in response to the dangerous mood of the capital that in 1782 a royal order was issued, stating that to prevent a shortage of wood for fuel, "the King forbids the erection of any new factories within a radius of fifteen leagues around the capital." Whatever the danger of a fuel shortage, the danger of the mob was greater.

Even more than solvency, Louis and his court craved the goodwill of the people. The popular cause of the age in France was American independence. It was his illusion that by supporting republicans abroad he could strengthen the monarchy at home—that the cheers of crowds augured security. Especially he wished to be admired and applauded by the enlightened writers and philosophers who then set the tone of French opinion. "We glory," he said, for their benefit, "that the France we govern is high-spirited and free."

To prove his support of freedom, he had encouraged his Foreign Minister, the Count de Vergennes, to plunge into open war against England in America's support. Once committed, there could be no withdrawal. Deep and deeper into the financial vortex he was sucked, until there was no money even to pay his household staff, until the word "tax" had become an epithet throughout France.

Vergennes and the King were eager to see an end to a struggle which France had entered in the hope of crushing an overextended British empire, only to become overextended herself. For one thing, her foreign trade had been seriously hurt by roving British naval squadrons. For another, Vergennes, in order to persuade Spain to enter the war against England, had made a troublesome promise to Floridablanca. Not only British lands east of Louisiana, on the Gulf of Mexico, had been assured to Spain, not only the expulsion of British colonists from Honduras, but most important,

France had agreed to go on fighting until Gibraltar was once more in Spanish hands. In the face of a long and costly siege by the French, the coveted citadel had proved irreducible. Now the tough-minded Florida-blanca was bluntly demanding that Vergennes find a satisfactory alternative to recompense Spain for her efforts against the British.

It was all very well to announce to the world that the French motive in fighting England was an idealistic desire to assure American independence. Many European liberals, as well as Americans, were comforted by the notion. But the rights of man and the sacred liberty of peoples did not concern Vergennes very much. He was a man who had become gray in diplomacy, and who had seen too much of life and politics to kindle over a new slogan. The war for him had never been more than another round in the ancient dynastic struggle between France and England. In this, his larger hopes had been thwarted at every turn. A plan to invade England across the Channel came to nothing. A British fleet under Admiral George Rodney smashed France's finest squadrons in the West Indies. A notion of bringing Prussia, Austria, and Russia into alliance against England evaporated when these nations decided instead to seize the opportunity to partition helpless Poland. Vergennes conceived and secretly supported the "League of the Armed Neutrality," a Baltic coalition of neutral states led by Russia, and supposed to menace England; but it shriveled until Catherine II disdainfully referred to it as the "League of Armed Nullity." The Dutch, not the French, benefited most from the Caribbean trade which England lost during the war. Acting on the principle that political isolation is fatal to a belligerent power, Vergennes had attempted to isolate England, but he had not sufficiently reckoned on the high cost of his own foreign alliances. The defeat of the British in the American colonies was in his eyes only meager consolation.

To make matters worse, Franklin was urging his consent to yet another inadvisable loan to the Americans. Robert Livingston had gloomily written to the doctor, "It is my duty to confide to you that if the war is to be continued in this country, it must be to a great extent at the expense of France." Congress, Franklin was informed, had been able to collect from the states not even one tenth of the five million dollars estimated to be required for the expenditures of the next fiscal year. Massachusetts, Rhode Island, and Virginia had rejected the request of the Congress for a federal tax on imports. In the face of this bleak news Franklin had to push again and again at Vergennes. He did not conceal from Jay that he sympathized with the French minister and admired the courage and skill with which he juggled the enormous burdens of his office. At the first opportunity, he drove his fellow commissioner to Versailles to pay formal respects to Vergennes.

3. *No One Could Be Trusted*

There was an epidemic of influenza in Paris at the time, and Jay, fatigued by his long journey from Spain and hours of concentrated talk, began to run a fever. It took a strong constitution, in those days of punishing travel, to represent one's country abroad—which perhaps explains why so many of the noted statesmen of the period were exceptionally long-lived. Jay's malaise first showed itself in a sudden lowering of his spirits. He was seized by a dislike of French society, not for its social iniquities or political follies, but for its carefree indulgence of the senses, its open concentration on amorous conquest, its ceaseless preoccupation with fashion, its dilettantism, its love of flippant wit. A fundamentalist in religion, taking his Bible literally, he was repelled by everything that Paris stood for. His was a serious world, and he could not forget that he spoke for a new nation at a turning point of history. He appears to have suffered from the obscure and uncomfortable sense of being excluded, which a man of action is likely to experience in a foreign country whose language he speaks only haltingly and crudely. Out of a strain of prudishness that was in him came the conclusion that the French "were not a moral people and did not know what it was." Franklin's easy acceptance of French ways and French ideas he found incomprehensible and even a little shameful. He was depressed, too, for he was a fastidious man, by the casual attitude of the citizens of Paris, especially in the unscented classes, toward the disposal of garbage and ordure, and the washing of linen. The smells, filth, and squalor of the purlieus of Paris at that time startled even those who knew the slums of London, and were a factor, it has been suggested, in the almost total withdrawal of aristocrats from any physical contact with the poor, and the bitter resentment of the French poor toward nose-wrinkling aristocrats.

Jay's anxieties quickly found a focus—Vergennes. His considerable ego had been abraded at their meeting by the cool courtesy which the minister had shown him, while making much of Franklin. Had the doctor been beguiled by the Frenchman? This was, Jay knew, the opinion formed by John Adams, when he had been in Paris a few years earlier. Vergennes's ivory smoothness and urbanity conveyed that all things diplomatic were somehow under his control. His was one of those subtle and skeptical and at the same time deeply Catholic minds, which so often used to appear in the French ruling classes, a mind conditioned by Europe's long and bitter experience of the human predicament; and the Protestant Jay, who for all his legal training and accomplishment was in many ways an unsophisticated man, was repelled and intimidated by it. To trust such a man, as Franklin clearly trusted him, could, he felt, only be prejudicial to American interests.

The orders which the Continental Congress had sent to its commissioners now took on a sinister connotation for him. "You are . . . to undertake nothing without their [the French government's] knowledge and concurrence, and ultimately to govern yourself by their advice and opinion." Was such a policy compatible with the honor of a sovereign nation? Had the Congress been corrupted by Vergennes's agents in Philadelphia? It seemed to Jay that in this instruction the American birthright had been sold for a mess of French promises.

He had the feeling that conspiracy and espionage were all around him. Franklin was so used to surveillance by French and British agents that even when he suspected some of his servants he did not discharge them; he preferred spies he knew and liked to those who might replace them. Jay was less philosophical, almost obsessed by suspicion, epecially of the French. Much as he revered Franklin, he feared the consequences of letting the old man, with his Francophile leanings, negotiate alone for peace and the American future. Hurriedly Jay wrote to John Adams, saying that he was much needed in Paris, but Adams was then in the thick of arrangements for the Dutch loan, and could not leave Amsterdam. When Jay's fever grew worse and chills and coughing forced him to bed, the world looked black to him.

4. "Mr. Jay Is a Lawyer"

Several weeks of a hot summer went by before Jay was well enough to receive visitors, but then Franklin brought reassuring news. Lord Shelburne had become Prime Minister, with the fast-rising Pitt as his Chancellor of the Exchequer. Oswald was once more in Paris, empowered to resume negotiations. The French had approved an arrangement under which America would negotiate separately with the British, on the understanding that Vergennes would be kept fully informed of progress, and that no terms would be concluded without his assent. Franklin had put Oswald off until Jay would be well enough to participate in the talks. With fears somewhat abated, and strength returning, Jay suggested that Oswald call on him so that they could become acquainted without further delay.

A few days later—it was then early August—Oswald appeared at Jay's house, and formally presented his credentials. As Jay took the paper in his hands and read it, anger boiled up in him. No mention was made of the United States of America. Shelburne had empowered Oswald only to deal with the commissioners representing "the Colonys." The words were like a slap in the face. With the cold precision for which he was known when he sat on the judge's bench, Jay said that he could not admit Oswald's powers so long as they failed to designate the independent United States of America by their correct title. When Oswald remarked that Dr. Franklin had not raised any such objection, Jay retorted caustically that

Mr. Adams, with whom he had corresponded, agreed that prior recognition of American independence was indispensable to the peace negotiation, as the Congress had long since stipulated. Unless independence were promptly and unconditionally granted, America, Jay strongly hinted, would pursue the war against England with full vigor, and with the support of her allies.

Taken aback by this blunt challenge, Oswald went directly to Franklin, only to find that while the doctor's welcome was friendly, he was disposed to agree with Jay. If he had not previously seen fit to challenge Oswald's powers, Franklin said, it was perhaps because he had not fully grasped the significance of the point. "Mr. Jay is a lawyer, and might think of things that do not occur to those who are not lawyers." Now that Lord Shelburne was head of the British Government, what justification could there be for further postponement of recognition? In the face of this united front, Oswald could see nothing to do but return to London, report to Shelburne the hardened mood of the American negotiators, and ask for revised powers.

CHAPTER THREE

The Rayneval Affair

1. *Whose Land?*

Jay and his wife were pleased at his having made himself so strongly felt by the British. As soon as he was able to leave his house, he sought further action. It seemed to him that the time had come to demand that Spain clarify her attitude toward America's future, and in a determined frame of mind, he called on Count d'Aranda, to whom Franklin had provided an introduction.

He found that the Spanish loan was still a mirage; Aranda had received no authorization from Floridablanca to arrange it. But in the course of their talk, the ambassador brought out a map of America which Jay found intensely interesting, if alarming. It showed the thirteen states confined to the Atlantic coast, with Canada British, and virtually everything south of the Great Lakes and west of the Alleghenies, Spanish. Swallowing his wrath, Jay remarked that the map overlooked American rights in much of this territory. Aranda reminded him of his conversation with Floridablanca in Madrid, when America had offered to give up her alleged navigation rights on the Mississippi. At Jay's denial that his country's claim to extend west of the Alleghenies had in any way been prejudiced, the Spaniard merely shrugged. Presently Jay caught an implication that France had approved the settlement indicated on the map, and that the vast territories east of the Mississippi were to be Spain's compensation in lieu of Gibraltar. At this he realized that he was out of his depth; he took himself off and drove hastily to Franklin's house.

Franklin no more than Jay liked the sound of Aranda's statements. The best thing, he thought, would be to discuss the matter frankly with Vergennes, and he arranged an appointment. Early on the morning of August 10, they visited the Foreign Ministry at Versailles, where they were courteously received by Vergennes and his chief assistant, Gérard de Rayneval, a quiet, thoughtful, unsmiling man of middle age. Jay spoke of Aranda's map and strongly presented the American position, much as he might have presented it in a court of law. He had a fairly good case, especially as it applied to America's interest in the great triangle of forests and prairie bounded by the Ohio River, the Great Lakes, and the Mississippi. George Rogers Clark had shortly before led a small body of troops through the heart of this country. On the strength of his achievement, Congress had announced that "if a right to said territory depended on the conquests of the British posts within it, the United States have already more extensive claim than Spain can acquire, having by the success of their arms obtained possession of all the important posts and settlements on the Illinois and Wabash." This was an exaggeration, as was also an estimate that twenty thousand American settlers were already in the Ohio valley, but there was a core of fact in the argument.

Rayneval answered for France. He was a specialist in American affairs and his brother, Conrad Gérard, was then minister to the Continental Congress. Precise logic, in the rigid French tradition, was at once his forte and his weakness; he had a passion for clarity and finality. If the American claim was based on mere physical possession of the region, then it was empty, he held, for the actual owners of most of the land were Indians, who greatly outnumbered the white settlers. This being so, the disposition of the Indian tribes must be given decisive weight. He was then preparing a long report, showing in unanswerable detail, tribe by tribe, that the Indians of the lands north of the Ohio accepted the suzerainty of the British crown. This region had long been claimed by England without contest; it was rightfully hers, and if, as a penalty of defeat in war, she felt constrained to cede it to Spain, then it would legally become Spanish territory.

Technically, it was an argument difficult to rebut. The heart of Jay's position was simply the knowledge that America had whipped England, and was not going to let any other nation walk off with the spoils. The western lands were an indispensable part of the American dream of future greatness. But Jay could hardly say this to the French, whose military aid had made the American victory possible, who were America's financial patrons and seniors in diplomacy. He was further exasperated when Vergennes, turning to Franklin, advised the American commissioners to moderate their demands on England—not to insist on recognition of independence prior to the peace negotiation—not to demand Canada, or fishing rights off Newfoundland. By asking too much for herself, America might prejudice the just claims of France and Spain, which were as important to them as America's aspirations were to her.

Franklin, as usual with him when he was hard pressed, preserved an enigmatic silence, and both sides maintained the forms of courtesy. As soon as the Americans were in their carriage, Jay's choler exploded. Vergennes, he felt, was about to betray America, and it struck him as strange that Franklin was not as exercised as himself. Franklin tried to soothe him. Vergennes was after all a Frenchman, and thought of France's interests first, as was his duty. So far as Franklin knew, he had never broken his word once it had been given. Patience and persistence were the qualities likely to be most productive for America. There was no doubt, Franklin said, that "we should insist on the Mississippi as our western boundary." But he had also to consider his status as a friend of France, for he was still pressing Vergennes for the needed loan. In view of their instructions from the Congress, he did not see that there was any action to be profitably taken at the moment. It was his belief that Shelburne and Oswald were sincere in their avowed intention to make a peace which would wipe away America's hard feelings toward England, and that they would not consent to give the western lands to Spain. All this seemed to Jay to be mere evasion, mere pusillanimity in the face of a major challenge. Both men felt a strain in their relationship when they separated.

2. Oswald Is Pleasantly Surprised

A few days later a sudden gallstone attack, the first of the many which were to plague Franklin for the rest of his life, confined him to his home, in a state of great pain. Jay, brooding alone over the problem of the Mississippi, concluded that if Vergennes maintained his stand, if America's hopes for the west depended solely on the British, a different attitude towards England was indicated. At the beginning of September, Oswald returned from London, and was startled to be greeted by a Jay amiable and conciliatory. The merchant, who was rapidly learning the rules of the diplomatic game, quickly revised his own tactics, which had been prepared for a very different situation. Lord Shelburne had been shaken by his account of Jay's earlier toughness. The Prime Minister's political career depended on success in arriving at a quick peace; precariously placed as he was he could not take the risks of protracted bargaining. As a result, Oswald had been authorized to make extraordinary concessions. Fishing rights would be granted; troops would be promptly withdrawn; the question of Canada would be left open for negotiation; even the issues of the Loyalists and of pre-Revolutionary debts might be dropped, if the Americans insisted. Oswald carried a secret letter from the Foreign Office, to be used at his discretion: "His Majesty is pleased, for the salutary purpose of precluding all further delay . . . to waive every stipulation by the treaty for the undoubted rights of the merchants whose debts accrued before 1775 and also for the claims of the [Loyalist] refugees for the compensation for their losses."

In effect, Shelburne was prepared to give America almost everything that Franklin had asked for in his first tentative outline of terms. But when Oswald found Jay suddenly malleable he adopted a tone of statesmanlike reserve, such as he had never used with Franklin. His only encouragement for Jay was the news that Parliament would soon be asked to pass an Enabling Act, empowering him to treat with America as an independent nation. Meanwhile, should they not proceed to work on a preliminary draft of the treaty, without further delay? Overlooking his earlier insistence on recognition prior to negotiation, Jay readily acquiesced.

As the new talks with Oswald were about to get under way, a messenger brought Jay a letter which, he was surprised to find, had been written by Rayneval, in his own hand. Courteous but urgent in tone, the note expressed Rayneval's hope that Jay would on reflection see the wisdom of the view which had been discussed at their last meeting, as to the advisability of limiting the territorial aspirations of the American government. A postscript added that he expected to be absent from Paris for some days.

Instantly Jay suspected a French scheme to settle the cession of the western territory behind America's back. In a letter to Livingston he wrote, "The perusal of this memoir convinced me that this court [France] would . . . oppose our extension to the Mississippi." As for Rayneval's mysterious absence from Paris—where would he have gone but to London? The next morning he made inquiries at Versailles, and learned that Rayneval, after having met with Aranda for a long talk, had left Paris secretly and mysteriously. This to Jay's mind was conclusive, and he rushed to Franklin's house to report that the French plot against America had reached the point of crisis.

3. A Matter of Conscience

There was only one way, Jay insisted, to counter the French move—to open secret negotiations with Shelburne, immediately, for a separate peace in which France would not be consulted. Franklin, who was feeling barely well enough to talk, shook his head and mustered arguments. The proposal threatened the French alliance which had made possible the success of the Revolution. Their instructions from the Congress ruled out a separate peace. As soon as America showed distrust of her ally, much of her bargaining advantage would be lost. On the evidence at hand, there could be no moral justification for breaking their pledge to maintain close liaison with the French during the peace talks. Was it not possible that Jay had misread the purpose of Rayneval's mission to England, if in fact he had really gone there?

While raising objections and questions, Franklin did not flatly reject Jay's idea. He was too shrewd and experienced not to allow for the possibility that Jay's interpretation of the situation might be right. But it was not caution alone that made him decide to avoid a commitment. Enfeebled by pain, he was profoundly aware of his age and the ebbing of his physical powers. It was on Jay and Adams that the heaviest burden of responsibility for the peace would fall in the future. If the younger men overruled his judgment in dealing with England, that was no reason to let the unity of the American commission be weakened; and so he limited himself to pointing out the dangers of Jay's stand.

A formidable question of conscience now confronted Jay. Obedience to the orders of the Congress might undermine the future of his country, as he saw it; but how would defiance of these orders be regarded? More than political judgment was involved here. He was an ambitious man, and the temptation to demonstrate his personal force was strong in him. Many of his contemporaries observed that for a man so able and so successful his need for surface recognition was singularly intense. He enjoyed flattery (and it did not have to be very subtle) as other men enjoyed wine, and with the same heady effect. "Mr. Jay's weakness," a British agent reported to his government a few years later, "is Mr. Jay." At this moment, he was more than a little frustrated, for contact with European diplomats had brought home to him the fact that he was regarded as distinctly secondary to Franklin.

Like George Washington on the other side of the Atlantic, Franklin's fame made his compatriots in Europe seem unimportant by comparison, even an Adams, even a Jay. The shadow of a truly great man always falls very dark on ambitious heads near him. Jay had been a little taken aback to discover the almost worshipful affection and respect with which the doctor was regarded by Europeans of all classes, from dukes to stable boys. An epigram about him written by Turgot (in Latin) summed up the general feeling: "He snatched the lightning from the sky and the scepter from tyrants." And women—young and beautiful women—simply adored him, as if they saw in him the vital force, the humor, and the kindness they wished their husbands had. Fond of Franklin as he was, Jay could not fathom the secret of his ageless charm, but he knew that Sara Jay felt it, and even the children loved to visit the doctor's house. While Jay's expressed feelings about Franklin never descended to the level of open envy and petty resentment revealed by Adams, the desire to dominate in this situation, to prove his independence of the old man, was very strong.

There was at that time in Paris an Englishman named Benjamin Vaughan, an old friend of Franklin, and the publisher of many of his books and pamphlets. This did not, however, prevent him from being at the same time an agent of Shelburne, reporting regularly his conversations with the American envoys. Both sides were apparently aware of his divided allegiance, but used him as a go-between without serious qualms. Vaughan had sensed and communicated to London Jay's doubts of Vergennes, doubts which it was obviously in England's interest to encourage. The very day after Jay learned of Rayneval's departure for London, the British managed to put into his hands a letter which galvanized him into action. Written to Vergennes by Barbé-Marbois, a young French diplomat in Philadelphia, the letter suggested a means by which differences between the southern states and New England might be used to block America's claim to share in the Newfoundland fisheries. How the British had managed to intercept this dispatch Jay did not learn, but he read it with a sense of outrage, as tangible proof of all that he had suspected of Vergennes. Again he drove to Franklin's house—and again the calm response frustrated him. The document, Franklin suggested, came too apropos; might it not be a British forgery? In any event, it was not written by Vergennes, but to him, and so could hardly be taken as representing French policy.

Barely controlling his temper, and with no further consultation with Franklin, Jay sought out Vaughan and asked him to go to London with a private communication for Lord Shelburne. He went so far as to express the hope—or at least Vaughan so related to Shelburne—"that your Lordship, as a wise man, would take the moment to associate to yourself those that had quitted you and were inclined to return to you." Specifically, Vaughan was to ask the Prime Minister to authorize Oswald to treat secretly with the Americans in working out a separate peace, without reference to France.

4. The Gamblers and the Stakes

It was perfectly plain to Lord Shelburne that Rayneval's mission to London had been timed to catch British morale at its lowest. For some months agents in France had reported that French shipyards were turning out warships carrying unprecedented defensive armor—heavy thicknesses of wood and iron, such as would enable an attacking cruiser to move in close to a fortress for a crushing bombardment—and what fortress but Gibraltar could justify such an effort? Then in late August came word that squadrons of the French fleet had gathered off Bordeaux and sailed south—for what purpose, if not to join the ships of Spain for a supreme assault on the Rock? For months the British Navy had been unable to land supplies for the hard-pressed Gibraltar garrison, and the possibility of its surrender had been seriously discussed in a cabinet meeting. It was in an atmosphere of gloom engendered by this expectation that Rayneval appeared to outline the French terms for peace.

Shelburne received him courteously, while finding excuses for putting off serious talk. His chief if tenuous hope of advantage lay in reports from Vaughan that Jay seemed to have turned against Vergennes, and he wanted to give this development a chance to mature. First, M. Rayneval, even though his visit was unofficial and secret, must attend court, and make his bow to His Majesty. (The serious Frenchman had brought no court clothes with him, and went through the ceremony wearing a plain black suit—a lapse which caused the King to take an instant dislike to him.) Another day, another excuse—but finally Shelburne had to sit down with Rayneval in a private conference.

Contrary to Jay's expectation, Rayneval had little to say about America. He sketched a large scheme for world peace, involving British concessions to France in India, in Ceylon, in the West Indies, in the Grand Banks fisheries. The Prime Minister remained attentive but non-committal. As to Spain's demands, Rayneval spoke of the withdrawal of the English from Central America, and the surrender of Florida; he merely threw out the possibility that the British might keep Gibraltar in exchange for territory west of the Alleghenies. When Shelburne showed no interest in the suggestion, Rayneval quickly veered off to other subjects. He was disappointed by the Earl's refusal to follow the logic of his peace terms; that night, in a letter to Vergennes, he wrote that "sentiment, more than reason, influences his [Shelburne's] mind."

The Prime Minister was, however, far from sentimental in the matter. Franklin had convinced him that England's best chance for a quick peace and a healthy future relationship with America lay in a bold break with the past, in a policy of forthrightness and generosity. It was in this spirit that he had prepared to meet Franklin's demands. In doing so he knew that he would invite raging criticism from enemies in Parliament, but he believed he could counter their onslaught with the argument of necessity. While France and America stood firmly together, while the British military position deteriorated, what was England to do? The price for immediate peace was high but delay might drive it higher still.

This was his position on September 12, 1782, after his second meeting with Rayneval. It changed the next day, when the elated Benjamin Vaughan came to him with John Jay's message. For Shelburne, the implications of the overture were tremendous. If a wedge could be driven between America and France, the terms of peace would be far less onerous for England. If Jay and Adams were to lead the American side of the negotiation, then he would be justified in reconsidering the conception of the peace on which he had agreed with Franklin. The King might be appeased, the Whig opposition mollified.

Shelburne was too experienced not to look twice at Jay's gambit, and he questioned Vaughan closely. Could the *démarche* be a subtle trap on the part of Vergennes? Could Jay be relied on to stand firm against French pressure? Would Adams and Franklin support him? Might the French, angered by the American default, insist on continuing the war? On full consideration, the chance was too good to be missed, and he wrote to Oswald to begin secret negotiations with Jay. But he added soberly, "There never was greater risk run. I hope the public will be the gainer, else our heads must answer for it, and deservedly." Parliament, at his request, empowered Oswald "to treat with the Commissioners appointed by the Colonys under the title of the Thirteen United States"—a wording sufficiently ambiguous to pacify King George on the one hand and to satisfy John Jay on the other.

Rayneval, knowing nothing of the American action, was still seeking by patient logic to persuade British officials to his scheme of peace, when all at once the ground of his mission was cut out from under him by sensational news from Gibraltar. The famous red-hot cannon balls used by the British gunners on September 13 had set fire to the finest ships of the French fleet and driven them off in distress. Hope of supplying the beleaguered garrison soared again, and as England went wild over the victory, Rayneval threw up his hands and returned to France.

He found Vergennes profoundly depressed by the failure at Gibraltar, the nagging of Floridablanca, and the unexpected firmness of Shelburne. The aging minister was staking his career on a peace which would not injure his country's *amour-propre*. In spite of the disasters which had overtaken the French fleet, in spite of financial crisis, the people still regarded themselves as victorious, and expected a treaty that would support this conviction. The perils of further war for the monarchy were little understood. Vergennes had long since learned that it is far easier to persuade a nation to the sacrifices of war than to the compromises of peace. At court, he was often urged to continue fighting in order to shatter the British empire beyond repair. A highly vocal party of war-to-the-end aristocrats, led by the young Marquis de Lafayette, was especially troublesome. "That vain and insolent young man," as a British ambassador called him, had found the battlefield an easy short cut to fame, and was blowing hard on the dying embers of war.

In short, matters were going badly, and Vergennes could see no solution but a new diplomatic approach to Shelburne. Let Rayneval return to London, with modified terms of peace; Vergennes's own son would accompany him, to lend weight to the mission. Let them express to Shelburne the hope that England would not this time bar the way to peace, and the warning of disaster if she did. Let England be reasonable, yield up Dominica and Ceylon, and France would do her utmost to make sure that she was compensated by easy terms with the Americans. At this stage, Vergennes had still heard nothing of Jay's violation of the orders of Congress. Like Shelburne, he was deeply conscious of gambling his career and reputation on the draw of a card. To leave no doubt that he sincerely sought a fair and reasonable treaty with England, he wrote a long private letter to the Prime Minister, concluding it with a rueful little sentence: "Eh! What I would not risk to be useful to mankind!" The sigh in the words was not lost on Shelburne. Both men had put all their stakes on the table, and both were fated to lose.

5. *The Gentleman from Massachusetts*

It was September when John Adams finally appeared in Paris, where Jay awaited him with considerable uneasiness. He counted on Adams's well-known dislike of Vergennes, for they had met and clashed a few years earlier; but the New Englander was not a predictable man. On his attitude toward Jay's mutiny against the Congress much might hinge, including the political future of John Jay. Adams's long history of zealous effort for the Revolution and his stubborn quality in strategy and debate had given him great influence in America. Technically, he was the official head of the commissioners, for his had been the first name approved by the Congress for the peacemaking task. A word from him to Philadelphia could be decisive.

It was a relief to Jay to find his opinionated colleague wholly enthusiastic about the new development. In Adams's view, Congress, by aligning America rigidly with France, had ignominiously "surrendered their own sovereignty into the hands of a French minister. It is a glory to have broken such infamous orders!" He warned the Philadelphia politicos that if their ministers abroad suffered themselves to be intimidated, the Mississippi boundary would be lost. He reminded Secretary Livingston that with the transatlantic mails requiring more than a month, often two months each way, the commissioners could not be handcuffed by the need to wait for instructions from Philadelphia. To his diary he confided that Jay was probably honest, but that "Franklin's cunning will be to divide us; to this end he will provoke, he will insinuate, he will intrigue, he will manoeuvre." As for Vergennes, he said flatly, "He means to keep us down if he can."

Whatever satisfaction Jay had found in challenging Franklin's judgment was vastly multiplied in the mind of Adams, who was beset by morbid suspicion of the doctor's good faith. Although the phrase had not yet been coined, guilt by association was already a weapon of politics. Franklin's son was a traitor in American eyes; his former associate in Paris, Silas Deane, had been charged with misappropriation of public funds; and the author of the reckless charges against Deane, the malignant Arthur Lee, had written to the Congress that Franklin himself was "concerned in the plunder, and in time we shall collect the proofs."

As a man who had worked at the very heart of American politics, Adams knew better than to let his opinions of men be swayed by mere accusation —what patriot had not been attacked and abused by enemies? But he joined with Lee in questioning the disinterestedness of the doctor's devotion to the revolutionary cause.

Everyone was aware that Franklin, philosopher though he was, in his younger days had an eye for business, and liked to turn a dollar as well as

the next man. During his pre-Revolutionary service in England, as agent
for the Massachusetts colony, he had put a finger into more than one speculative pie, and pulled out more than one plum. One could put two and two
together, and if so inclined, read the sum as scandal. For example, Franklin
had acquired substantial holdings of land in Nova Scotia, which would be
worth little to him unless they became American territory; could this be
the reason why he was so insistent on the cession of Canada? As for his
failure to demand the Mississippi boundary from the outset—might not
his stock in the Illinois-Wabash Company provide the answer? This speculative venture, backed by British capital, was founded on large tracts of
Illinois prairie acquired from Indian tribes. If the title of the tribes was
confirmed by England, the stockholders might still validate their holdings
and reap vast profits, but if the region should be ceded to the United
States, the company's claims would be wiped out. Seeking the reason why
Franklin had written the memorandum on Canada, and why he resisted
Jay's effort to deal directly with Shelburne, Adams considered that he might
be craftily seeking to keep the Mississippi lands in British hands for the
benefit of his own pocket.

Later, Adams encouraged Congressional inquiry into Franklin's service
as commissioner; and only reluctantly was he finally persuaded to express
publicly his confidence in the doctor's honor and loyalty. In Paris, in 1782,
animosity and suspicion ran away with him. To Franklin's mild attempts
to explain his first statement of terms to Oswald, in which mention of
the Mississippi was omitted, he paid little attention. And yet the facts
were so obvious, so simple, as to need no explanation. Before the Revolution,
the British had formally annexed the territory north of the Ohio and east
of the Mississippi to the province of Quebec, and it was so shown on the
English and French maps of the period used by Oswald and Franklin. In
asking for Canada, Franklin had also been asking for the Mississippi boundary, and had not thought it necessary to say so. But neither Adams nor
Jay was convinced of this.

Like Jay, the stern New Englander felt that Franklin's open delight in
the color and vivacity of French society was a sign of dangerous weakness.
Like Jay again, there was in him a need to prove his personal ascendancy
in the contest for fame which he conceived to be taking place between himself and Franklin. In one of his letters home he recounts compliments paid
him in Amsterdam, and one especially which elated him; a Dutch official
had called him "the Washington of negotiation." He could not resist adding, "This would kill Franklin if he should hear of it" . . . a remark which,
while grossly misreading Franklin's nature, revealed much about Adams's.
Franklin, on his part, accepted Adams's hostility with quiet tolerance. He
had learned early the importance of not wasting energy in trying to be

better than others. Simply to be better than the man he used to be had been his own lifelong aim; and displays of envy in others surprised him more than they hurt him. In his view, Adams was "an honest man, often a wise one, but sometimes, and in some things, absolutely out of his senses."

Adams brought to Paris not only his personal endorsement of Jay's secret approach to Shelburne, but also news of a kind calculated to stiffen American spines. Holland had at last agreed to lend the American government a sum large enough to tide it over current difficulties. This was a triumph all the greater because it had not long before seemed beyond hope. In the first year of his mission to the Hague, Adams had found the political atmosphere so cold and depressing that he wrote of himself as "a man in the midst of the ocean negotiating for his life among a school of sharks," and he suspected Holland's negotiators of being in the pay of England. The fact was, however, that prior to Lord North's fall the prospering Dutch bankers and merchants saw no reason to risk capital in a loan to an upstart republic with a dubious future. They preferred to lend their money to European nations with good credit. Even British interests, as the war approached its end, were able to borrow in Amsterdam—but not the Americans.

To the Dutch it seemed probable that the union of the states would soon dissolve; one of them, South Carolina, had entered into separate negotiations with them for a loan on its own account. Many of Holland's nobles, led by the Prince of Orange, were flatly opposed to American independence. It took Shelburne's rise to power in England to alter the Dutch attitude. Convinced at last that America might survive as a unified country, and foreseeing its commercial importance, Holland recognized the new republic; Dutch financiers offered a loan of guilders equivalent to $3,600,000.

Adams exulted over this event as the financial salvation of his country, and he was perhaps not wrong. In a letter to Secretary Livingston he even boasted that his work in Holland had stimulated Shelburne to make his first overture to Franklin. This was totally without foundation; the fact was that Shelburne's appointment paved the way for the Dutch loan. Nevertheless, Adams's success confirmed in hard commercial terms the military victories of the Revolutionary War, and helped to set the stage for the ensuing peace conference.

CHAPTER FOUR

Pandora's Treaty

1. *"Hanged or Applauded?"*

As the next round of talks with Oswald began, with Franklin still confined to his house, neither Adams nor Jay fully realized how far the British position had changed. Oswald had been reinforced by a career diplomat, Henry Strachey, who had aggressive and resilient qualities which the merchant lacked, who argued every disputed point tenaciously, and who privately considered Jay and Adams great quibblers. He was surprised by their readiness to forget about Canada while insisting on the Mississippi boundary—which Shelburne had never intended to contest. On the two most controversial issues—the debts and the Loyalists—he persuaded them to accept the British position. A sly suggestion that the Americans were trying to swindle British merchants who had advanced them credit in good faith touched a nerve in the rigidly moral Adams, and he capitulated, growling, "We don't want to cheat anybody." It was thereupon agreed that "the creditors on either side shall meet with no lawful impediment"—a phrase which was to haunt the Americans in the years ahead—"to the recovery of the full value in sterling money of all bona fide debts heretofore contracted."

The problem of the Loyalists, which Shelburne had been ready to wipe off the slate, was a sticking point. Strachey contended that eighty thousand or more of these unfortunates were destitute exiles in Canada and England, their properties gone, their lives in danger should they dare to return to their homes. At first, the Americans stubbornly closed their ears to all such appeals to humanity. Their position was complicated by the fact that George Washington, in accepting Cornwallis's surrender, had stipulated that captured Tories should be made to stand trial as war criminals—a "sublime decision," John Adams called it. Franklin was well enough to attend some of the meetings at which the issue was discussed, and with an anger unusual in him, summed up his stand: "Your ministers require that we should receive again into our bosom those who have been our bitterest enemies, and restore their properties who have destroyed ours, and this while the wounds they have given us are still bleeding!" In the end, however, he gave in to Jay and Adams, who led the way to a compromise. While it would remain with the several states of the Union to determine the treatment to be accorded the Loyalists, Congress would "earnestly recommend" that the confiscated properties be restored or paid for. A pious declaration to the effect that there would be no further persecution of Loyalists was also included.

While America's north and west boundaries were settled without much difficulty, when it came to the determination of her southern line the Englishmen were forced to straddle. Under pressure from Vergennes, Shelburne had agreed to return to Spain both the Florida peninsula, which England had taken from the Spaniards twenty years earlier, and the region known as West Florida, including the Gulf coastal plain as far west as Louisiana. This was a decision the easier to make because Spanish troops had occupied these regions. As Shelburne told Parliament, trade with the Floridas was too insignificant to justify a war. But how far north did the Spanish acquisitions extend? When Adams and Jay pressed for a clear statement on the matter, Oswald finally agreed that, since Spain was to have the Floridas, the dividing line between West Florida and the United States should be established at the thirty-first parallel, just south of Natchez. There was no such restriction, however, in the treaty then being drafted between England and Spain. The consequence was that in the Spanish view the Floridas comprised all territory formerly held by the British under that name, and they claimed land as far north as the Tennessee River and beyond. It took no great prescience to see that a Spanish-American quarrel was in the making. But the men of 1782 were too busy with more urgent problems to do anything to prevent it.

Almost every major position which Franklin had taken with the purpose of preventing future war between England and America was lost in the draft of the treaty which emerged from the talks of late October. The broad conception to which he had persuaded Shelburne, based on the belief that a wholehearted British effort to conciliate America would lead to an era of good feeling and active trade by which both countries would greatly profit, was now jettisoned. In the perpetuation of the long boundary between the United States and Canada, he foresaw bitter conflict; in the matters of the debts and Loyalists, endless dispute.

He was perhaps even more disturbed by the shunting aside of another of his proposals to Shelburne—the immediate preparation of a commercial agreement which would establish free trade between the two countries, with full reciprocity of treatment for ships, cargoes, and seamen. Oswald and Strachey made no mention of this agreement. Adams and Jay appeared to consider it of secondary importance. Gloomily and prophetically, Franklin remarked to Vaughan that the opportunity "had been missed and might never return." But he would not stand in the way of Adams and Jay, to whom the prevention of wars to come was a notion too theoretical to merit much attention, and who emphasized what they conceived to be the realities of the situation. They had achieved all that America dared hope for, they were convinced, when Shelburne agreed to recognize the independence of an America stretching north to Canada and west to the Mississippi. England would evacuate "with all convenient speed" the chain of forts and trading posts which she had established on the American side of the Great Lakes and the St. Lawrence River, and which was the backbone of a large and profitable trade in furs. And there was more. The British would open the Grand Banks to American fishing vessels—a gain dear to the heart of the man from Massachusetts. ("When God Almighty made the banks of Newfoundland," he said hotly to Oswald at one meeting. ". . . if Heaven in the creation gave a right, it is ours at least as much as yours"; and the Scot, who had been instructed to yield the point, appeared to give way to so much ardor.) If to obtain these great advantages, America made some concessions to British pride, were they not fully justified? At the end, Adams and Jay were pleased with what they had wrought, and the British were not dissatisfied. "If," wrote Strachey to Shelburne, "this is not so good a peace as was expected, I am confident that it is the best that could have been made. Now are we to be hanged or applauded for thus rescuing England from the American war?"

2. *The Diplomacy of Necessity*

As the time approached for signatures to the articles, the three Americans faced a serious problem: What were they to tell the French? They had ridden ruthlessly over their instructions from Congress and their agreement with Vergennes. Their need now was to find a way to enable Franklin to preserve friendly relations with the minister, for the Dutch credits would not last long, and France's continued financial support was indispensable to America. Franklin himself suggested a formula: let the French be given to understand that the commissioners had agreed merely to a preliminary statement of conditions to be included in a final treaty, still to be negotiated. A letter from the Americans went to Vergennes at the same time that they dispatched a copy of the articles to Philadelphia for Congressional approval.

The news that they had gone so far in establishing peace terms without consultation with him could hardly have surprised Vergennes. His system of espionage was one of the strong spots of the French regime, and it was unlikely that such a negotiation as the commissioners had been carrying on with the British could have escaped his notice or been misinterpreted. His failure to reply at once denouncing the American action implied his willingness to accept the situation. After some days he cautiously expressed his gratified surprise at the many concessions made by the British who, he remarked, "do not so much make peace as buy it." He took it for granted that the French-American alliance was in full force, and that the provisional articles required French approval before they could become effective. "It were sufficient," he wrote, ". . . that the two negotiations proceed at an equal pace, provided that the final efficacy of each depends upon the signature of the other."

Privately, Vergennes was pleased by one aspect of the new development —its impact on his relations with Spain. It would now be clear to Count Floridablanca that Spain had little to hope either from England or America, and so might do well to moderate her demands on France. But whatever the diplomatic advantage that he could extract from the changed aspect of affairs, he could not let the Americans deal so cavalierly with the interests of France without some reproach. A stiff note presently went from him to Franklin, initiating one of the most masterly and famous exchanges in diplomatic history. "I am at a loss, sir, to explain your conduct and that of your colleagues . . . You are wise and discreet, sir; you understand perfectly what is due to propriety; you have all your life performed your duties. I pray you to consider how you propose to fulfill those which are due to the King."

Franklin was able to deny, on his part, any want of respect to the French King, "whom we all love and honor." Jay's action in keeping the talks with England secret he construed as perhaps a neglect of a point of propriety, but certainly not a violation of the terms of the alliance. The incident must not be allowed to rupture the friendship of the two nations, after they had fought together so long and bravely. "The British, I just now learn, flatter themselves they have already divided us. I hope this little misunderstanding will therefore be kept a secret, so that they will find themselves totally mistaken." It was essential, Franklin conveyed, to preserve the fruits of common victory. And how sad if the costly American effort were after all to fail for lack of money!

The one thing Vergennes dared not contemplate, after so much expenditure of French blood and money in the American cause, was a full turning away by the United States from France and toward England. The French government, and perhaps even the monarchy itself, would be swamped by the disgust and ridicule resulting from such a disaster. Empty or not, the royal treasury had somehow to find money for another American loan. In a short time Franklin was able to report to a relieved Congress that a new credit of six million livres, then roughly equivalent to one million dollars, had been offered by France. This sum, coming on top of the Dutch loan, enabled the feeble American government to keep afloat in a stormy sea of debt. But for France the financial effort involved in making the loan was another step along the inflationary road that led to the revolution of 1789.

As for the Congress, when it heard of Jay's disobedience and Adams's mutiny, it grumbled, it threatened, it orated, but it yielded. Every delegate knew that further war threatened havoc. As England was driven by the need to rescue her infant industrial capitalism from suffocating economic pressure, as France struggled to stave off the financial collapse of the bankrupt monarchy, so the newborn confederation of the United States needed peace to survive. In the final test, the large authority granted to Jay, Adams, and Franklin stemmed less from anything stated by the Congress than from utter necessity.

3. *Shelburne Is Destroyed*

In Whitehall, the postwar tide of liberalism was ebbing fast. Vaughan wrote to Lord Shelburne, telling of Franklin's concern over the failure to provide a proper basis for future Anglo-American trade. Belatedly the Prime Minister began to draft a commercial agreement, which was everything that the doctor could have desired. Ships of the United States when laden with goods of their own country were to be allowed to enter all ports of the British Empire, paying only those duties required of British vessels. Trade between America and the British West Indies and Canada was to be entirely free of duties. Shelburne wrote into the document his conviction that "a peace is good in the exact proportion as it recognizes that [free-trade] principle," and prepared to fight for its approval by Parliament. A bill authorizing the agreement was introduced in the Commons by young William Pitt, then Shelburne's Chancellor of the Exchequer. If, Pitt argued, unrestricted trade with the American colonies had been profitable to England before the Revolution, then unrestricted trade with the independent and now more populous states must prove even more profitable. Above all, let them exchange goods freely with the West Indies, where American raw materials were urgently wanted. The influential Edmund Burke agreed, but on other grounds: it was to England's advantage to keep the United States an agricultural country and supply its demands for manufactured goods. "They will not rival us in manufactures . . . Do not treat them as aliens. Let all prohibitory acts be repealed."

While the draft commercial agreement was being scrutinized by Parliament, another major issue came to the fore. Shelburne knew how much total withdrawal of British troops from American soil meant to the new nation. As his government set about the complicated four-sided negotiation aimed at final treaties with France, Spain, Holland, and the United States, he issued orders to the British troops which still occupied New York to sail for Canada as soon as possible, and this was done. A similar letter of instruction was drafted for the Governor of Canada, looking toward early evacuation of England's eight posts on the southern side of the Canadian border. But before this letter could be sent, a delegation of Canadian fur traders arrived in London, and supported by influential British investors, angrily protested the yielding of the posts. Was it the purpose of the government to deprive them of their profitable trade with the Indians across the lakes —a trade then valued at £140,000 per year? The very least that the Canadians expected was a delay. They had accumulated at the forts large quantities of guns, knives, blankets, whisky, and cloth with which to pay Indian trappers for their furs, and it was their contention that they should be permitted to complete the exchange of their merchandise, which would otherwise involve a heavy loss. The British government, after all, had promised no more than to evacuate the forts "with all convenient speed." It was a flexible phrase.

Simultaneously, in January 1783, heavy pressure was exerted on Shelburne by the War Office, which warned of the effect of the cession of the posts on the Indians of the region. The Governor of Canada, General Haldimand, was quoted as saying that if the United States should some day attack Canada, the allegiance of the tribes could be of decisive importance. Thousands of Indians had become economically dependent on the British traders, not only for manufactured goods, but for food, since in the lean years provisions from the forts helped them survive. "They are a part of our family," wrote a British general in command at Fort Detroit. The Department of Indian Affairs at Montreal declared that rumors of the transfer of the posts were already causing great unrest among the tribes, who felt themselves betrayed. None of this would have been in the least surprising to Franklin, who knew from personal experience the psychology and economics of the frontier, and had made his original demand for Canada with one eye on the fur traders and the Indian problem. To Shelburne, however, so much concentrated resistance was highly disconcerting. To put off a decision on the western posts until he could get his bearings was the obvious move.

Then all at once the power to make the decision slipped forever out of his hands. The unforgiving Charles James Fox, impatient for his revenge, unexpectedly and cynically joined forces with his old enemy, Lord North, to form an overwhelming coalition against Shelburne. When heavy Whig attacks were made on the Prime Minister in Parliament and the Tories remained silent and indifferent, Shelburne hastily turned to the throne. But his hope that George, who he fancied had become his friend, might again intercede for him with North quickly dissolved; the King was sympathetic, he was even indignant on Shelburne's account, but he did nothing. In later years, the Earl came to the conclusion that George had secretly encouraged the Tory leaders in their callous conspiracy with Fox. The Psalmist's admonition against putting trust in princes is easily forgotten in the aura of royalty, even by case-hardened politicians. The minister had lost sight of the fact that with the American treaty written, there was little reason for the King to be concerned for him. With the acceptance of his resignation, he sank swiftly into the limbo of outmoded statesmen.

A new government, in which Fox as Foreign Secretary was the dominating figure, promptly succeeded him. When the news reached Paris, it aroused almost as much speculation as had the fall of Lord North a year earlier. For the Americans, the great question was whether Fox would disavow the work of Oswald and Strachey. This he could easily have done, since the provisional articles had not been formally approved by either government. The pace of the peace talks slowed while the British envoys awaited instructions from Fox. Meanwhile, inspired articles full of threats against America began to fill the London press. Sir Henry Clinton stirred enthusiasm with the claim that with ten thousand fresh troops he could recapture all thirteen colonies for England. The *Morning Herald* reported that odds of forty to one were being offered that the treaty with America would not be signed, or if signed would not include the provisional articles agreed upon a few months earlier. Oswald was to be recalled by Fox.

If all this was propaganda calculated to alarm the American envoys in Paris and weaken their bargaining power, it failed of its purpose. They were saddened but not shaken. Adams wrote to his wife Abigail in Massachusetts that the chances of peace had greatly diminished, and that he considered another military campaign probable. But he was soon reassured by word that England would after all abide by the provisional articles. The man chosen by Fox to replace Oswald turned out to be another old friend of Franklin's, David Hartley; and the remaining business of the peace conference went on at a brisk pace. The Treaty of Paris was signed by the combatant powers in September 1783. But all hope had vanished for the commercial treaty and the early evacuation of the western posts.

4. *The Trouble With Treaties*

When Ben Franklin said of the treaty of 1783, "There never was a bad peace or a good war," it was in his mind to influence American opinion in favor of ratification. He knew, however—none better—that there never was a bad peace that did not invite another war. And the treaty made for a bad peace, in the sense that it failed to anticipate the predicament in which the governments concerned would find themselves when they attempted to apply its provisions. Its negotiators had packed a Pandora's box full of future controversy. The document which they produced at Paris marked a cessation only of hostilities, not of hostility. As events proved, there was hardly a clause in it which was not provocative of strain and recrimination.

America's reach to the east bank of the Mississippi brought to a head the bitter question of navigational rights claimed by the Spanish, while the obscurities surrounding the area of West Florida spelled trouble in the south.

England continued to hold the forts and trading posts which she had promised to relinquish. The terminology of the fisheries clause proved to be ambiguous, for while the Americans believed that their right to fish the Grand Banks had been recognized, the British had managed so to word the article as to convey that they were granting a "liberty" which might be withdrawn; and recriminations followed. The American states, disregarding the injunctions of Congress, held on to confiscated Loyalist properties; and lynchings of Loyalists who had the temerity to appear in person to press their claims added to the British sense of outrage. As for lawful debts owing to British subjects, and estimated in England at the time to have a value approaching $25,000,000, an easy settlement could hardly have been expected by the signers of the treaty. Two decades more would elapse, and much mutual abuse, before the United States finally paid England the sum of $2,600,000 to settle these claims. Similarly disregarded was a provision calling on England to reimburse Americans from whom British troops had taken some three thousand Negro slaves. These had allegedly been given their freedom, and London held back from any serious approach to indemnification, pending settlements of the claims of Loyalists and of merchants' debts.

Even the boundary with Canada, which the negotiators thought had been fixed beyond cavil, sixty years later became a source of irritation so violent as to bring the two countries close to war. The Maine boundary dispute of 1842 grew in part out of Anglo-American differences as to the line agreed to by Oswald. By then the map which had been attached to the British copy of the treaty had disappeared from the archives of the Foreign Office.

Not that there is much reason to suppose that a better peace could have been made, given the circumstances of the moment. Shelburne and Franklin, making a heroic try to write the terms of peace in a way calculated to avert future war, could not find around them the generosity and understanding needed for success. The resulting treaty dealt only with problems, not with purpose. Changing conditions made it obsolete almost from the moment of signature. This early obsolescence (which is characteristic of most treaties) subsequently throttled the affirmative efforts of British and American diplomacy. The statesmen who came afterward were forever picking up the debris from the decayed treaty—like architects put to cleaning streets, and given no time to create new structures. Both nations were as reluctant to admit the out-of-dateness of clauses which seemed to favor them as children are to hear a familiar story told with a different ending. The treaty, they pretended, was a permanent contract. Attempts to enforce it provoked disputes which grew to huge proportions before the need for revision was admitted by both sides. By that time, healthy compromise had become exceedingly difficult to effect. This was a point clearly understood by Franklin. He recognized that arrangements designed to avoid future war must be adopted while the desire for peace is hot, that if the treaty makers do not seize the moment of hope and act with resolution they are unlikely to produce in the end anything more than the terms of a temporary truce, that once a war has ended and the pressure groups in the nations begin to make themselves heard, the chances of a lasting peace steadily diminish.

The treaty was hardly signed before the Fox-North coalition dissolved, and a new government, with William Pitt as Prime Minister, took office. So far as Anglo-American relations were concerned, nothing changed. The adverse drift continued. Shelburne's efforts to heal the wounds of war and promote Anglo-American friendship had lost almost all support in Parliament. The treaty itself was not in danger; its ratification would be carried through for the sake of England's internal economy. But as Shelburne and Franklin both knew, a treaty gives little hope of enduring peace unless the spirit behind it is genuinely amicable.

PART TWO

THE TROUBLE BEGINS
1783—1792

CHAPTER ONE

Second Thoughts of a Secretary of State

1. *With All Convenient Speed*

With the treaty out of the way, the American commissioners separated, each to pursue a new phase of his career. John Jay exchanged a formal bow with Vergennes, and gladly set sail with his family for Philadelphia, where he was scheduled to replace Livingston as Secretary of State. John Adams went to London as minister to the Court of St. James, a post for which he had long been eager, as carrying more prestige than any other American diplomatic appointment, including Franklin's. The ailing but still lively doctor could not have cared less. He was pleased by the action of the Congress in providing him with a competent subordinate to help look after America's affairs in Paris, thus making it possible for him to devote more time to writing and scientific investigation.

As the only one of the three peacemakers to return at once to the United States, John Jay was given a fine welcome, and was the honored guest at many a banquet. In taking over his new position at the heart of the government, he was under the impression that England seriously intended to fulfill her treaty obligations. It was something of a shock to him to find otherwise. Adams reported from London that the Duke of Leeds, Pitt's Foreign Minister, seeking to justify England's delay in evacuating the western posts, had made an excuse so perfunctory as to be offensive. It was not feasible, Leeds said, to abandon the posts before American troops were ready to occupy them, for hasty action would invite bloody Indian uprisings. Adams's reply that American garrisons could soon be ready, so that delay was unnecessary, was shrugged aside.

The Congress then sent special agents into the Great Lakes area for the purpose of reassuring and conciliating the hostile tribes. This move proved wholly futile. British commanders of the forts promptly took steps to frustrate the work of the agents by persuading the important Indian chiefs to ignore them. The situation on the border steadily deteriorated. Early in 1784 a group of chiefs approached the British with the proposal that their tribes make open war on American settlements to the south. The official British reply was a recommendation to the Indians to "desist from hostilities," but the words were uttered with a smile. Soon thereafter, braves of the Great Lakes region, carrying British muskets, attacked several settlements on the American side and massacred the inhabitants.

When word of this outrage reached Adams in London, and he made an incensed protest, he was told that the Indian forays were merely evidence of American inability to control the tribes. Jay and Adams now pressed hard on Leeds, asking him to define the phrase "with all convenient speed," and to indicate a specific time for the evacuation. The Foreign Secretary was somewhat uncomfortable; unless England were to throw caution aside, and openly reveal her intention to ignore her obligation under the treaty, she needed a better pretext for clinging to the posts. Events played into his hands. The legislature of Virginia, dissatisfied with the article of the treaty dealing with pre-Revolutionary debts owed to British merchants, passed a law deliberately exempting its citizens from the necessity of paying such debts. Here was a "lawful impediment" to the collection of the debts, such as the Treaty of 1783 had too optimistically promised to prevent. From London's standpoint, this contemptuous snap of the fingers toward Congress by a powerful state came at the perfect moment. Whatever England's loss in Virginia, it was offset twenty times over by her gain in Canada. She could now allege that she was holding on to the western posts only in reprisal for an American violation of the treaty. With the certainty that the diplomatic tangle would take years to unsnarl, Pitt bluntly issued an order to his commanders on the Canadian border to stay where they were.

Patriotic fury ran through the American states like a fever, and John Jay's exasperation burst into a public warning. The posts in British hands, he declared, were "pledges of enmity; and the time must and will come when the seeds of . . . hatred, which such measures always sow, will produce very bitter fruit." In the same pessimistic vein, Franklin wrote from Paris that it was "essential to be on guard against the British . . . England still hopes that some disunion among ourselves may afford them an opportunity of recovering their dominion . . . We cannot be too careful to preserve the friendships we have acquired abroad . . . since we know not how soon we may have a fresh occasion for friends, for credit and for reputation."

With all this, the breaches of the treaty were not allowed to prevent its ratification in 1784, both in London and in Philadelphia. There was, however, a difference in spirit between the two countries in accepting it. The experienced British had their tongues in their cheeks; the Americans their lips compressed.

2. The Nearer to England, the Farther from France

Within a few months after he had vigorously denounced British high-handedness, John Jay suddenly shifted his ground. His first and, there is no reason to doubt, genuine indignation at England's violations of the treaty gave way to a certain judiciousness, and then to an extraordinary tolerance. In his heart he had always been more conservative than in his official words;

his inner identification was always with the aristocracy; he drew back with alarm from the hot radicalism of the angry Thomases, Paine and Jefferson. Benjamin Vaughan's letters give some reason to believe that Jay's insistence on approaching Shelburne directly in 1782 was based in part on his belief that close ties with England would give far more security to American men of property than would any alliance with France. This hidden core of pro-British feeling only awaited a favorable time to assert itself in his public policy. And the time had come. A new and powerful influence had begun to mold the American economy. Trade with England was gathering momentum. Important merchants, especially in the northern states, were urging that in the interests of good business a milder tone be adopted toward the British. Prominent among the advocates of restraint was the persuasive Alexander Hamilton, who in spite of his youth—he was then twenty-seven years old—commanded respect from Jay as from every other man of affairs in America. Hamilton was convinced that in view of the weakness of the Confederation and the troubles among the states it would be folly to antagonize England further. While he never openly said that he expected America soon to return voluntarily to the British empire, it was widely believed that this was his conviction, and many wealthy men shared it.

Jay himself, in 1784, privately questioned America's chances of survival as a unified country, if she insisted on independence. For the Continental Congress was bankrupt. Lacking power to tax the citizens of the constituent states, it had been forced to support its undertakings by foreign loans and the sale of bonds. Now, with credit exhausted, its debts huge, it could do nothing to prevent these bonds from depreciating until they sold at half their face value or less. A kind of financial anarchy was spreading through the land. Scarcity of specie made it increasingly difficult for debtors to meet taxes, mortgages, and bills. The rural areas especially felt the pinch. Throughout the country evictions, foreclosures, and bankruptcies became more and more prevalent. A popular demand arose for measures which would in effect repudiate old debts—such as the printing of inflationary paper money. In Massachusetts, Daniel Shays led fifteen hundred angry farmers in an armed revolt which testified to the depth of feeling in the debtor class, and which threw the legislatures and courts into a panic from Boston to Savannah.

A dim hope of economic salvation for the Confederation lay in one direction only—an increase in trade large enough so that duties levied on importations could meet some of the more pressing obligations of the government. But where would these increased duties come from, if not from British cargoes? Even before the war had ended, Massachusetts concerns had been in touch with correspondents in England to negotiate for goods and credits. Revolution or no revolution, the old habits of doing business were not to be broken, especially when they were supported by a common language and by similar commercial usages. British manufactures were far more to the taste of the American market than those of France. The comparison with homemade products was even more advantageous for England. American-made blankets, for example, used shoddy wool, and soon disintegrated, but British blankets were warm and sturdy. American muskets were said to be less true than the British, American iron to rust twice as fast. Among the Indians, it had become common to speak of any inferior product, regardless of its origin, as American.

Control of credit alone gave England the upper hand. By granting credit on a single cargo, a British merchant could bind his transatlantic customers to him. Before the American buyer could obtain another cargo he would have to pay for the last one; to get money to meet his debt he would have to dispose of the cargo already received; in selling these goods he established the market for similar shipments to come. The conclusion of the first deal with a British supplier locked the American merchant into a fixed credit and marketing pattern—and after seven lean years the eager Americans were not disposed to haggle.

By 1784 American trade had become almost as dependent on England as it had been in colonial days. The British were taken by surprise. They had expected stiff competition from France. Before the peace treaty was signed, and when they had not as yet put any substantial amount of shipping into the transatlantic run, England's press reported with alarm that the French had provided 160 ships and 3400 sailors to carry cargoes to America. The London *Chronicle* of December 3, 1783, went so far as to complain that "France's exclusive attitude toward American trade is the principal obstruction in the way of peace." What was not then realized in London was that the French merchants were for the most part still caught in the fallacies of primitive capitalism, with its extreme caution in the granting of credits, its indifference to customer preferences, and its demands for prompt payment in specie or bullion. This antedeluvian attitude, coupled with the language barrier, made it impossible for the businessmen of France to obtain a firm hold on the American market during the war years. In spite of all the friction between England and the United States, their economic ties were soon too strong to be broken. In the words of a shrewd Frenchman, Talleyrand, reporting this situation to his government a little later, "The first years after a war are decisive in determining the commercial systems of states."

As Jay saw it, the entire policy of France toward the United States was founded on a false assumption for which Vergennes was largely responsible —that the new republic, if kept in a weakened economic condition, would be dependent on French protection, and so would serve French political interests. It was on this assumption that France insisted on extraterritorial

privileges for her consuls in American ports, giving them the same kind of
power that representatives of the United States were to demand in China
a century later. To add to the growing misunderstanding between the two
countries, Vergennes persistently reproached Thomas Jefferson, who had
succeeded Franklin in Paris, for American delay in paying back the wartime
loans made by France—a demand the more irritating because it was so impossible of fulfillment.

3. An Act of Treason?

The new line of Jay's thinking showed itself in a report which he made
to the Continental Congress on the subject of the western posts. Many
delegates were astounded by its unconcealed justification of England's
position. Jay did not say that, for the sake of British trade, the United States
had to be prepared to make political sacrifices; on the contrary, he based his
argument on the moral ground that the United States had herself been
guilty of so many treaty violations that it had little right to object to England's; but the sophisticated understood the economic urgencies that lay
behind.

Historians have since learned that Jay, at this time, was guilty of an act
which on the surface seems so gross an indiscretion that he has even been
accused of something very like treason. Although his report to the Congress
was secret, he deliberately allowed its contents to become known to the
British Government. His confidant in the matter was England's consul in
New York, Sir John Temple, a prominent figure in the rarefied social circle
of the Jays, and one of their close friends. Through Temple, word went to
London of Jay's stand on the western posts.

Compared with Washington, Franklin, or Jefferson, John Jay was a man
of limited horizons, but in practical affairs his sagacity, realism, discretion,
and integrity were respected by the keenest observers of his time. The question of his motive in acting as the voluntary agent of a late enemy intrigues
the mind. Did he do his country a disservice? It is true that if England had
had any intention of modifying her stand on the western posts, Jay's remarkable candor must have made her rulers grin. Was he seeking to establish
himself as their friend, in the expectation of an early return by the United
States to the imperial British fold?

This interpretation is almost certainly as wrong as it is cynical. There are
strong reasons to believe that Jay was playing an honorable if dangerous
game. He was in a position to realize, as few Americans then did, that
England had the whip hand, and her hard use of the economic lash might
have altogether undone the American Government. The temptation in
Whitehall to bear down heavily could only be increased by the fulminations
against England then current in the American press and in the Congress. In

communicating a state secret Jay was almost certainly attempting to mollify the British Cabinet, by letting them know without delay (for they would soon find out anyway; since when has Congress long kept a secret?) that at its center the American Government was disposed to a peaceful, negotiated settlement. Far from serving Temple, Jay was using him in the interest of the Confederation. This may have been appeasement, but only in the narrowest sense could it be termed a betrayal of trust. If Jay's action was treasonable, then every statesman who has with calculation leaked the information which he wanted his antagonist to know—a category which includes the best and ablest of them over the ages—would be a traitor.

4. The Disunited States

It did not need Jay to make England realize that responsible men in America were willing to see their government pay almost any political price to insure a steady flow of transatlantic trade. The intention to squeeze the Americans had been openly revealed in the British press and Parliament for months before. Lust for quick and easy profit was rampant among British businessmen. Forgotten now were Adam Smith's reasoned plea for free trade and Shelburne's high-minded talk of enduring peace. The United States had become again the land of the golden fleece, and the shears were in England's hand. All that the British manufacturers and merchants wanted before backing a governmental policy calculated to put the upstart Americans in their place was assurance that there would be no serious reprisals, and this was promptly forthcoming. A pamphlet written by one of the most influential of England's business leaders, Lord Sheffield, and called *The Commerce of the United States*, scored an instant and large success by asserting that England had nothing to fear from the former colonials. Why, Sheffield demanded, should the Americans, having insisted on their independence, be given more consideration than any other foreign nation? Why should their ships be permitted to participate in the lucrative trade with the British West Indies? By leaving her commerce with America free of treaty obligations, England could exert all needful pressure on the individual states, which would never be able to stand together.

All that was insular and reactionary in British tradition responded to Sheffield's argument, and it captured the government. Leading British politicians of both parties rallied to an aggressive economic policy, until William Pitt found it expedient to change his mind on the subject of free trade, and threw down the commercial gauntlet to America. An order followed to the effect that trade between the United States and the British West Indies could be carried on only in ships built in England and owned by British subjects. Major American exports, such as fish, were banned from British colonies. The embittered John Adams wrote to Jay from London,

"This order is issued in full confidence that the United States cannot agree to act as one nation." This was the heart of the matter. When Massachusetts in a surge of patriotic anger passed laws excluding British merchandise, Connecticut promptly invited British cargoes into her harbors, and profited thereby. George Washington confessed to Lafayette, "It would be idle to think of making commercial regulations on our part. One state passes a prohibitory law respecting some article, another state opens wide the avenue for the admission."

Sheffield proved a sound prophet. Although Americans railed at England's brutal commercial tactics and claimed that she sought to ruin the states, although British anger flared when Yankee smugglers wormed their way into the prohibited West Indies, the essential fact is that the volume of trade between the two countries soon exceeded all previous records, with England showing a heavy credit balance. The time was only a few years away when America would absorb 17 per cent of all British exports, under conditions exceptionally profitable for England's manufacturers and merchants, while three fourths of all American commerce was with England.

5. *"The Touch of a Feather"*

The great question in Jay's mind was: even if the Confederation were saved from internal collapse, could it maintain its territories intact against external pressure? England's agents in Vermont were intriguing with the canny Ira Allen and his brother Ethan, who hoped to link their state with Canada and avail themselves of the St. Lawrence outlet to the sea. To the west, the frontiersmen of the Ohio valley were being tempted by offers from the Spaniards to the south and the British to the north.

Most immediate and dangerous of these threats was that from Spain. Rebuffing all American objections, the Spaniards had occupied Natchez and announced a claim to lands as far north as Kentucky. Their subversive activities among the frontiersmen in this area were backed by strong arguments. Protection from Indians? Mighty Spain if she chose could assure it to the American settlers of the west, the puny United States could not. A market for surplus crops? The Alleghenies, with their hopeless roads, barred the way of wagon freight to the east, but to the south was New Orleans and a gate to Europe—for cargoes permitted to travel the Spanish-controlled Mississippi.

To drive home the point, Spain encouraged the savage Indian tribes of the Tennessee Valley with rifles and supplies. A long series of murderous forays against the settlers followed, similar to those stimulated by England in the Great Lakes area. Simultaneously, the Mississippi was closed to American shipping.

The freedom of the Mississippi was a cause in which many Americans were ready to spill their hearts' blood, and news of Spain's denial of the river to the western settlers shook the country. Jay made a powerful protest to Madrid, asserting "that God Almighty had made that river a highway for the people of the upper country to go to the sea . . ." and that the Spanish action threatened the survival of the settlers of the West. The frontiersmen themselves were of two minds. They were strong violent men, to whom direct action came naturally, and wild schemes to form an army and descend in force on Natchez and New Orleans flourished among them. At the same time, cool calculation suggested another solution—separation from the United States. If the thought of accepting Spanish rule was intolerable, there was always England, whose agents, moving freely through the countryside, spread glowing promises of a safe and prosperous future under British protection.

So dangerous was this threat considered by American leaders that George Washington himself undertook to make an investigatory trip to "the western country." His interest was the greater since he himself owned enormous tracts of land there—land which was to make him an extremely rich man for his time. On his return, in October 1784, after covering 680 miles on horseback, he wrote Benjamin Harrison, then Governor of Virginia, of the need to help and conciliate the men of the frontier: "The flanks and rear of the United States are possessed by other powers, and formidable ones, too . . . The western settlers (I speak now from my own observation) stand as it were upon a pivot. The touch of a feather would turn them any way."

6. *The Diplomacy of Don Diego*

The situation, as Spain saw it, favored a strong diplomatic offensive. As agent for this purpose, Count Floridablanca in Madrid selected a gentleman of good family, courtly manners, and lofty self-esteem, Don Diego de Gardoqui. From Spain's high-chinned viewpoint, as expressed in correspondence during 1786, the problem was relatively simple. Louisiana and the vast lands west of the Mississippi already belonged to Spain. So did the Florida peninsula and West Florida. One of Floridablanca's chief aims was to consolidate and develop these rich holdings. The United States, trembling on the brink of disintegration, was to be asked to recognize the Spanish claim to the Tennessee Valley, and Spanish sovereignty on the Mississippi. If the matter could be settled to Spain's satisfaction in no other way, Floridablanca was willing to grant certain trading concessions to American merchants in exchange. On the appeal of this *quid pro quo* he put great reliance, for the profits and duties of trade with Spain could go some distance to lift the struggling American Government out of its financial miseries.

A considerable sum of money was put at the discretion of Gardoqui to enable him to ingratiate himself with American political leaders. In his use of it he revealed a dexterity worthy of a space-age public-relations man. A Spanish jackass for breeding purposes was presented to George Washington in the name of Spanish King Charles III—a gift greatly appreciated at Mount Vernon. To an influential member of the Congressional Committee for Foreign Affairs, Gardoqui personally made a "loan" of $5000. To John Jay, he offered luxurious and lively entertainment in an expensive New York mansion rented for the purpose; and he went to great lengths to win the good will of the beautiful and influential Mrs. Jay, accompanying her to dinners, soirées, and dances. "I am acting the gallant," he meticulously reported to Floridablanca, ". . . in the King's best interest." It was his firm belief that Sarah Jay molded her husband's opinions.

A vigorous movement in favor of Gardoqui's proposed treaty gained head among American merchants along the Atlantic seaboard. The prospect of a handsome return from the Spanish trade made the struggle over the Mississippi secondary in their eyes. Whether as a result of mercantile pressure, or Gardoqui's persuasions, or the logic of the times, or all three, John Jay changed his mind about the highway to the sea made by God Almighty for the use of the people. Instead, he came to the conclusion that in the trying years ahead the country stood to profit far more from ocean trade with Spain than from the thin river traffic of the struggling western settlements. George Washington, too, admitted that for years to come loss of the navigational rights of the Mississippi would not work a great national hardship. As Jay pointed out, those rights would be denied to Americans whether Spain's offer was accepted or not. By coming to terms with Spain, America, in a state of financial extremity, would give up nothing that she tangibly possessed and would gain income of great and immediate importance.

Speaking in his capacity as Secretary of State, Jay urged Congress to allow him to negotiate a treaty in which America's claim to navigate the Mississippi would be suspended for twenty-five years, in return for commercial advantages to be conceded by Spain. A tornado of protest rose, its center in the southern states. There wealthy men had been buying large holdings of western lands. If these lands were to be sold at the anticipated profit, settlers had to be attracted in large numbers; and how attract them if their chief trade route was closed? Delegates in the Congress thundered for days against Jay and the Spaniards. The wrath of Patrick Henry, whose western investments were very large, stirred southern hearts when he roared that he would "rather part with the confederation than relinquish the navigation of the Mississippi." The South was confident that even without northern help it could force the Spaniards to come to terms. Soon Jay realized that the treaty could never be ratified under the Congressional rule requiring approval by two thirds of the states.

His effort, however, produced a result which he had not anticipated, and did not want. It brought into sharp focus serious differences in regional interest which were to be felt in American politics for decades to come. Northern financiers and men of business were exasperated by the obduracy of southern land owners. Western farmers felt themselves betrayed by eastern merchants who would let them become "vassals of the merciless Spaniards." In time, flaring tempers died down; so did threats of separation from the Union; but throughout the frontier hatred of Spain was coupled with grim distrust of the magnates of the coastal cities.

Angry as the westerners were, they recognized the advisability of avoiding extreme measures until they were strong enough to force the issue of the Mississippi. The time would come—so their leaders prophesied—when decaying Spain would be unable to stand against the growing numbers of farmers, hunters, and boatmen who were steadily pushing into the forests of the Blue Ridge, the Cumberlands, the Great Smokies, and the valleys of the Ohio and Tennessee. Moreover, they had friends in high places. Thomas Jefferson, already identified with agrarian policy, promised that patience now would be rewarded later. In a letter written from Paris, he went so far as to suggest that the best time to use force against the Spanish territories would be when the great powers of western Europe were next engaged in war.

Even so, the leash holding back the turbulent river men, the "Kaintucks," from an assault on Spanish posts was exceedingly flimsy. And Spain was not slow to recognize the precariousness of her own position. Her first efforts to put a check on the settlers took the form of bribes to American frontier leaders, such as the ineffable General Wilkinson, who for years afterward served as a Spanish agent while occupying major posts in the American Army and government. When Wilkinson and his kind proved unable to control the passions of their followers, Spain tried to ease the strain by granting permission to American boats and rafts to bring certain limited cargoes down the Mississippi upon payment of high fees and duties. This grudging measure, however, in no way diminished the latent bellicosity of the frontier. The ingrained determination of the old Southwest to drive Spain out of the Floridas and to teach the pro-British eastern merchants a lesson was to play a significant part in America's policy as 1812 approached.

CHAPTER TWO

America Becomes Capable of War

1. *"Ill-treated Abroad . . . Consolidate at Home."*
While engaged in his fruitless negotiation with Gardoqui, Jay was simultaneously trying to cope with other potential enemies of the United States, notably the pirates of Morocco, Algiers, Tunis, and Tripoli. It had become the custom of England and the continental powers to pay annual "protection money" to the rulers of these states for the safe passage of their merchant ships through the Mediterranean, since the tributes came to less than the cost of a naval war. So long as American colonials had sailed under the British flag, they too were spared from attack. But after the Revolution the unprotected Stars and Stripes on a masthead invited a swarm of ruthless rovers. Seizure of ships and enslavement of crews became so common that in the late 1780s it was a rare American merchant who dared send a cargo into Mediterranean waters, and a rare sailor who would sign up for the voyage. The British, profiting by the elimination of American competition, may have secretly encouraged the Barbary corsairs. So at least Ben Franklin thought. In a letter to Livingston, he quoted a London merchant as saying, "If there were no Algiers, it would be worth England's while to build one."

In 1787 an envoy sent by Jay persuaded the Sultan of Morocco to accept an annual tribute amounting to about $9000 a year for the right of American ships to pass his coast unmolested. Algiers and Tunis, however, continued their depredations, and the Dey of Algiers, unable to extract what he considered his due from the impoverished Americans, even threatened them with war. The humiliation of these events added to the resentment then mounting in American minds over Spain's closing of the Mississippi, over France's demand for extraterritorial rights in American ports, over British retention of the western posts, and over Indian aggressions.

Fear of a large-scale Indian war especially agitated the frontiers as the decade wore on. In 1786, Joseph Brant, the remarkable Mohawk chief and Christian zealot, was sent under official aegis to London, where he formally asked Pitt's government to aid the Indian Confederation to protect its lands against the United States. He came back with great confidence, telling the tribes that England wanted them to "stick to their rights," that the American union was falling to pieces, and that many new guns and much ammunition would soon be in their hands. The fact was that Pitt had become almost indifferent to American views on the western posts. His chief concern in the matter had always been the possibility that in the event of open war, France and Spain might decide to join the United States in another effort to wrest Britain's transatlantic possessions from her. Now such a development could be ruled out. He had just prevailed on the French to sign an unprecedented commercial treaty based on free-trade principles. Traffic was booming across the English Channel. It was altogether unlikely that King Louis could just then be tempted into an unnecessary war.

To the American people, the times seemed full of dark omens. Yet the man most intimately concerned with the diplomatic aggravations of the time, John Jay, was not altogether displeased with what he saw. A resourceful nation, like a resourceful person, he was aware, could benefit even from misfortune. He believed that infringements of America's self-respect, painful as they were, could contribute mightily to the country's future, if they moved the thirteen states toward genuine federation. "The more we are ill-treated abroad," he foresaw, "the more we shall unite and consolidate at home." This penetrating utterance came shortly before the Constitutional Convention assembled at Philadelphia in 1787, for an undertaking then considered by many to be hopeless.

The mood of the Convention was deeply colored by concern over the weakness of the central government in its dealings with other nations. While there was little open discussion of foreign affairs on the floor, every man present knew that as long as the actual military power of the country remained in the hands of the separate states, defeat in war by England or Spain was an ominous probability. Elbridge Gerry of Massachusetts flatly expressed the harsh truth: "If the convention does not agree upon a compromise a secession will take place, and some foreign sword will do the work"; while Washington warned against letting the country sink into "wretched and contemptible fragments of empire."

In the knowledge of America's military insecurity, the bitter disputes between slave states and free states, between large and small states, between commercial states and agricultural states, had to be compromised. The remarkable intellectual and moral qualities of the fifty-five men who met in Philadelphia to draft the Constitution caused Jefferson to describe them as "an assembly of demigods," but it is doubtful that even they could have found agreement if they had not been commonly animated by a sense of desperation. The Constitution, "the greatest work ever struck off at a given time by the brain and purpose of mankind," in Gladstone's language, was, at bottom, an act of self-preservation. The logic of national security was unanswerable. Failure to establish a strong union would invite secession by one or more states; secession would invite foreign intervention and war;

war fought under the weak leadership of a divided Congress might well mean the end of independence. Radicals like Albert Gallatin and James Monroe, who feared abuses of power by a strong central government and so would have preferred to grant no power to be abused, finally succumbed to the unanswerable fact that only the ability of the nation to organize a swift common defense against an enemy could assure adequate protection to all of its regions.

In the writing of the Constitution virtually the only great function of the national government which was not in some way compromised with state interests was the authority to wage war. The states were allowed to have their own militia, but "to provide for the common defense," Congress was given power to raise and support armies, to build and maintain a navy, to make rules for the government's land and naval forces, to provide for the organizing and arming of the militia, and to declare war; while the President was made commander in chief of all the armed forces. This ready abandonment of military pretensions by the states stands in interesting contrast to the painful adjustments which had to be made among them on other major issues. Where slavery was concerned, or the right of secession, or the right of the national government to coerce a rebellious state, the Constitution omitted anything that might have caused the southern states to refuse ratification. The compromises made in these matters were essentially denationalizing, and together they helped to pave the way for threats of secession in 1804, 1808, 1820, 1833, and 1850, and finally, for the Civil War. But behind the clauses dealing with matters military were the uninhibited energies of nationalism.

2. "With All Its Faults . . ."

When it came to approval of the Constitution by the individual states, however, even fear of external enemies was not in itself enough to assure victory. In the state conventions the chief motive for ratification was not national, but local—not danger from abroad, but from angry men just outside the door. The property owners from among whom the delegates were largely chosen were inclined to keep as much power as possible in their respective state governments, over which they could exercise easy control. Many of them found the far-reaching powers granted by the Constitution to the federal administration highly objectionable. But the economics of the Constitution were irresistably attractive to them. For it did what no single state could do—it guaranteed property rights against the penniless mob; and it backed that guarantee with the powers of a federal judiciary—which, in the final test, meant federal guns. According to John Adams, Shays's rebellion in Massachusetts had more to do with the state convention's approval of the Constitution than any other factor. "It was under the effect of this panic," he wrote, "that the delegates had been elected, and that they acted."

Precisely the same feature that made the Constitution attractive to men of property created rampant doubts among the poor. Townsmen in the streets and farmers in the fields, who had been forced by hard times to sell depreciated bonds of the Continental Congress, felt that they had been swindled. Were the bonds now to be redeemed at par for the benefit of the canny speculators who had bought them at their cheapest? Poor men were resentful, too, of their local mortgagees, who had lent them inflated money and expected it to be paid back in hard dollars. Daniel Shays's sympathizers, whose numbers were growing in every state, saw in the Constitution an end of hope of legal repudiation of debt. There was little virtue for them in a strong central government, "one object of which" as Hamilton bluntly said, was "to restrain the means of cheating creditors." Thousands of Americans felt that one man's cheating was another man's justice.

Others were deeply disturbed by the failure of the Constitution as drafted to guarantee them the full political equality promised by the Declaration of Independence. If the truth was held to be self-evident that all men were created equal, why did not the Constitution sustain this principle openly in the law of the nation? This was a question raised by Thomas Jefferson, who was troubled by the failure of the document to include a Bill of Rights. If public opinion polls at the end of 1787 had been able to exert the power that they acquired in the twentieth century, it is unlikely that the Constitution as we know it could have been ratified. Leaders in many of the states found it necessary to mollify their citizens by promising to work for immediate amendment of the Constitution. The consequence was the adoption, two years later, of the nine amendments which form the Bill of Rights.

In spite of all grumbling, the sense of a common cause gradually prevailed over sectional and class feeling. Benjamin Franklin's last speech before the Constitutional Convention at Philadelphia, and the last major address of his life, expressed what was in most hearts: "I agree to this Constitution with all of its faults, if they are such; because I think a general government necessary for us, and there is no form of government but what may be a blessing to the people if it is well administered."

With Washington elected first President a thrill of nationality discovered ran through the country, a great wave of pride in new-found status as a power among the world's powers. The United States now had within it the potentiality of waging war, with all the resources of the country pitted against any nation which encroached on its institutions or interfered with its expansion. From this time on, American history would be marked by frequent popular pressure on the government to invoke its war-making powers. At any provocation from abroad, there was always some offended and vociferous region, economic class, or racial or religious group which felt that compromise was unthinkable and war the only recourse for the nation.

CHAPTER THREE

The Nootka Crisis

1. *Pitt and Miranda*

When John Jay was asked by the grateful George Washington to choose the post of his preference in the federal government, since he could not be President, he decided, after consultation with Mrs. Jay, to become the country's first Chief Justice of the Supreme Court. A new Secretary of State had to be found, and Washington recalled Thomas Jefferson from France for the assignment. Adams had already arrived from England to be elected Vice-President. To Washington, Jay, and Jefferson he gave advice not to replace him in London. It was time, he felt, to repay the British in kind for their insulting refusal to send an accredited minister to the United States, and for the indifference which he had encountered at the Court of St. James. He had been treated there, he recounted, "with a dry decency and cold civility which appears to have been the premeditated plan from the beginning."

England was, in fact, feeling the optimism and self-assurance of booming business, and was not disposed to make concessions to her rebellious off-spring across the sea, or to anyone else. William Pitt, then thirty years of age, was a Prime Minister to delight John Bull—aristocratic, handsome, gifted, astute—and above all, successful. His was the Midas touch in diplomacy—every treaty that he signed turned to gold. In almost every corner of the earth England's trade prospered.

Almost every corner. But not in South America, not in Mexico, not in the Floridas and Louisiana, not in Cuba. Wherever the Spanish flag flew, there British trade was excluded. For the ambitious Pitt, this was a situation to be soon corrected. His perceptive eye saw on the map that Spain's immense empire, then at its peak, had expanded beyond her ability to defend it. Concentrating on ways to break the Spanish monopoly, he encouraged the famous Venezuelan revolutionary, Francisco de Miranda, precursor of Bolívar, to come to London, where he hoped to find British support for the overthrow of Spanish rule in his country.

Miranda's plan was to set up a vast independent monarchy on the shores of the Caribbean, opening to England as her reward the golden trade of the Latin-American countries. For Pitt this was a dazzling dream. After meeting several times with Miranda, he submitted the project to his cabinet.

The risks were evident, but no serious objection was raised. If a suitable pretext for war with Spain could be found—and if France could be persuaded to remain neutral—why not?

2. *The Pretext Is Found*

Nootka Sound was only a remote spot in a largely unexplored continent, a small anchorage on the western shore of Vancouver Island, but in 1789 it loomed suddenly large in world diplomacy. For years the markets of Europe had heard rumors that wandering cargo ships occasionally picked up seal-skins and other furs from Nootka's Indians for a pittance, carried them across the Pacific to China, and there sold them at extraordinary profit for the adornment of wealthy mandarins. As to which country owned Nootka, there had long been mild disagreement. Spain contended that the entire west coast of North America was hers, under an old papal pronouncement; and besides, it was a Spanish explorer, Juan Pérez, who had discovered Nootka in 1774. All this England brushed aside, recalling that Captain James Cook had first made Nootka's commercial possibilities known, and that the first ship to trade there had been British.

Two flags might have been company, but three was a crowd. When at the end of 1788 news came that Russian ships had begun to buy Nootka furs, in quantity, Spain and England moved into action. The Viceroy of Mexico, who had jurisdiction over all Spanish territory to the north, ordered several men-of-war to Nootka, with orders to establish a permanent settlement. At about the same time, several British merchant vessels sailed from England with a similar purpose. One of these flew the flag of Portugal, to mislead any Spanish warships encountered on the way.

Spain's ships were the first to arrive, and when the British merchantmen hove to in the inlet, they saw the Spanish flag on the shore, while Spanish guns were trained on them from the nearby cruisers. Ignominious surrender was the only recourse, and the British crews were taken ashore. A nice question of judgment now arose for the Spanish commander. He had been given large authority, but he had no wish to provoke reprisals. After a difficult interval he released the men and the ships flying the Union Jack with a warning to respect Spain's waters. But the ship which had anchored under Portugal's colors, it seemed to him, could properly be regarded as fair prize; plainly an English vessel, it had flouted maritime law. This ship was accordingly held.

Long weeks elapsed before word of the humiliating affair reached London and the ears of Pitt, and then in garbled form, making it appear that all of the British ships had been confiscated and the crews subjected to long and harsh imprisonment. The providential timing of the news must have made him smile inwardly, even while he frowned for the benefit of Parliament. Spain's calculation in colonizing Nootka was perfectly obvious; England, she felt, would not fight for so small a gain, especially when France's King had pledged himself to stand together with his cousin, Spain's Charles III, in the event of war. But what Pitt knew, and what Charles and Count Floridablanca had not yet realized, was that the Bourbon "family compact" had been made obsolete by recent events in France. In that summer of 1789 the impoverished Louis XVI was in no position to help anybody, not even himself. The new National Assembly had become a major force in the French Government. Pitt's agents in Paris reported that it was showing a revolutionary spirit, limiting the royal power by an assertive Constitution, defying the king to raise taxes without its consent. Confronted by intrepid radicals and by his abysmal financial needs, Louis would be hard put to it to persuade his country to war on Spain's behalf, regardless of the royal honor.

What better moment for England to puncture the inflated balloon of Spanish pride? A stern note went from London to Madrid: England demanded not only the return of her ships and payment of a large indemnity, but also Spain's abandonment of all her claims in the region around Nootka, and a share in South America. Reading the British ultimatum, Floridablanca and Charles III were astounded by its warlike tone. The Foreign Minister uneasily suspected something of Pitt's reasoning, but in the mind of his royal master there was no doubt whatever that cousin Louis would keep his word, that the disturbances in France were merely a passing wind. He agreed to release the seized ships and the crews, if these were still being held, but beyond that he would not go. The first Spanish reply to Pitt was in effect a haughty rejection of his ultimatum—no more and no less than he had anticipated.

Reports from Spain's embassy in Paris continued to give Charles and Floridablanca the impression that Louis was master of France, and even the first violence of the Revolution in July did not deceive them. At Spanish urging, the French Royalist party introduced into the National Assembly a resolution calling on France to support the Bourbon alliance. The great Mirabeau himself, thinking it wise to strengthen the slipping hand of the King, for a time supported this measure. For one or two days there seemed to be a possibility of its adoption, but thereafter, as upheaval continued in France, radicals in the Assembly charged that the King's real purpose in asking for war powers was to effect a counterrevolution, and do away with the new constitutional government. Against this argument, the war party had no chance. Dismayed royalty in Madrid suddenly realized that it could no longer hope for anything from tottering royalty in Paris.

3. *The Ardent Young Men of England*

Wasting no time, Pitt gave orders to make the British fleet ready for war. A great propaganda got under way to win popular acceptance, not for a fight, which the people were ready to welcome, but for taxes, which they were not. London newspapers announced that Pitt had warned King George of impending war. One of the British merchant captains seized at Nootka was brought to London with inflammatory tales of humiliations suffered at Spanish hands, and after hearing his story Parliament voted £1,000,000 to bring the navy to fighting strength.

When this word came to Madrid, the trapped Spanish King wrote a desperate circular letter to all the crowned heads of Europe asking them to use their influence for peace. He was shocked by their indifference. Diplomacy of an extraordinary ruthlessness had forestalled him. Pitt had brought into the Foreign Ministry a brilliant young scion of the Grenville family, William Wyndham, soon to become Baron Grenville and to supplant the Duke of Leeds in the cabinet; and together they had concocted a Machiavellian strategy. Russia, they knew, was interested in Nootka and was thus a potential ally of Spain; so they used British gold and some provocative incidents to incite Turkey and Sweden to invade the Czar's territory, and keep the bear off balance. The thoughts of the Austrian emperor were similarly diverted from possible intervention on Spain's side by encouraging the King of Prussia to press a claim to territory held by the Hapsburgs. France was coldly advised to remain neutral, Holland sharply told that if she lent support of any kind to Spain naval and commercial reprisals would be taken against her.

The aggressiveness of Pitt and Grenville made some of their elders rear back in alarm. Lord Shelburne, who had been made Marquess of Lansdowne, warned Parliament that Pitt was leading the country into foreign embroilments which once begun, would not easily be ended, and might lead anywhere. Speaking with hot irony, he said, "From this era the pacific system was rejected; the ancient language was revived. France was again held out as our natural enemy; England was thought equal to dictate to the whole world . . . our resources were inexhaustible, and our power not to be resisted . . . Holland was obliged by force . . . to return to our alliance. France was dictated to; the Turks were excited to murder the Russians . . . and all this was to be made to terminate in Nootka Sound!"

Only toward the United States did Pitt consider the moment advisable for a softer tone. In May 1790, when the Nootka crisis was at its peak, he instructed the Governor of Canada to reverse his policy, hold the Indians in check, and make every effort to cultivate American friendship. England, it was clear, might need permission to march troops across the territory of the United States in order to seize Louisiana and the Floridas.

4. America Takes a Stand

The Nootka controversy, mushrooming suddenly into the threat of war, was to prove strangely important in the history of American foreign policy. When word of England's war preparations reached the United States, the country guessed that Pitt's objectives would include New Orleans, Louisiana, and the Floridas. The question arose: what should be done if England sought to transport troops across the American territory? Would refusal result in a British invasion of the United States? Old Revolutionary soldiers grimly welcomed the prospect, but many voices asked, "Why risk a useless war with England?" Anglophile business men in the East joined with eager western settlers in demanding that the United States help the British oust Spain from the Floridas, in return for a division of the spoils. When a British scheme for leading Creek and Cherokee braves against the Spaniards was proposed to Governor William Blount of the Tennessee territory, he readily acquiesced.

A British agent, Lieutenant Colonel Beckwith, approached Alexander Hamilton to confide that his government's plan was to march an army southward from Detroit against the Floridas. With this news Hamilton went to President Washington, and quoted Beckwith as saying, "Should a war take place . . . the United States would find it to their interest to take part with Great Britain." Calling a meeting of his advisers, Washington put the problem before them. Although Hamilton privately favored an Anglo-American military alliance against Spain, in the cabinet he was guarded, merely recommending that the British be given permission to cross the western territory if they asked for it. John Jay followed Hamilton's lead and advised a wait-and-see policy, while allowing the British to cross. Jefferson took the other side. He had been working to improve American relations with Spain; and Count Floridablanca, anxious to assure the neutrality of the United States, appeared willing to negotiate further relaxation of restrictions on Mississippi River traffic. Was it not more desirable to have weakened Spain as a neighbor to the south than arrogant England? And what of the military and trading posts still held by the British on American soil, in violation of the treaty of 1783? Refuse the British request for permission, Jefferson urged; stay out of the war if possible, but remain friendly to Spain and above all to France.

Vice-President John Adams and Secretary of War Henry Knox advocated a more determined neutrality. They felt that Washington should sternly resist pressure toward war from both sides. Years before, Adams had told Richard Oswald in Paris, "It is obvious that all the powers of Europe will be continually maneuvering with us, to work us into their real or imaginary balances of power . . . But I think it ought to be our rule not to meddle."

This was the counsel which finally prevailed with Washington. America's policy of non-involvement in European wars was first formulated at the time of the Nootka controversy, and it was to remain intact until 1812. The principles which were later embodied in the Monroe Doctrine also emerged from this decisive meeting, when Jefferson was instructed to warn the British that the United States could not be indifferent to a change in neighbors to the south.

War over Nootka never came, for the extent of England's military advantage was painfully obvious to the experienced Floridablanca. His career was about to be smashed by this crisis, which marked the beginning of the decline of the Spanish empire; but by sparing Spain a hopeless war he at least slowed that decline. Overlooking all provocations, and putting up a strong diplomatic rear-guard action, he retreated far enough to deprive England of her pretext for war. Nootka and the surrounding area would be yielded up, he told the British ambassador in Madrid. Monies would be paid. Even concessions in South America were possible. But if England persisted in trying to force Spain to her knees, his country would fight to the death.

By this time, Miranda's revolutionary scheme had lost some of its luster for the British Government. Influential Englishmen reminded Pitt that the internal troubles of France had come largely as a result of her support of the American Revolution, and drew the inference that it was unsound policy for any European monarchy to encourage colonial rebellion against any other. In prolonged and patient conferences between Floridablanca and British diplomats, the threat of war was talked away. England moderated her sweeping demands for territories in South America, and Spain on her part agreed to limited British settlements there.

America, too, as it turned out, eventually gained land from the Anglo-Spanish settlement. Owing to the inadequacy of the maps then available, the area ceded by Spain to England in the Pacific Northwest was only vaguely defined. The resulting uncertainty aided the United States in working out an intricate deal with Spain in 1819 for a vast part of the region, including the present states of Washington, Oregon, and Idaho. When England entered a counter-claim, the argument grew into a serious threat of war. The Oregon controversy of 1844—"Fifty-four forty or fight!" —was in some sense a repercussion of the Nootka Sound affair of 1789.

CHAPTER FOUR

Grenville Vs. Jefferson

1. *Success for Little Turtle*

William Pitt was an astute manipulator of Parliaments and public opinion, he was perhaps a genius of political persuasion, but unlike his tremendous father, he had little feeling for the deeper currents of international relations. When the Earl of Chatham was Prime Minister he kept all aspects of foreign policy under his direct supervision, for he knew, as all great statesmen come to know, how frequently broad policy is twisted and distorted and remade in practice, how almost painfully its outcome may depend on a detail of execution or an unforeseeable response by an adversary. Not so his son. Increasingly Pitt yielded command of diplomatic affairs to the aggressive Grenville. The chief permanent official of the Foreign Office at the time, Sir James Burges, commented with amazement that Grenville "is rapidly gaining a preeminence . . . Pitt gives way to him in a manner very extraordinary . . ."

At the time of the Nootka crisis, Pitt was inclined to pacify the United States by yielding up the western posts, but Grenville's mettlesome opposition overbore him. And afterward, when there was no longer need to exercise restraint toward the Americans, the Foreign Minister took overt command of British policy toward the United States. His motto might have been "When in doubt, act." The situation across the Atlantic was cloudy, so he introduced a little lightning. New instructions went to the Canadian authorities to put maximum pressure on the Americans. One immediate effect was a lowering of prices on the American border for British-made rifles, scalping knives, blankets, and whisky. Eager Indians came in a steady stream to England's Great Lakes trading posts, and went away again to spread the rumor that the long-awaited moment was near when all the western lands would once again belong to the tribes under the benevolent protection of the Great White Father in the red coat, George III.

All this was related, in Grenville's eyes, to his personal belief (which Pitt did not share) that England would soon be at war in Europe. It seemed to him that fear of the Indians might produce a chastened mood in America, and prevent her from trying to seize the border posts at a moment when England could not reinforce them. The results of his strategy were promptly felt when a number of strong tribes in Michigan and Ohio were organized into a loose military combination frankly aimed at the systematic destruction of American settlements. Their leader was the Miami chief, Little Turtle, a highly intelligent and capable warrior; and his first raids revealed so much power, and were so ferociously executed, that the frontiersmen sent out hurried appeals for aid to Philadelphia.

Secretary of War Henry Knox responded by dispatching an expeditionary force to deal with the menace. Its leader, General Josiah Harmar, knew the western forests, and his troops engaged Little Turtle's braves in a series of inconclusive running fights, until, hampered by heavy casualties and lack of supply, he was forced to withdraw from the region. At once the Indian raids were resumed, even more savagely than before, with bloody massacres of helpless white families. For more than a year thereafter, repeated outcries to the government produced only promises of help for the settlers, until in 1791 President Washington, beset by a thousand cares, responded with an order to muster and equip a small army. About fifteen hundred troops, most of them raw, were assembled in southern Ohio under the command of General Arthur St. Clair, who had been made Governor General of the Northwest Territory.

St. Clair was one of those officers, to be found in every war, who somehow manage to command the respect of politicians, press, and public through sheer personality and charm, and without much regard to actual military accomplishment. He was the man who, during the Revolution, had surrendered Fort Ticonderoga to the British without firing a shot. His plan in the Indian war was simply to close in on the villages of the Miamis and destroy them, as the quickest way to break the morale of the tribes, but he had not reckoned on the sagacity and mobility of Little Turtle. While his column was moving through the forests, it was flanked on both sides by scores of disciplined Indian detachments, and under heavy fire it broke and fled. The defeat was not so complete as that which Braddock had sustained on the Monongahela in 1755, but it was bad enough, and left the western settlers in a plight even more desperate than before.

England's elated commanders in Canada hardly bothered to deny their complicity in Little Turtle's successes. It was taken for granted on the border that open war between England and America was on its way. British garrison commanders began to reveal a studied contempt which fretted American nerves almost as much as the Indian attacks—as when an English colonel at Niagara refused to permit Americans in the vicinity even to view the falls.

2. *Pitt Predicts Peace*

At first, neither Pitt nor Grenville had been greatly disturbed by the upheaval in France. Rather they were delighted to see the military power of the French weakened, as they thought. In the Nootka affair, they hastened to extract benefit for England from confusion in Paris. Pitt's liberal wing of the Tory party even joined with the Whigs in approving the Revolution's early achievements, such as the establishment of constitutional government in France and the discarding of antiquated commercial practices which had hampered the importation of British goods. When Charles Fox and Edmund Burke tearfully dissolved a lifelong friendship in a turbulent Parliamentary debate on the revolution, with Burke predicting that it would "inevitably promote tyranny, anarchy and revolution" in other countries, and Fox descanting on its blessings, Pitt remained quietly neutral. He was not to be swayed either by the rhetoric of young intellectuals like Coleridge and Wordsworth, who were organizing democratic clubs and writing pamphlets in praise of French republicanism, or by the hundreds of French aristocrats then pouring into England with tales of horrors endured at the hands of sans-culotte mobs. For several years, although the upper levels of British society in which his roots were fixed were in a state of high agitation, Pitt held to the opinion that England had no reason to intervene in a purely French imbroglio. Although Pitt allowed Grenville to encourage the formation of an Austro-Prussian alliance against France, direct British participation in the war was so far from his thoughts that he opened Parliament's spring session in 1792 with a speech in which he congratulated the nation on the prospect of a long era of peace, and even proposed the remission of certain taxes.

The country responded with enthusiasm to this sunrise view of the future. The general opinion was that the continental armies then on the move against France would quickly settle the account of the Marats and Dantons. Even the down-to-earth Grenville shared this belief; neither he nor Pitt seems to have sensed the fanatical temper of the French revolutionaries, so that they were caught off guard by the subsequent march of events. It was not until late in the year, when French troops singing the "Chant de Guerre," later known as the "Marseillaise," won the decisive battle of Jemappes and swarmed into the Austrian Netherlands that Pitt bowed to the pressure for war. His decision was taken then not only for strategic but also for practical commercial reasons. The estuary of the Scheldt River, long under Dutch control, was regarded by British mercantile interests almost as their own. When the French compelled the Dutch to open the Scheldt to their ships, dread of being cut off from a major European market convulsed the British counting houses.

Chauvelin, the French ambassador to England, and a man as astute as he was devious, sensed the danger. Without delay, he called on Pitt to persuade him that England was in no way menaced, that her ships need not be denied the navigation of the Scheldt. He was abruptly dismissed. Once the specter of French commercial competition raised its head, the British

government hastily reached for its sword. Grenville wrote in a private letter
that England's aim was "to restrain the progress of French arms and French
principles, even though we should not be the immediate object of attack."
But to England as a whole, long-range military strategy and ideology were
far less compelling as motives for war than the immediate threat to the
flow of commerce on which her survival was felt to depend.

Many liberals in Parliament, including Lord Lansdowne, urged Pitt to
settle differences with the French by negotiation. Pitt replied with a remark
which the heads of conservative nations have been making about foreign
revolutionists from the beginning of time, that there was no government in
France with which to negotiate. In a fiery speech, the former Prime Minister
accused Pitt of evading the issue, reminding him that a similar argument
had been used to prevent negotiation with the American Congress in 1776.
The result in the present case would be equally disastrous, Lansdowne
predicted. Beyond this, he believed, quite correctly, that the government
planned to use intervention in France as an excuse to suppress British
liberties and block impending social and economic reforms. But Cassandra's
voice is seldom heeded. In a short time, the writ of habeas corpus was
suspended, public protests were forbidden, the liberty of assembly sharply
limited, and Britons who had openly sympathized with the Revolution
found themselves in danger of being tried for treason. In leading England
against European radicalism, Pitt had shifted his domestic ground far to
the right.

It was Grenville who composed the royal manifesto which made the war
certain. In November 1792, King George called on the French people "to
join the standard of an hereditary monarchy," and "to unite themselves
under the empire of law, of morality and of religion." A few weeks later, the
appropriate retort came from the French National Convention, which had
replaced the Assembly—a decree urging the subjects of every monarchy in
Europe to rise in rebellion against their king. The Convention then set
about the trial and execution of Louis XVI, and formally declared war on
Great Britain.

3. "Clamors and Combinations"

In the United States, the political implications of the Revolution were
profound, greatly accentuating partisan differences, and speeding the rise
of the two-party system. A frenzy of rejoicing that swept delirious crowds
into the streets of every American city was the initial reaction to the fall of
the Bastille. As de Tocqueville remarks, the French Revolution transcended
the merely political. It had at first a religious character, with a universal
appeal to humanitarian sentiment. A few men of large affairs regarded this
outbreak of "Bastille fever" with misgivings, but in 1789 most people in all

classes saw in the Revolution the dawning of a new era of republican triumph, made possible by a "spark from the altar flame of liberty on this side of the Atlantic." Banquets were held, orations poured forth, streets were renamed to celebrate the event. In Boston, Royal Exchange Alley became Equality Lane.

After the overthrow of the monarchical Lafayette government in 1792, sentiment began to change, especially in the high places of American government and finance. Hamilton, asked if he were a friend to the Revolution, flatly replied, "I hold it in abhorrence." To the people generally, however, the downfall of the French King was merely the natural and proper goal of the Revolution. They longed for the defeat of the European monarchies then organizing for the war against the First Republic. Jefferson, as a spokesman for this sentiment, wrote: "God send that all the nations who join in attacking the liberties of France may end in attainment of their own."

Up to this time Jefferson and Madison had found difficulty in organizing an effective radical party, largely because of Washington's warnings against factionalism. The popularity of the French Revolution helped to solve their problem, by providing a psychological springboard for the launching of the Republican Party—later to be the Democratic-Republican, and finally the Democratic Party. This move was, of course, expressive of much more than political rivalry. Powerful economic forces were then pounding at American, as well as at French attitudes. It had become apparent that Hamilton's financial policy was grossly favorable to the commercial interests of the eastern cities. When, under his influence, Congress permitted private individuals to own the stock of the Bank of the United States, with its monopoly of government financing, there was an explosion of anger among the Jeffersonians. In July 1791, Madison bluntly declared that subscriptions to the stock by wealthy New Yorkers and Philadelphians were "a mere scramble for public plunder . . . by those already loaded with the spoils . . . The stock-jobbers will become the Praetorian band of the government . . . overawing it by clamors and combinations."

The animosities engendered by the dispute over the bank quickened cleavage on other issues. Large commercial enterprises in New England and New York, growing rich on Anglo-American trade, feared that if Pitt intervened openly in France, popular sentiment in America might push the United States into war on her side. The danger was the greater because Americans who owed debts to British merchants saw in such a war a chance of avoiding payment. Many southern plantation owners were in this position. Although they drew back from Jefferson's radicalism, they helped to make his pro-French and anti-British Republican Party strong in their states.

Pitt was not unaware of the dangers for England inherent in the rise of the Republicans under Jefferson. Fashionables in London, to be sure, still professed to sneer at Philadelphia's diplomatic pretensions, and to regard Americans as ungrateful colonials who would presently learn to their cost the enormity of their revolutionary error. But the Nootka incident and America's refusal to become involved in Europe's disputes had brought home to the British government the fact that the United States, under its new Constitution, was a unified power to be reckoned with. If Jefferson, as Secretary of State, should be given his way, the United States would be likely to inflict severe reprisals for injurious British actions. Congress, agitated by England's denial of American trade to the British West Indies, had already considered a bill drafted by Jefferson and designed to curtail British imports. Only Hamilton's energetic efforts had defeated this measure. The London press was full of uneasy mutterings, for England's unprecedented level of prosperity could be gravely damaged by American discrimination against her commerce.

4. *The Grenville Strategy*

Until the rise of the Republican party, Pitt and Grenville had been content to rely for news of America on British consuls and roving agents, such as Beckwith. The threat implicit in Jefferson's large popular following caused Grenville to feel a need for closer study of American opinion. He was strongly influenced by Hamilton's view, reported in letters from Beckwith, that apparent British indifference to America was playing into Jefferson's hands. When in 1791, Grenville decided to send a minister plenipotentiary to Philadelphia, Hamilton was mightily pleased, telling Beckwith that the news would "put an end to the suggestion . . . that we are held in little consideration by the English government."

Grenville's envoy, George Hammond, proved to be a young man of considerable diligence and common sense—perhaps the ablest of a series of British ministers whose prevailing inadequacy helped to grease the slide leading to the War of 1812. It is true that he associated largely with wealthy Federalists in Philadelphia, and, marrying the daughter of one of them, appears to have borrowed his views of American political life exclusively from their partisan prejudices. It is true also that at every turn he consulted with Hamilton, ignoring Secretary of State Jefferson so far as he could. But since Hamilton and his Federalist following were England's friends, it would have been arrant folly for Hammond to fail in cultivating them. To frustrate Jefferson was the Grenville policy, and the young Englishman studiously applied himself to his task.

Soon after Hammond's arrival, Jefferson wrote him a letter clearly stating the claims of the American government under the treaty of 1783. Before the minister replied, he had to await instructions from Grenville. These came three months later, and consisted in essence of an accusation that the United States had not kept its own engagements under the treaty. To this Jefferson retorted with a brilliant and detailed analysis of the still fluid American position on the debt provisions of the treaty and the honest effort made by Congress in behalf of the Loyalists, as compared with the unmistakable, emphatic, and overt violations by the British in connection with the western posts. After a year without a response, Jefferson asked Hammond when one might be forthcoming. The usual formula, "I am waiting for instructions from my government," meant nothing; no reply was ever made. The obvious implication of the silence was that treaty or no treaty, England did not intend to negotiate in the matter of the posts, and simply rested on the fact of possession. Jefferson next tried to persuade England to consent to the use of American ships in the importation of British goods. In another note to Hammond, he pointedly commented that during the century in which England had insisted on controlling the Anglo-American carrying trade, she had experienced three years of war to each five years of peace. The warning was clear; but still there was no answer.

Hammond's early letters to London assured Grenville that Jefferson's Republicans were not strong enough to dominate Washington, that Hamilton's influence would continue to keep American policy realistically tied to its bread-and-butter commerce with England, and that with Little Turtle's Indians on the warpath America would not dare to seize the western posts. There was therefore no reason to debate with Jefferson any of the British violations of the treaty of 1783. Uncompromising indifference continued to be the keynote of British policy toward the United States. No serious negotiations were undertaken to ease the mounting strain; nothing was done to reduce the force of American resentment. In spite of active commercial dealings between the two countries, the shadow of 1812 was already visible twenty years before.

PART THREE

SHADOW OF THE FUTURE

1793–1802

Persona Non Grata

1. *Friendly and Impartial*

News of the impending conflict between England and France reached Philadelphia early in 1793. The popular conviction was that the treaties of alliance and commerce which America and France had signed in 1778 were still in force, and would automatically bring the United States into the war. Most people welcomed the prospect. But in the eyes of some citizens, and those the most influential, a war with England held terrible danger, and the revolutionary change in the government of France justified America in reviewing its position.

The problem took on urgency when a note arrived from the National Convention in Paris, informing President Washington that a new French minister would shortly arrive in Philadelphia to replace the representative of the dethroned king. At a historic meeting of his cabinet on April 19, 1793, Washington put forward a number of questions, which had been drafted by Hamilton. Should the United States remain neutral? Should the French Republic's envoy be received, and if he was, would his admission constitute recognition of the revolutionary government? What position should be taken with respect to the French treaties?

On the issue of neutrality, there was no dispute; all the secretaries were unanimous in agreeing that the United States should if possible stay out of the war. So, too, with respect to recognition of France and acceptance of the new envoy. Jefferson had already expressed his doctrine of recognition (which was to remain in effect until the administration of Woodrow Wilson and the Mexican and Russian revolutions): "We certainly cannot deny to other nations the principle on which our own government is founded, that every nation has a right to govern itself internally under what form it pleases, and to change these forms at its own will . . ."

Dispute arose, however, in the matter of the treaties. In a fine-spun legalistic statement, considerably below the level of his usual style, Hamilton argued that the treaties were no longer binding on America. Jefferson rebutted with a good deal of heat. While he wished to avoid war with England as much as anyone, he said, he felt it only honest to admit that "the treaties between the United States and France were not treaties between the United States and Louis Capet . . ." Though both nations had since 1778 changed their form of government the treaties were not annulled by these changes. The sentiment of the rest of the cabinet was divided on the issue, and the meeting ended inconclusively. Three days later, Washington issued his Neutrality Proclamation—in which, however, the word "neutrality" was not used. American citizens were warned against giving illegal assistance to either of the warring nations, toward both of which the United States would remain "friendly and impartial."

To the country as a whole this pronouncement came as a shock and disappointment. John Marshall, already famous as a practicing attorney, later described the feeling of the time: "By a great proportion of the American people it was deemed almost criminal to remain unconcerned spectators of a conflict between their ancient enemy and republican France . . . The war was confidently . . . pronounced a war of aggression on the part of Great Britain . . . The few who did not embrace these opinions were calumniated as the tools of Britain and the satellites of despotism." In the popular mind, Washington and Hamilton were especially guilty of Anglophilia. In the characteristically unbridled style of the time, Republican orators denounced them as Benedict Arnolds, traitors, and Tories, and many sober observers believed that in the face of so much public resentment the government would be unable to maintain its position.

The arrival in Philadelphia of the French minister was awaited as the moment of crisis. It is tempting to speculate on the probable later course of history if he had been anyone but the incredible Citizen Edmond Genêt. A wiser diplomat representing France to America in 1793 might have compelled Washington to implement the alliance. Even as it was, the President's strong resisting hand was very nearly forced.

2. *The High Hopes of M. Genêt*

To understand Genêt's behavior in the United States, it must be taken into account that he was a prodigy, almost a genius. At the age of six, he had spoken classical Greek; at thirteen, he had already translated and annotated two historical works from Swedish; in his twenties he had served as ambassador to Prussia, Austria, and Russia. The world's applause was as familiar and necessary to him as the "bravos" of an audience to a temperamental star of the footlights. Young as he was, success for him had become a habit-forming drug, it was his tyrant. A fiery propagandist of revolution, a vivid speaker and writer, he saw America as a stage on which to perform, rather than as a nation to be comprehended. This attitude was his undoing. His errors, it seems plain in retrospect, grew out of his inability to fathom the American mind. He never grasped the essential fact that although the typical American is often sympathetic to rebellion he is instinctively hostile to revolution. In Genêt's time, the United States had already learned to cling tenaciously to its institutions while savagely criticizing the men who administered them. British political thinkers like Edmund Burke perceived that while the French were achieving a genuine revolution of classes, the so-called American Revolution had in reality been little more than a rebellion against an unpopular rule. But in Paris this distinction was not well understood. The National Convention was misled by the word "revolution," and by America's sentimental denunciations of kings and aristocrats into assuming an identity of interests between the French and American peoples. It failed to allow for the enormous gap which had developed between European and American ways of thought. One of Genêt's successors, Pierre Adet, was to discover this for himself. Trying to account for the—to him—shocking fact that Jefferson, with all his affection for France, was yet a determined neutralist, he bluntly wrote: "Jefferson . . . is an American, and as such he cannot sincerely be our friend. An American is the born enemy of all the peoples of Europe." It is a feeling which many a European diplomat since has shared.

Genêt had no grasp whatever of the extent of America's intellectual separateness from Europe. He saw only the people's fervid partisanship for underdogs, their hatred of tyranny, their love of a good fight, and on these attributes he traded. Selected for his mission by the National Convention after a brilliant success in annexing the city of Geneva to the French Republic, on his departure for America he had been given such instructions as might have been appropriate in seeking to revolutionize another Geneva. If the attitude of President Washington and the Congress should appear to be "timid and wavering," he was "to take such steps as . . . the exigencies may require to serve the cause of liberty . . . in expectation that the American government will finally decide to make common cause with us." His task, it was plain to Genêt, was to break any opposition within the United States by rallying an overwhelming public opinion to the side of France. And there was more. He was to regard the treaties of 1778 as still in effect, and to draw every advantage from them until such time as he could negotiate treaties even more favorable to France. The French government assured him that the provisions of the existing treaties would justify him in fitting out privateers in American ports to harass enemy shipping, and in commissioning Indian chiefs into the French Army for service against the British in Canada. Since Spain, eager for revenge on the regicides, had declared war on the French republic, her American colonies were to be attacked, and Genêt was authorized to expend large sums for the purpose of enticing the Kentucky frontiersmen into a march on Louisiana.

If the purpose of the National Convention had been to alienate America, instead of to secure her friendship, it could not have done better than to issue these instructions and entrust them to Genêt.

3. *The Voice of the People*

He began auspiciously enough, cannily selecting Charleston as his port of entry, since the sentiment of the South was especially favorable to France. Every detail of his arrival had been calculated. The French colors of the ship on which he came, *L'Ambuscade,* flew above an English flag, which had been turned upside down—causing old soldiers to remember that when Cornwallis's troops had marched out of Yorktown to their surrender, their fifes had played the tune called "The World Turned Upside Down." Slogans had been emblazoned on *L'Ambuscade's* masts: "Enemies of equality, change or tremble!" "Free people, you see in us brothers and friends." Although a consummate egotist, Genêt had energy, charm, and dash, and his first speeches electrified the cheering crowds at Charleston's water front. The women of the city especially were fascinated by his romantic bearing and dark, burning eyes. Asking no permission from anyone, availing himself of France's extraterritorial privilege, conducting himself like a ruler, rather than the envoy of a foreign nation, he plunged into work with immense zeal. Charleston's newspapers could hardly keep up with his speeches, orders, and pronouncements as he bought two swift brigantines, outfitted them as fighting craft, and sent them out to capture British merchantmen; as he instructed the French consul to set up a court of admiralty for the trial and condemnation of prizes brought to port; as he met with the governor of South Carolina and extracted tacit approval of his acts.

Then, with the plaudits of the town in his ears, he set out by carriage for Philadelphia, taking a long route through the back country where the Republican party and pro-French opinion were known to be strongest. In this way, he assured himself of a continuous ovation on a journey which lasted nearly a month. Every town through which he passed exploded with excitement. The Republicans took him to their hearts, wined him, dined him, orated at him, listened breathlessly to his every word. Accounts of his triumphs preceded him, and when he finally reached the outskirts of Philadelphia, cheering thousands were waiting to escort him to the residence prepared for him in the city. British-born William Cobbett described in his *Porcupine's Gazette* a fantastic Republican banquet given to Genêt the day after his arrival, and told satirically how, after the singing of the "Marseillaise," the cap of Liberty was placed on his head, "and it then travelled from head to head around the table, each wearer enlivening the scene with a patriotic sentiment." At this and many other functions in Genêt's honor, speakers pointed out the contrast between the young Frenchman's democratic ways, his warm fraternal embraces, his readiness to talk to anyone, and the austere and almost regal bearing of George Washington, with whom it was difficult for any except the most prominent to obtain an audience.

The first jarring note for the new minister had come during his journey northward, when he heard of the Neutrality Proclamation. This was a challenge to the very heart of his mission, and he did not intend to let it pass. Next, he heard that the President had decided to forbid the commissioning of privateers in American ports. His anger grew, for the harrying of British commerce was a major objective of French strategy. And with reason; for Grenville was then busily seeking diplomatic agreements with European neutrals to prevent needed food supplies, notably grain, from reaching the French West Indies, and the only reply France could make was to disrupt England's West Indian trade by the use of privateers out of American bases.

Destruction
of French
Navy

Genêt was hotheaded, he had exalted notions of himself, but he also had courage. As he saw it, only one course was open to him—to ignore the American government's declarations. This he was bold enough to attempt. The roars of the crowds had convinced him that the American people would soon compel Washington to reverse his stand, and that a break between the United States and England was imminent. Every day brought news to strengthen his confidence. The Republican press reported that Grenville had treated with silent contempt Jefferson's notes on the western posts, that England was now openly encouraging Indians of the Great Lakes region to set up an independent state of their own. Under such provocation, how could Genêt's privateers be denied the freedom of American ports? They were America's reply, as well as France's, to British aggression.

4. *"Old Washington Envies Me"*

The *National Gazette*, edited by Philip Freneau, a protegé of Jefferson, and a member of his staff in the Department of State, went so far as to assure Genêt that the treaties of 1778 would be upheld, for "thanks to our God, the *sovereignty* still resides with THE PEOPLE, and . . . neither proclamations nor *royal demeanour and state* can prevent them from exercising it." It was an open secret that Washington, deeply hurt by Freneau's attacks, had asked Jefferson to end his sinecure with the government, and that the Secretary had courteously but firmly declined to do so. All the auguries seemed so favorable to Genêt that he could not resist writing to the Minister of Foreign Affairs in Paris of "the enthusiasm and entire devotion of our brothers in the United States" and to assert that the Neutrality Proclamation was a dead letter.

From this time, he took the bridle off his tongue. When two citizens of Charleston who defied the proclamation by enlisting on one of Genêt's privateers were arrested, he denounced the government in print for its crime

Singletary

"against the common and glorious cause of liberty." The President, he dared to tell Jefferson, had exceeded his powers; only Congress had the right to determine "that this solemn engagement [the treaty of 1778] shall not be performed . . . [and] to shackle our operations." He convinced himself that when Congress returned to Philadelphia after the summer, the House of Representatives, with a Republican majority, would force the President to withdraw the proclamation, if he had not already yielded to public pressure by that time.

It was in this state of mind that he finally presented his credentials to Washington—a ceremony which he had deliberately put off until the power of his position should be made clear. In spite of all that he had heard of the President, he was disconcerted by the interview. There was something about Washington's majestic presence and reserved force which intimidated even his friends; and Genêt was received with the barest and coldest formalities. The President, while speaking briefly of the friendship of the United States for France, said not a word of the revolution. It was rumored that he had been disgusted by the bloody turn of events in Paris, to the point where he would have preferred a return to the old monarchy, if that had been possible; but Genêt hardly expected to be received in a room, from the walls of which there stared at him medallion portraits of Louis XVI, who had gone to the guillotine only a few months before, and of other members of the royal family.

The Frenchman then became as aggressive as the President was aloof. Vehemently he protested the decision on the privateers; urgently he demanded that the United States abide by the treaty of 1778, which implied permission for all his actions. He was heard out, and no more. When he went away he was chilled and angry, unable to understand Washington's indifference to his logic, determined not to be put off his course. An explanation of the President's attitude presently occurred to him: no doubt it was due to personal pique. "Old Washington," he told his admirers that night, "envies me my success."

And success it almost was. If any other man than the rocklike Washington had been his antagonist, the Genêt tempest would almost certainly have swept the United States into war. Genêt's techniques of propaganda strongly suggest the methods used by twentieth-century Soviet emissaries in weak countries. He specialized in crowds. At one time ten thousand Republicans swarmed through Philadelphia's streets and threatened to drag Washington out of his residence if he did not at once declare war on England. It was Genêt's belief that the methods used by Danton and Marat in organizing the Paris communes could be applied anywhere to inflame the passions of a frustrated citizenry. The machinery of his day for keeping the mass of Americans misinformed was primitive by later standards, but he used it like

a master. Ugly rumors about the administration spread from his house. His
secretary, hand-picked for ability with the pen, assisted Republican fanatics
in composing scurrilous attacks on the President, reviving the old canard
that he had monarchical ambitions. Elaborate symbolism was employed; at
a dinner for Genêt attended by the governor of Pennsylvania, Thomas
Mifflin, each guest plunged a knife into the head of a roast pig to show
approval of the fate of King Louis, while cries of "Death to the tyrant!"
rang through the room. Woodcut prints showing the President being
guillotined were distributed. The streets of Philadelphia at night resounded
with American voices singing the "Marseillaise." Day after day mobs
gathered in front of Washington's house and shouted his damnation. The
weary President swallowed his gorge and continued to go imperturbably
about the business of government, but it was John Adams's opinion, as he
looked back in later years, that pure chance, in the form of an epidemic of
yellow fever, had rescued Washington from an otherwise hopeless situation.
When the first news of the disease was published, fear of contagion swiftly
overcame political frenzy, and the potentially violent crowds could no longer
be assembled.

The epidemic notwithstanding, Genêt's power for a time continued great.
Paying no attention to the prohibitions of the government, relying wholly
on public opinion, he proceeded to buy and equip fourteen more privateers in Boston, Philadelphia, Charleston, and Savannah. The resentful
Washington saw himself flouted by the minister of a foreign power whose
ships defiantly combed American waters and brought more than eighty captured British merchantmen into American ports as prizes. But Genêt's grip
on the American mind made it necessary for the President to bide his time.

Even Jefferson, who at first had been on extremely friendly terms with
Genêt, soon found his arrogance insupportable. When Hammond, the
British minister, protested the ship seizures, and the Secretary of State formally expressed to Genêt the concern of the American Government, he
was sharply rebuked, in the spirit of a master scolding a stupid apprentice.
Genêt, it was obvious, conceived of himself as the leading player in the
drama of the time—a combination of Caesar and Tiberius Gracchus.
Thereafter the man who had drafted the Declaration of Independence
concealed his feelings under a mask of formality. "Whom God would destroy he first sends mad," was a quotation well known to him.

5. Hamilton's Hidden Hand

To the far-seeing Alexander Hamilton, Genêt's assumption of almost sovereign powers and his unceasing revolutionary agitation were by no means
unmixed worries. He knew how small a pin it takes to burst the bubble of
popularity in American politics. One of his agents, of whom there were

many in Philadelphia, reported to him that Genêt was planning a particularly offensive violation of Washington's ruling against privateers. The English brig *Little Sarah* had been brought into port a short time before as a French prize, and lay at anchor in the Delaware River, awaiting an American court's adjudication. Hamilton's information was that Genêt was secretly equipping the vessel as a privateer. Such an act, performed in Boston or Savannah, might have been only another item in the rapidly growing list of disputes between the United States and Genêt. The slowness of communication with other cities could explain previous failures of the government to intervene in time to prevent the Frenchman's previous privateering ventures. But to defy the Administration under its very nose—this was another matter. There could be no excuse except supine weakness for permitting Genêt to bring off this coup, which might well destroy whatever remained of the government's prestige.

Messengers were sent to all members of the Cabinet, summoning them to an emergency meeting. The other secretaries shared Hamilton's alarm and, when a further report from the waterfront verified that the *Little Sarah* was making ready to sail, decided that military measures were required. Technically, however, the violation fell within the jurisdiction of the state of Pennsylvania, and the federal government could not constitutionally take direct action. Accordingly, the cabinet rose in a body and hurried to the house of Governor Mifflin.

Like almost every one else in authority, the Governor had begun to find Genêt tedious, but respected his power. As a first step he dispatched an aide to call on the Frenchman with a courteous request to detain the ship, and to inform him that if this were not done, the Governor would have no choice but to call out the state militia. Genêt reacted to this threat like a wounded panther, with a snarl and all claws showing. Let the government dare to call out the militia! They would see for themselves that the people were the real sovereign of the nation. He would appeal to the people against the President and the government! The aide, who was Pennsylvania's Secretary of State Dallas, realized that Genêt was virtually threatening to head an insurrection and, profoundly shocked, he drove back to Mifflin.

A few minutes later, a company of the state militia was ordered to the wharf where the *Little Sarah* was tied up, with instructions to use force if necessary to prevent its sailing. Notice of this action went to the cabinet, again in session, and keeping the matter very much a secret. The news delighted Hamilton, but disturbed Jefferson, who recognized the dangers that Genêt was conjuring up, not only for the government, but for the Republican party. It was essential, he felt, to prevent violence. In a last attempt to bring Genêt to his senses he took it upon himself to call at his house and urge him to detain the ship voluntarily, until there could be a proper settlement of the dispute. Genêt began a violent outburst, but suddenly checked himself, and became quite reasonable. There had been a misunderstanding, he assured Jefferson. True, it was intended that the vessel should drop down the river to another anchorage, but not with the intention of putting out to sea. This statement Jefferson chose to construe as a promise. He notified Governor Mifflin of the changed situation, and asked him to withdraw the militia. A few hours after this had been done, the *Little Sarah* slipped down the Delaware and was off on its hunt for British prizes.

It then became Jefferson's unpleasant duty to explain matters to the President. Washington exploded: "Is the Minister of the French Republic to set the acts of this government at defiance *with impunity?* And then threaten the executive with an appeal to the people?" The Secretary's position was awkward. He was only too aware of his own previous zealousness on Genêt's behalf. Himself disliking the Neutrality Proclamation as a "milk and water document." he had given indirect encouragement to some of Genêt's propagandist efforts, including the move to persuade the Kentuckians into action against Louisiana. His defense of his friend Freneau also stood thornily between him and Washington. The time had come, he saw, for a tactical retreat, and his expression of outrage over Genêt's behavior matched the President's. Writing to James Madison that night, Jefferson warned him that the Republicans had to abandon Genêt or be wrecked by him.

But the imp was out of the bottle, and could not easily be put back. The Republican press, not yet aware of the change of attitude in the high councils of the party, seized on the *Little Sarah* incident, defending Genêt, excoriating the President, denouncing Governor Mifflin for making the militia "tools of design and dishonor." The newspaper *Aurora* even hinted that Washington was preparing to go to war against France, and Freneau editorialized in the *Gazette:* "The minister of France will, I hope, act with firmness and spirit. The people are his friends and the friends of France. She will have nothing to apprehend, for as yet the people are the sovereign of the United States."

The Republicans, Hamilton saw, were sitting nervously on their own petard; all that was necessary was to touch a match to it, and let it hoist them. This he did, using the device of the journalistic leak, already familiar to government officials anxious to disclose confidences without responsibility. By communicating to his friends, Chief Justice John Jay and Senator Rufus King of New York the previously secret story of the effort to prevent the *Little Sarah* from sailing, he made sure that within a few hours William Cobbett, whose violent paper set the tone for the Federalist press, would be writing an account of Genêt's threat to appeal to the people over the President's head. As the news gained currency, Republicans who had eagerly lent themselves to vilification of Washington came to understand that Genêt, the representative of a foreign power, had insulted and threatened not one man merely, but the government of the United States. Here was an issue which any but the hopelessly partisan could recognize as transcending party. From this moment Genêt's influence waned as former adherents fell away from him, shamefaced, by the thousands.

6. *"Burned-out Comet"*

Genêt for some days seemed unaware that his love affair with the Republicans had ended. A shock from another quarter preoccupied his thoughts. Word had come from Paris that not only had the power of the Girondist party been broken under the pressure of the Jacobin radicals, but Marat had been assassinated, Danton's star was falling fast, and the self-hypnotized Robespierre was master of the hour and of the guillotine. For Genêt this was pure disaster, since it was the Gironde which had pushed him to prominence. Promptly thereafter he received an ominous rebuke from the National Convention's Executive Committee, which informed him that he had never been instructed to regard himself as "the head of an American party . . . We cannot recognize any authority in the United States beyond that of the President and Congress." He was still trying to regain his balance from this blow when the American Congress, reconvening, dealt him another. Following Jefferson's lead, the Republican majority in the House gave approval, however tepid, to the Proclamation of Neutrality and the President's course of action.

Washington and the cabinet agreed that the moment was ripe to demand Genêt's recall, but there was still plenty of fight and impetuosity left in the young Frenchman. When he received a copy of Jefferson's letter to Gouverneur Morris, then American minister to France, asking him to initiate the recall, Genêt promptly demanded that Congress inquire into the administration's motives. Publishing his instructions from the French government and his correspondence with Jefferson, he asked "the American people, whose esteem is dearer to me than life," to "judge if I have been worthy." He went even further, negotiating secretly with the headstrong George Rogers Clark to lead an expedition against the Spanish provinces. For this purpose, he planned to use money which the Congress had agreed to send France as an installment on the old debt and an earnest of good will. But here again he was thwarted by Hamilton, who had foresightedly taken steps to keep the gold out of Genêt's hands. It was only the Frenchman's inability to supply adequate financial support that prevented Clark from raising a Kentucky army for an assault on New Orleans.

Hamilton summarized the new public attitude toward Genêt when he called him "a burned-out comet." Nevertheless, until his immediate successor, Fauchet, arrived from Paris, the young man managed to keep constantly in the news. He was greatly pleased when the French government, while recalling him, simultaneously demanded that the President recall Morris, whose royalist sympathies had led him also into meddling with the internal policies of his host country.

To the end, Genêt carried himself with an air. He had thrown away his country's unique chance to win America to her revolutionary side; but he was still pleased with himself. He did not even appear greatly concerned about deportation to France, where Robespierre's guillotine almost certainly awaited him. Washington, however, had no desire to make a martyr of the young man, and Genêt retreated from Philadelphia only as far as New York. There he was made much of by Republican society, for was he not famous, animated, and single? In time, he married the daughter of Governor Clinton, and settled down to domesticity—after so much grandiloquence, a tame ending.

CHAPTER TWO

The Successful Man

1. *The Hamiltonian Style*

A significant contrast to Genêt's conduct was provided by England's minister, Hammond. Unfailingly cautious and correct, he stayed out of the public eye, and put his faith in Hamilton. It was a faith well placed. Hamilton not only prevented Genêt from financing Clark's march on Louisiana and made maximum political capital out of the *Little Sarah* affair to England's benefit, but he greatly strengthened Hammond in official disputes, and openly defended the British position against Jefferson's thrusts. In his dispatches to Grenville, Hammond always referred to Hamilton as his "confidential quarter"—"I learn from a confidential quarter"—and he was often able to give the Foreign Office information known nowhere else except in Washington's cabinet.

The English minister regarded Hamilton with profound respect, for there was an aura of infallibility about him. This was before the period of his amorous scandals, and the handsome, articulate, easy-mannered man had the great world at his feet. No matter what enterprise he engaged in, he seemed to succeed. It had been so all his thirty-five years—as a student in King's College, as an officer on Washington's staff during the war, as a lawyer in New York, as a member of the Continental Congress, as coauthor with Madison and Jay of the *Federalist Papers*, as leader of the Federalist party, and now as Secretary of the Treasury, with authority second only to that of Washington himself, and with influence second to none. Even the Odysseus-like Jefferson, with his thousand skills, seemed unable to stand against him. Hamilton's victory in the Genêt affair had given him a distinct advantage in their historic contest for power to shape the American destiny. Chance had favored him then, and it continued to help him extract success from apparently hopeless situations until the withdrawal from public life of the greater man, Washington, to whom he had linked his destiny. Thereafter nothing went right for him. It was as if Washington had been his guardian angel, or perhaps a father-divinity, to win whose approbation the younger man felt impelled to live and work at his top level of performance. Without Washington, the incentive to greatness was somehow lost. He who had been the star-blessed became suddenly the star-crossed. Hamilton's judgment faltered, his political enterprises failed, his business speculations went awry, his adultery became a public issue, his name was tarnished by hints of corruption, and in the end he allowed himself to be seduced into his grotesque and fatal duel with Aaron Burr. But while he served Washington, Hamilton seemed to have the gift of transmuting every disaster into triumph. Again and again his alert and vigorous response to chance prevented his policy from foundering at moments of crisis.

His feeling for the right moment was never more clearly revealed than in connection with the notorious Order in Council issued by the British government on June 8, 1793, authorizing British warships to seize American vessels carrying grain to France and her colonies. The story of this order, as uncovered by S. F. Bemis in his remarkable study, *Jay's Treaty*, and as traced through other sources, indicates how featly Hamilton walked the unstable tightrope of public opinion. Preliminary and secret notice of the order was dispatched by Grenville early in June, and reached Hammond in July. Simultaneously, the British Admiralty sent instructions to squadrons of the fleet then operating in the West Indies. The intention was to disclose the existence of the order to the American government only after the initial ship seizures had been made.

Hammond feared that if news of the order came to America as a complete surprise, the resulting sense of outrage and shock might be enough to push the nation into war. He felt that he needed Hamilton's advice, but at first he dared not take the risk of sharing the dangerous secret even with so good a friend of England. On the other hand, it was obvious that failure to give Hamilton preliminary warning might create a serious breach between them, and remove the "confidential quarter" on which he and England's position in America so largely depended. When, in early August, Hamilton confided to him, with much satisfaction, that Genêt's recall was about to be demanded, Hammond felt that he could no longer safely defer speaking of the order. It was his hope, he told Hamilton anxiously, that the American public would not gain a "wrong impression" of England's policy.

The information shook the usually unemotional Hamilton. The order, he said was "harsh" and "unprecedented," and he warned that the American government would react strongly. But his fundamental position was in no way altered. Immediately he sought ways to prevent the inevitable blast of anti-British feeling from getting out of control. Could Hammond, he asked, provide him with an exposition of the order which he could use in the Cabinet to meet the attack which was to be expected?

Hamilton's was not a mind to overlook the likelihood that the British would move first and inform his government later. Nevertheless, he said nothing of the order to the Cabinet, and no warning was given to American ships then about to sail for the West Indies. The core of his politics was the conviction that in the long run what was good for England was good for the United States. It was possible for him to respect Hammond's confidence without serious misgivings as to his own loyalty, for the damage had been done, the order was an accomplished fact. From his standpoint as a statesman the fate of a few, or even a good many merchant ships was less important than the prevention of war; from his standpoint as a politician, there was every reason to delay public knowledge of the new trouble until the affair of the *Little Sarah* had been fully exploited by the Federalists, and Republican prestige further deflated. It was not until August 24, when Hammond sent Jefferson an official notification of the Order in Council, that the American government officially learned the alarming facts.

2. "Rule, Britannia"

Grenville's scheme in persuading Pitt to issue the June Order in Council was aimed primarily at cutting off American shipments of wheat to France's undersupplied and restive West Indian colonies, long coveted by England. He did not, however, lose sight of the fact that the seized cargoes and ships would be of considerable benefit to British military forces and colonists in the islands. A color of legality was needed for the move. It was found in a long dormant British policy which England had used a generation earlier to discourage Dutch merchants from trading with France during the Seven Years' War. Its essence was that in time of war a neutral would not be permitted to trade with a belligerent unless the trade route in question had previously been open to the neutral's ships carrying similar cargoes. Known as the Rule of 1756, this arbitrary policy was based wholly on the power of the British navy to exact compliance. As the British saw it, the rule barred American exports of grain to the French West Indian colonies, where the grain trade had formerly been a monopoly of France.

While the order proposed merely to "detain" any neutral vessels seized, to purchase their cargoes and to pay freight and demurrage to their owners, no one could doubt that these pledges would mean only so much as the British Admiralty chose to make them mean. At the very moment when dismayed merchants in Philadelphia and New York were reading the order, England's warships were at work rounding up scores of American ships in West Indian waters and sending them to British ports as prizes. A few days later, when word of the seizures was brought to the mainland, a wave of fury swept the country, and the fact that most of these ships were of small tonnage did not lessen the shock. But Hamilton was prepared. At once he proposed to the Cabinet that a sharp protest be made to London, through diplomatic channels. Jefferson thought mere protest inadequate, and wished to ask Congress to sanction measures which would sequester all British ships then in American ports, and exclude further British imports until the Order in Council should be rescinded. But when Washington sided with Hamilton, the Cabinet contented itself by sending a strongly worded dispatch by fast boat to the American minister in London, General Thomas Pinckney.

The resulting conversation between Pinckney and Grenville fully exposed the British point of view. Pinckney began by expressing his country's deep concern over the situation. Feeling in America was especially intense because of the high-handed and arbitrary nature of the British action. The Rule of 1756 had no valid basis in law. He quoted a counterrule promulgated by Frederick the Great, holding that "the goods of an enemy cannot be taken from on board the ships of a friend," and a former British commercial arrangement with the Dutch, which stated that "free ships make free goods."

Grenville's polite reply was that many a famous European legal authority —Vattel, Grotius, Puffendorf—could be cited to justify the British position. With great earnestness, he said—as how many heads of state have said since —that this war was different from other wars, and so imposed different requirements on neutrals as well as on belligerents. A French victory, he warned, would endanger America, ocean or no ocean. The enemy had "armed almost the whole laboring classes of the French nation" for war against Europe. Was England to stand inert while a country with nearly three times her population mobilized on so unprecedented a scale? France's aim was plainly to subvert the established order of society everywhere. French secret agents had attempted to foment rebellion in England against the Crown. In dealing with so ruthless, cruel, and anarchic a power, the British were entitled to use every means available to them.

As an American officer who had fought against Tarleton's raiders during the Revolutionary War, Pinckney knew something of ruthlessness and cruelty, and that these characteristics were not limited to any one people. He was aware, too, that the French Republic's vast military effort had been stimulated by enemy invasion and by the counter-revolutionary activities of aristocratic émigrés, aided by England and the German states. Nevertheless he could understand the British feeling. Under the ambitious leadership of Robespierre, the French had begun to assert an almost religious mission to give revolution and liberty to the world. A kind of republican-international was taking shape, and other nations were staggered by the impact of French ideas on their tradesmen and urban laborers.

As usual, the statesmen of the established governments failed to comprehend the power of the energies released by popular revolution. A new and terrifying kind of war loomed ahead. When the old monarchies had fought, statesmen regarded war almost as a game, in which the side accumulating enough counters—victories of its army and navy—would win certain territory or commercial benefits. The aim was not unconditional surrender by the enemy, but advantageous compromise; not the overthrow of governments, but readjustment in their relative power. This conventional and comfortable scheme of war was now shattered. From the moment that French conscripts, shouting the "Marseillaise," beat the professional troops of Austria and Prussia, the doctrine of total war was in the air, although the phrase would not be invented by Clausewitz for another few years. And the French had gone even farther than universal conscription; they had begun to produce improved and standardized rifles, artillery, and ammunition, permitting relatively rapid reloading. Their troops consequently had a significant advantage in firing power. Concealed from public view by the flamboyant Robespierre, the far abler Lazar Carnot was organizing an army such as Europe had never before seen, and which in a few years would provide Napoleon Bonaparte with the essential tool of victory.

Pinckney was aware that England's entire strategic and commercial position on the continent was endangered. It was only natural that her resentment should pour in a torrent from press and pulpit, that fear of the Revolution should spread from the aristocracy into all classes, until the nation which only a few years earlier had sympathized with the French people in their revolt against feudal miseries came to regard them as murderous monsters. Noble blood had spurted under the executioner's ax on many a British scaffold, but there seemed something horrible and obscene in the mechanical efficiency of the guillotine and the scale of its exactions. Grenville's conviction that nothing could be allowed to interfere with the overthrow of the "guillotine republic" had become the sentiment of the British people.

The Foreign Minister conveyed to Pinckney that if his policy bore hard on neutrals, the fault lay in their neutrality. While he did not use the word "crusade" he made it clear that to crush the French republicans was a moral obligation on all right-thinking nations. It was no use, Pinckney saw, to debate either the legality or the morality of the Rule of 1756 with the Foreign Secretary; so he turned to the practical side of the issue. If the sole purpose of the British Government was to bring republican France to her knees, he asked, then how could the controversial order be justified? It was evident that the French people would not starve for lack of American grain. Wheat in France was far more abundant and cheaper than in England. Obviously the target of the order was not France, but the French West Indies, one of America's major markets, and no military threat to England. This being so, it was only fair and reasonable to expect the prompt release of the seized American ships and sailors, with proper indemnity; yet the British courts of admiralty had made no real effort to dispose of the cases brought before them by the injured American shipowners.

There the matter stood. Maintaining his pleasant demeanor, the hardheaded British minister fell back on diplomatic generalities, and Pinckney knew that his oral protest would be ignored. Behind Grenville's attitude was the conviction that America was neither able nor willing to fight for her neutral rights. Pinckney said as much in the discouraged report that he sent off to Philadelphia.

3. *Jefferson Resigns*

The next move was up to Jefferson. Using temperate language, he composed a formal note which Pinckney was to deliver to Grenville, and which detailed the illegality and inconsistencies of the British order. If it was not neutral to export foodstuffs to the French possessions, was it neutral to export them to England? The Order in Council, said Jefferson, threatened the prosperity of American agriculture, and he warned that it might mean the end of American neutrality.

All this was for the record. He had no hope of achieving a result from words alone, so long as Washington continued to back Hamilton's passive attitude in the face of British provocation. Jefferson suspected, too, that Hamilton kept Hammond continuously informed of the confidential decisions of the cabinet. Under these conditions, no change in British policy was to be expected. Diplomatically, the United States had been put in a hopeless tactical position, with no power either to persuade or coerce, and for this Jefferson put the blame squarely on Hamilton.

He was especially irritated by Hamilton's repeated implications that the Republicans sought a war with England. While this was true of a strong segment of the party, the ranking Republican leaders, Jefferson and Madison, saw war only as a last and desperate recourse. War implied debt, heavy taxation, centralization of power in the Executive, large armaments, a big navy, threats to civil liberty, suspension of constitutional rights in a word, disaster to the democracy to which Jefferson had pledged his life. He believed that war was unnecessary—that commercial retaliation would be enough to protect America against any power which aggressed against her trade. Over and over he repeated this, and he wrote it into a comprehensive report which he submitted to the Congress. But still Hamilton persisted in spreading the rumor that the Secretary of State was advocating war with England. And this was not mere politicking on Hamilton's part. He was genuinely convinced that, confronted by such economic reprisals as Jefferson was promoting, the British would declare war.

The enmity between these two brilliant partisans was a source of constant worry to Washington, and more than once he attempted a reconciliation. But their minds were too clouded by political passions, and they were too far apart in belief to permit compromise. The President's efforts merely intensified their dislike for each other. To Jefferson it seemed unmistakable that Washington, who prided himself on standing above party, was at heart in Hamilton's camp, and was being used by him. Late in 1793, feeling that he could no longer accept the Cabinet's policy, he determined to resign his post, and work with his party to drive through Congress the anti-British economic legislation that he wanted. It was only with great reluctance that Washington agreed to let him go, for he disliked the political implications of the resignation, and was unwilling to lose Jefferson's talents. Whatever their disagreements, greatness called to greatness when they met.

4. "... War ... Inevitable ..."

Pinckney in London was as disturbed as Jefferson, and lonelier. In November 1793, he wrote that England's attitude "seems to render our taking part in the war . . . inevitable," and began to plan his departure for France. Nevertheless, when he received Jefferson's written protest on the Rule of 1756, he dutifully presented it to Grenville, and the Foreign Secretary acknowledged it in correct terms. Pinckney had no way of knowing that the note was already too far behind the march of events to have any significance. The British government was about to issue a new Order in Council yet more drastic than the last. Dispensing even with the appearance of legality, going far beyond the Rule of 1756, it directed British naval commanders to stop and detain all ships trafficking with the French colonies, regardless of whether or not such trade had been permitted before. In effect, the new order interdicted all American commerce with the French West Indies, and not only in grain, but in lumber, fish, leather, sugar, and the like.

As before, Grenville was not content merely to announce this measure; he timed its release in the way most injurious to America, signing it early in November, but not making it public until special squadrons of the fleet, sailing from England, could reach West Indian waters. Then, with warships poised for action, Grenville at last told Hammond to notify the new American Secretary of State, Edmund Randolph. By the time the Cabinet heard the news, calamity had already overtaken the country's merchant marine. Two hundred and fifty American cargo ships were plying their routes in or near the West Indies when the British cruisers bore down on them, and seized them without reference to cargoes or destinations. The American flag on a masthead was enough to cause any vessel sighted by the British to be taken to one of their own island ports, where cargoes were unloaded, and sailors flung into foul and fever-ridden prison ships, or impressed into the abominated service of the British Navy. Local admiralty courts did as they wished with ships, cargoes, captains, and crews. The only redress of the American owner of a seized ship was to engage in long and costly litigation before a high court of admiralty in England.

Accounts of these events, trickling into American ports early in the new year, evoked an anti-British outburst which surpassed even the demonstrations for Genêt. Newspapers denounced the British action as piracy on a national scale. Even Hamilton, called to express an opinion, denounced it as "atrocious." Many Federalists who had stood staunchly by England now cursed her as well as France. In southern cities crowds rioted, and hundreds of young men volunteered for the Army, while patriotic songs of vengeance to come rose in taverns throughout the land. A popular actor who appeared on a stage in a Philadelphia theater wearing a British uniform was booed and threatened with violence until he shouted to the audience that he was playing the part of a coward and a bully, whereupon he was cheered. In the face of this hysteria, Jefferson advised Madison, who was then leader of the Republicans in the House, to proceed with care. "I should hope that Congress," he said, "instead of a declaration of war, would instantly exclude from our ports all the manufactures, produce, vessels and subjects" of England until full satisfaction was forthcoming. It would harm the country less, he felt, to be impoverished by the diminution of trade, than to be made party to the European war. And although provocations multiplied, he continued to stand firm on this ground. When Algeria struck heavily at American ships in the Mediterranean, he wrote to his daughter, "The letting loose of the Algerines [sic] upon us, which has been contrived by England, has produced a peculiar irritation. I think Congress will indemnify themselves by high duties on all articles of British manufacture." When it came out that Lord Dorchester, the Governor of Canada, had told the Indian tribes that war was imminent, and they would soon recover their lands from the Americans, Jefferson still continued to urge only economic steps, until many bellicose Republicans became disgusted with what they considered his too great caution.

5. Hamilton Ascendant

A great part of Jefferson's reluctance to see the country go to war stemmed from fear of the large military powers assigned by the Constitution to the Executive. The simple core of his belief was a hatred of tyranny, political, economic, religious. Unlike Hamilton, who was a long-range planner, he was never willing to mortgage the present to a distant future. Intensely conscious of the unpredictability of politics, he could conceive of no distant reward that would justify the American people in waiving their democratic powers, for in history the future had too often proved to be the secret partner of the tyrant. Jefferson was a revolutionary, in the sense that he believed that violence was justified when reasonable talk could not free men from harsh oppression, but he could never have been a Robespierrist in 1793 any more than he could have been a Stalinist in 1953, for in both instances he would have had to support dictatorship and terrorism. During his mission to France he had warned friends among the Jacobins against excesses that were leading them away from democracy. The essence of democracy, in his mind, was limitation of the powers of the Executive. That is why he feared Hamilton, who wanted to make the Presidency more powerful than the Congress and the judiciary. Hamilton's Federalism, as Jefferson saw it, was a steppingstone to tyranny.

Conversely, Jefferson's enthusiasm for the common man seemed to Hamilton a sort of greasy sentimentality, which, if it were translated into policy, promised only anarchy. Both staunchly defended personal liberty, but the Virginian meant a reasonable degree of liberty for everybody, and the New Yorker a great deal of liberty for men of wealth and breeding. Neither was quite fair to the other. Jefferson thought Hamilton a hypocrite because he claimed to oppose monarchy while advocating a form of government monarchical in everything but name. Hamilton considered Jefferson a demagogue because, in order to maintain his partisan position, he was willing to see his country entrapped in a disastrous war with England. Yet, in the end, these two large spirits would prove that they were not, after all, so far apart as they had thought. When crisis tested them, Hamilton kept the nation true to its constitutional principles, while Jefferson kept the nation at peace. They were like rival stars exerting gravitational pull on the solar system. The very diversity of their ideas proved to be a stabilizing influence for the nation as a whole. Each needed the other to get the best out of himself, and to serve his country to the full.

Of Washington's personal integrity Jefferson had no doubts, but he believed the President to be so widely misled by Hamilton and the right-wing Federalists that he might be used as their tool in moves directed against the liberties of the people. On the one hand the Federalists were determined on no account to go to war with England; on the other they persistently asked Congress for large appropriations for an army and navy. This eagerness for arms, in Jefferson's opinion, could not entirely be accounted for by the commercial pressure of would-be military suppliers. He suspected a Federalist scheme to fight France while imposing dictatorship. Guns in the hands of an army under Hamiltonian leadership, he believed, would mean the end of the Republic.

In March 1794, one of Hamilton's disciples, Theodore Sedgwick, introduced bills in the House calling for a provisional army of fifteen thousand men, and giving the President power to lay a thirty-day embargo at his discretion on the vessels of any belligerent. A large number of Republican representatives saw no reason why they should not support this measure, which they assumed was directed against England. But James Madison, following Jefferson's line, warned that Hamilton was up to his "old trick of turning every contingency into a resource for accumulating force in the government," and the House voted down the Sedgwick bills. Instead, and to Jefferson's satisfaction, Congress instructed the President to impose a thirty-day embargo on all shipping in American ports bound for foreign destinations, denying him discretion in the matter.

Even when rebellion broke out in western Pennsylvania, when seven thousand determined citizens took up rifles to protest Hamilton's unpopular excise tax on whisky, and government revenue agents were tarred and feathered, Jefferson counseled against the use of force to suppress the trouble. Others agreed with him, if for different reasons. Governor Mifflin of Pennsylvania feared that the militia, if put into the field, would join the insurgents. Secretary of State Randolph thought it folly for a country so beset from abroad as the United States to use guns on its own people for the sake of a tax. "A calm survey of the situation," he declared, " . . . banishes every idea of calling the militia." But here Hamilton had his way. He was far ahead of his time in understanding the importance of preserving the tax structure and revenues of the nation, of maintaining orderly processes of administration, and of protecting government servants in the performance of their duties. "Shall the majority govern or be governed?" he asked unanswerably. ". . . Shall the general will prevail or the will of a faction? Shall there be government or no government?" He is also alleged to have declared in a cabinet meeting that "a government can never be said to be established until some signal display has manifested its power of military coercion."

The turn of events showed him strong, sound, and wise. Congress was not in session and Washington did not wait. He called out the militia of several states and put them into the field. A few shots were fired, the rebellion swiftly disintegrated, and the American people, realizing for the first time that the government was disposed and able to enforce its laws, felt the nervous elation of a child who knows that he deserves a spanking, and gets it. Jefferson criticized the President for "declaring a civil war" while "being so patient at the scoffs and kicks of our enemies," but it was apparent to the country that he and the Republicans had been seriously set back.

There was in Hamilton's general political position a financial logic that defied all challenge. His opposition to economic reprisals against England, for example, was based on arithmetic so simple that any backwoods Congressman could follow it. British goods constituted 90 per cent of the country's imports, and provided a great share of the government's revenue from customs duties and taxes. Repeatedly Hamilton reminded the country that exclusion of British imports would not merely incite England to war; it would shatter the government's financial structure, plunge it into debt, and stifle its executive branch. Jefferson, to whom ideology was more important than finance, believed that England's navy would be too preoccupied with the war against France to attack the United States, and that in the long run the internal economy would provide the necessary tax funds. This Hamilton considered naïve and dangerous folly. He was accused of playing into Britain's hands, and there is no doubt that he did, but it was in the sincere conviction that he was protecting America's future.

For a time, in the early months of 1794, the embargo advocates almost had their way. All Hamilton's hopes seemed about to be crushed under the weight of the bad news incessantly coming from England. Pinckney reported that Grenville had not yielded one comma of the Orders in Council, and had refused to review the problem of the western posts. Friction on the Canadian border worsened as Lord Dorchester continued to excite the tribes with promises of war. Under pressure from wrathful newspapers, Congress extended its embargo on exports to the belligerent nations for another month. It took all of Washington's influence, exerted at Hamilton's urging, to restrain the House from enacting legislation which would openly discriminate against British imports.

Then, as usual, the unforeseen came to Hamilton's rescue, in the shape of a new French policy. Genêt's successor, Fauchet, had become intimate with Secretary of State Randolph (a friendship which was finally to wreck Randolph's career) and accepting his narrowly Republican view of events, had given the French government a serious misconception of the trend of the partisan struggle in the Congress. In Paris, the Neutrality Proclamation, the embargo, which affected France as well as England, Jefferson's resignation, and the long patience of Washington in the face of the British ship seizures were taken to signify growing hostility toward the French Republic, and as meriting retaliation. The British had set an example of what could be done, safely and profitably, to vessels flying the American flag. Without warning, French cruisers began to prowl the Atlantic trade routes, capturing hundreds of American ships and cargoes bound for England; and their crews were treated with no less brutality than had been employed by the British navy.

Here was justification for Hamilton, and a bitter pill for Jefferson. Public opinion in the United States was confronted by proof that the French were as inimical as the British—and who would be so foolhardy as to suggest that America fight both?

6. Touch and Go

Unexpectedly, America's intolerable situation was somewhat eased by events on the European continent. A succession of French military successes set Prussia, Austria, and Holland to thinking and talking of peace with France. With the continental coalition showing signs of imminent collapse, England faced the prospect of fighting a long and dangerous war

single-handed; and it was evident to Pitt that this was no time to drive
America into France's arms, or to antagonize the British taxpayer by adding
another war to his burdens. Nor, at a time when the treasury needed every
pound which British exports could bring in, was it sensible to relinquish the
profitable American market. Without delay, he issued a new and modified
Order in Council, superseding those which had caused the trouble. America
would now be permitted to trade in non-contraband goods with the West
Indies. More, the British government would pay for seized cargoes im-
properly confiscated. About the same time, Hammond let it be known that
the incendiary speeches made by Lord Dorchester and his aides to the
Indians had not had the sanction of his government, and that Dorchester
had gone back to England.

This little burst of appeasement gave a momentary lift to American
spirits. The Republicans, including Jefferson, mistakenly saw in it a triumph
for the policy of embargo—an error which would have very large consequences ten years later. Hamilton, however, was aware that the new order
was no more than a diplomatic tactic concocted to meet an unexpected
crisis, and in no way indicated a change in the essential British attitude.
From his standpoint, the chief merit of the gesture by London was that it
made some doubtful senators and representatives draw back from Jefferson,
who was now demanding an act forbidding all commerce with England.

There was great danger, Hamilton realized, that at any time some new
provocation might be forthcoming which would swing the scales of Congress irretrievably against England. A new and bold strategy was needed if
the policy of neutrality was to survive. One of Hamilton's chief supporters,
the wealthy, ultraconservative, and highly competent senator from Massachusetts, George Cabot, took the initiative. Meeting with two equally important colleagues, Rufus King of New York and Oliver Ellsworth of
Connecticut, he proposed that the President send a personal representative
to London. Since Pinckney had been unable to make progress, let this
special envoy negotiate with Grenville on all the points in dispute between
the two nations. Only the sanction of the Federalist Senate and not that of
the Republican House would be required, so that if the right man could be
found, the enterprise would be approved. In that event the House might
be persuaded to withhold economic sanctions against England until the
outcome of the mission was known.

A good deal more than prevention of war was in the minds of the three
powerful senators. In some ways, their feelings were similar to those of
American isolationists just prior to World War II. The conservatives of 1940
feared that war with Germany, by linking America with Russia, would invite communism. The Federalists of 1794 feared that war with England
would send the United States down the path of revolutionary France. The

upper-class mood in both periods was expressed by John Marshall, when he later wrote: "That war with Britain . . . would throw America so completely into the arms of France as to leave her no longer mistress of her own conduct was not the only fear . . . That the spirit which triumphed in that nation . . . might cross the Atlantic and desolate the hitherto safe and peaceful dwellings of the American people was an apprehension not . . . entirely unsupported by appearances . . ." The mission to England was conceived by Cabot, King, and Ellsworth partly as a means to put England on notice that her provocative policy, by playing into the hands of the American radicals, invited social upheaval on the French model.

Word of the senators' meeting soon leaked out, and it became known that Hamilton was their preference for the task. It is doubtful, however, that men so shrewd and experienced as these seriously expected that the controversial Secretary would consent to go, or that if he did go, the House would co-operate to give him a chance of success. The suggestion of his name was more likely to have been a device to divert Republican attention away from the conception of the mission itself, by focusing opposition on the choice of the man. Meanwhile Hamilton had persuaded Washington that John Jay was the ideal man for the purpose, and together with Cabot and King, had brought great pressure on the Chief Justice to accept.

In considering the personal significance of Jay's response, it must be taken into account that he was considered, at that time, to have an excellent chance of supplanting John Adams as Washington's successor in the presidency, and the task which he was being asked to undertake was full of obvious danger to his political future. His initial reluctance gave way, however, as he considered the country's need, his party's plight, and the extraordinary opportunity to make history. He would accept, he said finally, if the anti-British bills sponsored by the Republicans and then pending in the Congress could be pigeonholed, since if enacted they would wreck the enterprise before it was begun. In a letter to his wife he explained his position: "The public considerations which were urged . . . strongly impressed me with a conviction that to refuse it would be to desert my duty for the sake of my ease . . ." There is no reason to doubt that he was writing from the heart.

As soon as Jay's consent was in hand, Hamilton quietly withdrew his name from consideration for the London mission, and the President sent Jay's nomination to the Senate. The debate was relatively brief. Eight senators were opposed on the ground that Jay had shown himself too favorably disposed toward England, but the other eighteen voted for him, and on May 12, 1794, he sailed. A warning from Washington to the House that it was of the utmost importance to defer legislation aimed at economic reprisals against England was received with grumbling, but it was heeded.

Once again, time had worked for Hamilton. A few days later, shocking news came from the west—news which could easily have destroyed his strategy if it had come before Jay's departure. The deputy governor of Lower Canada, John Simcoe, acting in the absence of the indiscreet Lord Dorchester, had virtually declared war on the United States by sending British troops thirty miles southwest of Detroit to build and garrison a new fort in the heart of Miami Indian country—territory unmistakably American under the Treaty of 1783. Simcoe was a man with a pathological hatred of America, an inflated conception of his own importance, and a fixed belief that the United States was planning an assault on the British-held western posts. A short time before, Congress had voted an army of five thousand men for the West, and Washington had appointed General Anthony Wayne to command it against Little Turtle's Indians. Such a force, Simcoe held, was excessive for a punitive expedition against the tribes, and could only presage war on Canada. On this assumption, he felt it necessary to prepare new defenses for Detroit, regardless of treaty stipulations and the effect on American opinion; and by distorting facts he managed to persuade Dorchester and Grenville of the essentiality of the new Miami fort.

This was a hard knock for Congress and the people to take without striking back. But with Jay en route to England, the President was able to still the clamor for immediate war. Angry senators were made to understand that regardless of the outcome of Jay's mission, an attack on Simcoe's new fort would for some time be out of the question, since General Wayne was still recruiting and drilling his army. Thus, in the precarious summer of 1794, the Hamiltonian policy still stood intact; there was still a chance of peace with England.

CHAPTER THREE

"This Damned Treaty"

1. *As Only the British Know How*

To Lord Grenville, the American negotiation was of secondary importance. Realizing that England, with a comparatively small population, had to rely heavily on the armies of allies while concentrating her own efforts on control of the sea, he was then immersed in a complex of subsidies, bribes, and secret treaties by which he hoped to keep Prussian and Austrian troops waging his country's continental battles with the French. The Viennese who first said "England expects every Austrian to do his duty" was quite right. For England, the conservation of manpower for the final battle was the strategy of survival. Grenville, more than any other, was responsible for the policy which wore down the armies of France for years before any considerable body of British troops was risked in the fighting.

His interest in a possible treaty with the United States grew primarily out of his desire to reduce, if he could not altogether prevent, American trade with the French, and so weaken the devil across the Channel. Did the United States want peace badly enough to consent to British maritime rules designed for this purpose? If not, then a transatlantic war would have to be added to England's burden. But although this was the essence of his American policy, it was by no means all of it. Like every statesman worth his salt, he knew better than to be negligent of weeds anywhere in his diplomatic garden. The spores of trouble traveled the winds, and were fertile; danger ignored in America could crop up multiplied in Europe or India. War with America would not necessarily be a disaster for England, but it was to be avoided if possible.

For this reason, the selection of John Jay as the American negotiator seemed to Grenville a good omen. Jay was a conservative by nature, an Anglophile, a member of Hamilton's inner circle, and a New Yorker, linked by tradition and interest to the merchants of the American North, rather than to the planters of the South. As a lawyer and an experienced statesman, he was not inclined to stand on abstract doctrines, but to work for practical compromises.

All this was good, but there were in Grenville's dossier on Jay indications even more hopeful. A personal description of Jay by a British agent who had known him gave him credit for good sense, patience, a long memory, and skill in argument, but went on to describe him as long-winded, opinionated, and above all, vain. "He can bear any opposition to what he advocates provided regard is shown to his ability. He may be attached by good treatment but will be unforgiving if he thinks himself neglected." Here was a clue that Grenville could follow. This was no Adams, with his Puritan stubbornness, no Pinckney, with his soldierly obedience to instructions. Grenville conferred with Pitt, and made his plans.

No American had ever received from the British so heart-warming a reception as that given Jay. With the perfection of style for which British diplomacy was—and is—justly famous, his hosts whisked him into a world of which he had read and dreamed—a world where aristocracy, talent, and elegance sat all around him. A glittering dinner at Lord Grenville's on the night following his arrival introduced him to the British Cabinet. A few days later Pitt himself entertained him. Invitations from the great houses poured in on him. He was taken to the bosom of British society, and coddled, and flattered. The intellects of England made much of him. Edmund Burke and Jeremy Bentham sought him out. Lord Chancellor Loughborough sent him a brace of grouse. The Bishop of London preached a sermon for him. Royalty itself joined in the game. Not only the King, but Queen Charlotte graciously received Jay; and she extended her hand to him, and he bowed, and kissed it. Word of that kiss was to go to the United States, and explode in the Republican press. "Men of America, he betrayed you with a kiss!" But Jay, in the summer of 1794, was indifferent to public opinion back home. How could provincial Americans be expected to understand the formal etiquette of the great world? His was the elation of a man who has at last come into his own. The aristocratic philosophy of politics, which he was later to express in a sentence: "Those who own the country ought to govern it," was irresistibly attractive to him. As the official negotiations began, he found himself sitting with men with whom he had drunk toasts of friendship the night before, men who did not conceal their admiration and respect for him. If he remembered the intensely patriotic John Jay of twelve years earlier, suspicious of every foreigner, he must have thought of him patronizingly as a manifestation of youthful naïveté.

Although he had been given some discretionary powers, his instructions were definite. He was to settle to America's satisfaction the conflicts arising out of the Treaty of 1783—especially the matters of the western posts and the slave seizures. He was to require England to make suitable compensation for her depredations under the Orders in Council, and to desist from further interference with American ships on their lawful occasions. If possible, he was to persuade the British to open their West Indian possessions to American merchants. In any event, he was to agree to nothing contrary to America's engagements with France. Jay must have been well aware that neither the President nor Hamilton expected him to follow these instructions to the letter, or even to the paragraph. In order to allay Jeffersonian fears, Edmund Randolph had been allowed a large hand in writing them; they represented one of Hamilton's subtlest deceptions. It was only because Randolph believed his instructions to be binding and so informed the French government that Jay was able to complete his mission without intervention by France.

To begin, Grenville seemed all courtesy and conciliation. He had no hesitation in saying that Lord Dorchester, in his incendiary speeches to the Indians, had overstepped his authority. It was not true, as his lordship had conveyed, that England intended to make war on the United States after defeating France. Dorchester, then in London, would be reprimanded. As to the situation created by Simcoe's action in establishing Fort Miami, it would be necessary to await reports of General Wayne's campaign against the Indians before taking action. If Wayne did not force war upon England by attacking British troops, it was possible that the western posts would be soon surrendered—provided, of course, that other elements of dispute could be settled.

This was a hopeful note. Jay was able to assure Grenville that the orders given Wayne by President Washington explicitly confined him to the sub-jugation of the warring Indians. No attack on the British, even on Fort Miami, was to be undertaken. Knowing Wayne's reputation for impetuous derring-do, however, Jay was by no means confident that a Canadian war would not blaze up while he was sparring with the British. He suggested to Grenville that they should at first avoid written communications, and talk informally "until there should appear a probability of coming to some amicable mutual understanding," since this was not a trial of diplomatic skill, but "a solemn question of peace or war between two peoples . . . on whose continued good understanding might perhaps depend the future freedom and happiness of the human race." To this statesmanlike proposal, Grenville readily acceded.

2. Below the Surface

The strongest card in Grenville's hand was Jay's patent desire to avoid war. For the rest, he held few trumps. The war with France was going badly. Austrian and German armies had been unable to prevent hard-hitting French troops from occupying the Low Countries and the Rhineland. Spain, having cast in her lot with England after the guillotining of Louis XVI, now regretted her bargain, and was veering again toward a French alliance. In England, taxes were rising, stock prices falling. Tories in Parliament were making their disappointment known; Whig liberals, headed by the irrepressible Charles Fox, never ceased to attack Pitt's heavy-handed suppression of civil liberties.

England's position in America was hardly more encouraging. She occupied the western posts, but illegally; the British navy could make rules for American shipping, but without sanction of treaty; in a war with the United States, England might inflict serious damage, but not without suffering the loss of profitable trade.

There was more. Below the surface of politics, pressure for peace with America was again being exerted on the government by the cloth makers, who owned England's principal industry. In 1792, an American, Eli Whitney, had invented a machine, the cotton gin, for mechanically extracting cottonseed from raw cotton, and so eliminating the slow process of hand-picking the seeds. Reports of his success, and of the imminent expansion of the American short-staple cotton crop, had aroused great interest and produced a radical change in the long-range plans of England's cotton importers. Until then, they had given little encouragement to American cotton growers, who had made their first plantings only during the Revolution, and whose production in 1794 was still negligible. Costly, long-staple Indian cotton, which required to be shipped 13,000 miles out of Bombay, around the Cape of Good Hope, was the mainstay of the industry. To preserve this arrangement was the policy of the immensely powerful East India Company, in which some of the cotton manufacturers themselves owned shares.

But as new power-driven machinery expanded the capacity of England's textile mills, the demand for raw cotton increased, and dissatisfaction with the high prices fixed by the East India Company became ever stronger in the Midlands. Manufacturers of the cheaper calicoes, especially, regarded the invention of the American cotton gin as providential. They could foresee a time when quantities of clean, accessible American cotton would fill the maw of their factories at costs far less than they had to pay for the Indian product. This was no time to be cut off from American trade. War with America might well result in the springing up of a rival yarn-spinning and textile-weaving industry in the States. Already a spinning machine comparing in efficiency with the jealously guarded designs of the British power-driven jenny had been built in America by an émigré Englishman named Slater.

To the disputing voices of Manchester and the East India Company were added those of another mighty economic power—the Liverpool and London shipowners. Their former traffic with the Continent had been reduced to a fraction by the war with France. To expand trade with America, and give them the carrying of it, was the only way to put their idle vessels to use. The great maritime insurance companies, whose business was languishing, seconded their views. In Parliament, in newspapers, in pamphlets, in memorials addressed to the Cabinet, men of business challenged Grenville's policy toward the United States as unnecessarily dangerous and provocative. What were the western posts, what the Canadian fur trade, compared to the health of England's economy? Let the government effect a settlement which would augment British exports to the United States, which would keep American ships out of the West Indian trade, which would give Manchester control of American cotton prices, and would assure the freightage of cotton to British shipowners.

All this Grenville found rather tedious. But the fact was inescapable that the politics of England were becoming increasingly an expression of economics. He had to try to fuse the requirements of commerce with England's wartime strategy.

3. *"He Nodded with a Smile"*

It came to John Jay as an enormous relief when dispatches from home, late that summer, told of Wayne's masterly success. After carefully drilling an army of nearly three thousand picked men, he had led them north to the Miami country, fanning them out in columns which made flank attack hazardous. Little Turtle tested the mettle of Wayne's troops in one or two raids, and promptly withdrew from the Indian command, recommending to the tribes that they make peace. But the other chiefs, heavily subsidized and supplied by Simcoe, refused to heed him, attempted to make a stand in the forests near Fort Miami, and were crushed in the decisive battle of Fallen Timbers. With the enemy dispersed and demoralized, Wayne advanced within a few hundred yards of the fort, under a flag of truce. There, in a critical parley, he and the British colonel in command agreed to leave the question of the ownership of the fort to the diplomats. The war predicted by Simcoe did not materialize.

While this encouraging news was in the making, the Foreign Office specialists whom Grenville had assigned to work with Jay outlined the British bargaining position. The old intractable questions of pre-Revolutionary debts owed to British merchants, of Loyalist properties, of the slave seizures, of uncertain boundaries between Canada and the United States, of British responsibility for American ship losses—why not refer these to joint commissions for settlement? Meanwhile, let the central issues be dealt with—the western posts and the matter of a commercial treaty. When the diplomatic language had been distilled away, the hard residue of the British proposal could be perceived. England was ready at last to yield up the posts. But to obtain this concession, America would have to accept British wartime restrictions on her commerce with the French, and confine her exports of cotton and certain other products to England, and to British shipping.

Jay, for all his desire to "accommodate rather than dispute"—his words to

Hamilton—argued these depressing terms. He reminded the British that the neutral powers of Europe had agreed to defend themselves, if need be, against the high-handed practices of the British Navy. If England's conditions were too stiff, America might find herself compelled to join the new Armed Neutrality.

This was a bluff; Washington and the Cabinet had secretly decided against such a course, and Jay knew it. What he did not know was that the British also knew it. Hamilton, in one of his startling indiscretions, had told Hammond that America would under no circumstances become involved with the European neutrals, and Hammond had promptly passed the word to Grenville. In consequence, the British diplomats listened to Jay's threat with the bland unconcern of a poker player who has seen his opponent's cards in a mirror. However, they made a small concession: American vessels of no more than seventy tons would be permitted to trade with the British West Indies.

If, during the negotiations, Jay's morale sometimes flagged in the daytime, it was buoyed up in the evening festivities of the London season. King George himself showed an unprecedented friendliness to Jay. It had its effect. Enthusiastically, Jay reported to Washington that "our prospects become more and more promising . . . A treaty of commerce is on the carpet . . . The King observed to me the other day, 'Well, sir, I imagine you begin to see that your mission will probably be successful.' 'I am happy, may it please Your Majesty, to find that you entertain that idea.' 'Well, but don't you perceive that it is like to be so?' 'There are some recent circumstances . . . which induce me to flatter myself that it will be so.' He nodded with a smile . . ."

4. The Realists

Late in 1794 Jay signed the draft of a treaty which began by saying, "There shall be a firm, inviolable and universal peace, and a true and sincere friendship, between his Britannic Majesty, and his heirs and successors, and the United States of America." It went on to say that the British would evacuate the western posts in June 1795. These were its only significant benefits for America. From Jay's point of view, they were enough to justify his signature. For all his vanity and susceptibility to his social environment, it was his own point of view as an American conservative, and not that of his British friends, which he had sought to express. The treaty meant peace, not war. It was "an entering wedge," in his words, for progressively better relations with England. There were many British men of affairs who felt that their government ought to make no concession whatever to America, but rather chastise her without delay, before she became too strong. Among them was the influential Lord Sheffield, who later said that Jay had "perfectly duped" Grenville into an inadvisable peace. Jay himself felt he had achieved the utmost that was possible. To him the details of the treaty were less important than the fact that England had voluntarily agreed to bind herself to an agreement with the United States.

Because the British made much of Jay, and he was pleased, the idea is widespread that he succumbed to their blandishments, but it is certainly an oversimplification of the facts. Jay and Grenville were both men of large experience and diplomatic insight. To both of them it was evident that the terms of the Treaty of 1783 had been weighted in America's favor primarily because France had then been America's partner in war. With French power no longer available to the United States in a transatlantic war, there had been a great change in her diplomatic position relative to England. Given the actual power potential of each side, the Treaty of 1783 no longer represented reality. Peace could be preserved only by mutual acceptance of a new treaty, the terms of which would reflect more accurately the real coercive force of each nation, its potential ability to injure the other by hostile economic or military action. It was not weakness or folly, but rather his view of reality that led Jay into fighting only a rear-guard action against Grenville's pressure.

In the light of subsequent American history, there is good reason to believe that he saw with exceptional clarity the actual positions of his country and of England as they stood in 1794. If the resulting treaty was deficient, its deficiencies were those of practically every treaty, arising from failure to anticipate and allow adequately for subsequent changes in the relative power potentials of the nations concerned. It was consequently doomed to early obsolescence; and the refusal of England to recognize its obsolescence would produce strains leading to the crisis of 1812. But even in respect to future changes Jay showed awareness. Recognizing that many articles of the treaty would be unsatisfactory to American opinion, he stressed the point that they were not necessarily permanent. As he wrote to Washington, "The commercial part of the treaty may be terminated at the expiration of two years after the war, and in the meantime a state of things more auspicious to negotiation will probably arise."

Jay and Grenville, when they met at the signing of the treaty, on November 19, 1794, both were gravely aware of the historic nature of the occasion. They had, in fact, advanced the principle of arbitration in international affairs farther than any statesmen before them. Grenville regarded Jay, he later said, as "a man valuable on every account," with whom he had achieved a great work, to which no reasonable objection could be made "except on the part of those who believe the interests of Great Britain and the United States to be in contradiction."

5. "An Old Woman's Treaty"

The draft treaty encountered its first storms at sea, when the fast boat to which Jay had entrusted it for delivery to Philadelphia ran into persistent westerly winds and buffeting waves. The crossing was in fact so slow that it created suspicion of a deliberate purpose on Jay's part. Had he planned with the ship's captain that the treaty should not arrive until after the adjournment of Congress? Whatever the truth of the matter, the document did not reach the Secretary of State until three days after the senators who would have had to be consulted had gone home. The Administration thus had time to determine its strategy, and it needed time.

Randolph's first reading of the treaty filled him with dismay. Jay had ignored nine tenths of his instructions. He had failed to provide for the cessation of impressment or compensation for ship seizures. He had accepted in principle the Rule of 1756, granting to belligerent England the right to dictate to neutral American commerce. He had consented to a British shipping monopoly of tropical crops grown in America. He had vitiated America's treaties with France by forbidding the fitting out of enemy privateers in American ports—an issue which the Genêt affair had left unresolved. The treaty's pretense of reciprocity was too thin to deceive anyone. Specifying that English ships of war would he hospitably received in American waters, it gave the same privilege to the non-existent American navy. As to the mixed commissions to which Jay assented for the handling of old claims, the arrangement greatly favored England. American claimants in London had to submit themselves to endless court procedures before commissioners could hear their cases, while British claimants in America were for the most part allowed to bypass American courts.

Washington, when the treaty was put in his hands, was less disturbed than Randolph. Jay's view that any negotiated treaty which made for peace was better than no treaty was also the President's. Hamilton came to his side at once, but now only in an unofficial capacity, for he had resigned from the Treasury. The rewards of a New York law practice had tempted him to leave the government, in order to rid himself of nagging creditors; and with an election not much more than a year away, he found it necessary to devote an increasing amount of time to his responsibilities as leader of the Federalist party.

According to a story of the time, Hamilton's first words about the treaty expressed disgust: "An old woman's treaty." His objection could hardly have been to its broad policy, which was his own, or to its one-sidedness, since he himself had cut the ground from under Jay in the matter of the Armed Neutrality. But the extremes to which the treaty went in its disregard for America's sovereignty over her own commerce were bound to multiply the difficulties ahead. Still, there it was. The decision taken by Washington, on Hamilton's advice, was to submit the treaty to a special session of the Senate, and not to publish it until after full ratification.

While the senators were making their laborious way back to Philadelphia, John Jay arrived from England; he had awaited spring weather before subjecting himself to the Atlantic crossing. The moment, for him, was critical in a personal as well as in a national sense. During his absence, Hamilton's influence had brought about Jay's nomination as Federalist candidate for Governor of New York State, and he had been elected only a few days before his homecoming. His acceptance of the new post, involving as it did his resignation as Chief Justice, was widely interpreted as a sign of larger ambitions. Everything depended on the public response to the treaty. If it were not unfavorable, Jay might easily become the next President; he had the backing of Hamilton, who had no illusions about his own chances of succeeding Washington, and was known to dislike the other major Federalist possibility, John Adams.

6. *Explosion*

For a few weeks, all went well. The Senate, convening in June 1795, solemnly imposed on its members an injunction of strict secrecy, and plunged into hot debate behind closed doors. Little by little outraged national pride gave way before the urge to peace and the profits of trade, but some clauses of the treaty went down hard, and one stuck in senatorial throats. This was a British attempt to restrict the tonnage of American ships in the West Indian trade, and confine them to the American market. It threatened for a time to prevent ratification, but Hamilton, as usual, came to the rescue. He had been in close touch with Hammond, and he was confident that if the Senate expunged the objectionable clause and ratified the rest of the treaty, England would accept the change. With this proviso to sustain self-respect, the bare two-thirds majority required for ratification was found, and the treaty, still secret, went to the President for his signature.

As it lay on Washington's desk, rumors of its contents began to appear in the Republican press. Letters signed "Franklin" were published in Philadelphia denouncing the document in vague but inflammatory terms. The Anglophobes needed no further encouragement. In Republican taverns, excited men harangued each other about the imminent betrayal of the United States by Jay, Hamilton, and the President. Wild rumors spread until credulity and passion, feeding on each other, exploded into violence. On the very day when Jay was inaugurated as Governor of New York, an effigy of him bearing the label "Sir John Jay" was placed in the pillory at Philadelphia, guillotined, and blown up with gunpowder.

Then on July 3, the influential Philadelphia newspaper *Aurora* printed the entire text of the treaty. Senator Stevens Mason of Virginia, it appeared, had decided that "duty to the nation" took precedence over solidarity with his colleagues, and had violated the senatorial injunction of secrecy. Philadelphia responded first, with a mass meeting which designated July 4 as a day of national humiliation. Like a torrent of flaming oil, the uproar then spread through the nation. The burning of effigies of Jay became a commonplace. Federalists as well as Republicans joined in the outcry. So staunch a conservative as John Rutledge of South Carolina, who had just been nominated by Washington to succeed Jay as Chief Justice of the Supreme Court, denounced the treaty. The South was rabid. In a Virginia tavern a speaker was cheered when he gave as a toast: "A speedy death to General Washington!" Even in Federalist New England, indignation rose to the pitch of frenzy. Patriotic old Samuel Adams, the Governor of Massachusetts, raged against Jay. Flags were lowered to half mast in Boston and crowds assaulted incautious citizens who dared to defend the treaty in public. In New York, Hamilton himself was attacked when he appeared to speak at a meeting. His forehead bleeding where a stone had struck him, he eyed the crowd, and said disdainfully, "If you use such striking arguments, I must retire." As he left the hall, crowds in the streets were shouting "Damn John Jay!" "Damn the British!" New York's growing Irish colony led the anti-British demonstrations. At one mass meeting, an Irish orator shouted to an appreciative crowd, "What a damned treaty! I make a motion that every good citizen in this assembly kick this damned treaty to hell!"

Washington had ridden out other storms, but "never since I have been in the administration of the government," he wrote, "have I seen a crisis from which more is to be apprehended." He saw America at a crossroads. If he signed the treaty, the country faced the risk of war with France; if he did not, "there is no foreseeing all the consequences which may follow, as it respects Great Britain." Nevertheless, unsatisfactory as he considered the treaty to be, he was determined on ratification, rather than "to suffer matters to remain as they are, unsettled." His was the gift of simplicity. He would not change his mind "unless circumstances more imperious than have yet come to my knowledge should compel it; for there is but one straight course, and that is to seek truth and pursue it steadily."

A serious administrative difficulty confronted him. All the members of the Cabinet were for ratification, except one—but that one was his Secretary of State, Edmund Randolph. His known pro-French leanings, and his close ties to Jefferson created suspicion that he would work to block the treaty's ratification. It was a danger not easy to avoid. To request Randolph's resignation without strong reason would have destroyed all hope of national unity.

Then occurred an incident curiously reminiscent of the method used by England to influence Jay in the Rayneval affair. On that occasion, the British had produced an intercepted French dispatch at the psychological moment. This time the rabbit in the magic hat was a letter written by the French minister in Philadelphia, Fauchet, to his government. Allegedly taken by an English officer from a captured French ship, there was in it an implication that Randolph might be willing to accept French money. The dispatch went to Hammond, and thereafter through Hamilton's hands to the Cabinet and the President. Washington, recognizing that there was no actual evidence in the letter to support an accusation against Randolph, hesitated to use it, but the moment came when he confronted Randolph, and in the presence of other cabinet members asked for an explanation. Randolph's quite truthful denial that he had been guilty of any impropriety might have carried more weight if it had not been known that he was on familiar terms with Fauchet. To be sure, Hamilton had been even closer to England's minister, but then Hamilton was no longer in the Cabinet, and in any event there had never been any hint of financial transactions between them. Shocked, embittered, and perceiving that Washington was determined to be rid of him, Randolph offered his resignation the same day. The way was clear at last for signature of the treaty by the President, and an exchange of ratifications with England.

7.   A Hint of Destiny

Viewed in very broad terms, Jay's mission to England succeeded in averting war because he made peace his prime objective not only in words, as diplomats generally do, but in action, as they generally do not. He went far beyond his instructions, beyond Washington's intention, beyond even Hamilton's wishes in order to obtain Grenville's signature on a treaty. The fact that America's national tradition was still young and not fully developed enabled Jay to take liberties with it that would be unthinkable for later American statesmen. In giving England the right to make laws of the sea for American commerce he did violence to his nation's sovereignty. But in spite of all the patriotic anguish that he caused, the heavens did not fall, the country was not crushed by humiliation, its future was not jeopardized. When the necessity of peace came in conflict with patriotic sentiment, the people chose peace, and followed Jay, even while they damned him.

Curiously, the chief and most immediate benefit experienced by the United States from the treaty came not from the Great Lakes, not from London, but from Madrid. An incompetent Spanish King, Charles IV, his self-opinionated Queen, Luisa, and a swaggering young minister, Godoy, had got far out of their depth in the stormy diplomacy of the time. Godoy, who had come to eminence by way of the Queen's bed, had persuaded

Charles that Spain should join England in defeating revolutionary France. This was not altogether a matter of ideology and of ambition for French territory. It was Godoy's expectation that an American war with England would soon break out on the Canadian border. If his assumption had been valid, not only would the security of Spain's threatened American colonies have been enhanced, but she might have seized the opportunity to extend them. Ignoring Kentucky's threats, in 1794 he revoked America's hard-won rights in the navigation of the Mississippi. But his calculations were based on a false premise—the imminent defeat of France. Almost immediately thereafter, the situation abruptly changed. The French, capitalizing on their military successes, poised an army on Spain's border, and warned of invasion if she did not withdraw forthwith from the British alliance.

Spain dared not risk the consequence of refusal, and a treaty of peace with France followed. But Godoy still counted on an Anglo-American war. As months passed and it did not come, his alarm grew. The rumblings in Kentucky were taking on an ominous note. There was great respect in Louisiana for the fighting qualities of the American frontiersman; and the few Spanish regiments in New Orleans, Mobile, and Pensacola were ill-equipped and underpaid. Unless America's attention was promptly diverted to Canada, Spain's empire north of the Gulf might be lost.

When Jay and Grenville, confounding European expectations, signed their treaty, Godoy's last hope collapsed. For the first time, he found it necessary to placate the United States. The new word went forth: Spain, like England, might consent to a treaty with America. No news could have pleased Washington more. Detaching Thomas Pinckney from his British assignment, he ordered him to Madrid, with instructions to take a firm line. The results were happier than anyone in Philadelphia dared hope. Under Pinckney's steady pressure, the Spanish government gave so much ground that the treaty which he signed in October 1795, proved to be one long concession. Free navigation of the Mississippi was granted without reservation. With it went the long desired right of Americans to deposit goods in New Orleans warehouses for export. The boundary of West Florida was definitely established at the thirty-first parallel. Spain furthermore promised to restrain Indian tribes in her territory from attacks on American settlements. Here was an unprecedented diplomatic triumph for America. When Pinckney returned home with the treaty, he was given an ovation the more impressive because of its contrast with Jay's reception a few months earlier. Few then recognized that Pinckney's Treaty had been made possible by Jay's.

The effects of the Spanish concessions were promptly felt and far-reaching. With the Mississippi open at last, the Kentuckians became less restive and disgruntled, began to regard themselves as a permanent part of the United

States, to shrug at agitators for separatism and secession. A new sense of unity, an optimistic faith in America's future uplifted the nation. The nationalist and expansionist spirit which decades later found expression in the phrase "Manifest Destiny" was born in those days of exultation over Pinckney's achievement. The South became ever more impatient for the time when Spain would be driven beyond the Gulf of Mexico. In the North, eyes turned covetously toward Canada. The next great wave of anti-British feeling, as it rolled toward 1812, would gain impetus from the surge of territorial aspiration which rose with the signing of the Jay and Pinckney treaties.

8. *The House Yields*

On March 3, 1796, the Senate gave unanimous approval to Pinckney's Treaty, and on the same day proclaimed Jay's Treaty to be in effect. By that time, the outcry against Jay and his work had lessened. It was as if the country's excitement had been spent. Perhaps outbreaks of yellow fever in a number of cities had a sobering influence, but the essential fact was that the treaty meant peace, and peace was what most people wanted, whatever they might have said in a moment of patriotic hysteria. Even further molestation of American ships by British naval vessels in contradiction to the spirit of the Jay treaty did not provoke anything like the anger of the year before.

For Thomas Jefferson, who had emerged into the open as the treaty's chief antagonist, and who even now continued to scheme for its destruction, the change in the popular mood was discouraging. He saw clearly that he could not safely rely on public opinion alone to invalidate "that execrable thing," as he called the treaty. But he had a final resource on which he thought he could rely. The joint commissions established by the treaty to settle controversial issues required governmental funds; such funds could be voted only by the House of Representatives; and the Republicans constituted a majority of the House. Without the consent of the House, the treaty, for practical purposes, would be nullified. "I trust," wrote Jefferson, "the popular branch of the legislature will disapprove of it, and thus rid us of this infamous act, which is really nothing more than a treaty of alliance between England and the Anglomen of this country against the legislature and the people." The House appeared of a mind to oblige him. Many of its members felt that it was their duty not only to defeat the treaty, but to prove the power of the representatives superior to that of the President—as in republican France. At the very time in the late winter of 1796 when the Senate was giving its final endorsement to the treaty, the House passed a resolution calling on the President to turn over to it his correspondence with Jay and other documents relating to the matter.

Washington immediately refused. The power to make treaties, he said with conviction, is vested exclusively in the President, with the advice and consent of the Senate. Once a treaty had been made, it was the duty of the House to assure its effectiveness. But the Republican majority, unimpressed, retorted by another resolution, asserting their right to deliberate on a treaty which could be implemented only if the House voted the requisite funds.

It was a nice point, which would not be settled until Andrew Johnson, in 1868, conceded that the House was entitled to debate the merits of America's treaty with Russia for the purchase of Alaska, and within limits had the right to refuse appropriations for it. Washington, however, faced far more than a construction of constitutional law. The entire future of the American nation was at stake. In the context of the time, a surrender to the House would have implied war with England; it would have implied a victory of American radicalism and danger for the propertied classes; it would have linked America to revolutionary France. In his view, the challenge of the House had to be resisted, no matter how. Hamilton wrote an urgent letter on this point to Senator Rufus King of New York. If appropriations for the treaty should be denied, he said, let the Senate encourage the President to put the treaty into effect without further reference to the House. "The glory of the President, the safety of the constitution, the greatest interests depend on it."

The House, meeting for the final day of the debate, was in a state of high tension. The Jeffersonians at first seemed to have every advantage, as they urged the representatives once and for all to denounce the treaty, refuse the President the required funds, and call for war. But the House as a whole gave an extraordinary demonstration of self-control. The serious and thoughtful debate that followed showed its awareness of the responsibility which it was assuming. A number of Republicans who had been communing with their consciences drew back from an open break with the President. Albert Gallatin, then making his mark as a congressman, confessed that "however injurious and unequal I conceive the treaty to be, however repugnant it may be to my feelings, and perhaps to my prejudices, I feel induced to vote for it, and will not give my assent to any proposition which would imply its rejection." As a compromise, he proposed that the House postpone the voting of moneys for the treaty until England gave assurances that she meant to abide by its professions of friendship.

The Federalist reply provided one of the great dramatic moments of the period—the famous speech by Fisher Ames of Massachusetts, for years afterward a staple of American education. Ames, although a right-wing Federalist, held the esteem of many Republicans as a man of ability and forthrightness, and a persuasive orator. A serious illness had long confined him to his bed, and it was in defiance of his physician's orders that he appeared at

Congress Hall. Frail, drawn, and tottering, apparently close to death, he rose to speak to a hushed House. The issue, he pointed out, was a simple one: "Shall we violate a solemn engagement into which this country has entered?" Honor was in the balance, and more than honor. To reject the treaty was to bring upon the Northwest all the horrors of another Indian war. "We light the savage fires, we bind the victims. This day we undertake to render account to the widows and orphans whom our decision will make —to the wretches who will be roasted at the stake!" As to war with England, what could it bring America except confusion and anarchy?

The most intransigeant Jeffersonians in the House listened to him spellbound as he touched upon a central truth of diplomacy—that negotiation, even if it merely marks time, even if it only postpones decision, gives altered circumstances a chance to reveal themselves, and so can help to uncover new areas of agreement in an apparently hopeless deadlock. "Even the minutes I have spent in expostulating have their value, because they protract the crisis and the short period in which alone we may resolve to escape it. Yet I have, perhaps, as little interest in the event as any man here. There is, perhaps, no member who will not think his chance to be a witness of the consequences greater than mine. If, however, the vote should pass . . . even I, slender and almost broken as my hold on life is, may outlive the government and constitution of my country." Men wept openly as he sat down, and John Adams, who was in the gallery, said in a broken voice, "My God! How great he is!"

The historical significance of Ames's speech is suggested by the vote which followed. By the skin of a majority—fifty-one to forty-eight—the House voted for a resolution to carry the treaty into effect. The press and the congressmen themselves had no doubt that without the emotional tide produced by the speech the resolution would have foundered. Some Republican skeptics spread a report that it was Hamilton who had persuaded Ames to leave his sickbed, and who had staged his mighty oration. Of this there could be no proof. In any event Ames, having done his work, lived on for many years.

9. *Scherzo Diplomatico*

Jay's Treaty was the law of the land. By late summer of 1796, England began at last to make good her pledge of 1783, by transferring the western posts to American troops. But as Thomas Jefferson saw it, the fight over the treaty was far from finished. It remained to him to thwart what he considered a plot of Hamilton and Jay to give England domination over American commerce. If in the election just ahead he were to win the Presidency, he could press for revision of the treaty, and above all, he could work to appease the just indignation of France. In the meantime, restraint on the part of the French was essential to his hopes. He stood before the country as an advocate of the French revolutionary cause. A weakening of America's relations with France inevitably weakened his own political status at home. Whenever France, in resentment against Washington's neutrality, harassed American shipping, it was the Republicans, not the Federalists, who were politically damaged.

After the ratification of Jay's treaty the French government seemed for a time ready to lump all Americans, Federalists and Republicans, in the same curses. They had reason to feel that they had been hoaxed. James Monroe, who in 1794 had replaced Gouverneur Morris as American minister to Paris, had revealed a totally indiscreet but engagingly sincere enthusiasm for the French Republic and all its works. France could not know how grossly Monroe was exceeding his instructions when he wrote to the revolutionary Convention and asked to be received "as the representative of their ally and sister republic," or when he exchanged fraternal embraces with the President of the Convention in the names of both their peoples, to the frenzied cheering of the delegates.

His entire stay in France was one long and heart-warming, if unconscious deception. France, he conveyed, could do no wrong in American eyes. Instructed to ask the French Government to compensate American shipowners for illegal ship seizures, he added astoundingly, and entirely on his own initiative, that if France later felt that the decree authorizing the seizures should be put into effect again, "my countrymen in general will not only bear it with patience, but with pleasure." Asked by France whether the United States might lend funds to aid her in carrying on the war against Europe's "impious coalition of tyrants," he acknowledged that he had no authority to answer the question, but conveyed his personal belief that such aid would be rendered. On the strength of this comforting assertion, the French issued decrees to compensate owners of seized American ships—only to find that they received nothing in return.

Even the announcement of Jay's mission to England did not dampen the zeal with which Monroe unwittingly conjured up illusion in the high places of the French Government. On the basis of the little that he had been told by Philadelphia, Monroe asserted to France's Foreign Minister, Delacroix, that Jay was "strictly limited to demanding reparations for injuries," and that there was no reason to fear the negotiation in London. As a result, the Directory, which had just assumed power in France, failed to protest Jay's mission to the enemy when it was first announced. The shock in Paris when the terms of the treaty were finally divulged was not lessened by the realization that Monroe sincerely believed his own statements. Only when it was too late did France let loose a blast against America's "betrayal" of her revolutionary principles. Still Monroe refused to be daunted. The Republican House of Representatives, he assured the French Government, would never vote the funds required to make the treaty effective. This time, when the event proved him a false prophet, he felt a certain embarrassment. But it was the honest embarrassment of the optimistic weather forecaster who is betrayed by the elements.

And like the weather forecaster, he was forgiven, since he had at least tried for sunlight. His adulation of the French Republic was so appealing in its simplicity that Paris spared him from personal blame. The word in the *salons* was that not Monroe, but the enemies of France in Philadelphia were responsible for the sinister turn of events, and an order from President Washington, recalling Monroe in the autumn of 1796, was taken as an affront to the French Republic. Ostentatiously the Directory tendered Monroe an impressive farewell banquet. There he sat avidly drinking in praise of himself and listening to bombastic threats against his President and his country, if they should persevere in their neutrality. He left Paris trailing clouds of Gallic glory.

Washington then announced the appointment in Monroe's place of a minister who provided the maximum contrast. Charles Cotesworth Pinckney, elder brother of the former minister to England, had studied at Oxford, attended a military college in pre-Revolutionary France, was a Carolina Federalist with aristocratic antecedents—was, in fact, precisely the man to send to Paris if the purpose was to antagonize the French Directory. That Hamilton had a hand in his selection is certain. It was very much to his interest, just then, to keep the Pinckneys in the national eye; Thomas Pinckney was his avowed candidate for the Vice-Presidency in the coming election, and his secret candidate for President.

Monroe's recall and Pinckney's appointment filled the American Republicans with forebodings. It was predicted that the French in reprisal would shortly resume their attacks on American vessels en route to British ports. Hamilton would certainly have welcomed such a development before the election; it would have crushed Jefferson's chances. But having spoken her mind, France saw nothing to gain by overt moves which would have undone the pro-French party in America. Her navy for the time being left American vessels undisturbed. A new French minister, Adet, was sent to Philadelphia with instructions to make it plain to the American people that the goodwill of France, with her formidable armies, was conditional on Jefferson's success at the polls. There followed the publication in the American press of open letters from Adet advocating Jefferson's election, and irritating a good many Americans to whom Genêt's interference in the country's internal affairs was only too vivid a memory.

10. Hamilton Stumbles

Against Jefferson, there stood John Adams. He was far from popular with the leaders of his party, but with Hamilton and Jay labeled as tools of the British, the Federalists had little choice in the matter. Adams's services in the Revolution, his long vice-presidency under Washington, his indisputable integrity, his aggressiveness as minister to England—all this made for votes. Nor could there be much debate over the Federalist selection for the vice-presidency. Thomas Pinckney was then at the zenith of his popularity—a Carolina man beloved of the South and liked in the North—the man who had stood up manfully to Lord Grenville and who had persuaded Spain to open the Mississippi. In Hamilton's eyes, Pinckney had one further qualification, and no small one—they got on together. This was especially important to him because of the instinctive antipathy which existed between Adams and himself. It was all too apparent that Adams, if elected, would seek his counsel as little as possible. To have at least the Vice-President responsive to him was sound strategy—especially as the office carried in the popular mind distinct connotations of succession to the Presidency.

Under the Constitution as it then stood, the people would not be voting directly for the presidential candidates. Instead, the voters in each state would choose among candidates for the legislature put up by the respective parties; the legislature would appoint the state's members of the Electoral College; and the electors would subsequently choose the President. Hamilton's thinking focused on the article of the Constitution under which each elector was authorized to vote for two presidential candidates, with the winner of the largest majority to be President, of the next largest, Vice-President. As the grand strategist of his party, he was supposed to assure that Adams and Pinckney would finish in that order, and both ahead of Jefferson. The auguries were auspicious, for the Federalists dominated in the populous northern states, and had substantial support in Maryland, Virginia, and the Carolinas; and although the South would certainly commit the bulk of its electors to Jefferson, the persuasive Aaron Burr, running against him, could be counted on to siphon off votes of Republican electors in the North.

In the early days of the campaign, Hamilton seemed dedicated to Adams, as his party's choice. Part of the time he spent with Washington, aiding in the preparation of the Farewell Address. The timing of the publication of the address, six weeks before the election, was recognized as giving aid to Adams. It was unmistakable that the pro-French Jeffersonians were in Washington's mind when he cautioned the American people: "Nothing is more essential than that permanent, inveterate antipathies against particular nations and passionate attachments for others should be excluded. . . .

The nation which indulges toward another an habitual hatred or an habitual fondness is in some degree a slave . . ."

To the members of his party Hamilton reiterated the need to exclude Jefferson from executive office at all costs. The Federalist electors had to be made to understand the importance of conserving every vote. Let each of them vote only for Adams and Pinckney, Hamilton counseled. It would be a risk to cast even a single sentimental vote for any other name on the list of candidates. If, when the votes were counted, Adams and Pinckney were to finish in a tie, no harm would be done. The election would then be thrown into the House of Representatives, with each state having a single vote. The Federalists, on this basis, would again be in control, and could designate Adams as President.

Northern electors pledged to Adams heard Hamilton's instructions with misgivings. It was all very well to tell them to cast their second vote without fail for Pinckney; but would every Federalist elector from Maryland and Virginia, who would unquestionably be for Pinckney, cast his second vote for Adams? Did Hamilton really believe that he could hold southern Federalists in line, when, as everyone knew, they were southerners first, and Federalists second? Adams, as a personality, was not popular in the South; and as a New Englander, he stirred up deep prejudices in southern hearts. It needed little political sagacity to foresee that some southern electors voting for Pinckney would throw away their second votes, rather than cast them for the spirit of Massachusetts. If at the same time the northern Federalists followed Hamilton's strategy, voting equally for Adams and Pinckney, Pinckney would be elected President, and Adams only Vice-President.

That Hamilton, one of the most astute politicians of his age, had overlooked this implication of his strategy was incredible. It dawned on those around him that the relegation of Adams to second place was precisely his objective. Later it became known that he had gone even farther in his attempt to undo Adams. To make sure that Virginia's Federalist electors would have no votes to spare for the New Englander, Hamilton had encouraged a movement designed to enter the name of Patrick Henry, the Old Dominion's favorite son, as a candidate. But Henry had cannily refused to dance to Hamilton's tune.

Suddenly Hamilton found himself facing a revolt within his party, and it quickly ran out of control. His power was on the wane; the rebels knew it, and were determined to keep faith with Adams. The result was that on the day of the vote the Federalists in the Electoral College no longer had any cohesion. Some of those from the North, having voted for Adams, failed to declare a second choice, while a number of Pinckney Federalists from the South, rather than support Adams, went so far as to give their second votes to Thomas Jefferson, who was, after all, a Virginia gentleman. In the tally, Jefferson came close to winning the presidency, with sixty-eight votes to Adams's seventy-one. Pinckney had fifty-nine and Burr thirty, with a few scattering. Hamilton had unintentionally made his archenemy Vice-President of the United States. Seldom have the interlocking chances out of which history is constructed produced a more ironic twist.

For the first time in his career, Hamilton had been severely set back. The private offices of both the President and the Vice-President would be closed to him. Yet there were consolations. Members of Adams's cabinet carried over from the Washington administration were thoroughly dominated by Hamilton, and would inform him and consult him at every point. And his policies remained intact. The conservatives were still in power, Jay's Treaty still held, the commerce on which America's financial solvency depended continued to grow. Above all, the threatened war with England had been averted.

CHAPTER FOUR

X Y Z

1. *Talleyrand on America*

The memoirs of statesmen show that international diplomacy often seems to its practitioners like a fascinating but never-ending dramatic performance, with Mars in the prompter's box. Men like Hamilton and Jefferson, deeply held by conviction as they were, nevertheless found a pleasure in the play for its own sake, and entered into their roles with a certain professional detachment. This John Adams could not do. His temperament, in which there was a great deal of self-righteousness and very little humor, caused him to see himself as coauthor, rather than as player in the spectacle—a coauthor arguing with a gloomy collaborator, and barely staving off a tragic dénouement. It would not have been possible for him to believe that the chief diplomatic episode of his Presidency, the notorious XYZ affair, would appear to later historians to have a distinct touch of *opera bouffe*. But it was *opera bouffe* with consequences. The traditional opinion of the people of the United States that European diplomats are smooth scoundrels bent on taking advantage of the inexperienced, upright American took root at this time.

The note of absurdity was introduced by one of the spectacular mountebanks of the age, Charles Maurice Talleyrand, who became Foreign Minister of France in 1797. For the previous several years, with his head forfeit in France, he had stayed safely in the United States, waiting for the great blood-letting to run its course. The former abbé and future prince was hard up, but he managed to earn enough for his needs by acting as correspondent for British merchants. He met Hamilton, who in spite of the Frenchman's cadaverous face and scrawny, limping figure, was rather taken by his style, and opened a number of doors to him. On his part, Talleyrand regarded Hamilton as the best mind he encountered in America. "He divined Europe," was his comment, suggesting that he had met a man almost as worldly as himself.

The *émigré* set himself to learn all that he could of American life. To an enlightened observer, the young nation was a fascinating hodgepodge of Old World traditions and New World enterprise, of English, Scotch, Irish, Dutch, French, Spanish, and Red Indian customs; of Tom Paine's creed of freedom and of Negro slavery. In Boston, Albany, New York, Philadelphia, Baltimore, and "the Federal City," then being built on the Potomac,

Talleyrand made extensive notes on the economic and political mores of the people. The convictions which he formed at this time became part of the explosive mixture of circumstance out of which the War of 1812 finally flamed. The chief of these convictions was that economic interest would always dictate the character of America's relations with other countries. Thus, her profitable commerce with England precluded any chance of a military alliance with the French. That such eminent men as Thomas Jefferson, James Madison, and James Monroe professed a strong sympathy for revolutionary France was all very well, and the names of Lafayette and Beaumarchais were always applauded in patriotic orations; but that this practical people, with their aggressive commercial outlook, would in high politics be guided by sentimental feeling for the past was, in Talleyrand's view, utterly unlikely. He knew his Machiavelli too well to count on the gratitude of governments. Jay's Treaty he considered to prove his point.

The assumption of power by the Directory in 1795 was the signal that Talleyrand had been waiting for. France's political pendulum, having swung as far as it could to the left, was now moving back again. Soon interventions on his behalf by influential friends in Paris, including Mme. de Staël, produced an annulment of accusations which had been made against him, and provided the documents necessary for his safe return to France.

To avoid another pitch-and-roll winter crossing of the Atlantic, he waited until the spring equinox had passed before going home. Meanwhile he used leisure to advantage, putting into polished form two long reports, the most important of which was entitled "A Memoir on the Commercial Relations between the United States and England." Dispassionately, clearly, and cogently he set forth the reasons why America was peacefully putting up with the most outrageous abuses by the British navy—search and seizure of cargoes, impressment of American sailors. Not national cowardice, but the tie of common profit was the essence of the matter. "The spirit of commerce makes men selfish." But sympathetic tradition also had to be taken into account. "There is something monarchical in the executive power of the American government." This tended, he thought, to create a link to British institutions.

2. A Little Squeeze

Soon after his return to Paris, Talleyrand read this paper to the National Institute of France. It made a strong impression, and his election to that august body followed—a sure sign that he had the favor of the Directory. When he accepted the Foreign Ministry, it was without illusions. Of the five Directors, two were notoriously corrupt and two thoroughly incompetent. France's war on the Continent was going less well, prices were high, business was bad, prisons were crowded, the people were grumbling. It was evident to Talleyrand that the Directory would not long survive. Sooner or later, one of France's ambitious generals would capitalize on popular discontent, make a *coup d'état*, seize power, and replace the present set of rascals with another. Talleyrand thought that the young Bonaparte, already idolized by half of Europe, was the ablest and most likely candidate for the task.

The flamboyant Paul Barras, who dominated the Directory, could see what Talleyrand saw, and had set about to accumulate as much money as possible before the débâcle. For Barras, one of Talleyrand's chief qualifications as Foreign Minister was his airy freedom from scruple. From the very beginning, the new minister played the game; in fact, his first gleeful words upon hearing of his appointment, were "I shall be rich, yes, immensely rich." When he died, a very old man, it was as the richest man in France.

In his eyes money was, as he said, "the only universal cult." Unlike Barras, however, he was selective in his pursuit of the franc. While he was a man of labyrinthine insincerity, while he was ready to fleece the representatives of other nations and to betray politicians in his own, he was at the same time sincerely devoted to the interests of France, as he saw them. It is not recorded that he ever took a bribe at the expense of French power. Within this limit, he was ruthless. If another nation wished to avoid punishment by one of France's conquering armies, then let it pay money, not only publicly for its treaty of peace, but before then, privately, to Talleyrand and the Directors, for the privilege of being heard. Portugal in 1797 provided a case in point. The Portuguese minister in Paris was compelled to put up a substantial *douceur* in order to interest Talleyrand in his plea for peace— and then was not accorded serious negotiation until he had paid as much again. Talleyrand's conception of foreign affairs was essentially feline. He liked nothing better than to use both paws in teasing his mouse. The total sum extracted from the Portuguese was eight million francs, of which three million went to Barras, and one million each to Talleyrand and the other four Directors. All this was hardly a secret. Talleyrand contended that such "distributions in diplomatic affairs" were sanctioned by custom, and even just. Portugal, for example, had profited heavily from wartime trade while Frenchmen bled for liberty. She owed something, therefore, to any Frenchman who was in a position to extort payment.

It struck Talleyrand that something of this sort might be done with the Americans, comparatively poor as they were. For purposes of squeeze, the situation was propitious. The Jay Treaty had facilitated the British blockade of French ports in the West Indies. France had a legitimate grievance. But this was only the beginning of her complaints against the United States. America's professions of neutrality were an affront to French sensibilities, proof that she had callously ignored her obligations as ally of France under the treaties of 1778. The American government had recalled the one truly sympathetic minister whom it had sent to Paris, James Monroe. The American people had failed to elect as President the one candidate on whom France might pin hope of friendship, Thomas Jefferson. To cap the list of offenses, Washington, before leaving the presidency, had attempted to replace Monroe by a noted southern Federalist, C. C. Pinckney, whose attitude toward republican France was known to be negative. From the French standpoint, there had been only one proper course to take, and the Foreign Office had taken it. A new search-and-seizure decree of extraordinary harshness went into effect against American vessels engaged in commerce with the British; and when Pinckney arrived in Paris he was not allowed to present his credentials. Instead, he was subjected to a number of petty indignities, and finally compelled to leave France under threat of arrest. This was in February 1797.

Talleyrand did not believe that the United States would go to war over such comparatively minor provocations as France had given her. The pivot of his transatlantic policy was the feeling that Americans would always follow the dollar—and many dollars were being made by their merchantmen in running the British blockade of the French West Indies. It was inconceivable to him that their needy government would throw away this source of income. Not that he failed to recognize the strength of the anti-French feeling among the Federalists. America's new Secretary of State, Timothy Pickering, was known to be spoiling for a fight with France. But President Adams himself seemed sincerely desirous of peace. Thomas Jefferson had declared "I do not believe Mr. Adams wishes war with France, nor do I believe he will truckle to England." That was good enough for Talleyrand. In any event, where could the United States find warships to match the naval might of France? To keep her on the defensive was obvious strategy, out of which might well come a *douceur* or two. Americans were good economists—and how much cheaper to bribe the Directory than to fight France!

3. *The Making Up of Minds*

When Pinckney's report of the treatment accorded him in Paris reached President Adams, he reacted strongly. France's action, he thought, indicated a complete rift to be followed by war. The spectacular successes of the French army in Italy under young Bonaparte had led to rumors that the continental coalition against France would soon collapse, and had aroused grave fears for the future of England, and eventually of America. The arch-Federalist, George Cabot, in a letter written in April 1797, gloomily recounts a conversation in which, replying to the statement that the power of England was at an end, he said, "All the civilized world would have cause to mourn if this should be true, for they would then be obliged to fight against France or give up their independence." The President saw no alternative to preparations for war, even though he still hoped to avoid it. A special session of Congress, he felt, was required.

In the interval before the Congressmen assembled he consulted with Pickering and others among his chief advisers as to the strategy to be followed. They were for the most part eagerly pessimistic, rubbing their hands over the unfortunate necessity of fighting France. Adams found more constructive value in a letter which he just then received from Joel Barlow, the American writer and sometime diplomat, and friend of republican France. Barlow, who was in Paris, suggested that the French might be willing to accept an American mission, the composition of which was not inimical to her. This idea attracted Adams, but his Cabinet roundly opposed it, especially Secretary of State Pickering, and the Secretaries of the Treasury and of War, Wolcott and McHenry. They held that the President was being duped, that America ought to go instantly to Britain's side against the terrible threat from France. McHenry argued that Adams "did not or would not perceive that the object of the French Government in this machinery was to obtain instead of being obliged to send a minister." He criticized the President's "precipitancy in taking the bait."

For a time it looked as if Federalist pressure might overcome Adams's disposition to peace. Here, however, he had unexpected help from Hamilton, who insisted that before the country went to war, France should be given an opportunity to receive another mission. If she refused, Americans could no longer doubt that their government had done all it could for peace. The country would then be united for war in alliance with England. Pickering and the others were pushed by this reasoning into grudging co-operation with Adams, and the question then became, who should be sent to Paris?

Pinckney had to be one of the mission; national dignity demanded as much, whether the French liked it or not. It seemed to Adams that a moderate Republican known to be friendly to France was also essential to the purpose. Pickering growled his opposition to "a piebald commission," but was overruled. The Cabinet canvassed several names, and sounded out Madison, who declined, and Jefferson, who declined also. Both felt that their country and their party were in great danger, and their leadership needed at home; and each suspected a Federalist plot to entangle him in a politically disastrous undertaking.

Finally Adams turned to an old friend, wealthy Elbridge Gerry of Massachusetts, who was a Republican, and whose family's shipowning interests were deeply involved in trade with France. His place on the mission settled, the third appointment had to go to a Federalist acceptable to the Hamiltonians, yet not marked as an enemy of France. At the suggestion of George Washington, the name of the rising Virginia lawyer, John Marshall, was considered. Marshall just then urgently needed money which his Richmond law practice could not provide, and the $20,000 emolument offered to him as commissioner would solve the problem for him.

When Congress convened, Adams, in a rousing address, declared his intention to convince France "that we are not a degraded people, humiliated under a colonial spirit of fear and sense of inferiority." He sharply rebuked the President of the French Directory, Barras, for derogatory remarks which he had made about the American government. He asked Congress to create a navy and to fortify American harbors for defense. But in the end he came to the three-man mission which he proposed to send to Paris.

The Republicans in Congress approved the President's nominations because they hoped the mission would succeed, and the Federalists because they hoped it would fail. Thereafter, Gerry and Marshall left by separate ships to join Pinckney. Marshall, taking advantage of his new status, provided himself "with a plenty of excellent porter, wine and brandy," as he told his wife; but for all that, he did not enjoy the prospect; neither diplomacy nor foreign travel was to his taste. "Oh God, how much time and happiness I have thrown away!" he wrote to his family from Paris a few months later.

4. The Talleyrand Gambit

A copy of the President's speech was delivered to Talleyrand before the new mission arrived in Paris, and he found some of its language offensive, as coming from a young upstart nation—"no more important than Genoa" —to glorious France. If there had been any question in his mind as to the procedure to follow with the Americans, it was now resolved. He would go as far as he could to make the President eat his words—short of war. For the period immediately ahead, at least, there were too many other commitments for the arms of France. With Prussia already out of the war, once Austria withdrew an invasion of England might be undertaken. And Talleyrand and Barras were also encouraging Bonaparte, who was becoming a little too popular and independent for their taste, in an ambitious plan of his to take an army to Egypt cut England's Mediterranean trade routes, and conquer the Middle East for France. While all this was going on, some easement of the troubles with America was indicated—but not until after the Americans had had a little lesson in the higher diplomacy. And not until the French privateers had been given more time for their raids on the American shipping lanes. Part of the profits thus obtained went to the Directory—so let the good work go on! By June 1797, when the American

Most of
them seized
in French
ports

peace mission was en route to France, the recent French decree had resulted in the seizure of 316 American vessels.

The first meeting between Talleyrand and the three envoys was at his
office, when they presented their credentials. He found them an interesting
study in contrasting types—Pinckney a plump man of affairs with a courtly
style; Marshall big, dark, and close-mouthed; the Bostonian Gerry, whom
Talleyrand had known in America, small and slim, with an inquisitive nose.
All of them he regarded as personalities of the second rank, and not worth
much of his time. His strategy went into effect at once. He regretted to
have to tell them that he was deeply occupied at the moment in preparing
a report for the Directory on France's relations with the United States; he
had no time for prolonged discussion just then; they would hear from him.

Surprised and uneasy at this cavalier reception, the Americans let a few
days go by before trying to see the minister again. Their request was ignored.
They tried once more—and were given an excuse so perfunctory as to be
insulting. Still they tried, only to be met with the open contempt of Talleyrand's clerks. The psychological pressure on them was increased when they
were visited by deputations of their countrymen, merchants and sea captains
who had been brought into French ports with their captured ships, and who
were desperate for help and advice. At last, however, a note came from a
minor official of the Foreign Office. For the Foreign Minister himself to
take time for negotiation with America was just then out of the question,
he told them. Certain persons had been designated to deal with them; they
would hear in good time.

More days passed; then one evening a gentleman appeared, and introduced himself as Jean Conrad Hottinguer, at their service, a Swiss, a friend
of the Foreign Minister. His name was known to Marshall, for Hottinguer
had raised money for a Virginia land speculation from which the lawyer
had once hoped to benefit. It was almost certainly this tenuous connection,
rather than the man's meager talents, which had caused Talleyrand to select
Hottinguer for the opening gambit. His manner was conspiratorial, stagy,
a little ridiculous; he alternated between hushed tones and strident eloquence. But what he said was plain enough. The President's speech to the
Congress had been studied by the Directory, and had aroused the utmost
irritation. Before the envoys could be received, passages of that speech
would have to be softened, the wound assuaged, evidence given of America's
friendship toward the nation to which she owed so much. If this evidence
were sufficiently concrete, negotiations could proceed. A sum of 1,200,000
livres, or $240,000, would first have to be given to Talleyrand for distribution
to the Directory. All that was required thereafter was an apology for the
President's speech, a loan to the French Republic, and withdrawal by

America of all claims of her citizens against France arising from the ship seizures.

The Americans restrained themselves, they did not rise in their wrath, but their attitude was sufficiently clear. Hottinguer went away disappointed, and for the next move, Talleyrand decided to use a stronger instrument. This was a French banker, a M. Bellamy, who had recently been in Hamburg, arranging for the terms of that state's capitulation to the Directory. He came with a copy of Adams's controversial speech, from which he read aloud the passages that had given offense. The Americans, he said, must realize that they were inviting nothing less than a disastrous war. The hopes of their mission depended on their willingness to give "satisfaction" to the Directory—that is, an apology. The negotiation could not proceed otherwise. Then according to Pinckney's account, he added, "But I will not conceal from you that, this satisfaction being made, the essential part of the treaty remains to be adjusted. You must pay money, you must pay a great deal of money."

How much money? Bellamy repeated Hottinguer's figure for the *douceur* —$240,000. Although less than customary, this sum would be acceptable. A loan must thereafter be made, in the form of purchases of bonds of the New Dutch Republic which French arms had established—say, to the amount of 32,000,000 florins—then approximately $4,000,000.

He seemed hardly able to believe his ears when Pinckney said that such payments were out of the question. Subsequently a note came from him, urging their prompt action, for Austria had capitulated to the French armies, and all the might of France could now be thrown against her remaining enemies. This letter went into a file, to which the envoys later added other notes from Talleyrand's emissaries, together with detailed accounts of all their conversations. With Bellamy making no progress, yet another go-between appeared, Lucien Hauteval, a Swiss who had grown rich in the French West Indies. But his statement varied hardly at all from Bellamy's, and was met by the Americans with the same bleak lack of response.

5. "No, No, Not a Sixpence!"

The moral issue did not trouble the Americans nearly so much as the political dangers involved. The pro-French Gerry, in fact, was inclined to think the sum demanded as a bribe quite reasonable, and an indication that Talleyrand was not planning to let the money go beyond his own office. As he wrote to Jefferson a few years later, explaining his motivations, "Fifty thousand pounds which as a *douceur* to be divided among the Directory would at that time have been spurned by them, might have answered the purposes of M. Talleyrand and the principal officers of his bureau."

Another meeting followed, a dinner, at which all six men were present. Hottinguer once more took the lead. He reviewed France's triumphant position on the continent. The Allied armies had been broken. Her triumph on the Continent was unquestioned. England could be considered as beaten. What, then, of America's relation to victorious France? Why should her envoys be surprised because the Directory had decided to take a more determined tone with her? In the world which the French Republic was reshaping, there could be no more neutrals. Those who were not for France were against her, and would be treated as enemies. The American mission, if they wished peace, needed to win the goodwill of the French Directory, not only by concessions in policy, but specifically by tangible payments and loans.

Receiving only a vague response, Hottinguer became impatient. "Gentlemen," he burst out finally, "you do not speak to the point. It is money—it is expected that you will offer money."

Marshall said he thought they "had spoken to that point very explicitly."

"No," said Hottinguer, "no, you have not. What is your answer?"

This was more than Pinckney could bear. "It is No!" he said sharply. "No, not a sixpence!"

Hottinguer and his friends asked the Americans to think again. Nothing, they urged, could be done in France without money. Bellamy stressed the fact that Hamburg and other European states had been compelled to buy a peace. Was it not evident that America would find the same strategy profitable?

The Americans were equally emphatic: M. Talleyrand should understand that their country ardently wished peace with France, but her national honor was even dearer to her. She had a right to be neutral; she would not lend France money under coercion; she would fight before she would surrender her independence.

Bellamy, realizing that the opposition was coming from Marshall and Pinckney, asked to meet with them alone. With the utmost earnestness he reminded them of France's military power, and the injuries which she could inflict on the United States. Remember, he urged them, the recent fate of the Republic of Venice when she insisted on her neutrality, and failed to heed the warnings of Bonaparte. The helpless city had been handed over by him to Austria, as part of the treaty under which most of Italy had become a satrapy of France.

"You may believe," he said, according to Pinckney's account, "that on exposing to your countrymen the unreasonableness of the demands of this government, they will unite in resenting them. You are mistaken. You ought to know that the diplomatic skill of France, and the means she possesses in America are sufficient to enable her, with the French party in

America, to throw the blame which will attend the rupture of these negotiations on the Federalists."

The retort of the Americans was unyielding. The conduct of France,
they said, was provocative and hostile. She had not received America's
envoys, not permitted them "to utter the amicable wishes of their country."
Hers was "the haughty style of a master." The Americans had been "told
that unless they pay a sum to which their resources scarcely extend, they may
expect vengeance . . ." Their self-respect would permit no further communication through intermediaries.

So they wrote to the minister again, waited two weeks, received no answer,
sent Pinckney's private secretary in person with a note, were curtly told
once more that the Americans would hear from Talleyrand when he was
ready. To their astonishment, the minister's next representative turned out
to be a woman, Mme. de Villette, mature and charming, who had known
Voltaire, and was on familiar terms with Talleyrand. The lonely Americans
accepted her gracious invitations with more gratitude, one suspects, than
can be read in their reports. She entertained them at luncheon one week,
at dinner the next, and with well-seasoned food and old wine, with a witty
anecdote and a winning compliment, with a hint here and a pretty impor-
tunity there, she tried to soften their attitude. Gerry especially found her
society delightful, and he and Marshall accepted her invitation to make
their lodging in her comfortable house; but she made no more headway with
them than had Hottinguer, Bellamy, and Hauteval.

It was through Mme. de Villette that they met Talleyrand's next spokesman, the great Pierre Beaumarchais himself. His claims on their esteem
were considerable: as a benefactor, for he had been the organizer of the
unofficial French aid given to the Americans in the first years of their
Revolution; as a client, for Marshall was acting as his lawyer in a lawsuit
against the American government to recover some of the money which he
had advanced; as a playwright, for all of them knew *The Barber of Seville*
and *The Marriage of Figaro*. He gave an impressive dinner for the Americans, who in return gave one for him. The persistent Bellamy thereafter
came forward with a new proposal, aimed primarily at Marshall. The
solution had been found—the Americans would after all preserve their
scruples, while Talleyrand would receive his *douceur*. It was very simple.
Let it be arranged that Beaumarchais should win his case in the American
courts. He would then take it upon himself to pay Talleyrand the required
$240,000 out of his own pocket. When the Americans explained that such
a scheme, while perhaps possible in France, ran counter to their principles
and to the ways of American courts, which were independent of the Executive, Bellamy was hurt and incredulous.

But time was running out, and against the Americans. Nearly six months had passed since their arrival, with French seizures of American vessels continuing, and President Adams impatient for results. Talleyrand was becoming more and more powerful in France, for General Bonaparte, the nation's new hero, had publicly displayed his friendship for the Foreign Minister.

Speaking one day to Marshall and Pinckney in Bellamy's presence, Gerry proposed that he call in person on Talleyrand to invite him to dine—a social call, as a friend who had exchanged visits with him in Boston. His associates were less than enchanted with this idea—they did not trust or like Gerry or his Republican politics—but they could hardly stand in his way. Bellamy, who had been looking for a chance to see Gerry without the others, volunteered to go with him to the Foreign Office. On the way he warned Gerry that the French navy stood poised to bombard and ravage American coastal cities if no arrangements were made. Gerry was shocked and angered. On coming into Talleyrand's office he asked him point-blank whether Bellamy had been authorized to speak for him. That was so, said Talleyrand; but he was apparently thinking only of the financial propositions which had been made in his name. To show his familiarity with those propositions, he wrote out in his own hand the suggested terms for the purchase of Dutch bonds, and showed them to Gerry. But he said nothing of the *douceur*, and a moment later he burned the paper on which he had written.

6. *Seduction of an American*

In spite of Gerry's efforts to soften Talleyrand, the position of affairs did not change. After another month, Pinckney and Marshall gave up hope of a treaty, and the record which they were preparing for the President became their chief interest. To complete their file, they drafted a long letter to Talleyrand, recapitulating all of America's complaints against France. They had some difficulties with Gerry, at this point, for he still thought that they ought to negotiate; the letter, he felt, was unnecessarily provocative. Finally, however, they argued him down, and it was sent. For weeks Talleyrand did not bother to reply. Instead, he allowed action to speak for him. The day after he received the letter, the Directory put into effect a new decree against American shipping—one which went beyond all previous experience. It instructed French warships to seize not only American vessels carrying supplies to the enemy, but even those which were bringing British goods to the United States; and it forbade the entry into France of any American ship whose manifest showed that it had touched at British ports.

Having shown the mice his claws, Talleyrand now offered a little hope. He met with the three Americans once, twice, and again; they all repeated themselves to boredom, and nothing was accomplished. Then, finally, he replied to their letter, writing, it was clear, largely for the record. The blame for the prolonged misunderstanding between their countries was to be put wholly on the American government, which had thought proper to send to France as envoys "persons whose opinions and connections were too well known to expect from them dispositions sincerely conciliatory." He contrasted the selection of the American mission with the sending of John Jay to the court of St. James's. Many an American, he knew, would agree. Then in a few concluding sentences, he proposed to deal with the one among the commissioners "who could be considered the most impartial."

In this bid for Gerry's collaboration, Talleyrand was reinforced by the knowledge that the new decree had hurt the American in more than his patriotic feelings. Under it, a number of his family's ships were liable to confiscation. Nevertheless, after heated discussion with Marshall and Pinckney, Gerry joined in signing a reply, in which they said, "No one of the undersigned is authorized to take upon himself a negotiation evidently entrusted by the tenor of their powers and instructions to the whole; nor are there any two of them who can propose to withdraw . . . while there remains a possibility of performing" their task.

Talleyrand felt that he knew better. That same day, April 3, 1798, he wrote to Gerry, saying that he supposed "Messrs. Pinckney and Marshall have thought it useful and proper . . . to quit the territory of the republic." On that assumption, he expressed himself ready "to resume our reciprocal communications." Gerry could no longer resist temptation. He had no authority to negotiate alone, he told Talleyrand, but he would remain in Paris to confer informally. This decision he justified to the others on the ground that if he were to leave, if the negotiations were to collapse completely, France, as Talleyrand had threatened, would declare war on the United States. Pinckney "warmly remonstrated"; Marshall lost his temper; but Gerry could not be budged.

Talleyrand had succeeded in splitting the American commission, but the douceur was now lost forever. He let his disappointment and vindictiveness show as Pinckney and Marshall prepared to leave Paris. Pinckney's daughter, who was with him, had become seriously ill, and had been sent to the south of France. When Pinckney asked for permission to visit her there, he was not refused, but he was kept dangling in Paris for frustrating weeks. Marshall received even more mortifying treatment. His application for the safe-conduct and passport essential to his departure was made a football in the French Foreign Office, and it was only after the sport had become somewhat tedious for its clerks that he was finally allowed to board ship for home in late April 1798.

7. *Danse Militaire*

All this time, "His Rotundity," as Republican newspapers called John Adams, was in a state of understandable impatience. Owing to adversities of the transatlantic crossing, a detailed report from his envoys in Paris did not reach him until March. When he finally heard of Talleyrand's demands for an apology, a loan, and a bribe, he was outraged in his feelings as President, but as a Federalist could not help but see the political possibilities of the situation. That publication of the dispatch would touch off a patriotic explosion costly to the Republican party was certain. Pickering counseled its immediate release. The President hesitated; he wished, he said, first to make sure that the persons of his three commissioners were safe. Meanwhile he reported to Congress that although every honorable effort had been made, the mission had failed. Let Congress therefore adopt measures "for the defence of any exposed portions of our territory"; and raise moneys for additional naval vessels and arsenals.

Jefferson, who as yet knew nothing of the report from the Paris mission, thought the President's message to Congress "insane." "So extraordinary a degree of impetuosity," he felt, could not be justified. But as Vice-President —an office which he described as "honorable and easy," in contrast to the President's "splendid misery"—he could do nothing. Although the House temporized on some of the proposed military expenditures, it voted appropriations for three frigates. Meanwhile, rumors of the report had begun to circulate, and the congressmen were agog to find out its details. No strategy could have helped the Federalists more than Adams's apparent reluctance to release it. The Republicans, even Jefferson, felt sure that his only reason for delay was that it contained nothing to justify his demand for armaments. In consequence, a resolution calling upon the President to "produce the papers" was introduced in the House and carried. Federalists who were in the President's confidence could hardly restrain their joy at this Republican blunder. "In the name of God, let them be gratified," chortled one of them as he voted for the resolution. After allowing the Republicans to urge him once or twice more, Adams consented to send the file to Congress.

The report as penned by Marshall and Pinckney, who were its chief authors, was incendiary enough, but the President made the one slight alteration necessary to give it maximum propaganda value. In the documents read in Congress, the names of Hottinguer, Bellamy, and Hauteval had been removed, and in their place appeared the mysterious initials, X, Y, and Z. It was a master stroke. The words "X Y Z Papers" took on instant magic, a one-second description of French perfidy and justification of Federalist policy. The Republicans were stunned as they read. It came to Jefferson and Madison that from the beginning of the mission this was the moment toward which the Federalists had been working, that they had never seriously looked for peace with France, but only for an exposure of Republicans as doubtful patriots. So far as Hamilton was concerned, the suspicion was almost certainly correct. His advocacy of the mission in private talks with prominent Federalists had been entirely in terms of practical political benefits to be derived. But even he could hardly have anticipated the scope of the windfall. It came at a time when Federalist sentiment seemed to be on the ebb, when the Republican power in the country was growing swiftly under the tonic guidance of Jefferson and Madison. If anything could blight their hopes, it was the XYZ Papers. The Jeffersonians were disgraced and discredited, Hamilton thought, forever. In terms of political appeal, what were the aggressions of Grenville compared to the insults of Talleyrand?

As the hail of criticism descended, many Republicans in the Congress ran for cover, switching their votes on all French questions to the Federalists. Despondently, Jefferson wrote to Madison, "Giles, Clopton, Cabell and Nicholas have gone, and Clay goes tomorrow . . . In this state of things, they will carry what they please." It seemed to him that war with France could no longer be avoided. A last-ditch Republican resolution designed to permit Gerry to negotiate alone with Talleyrand was overwhelmingly defeated. The Federalist press screamed its triumph. The government paid to have ten thousand copies of the XYZ Papers distributed throughout the country. Swiftly the war fever mounted. Even some Quakers threw overboard their pacifism and joined in the national frenzy. Pinckney's remark, "No, no, not a single sixpence," was embellished by patriots into "Millions for defense, but not one cent for tribute," and was shouted at every street corner. (The public did not know—and might not have cared if it had known—that an American ship was then on its way to Algiers with twenty-six barrels of dollars as a tribute for the Dey.) A new popular song swept the country and opened the floodgates of such a sentimental torrent as America had not previously seen. In theaters, in taverns, and in the streets, the people, with tears of fervor in their eyes, adulated themselves in song:

> Hail Columbia! Happy land,
> Hail ye heroes, heaven-born band!

Night after night, men sitting at dinner raised their glasses to such toasts as "Adams and Liberty!" "May the American eagle pluck out the gills of the Gallic cock!" "A fig for the French and the sly Talleyrand!" The arrival of John Marshall from France at this opportune moment lifted him to nationwide fame; wherever he went, crowds cheered him, bands played in his honor, orators called him another George Washington. Washington himself, within two years of death, was brought out of retirement by Adams to become commander in chief of an army for which Congress was to provide large sums.

Now began a curious *Danse Militaire* in the government, with the right-wing Federalists calling the tune. It was Washington's desire that Hamilton be made his second in command, which for practical purposes meant the acting head of the Army. Adams, full of resentments against Hamilton, tried to resist, but found no support except among his enemies, the Republicans. His Federalist cabinet was unanimously against him. With poor grace, he finally conferred the requested rank of major general on Hamilton. But the thought of the ambitious Hamilton leading the American Army was almost as obnoxious to the President as it was to Jefferson. He saw a sinister purpose behind Hamilton's and Washington's insistence. He could not believe that they seriously feared for the military safety of the United States. The French forces were fully occupied in Europe and Egypt. There was, Adams wrote, "no more prospect of seeing a French army here than in heaven." He could guess at Hamilton's purpose—to use war against France as an excuse to attack the American colonies of her ally, Spain—to conquer New Orleans and West Florida. There was even a proposal to venture the Army of the United States in Francisco de Miranda's long-heralded South American revolt; Hamilton was corresponding with Miranda and with the American minister to England, Rufus King, with this purpose, and Pickering also knew of the plan. Success on so vast a scale would make Hamilton the new national hero, and from that pinnacle to step to the Presidency would be easy for him. Already the British anticipated such a development. A future alliance with the United States was openly suggested in the British press. As soon as Hamilton's appointment as major general was announced England sent over a large quantity of cannon; the Admiralty arranged for an exchange of naval signals with American naval vessels; and a member of the royal family suggested that the British lend America a squadron of warships. With so much power in the hands of impatient Hamilton and his fire-breathing friends, who could tell what the end would be? "There may arise," Adams wrote gloomily, if muddily, "an enthusiasm that seems little to be foreseen." And again, "You cannot imagine what a horror some persons are in, lest peace should continue."

Fear of Hamilton's ascendancy, almost as much as his belief in the virtues of neutrality, held Adams back from a declared war on France. War would have made him more popular, but he sensed that it would apotheosize Hamilton. Adams had almost been cheated out of the Presidency by Hamilton's machinations in 1796; he did not intend to lose his second term in 1800. This is not to say that he allowed their feud to dictate the national policy. He sincerely believed that America's interests would be best served by peace. He was a genuine neutral. His anger at corrupt France did not make him forget his lifelong hostility to haughty England. One was as inimical to America as the other. Of all the leaders then in American public life, Adams was at that moment the most balanced and even-minded. Nevertheless even he might have bent to the hurricane and given the people the war they wanted if personal resentment of Hamilton had not stiffened his resistance.

It needed to be stiff. The steaming emotions of the country had no escape valve. Congress was racing wildly toward war. It passed a law virtually forbidding Americans to trade with France. It declared the treaties of 1778 to be void, having been violated by France. The Cabinet, working with Hamilton, drafted a speech for the President in which he was to affirm his determination not to make a new attempt at negotiation with France. There was every expectation that he would make his speech as written, and by so doing commit himself to the war party. But the Federalist leaders did not quite know their Adams. The President asserted himself by striking out the critical passage, and saying instead that he would never send another minister to France unless it was certain "that he will be received, respected and honored." Federalists were horrified by the hint that negotiation was still possible. Adams had deliberately played into the hands of Jefferson, who was striving feverishly to hold his party in line for steps short of war. Albert Gallatin took advantage of the President's moderation to make a remarkable speech in the House, sobering the representatives with the warning that the European war was coming to a close, and "it is not to our interest to enter into it."

In the decisive test, Congress, by a narrow vote, limited hostilities against France to defensive action. French warships and privateers operating against American commerce were to be captured, but French merchantmen were not to be attacked. For most Americans, it was a small distinction, but for purposes of diplomacy it was large enough to prevent open war and to shape future history.

8. *The Devious Route to Peace*

The late summer of 1798 found Citizen Talleyrand a good deal less full of himself than he had been a year earlier. France's Mediterranean fleet had just been demolished at Aboukir by Horatio Nelson; Bonaparte in Egypt was blockaded, and reports from him had almost ceased; English money and intrigue were known to be forming a new continental coalition against France, this time with Russian participation; dissension and plots threatened the Directory from day to day; the greed of Barras had become insatiable, and was threatening to swallow half the wealth of France. Under these conditions, the dispatches from America made unpalatable reading. The intensity of the reaction to the XYZ affair amazed Talleyrand: who would have thought the Americans to be so naïve? Reports from London said that the men of Whitehall, in their clubs, were toasting "Citizen Talleyrand, and Citizens X, Y, and Z, in gratitude for their aid to England." Even at home there was criticism of him: worse, there was laughter. He was familiar with the killing power of ridicule in politics, and hastily he composed a formal rebuttal to the charges of the American envoys. With an air of injury, he wrote of republican France's rebuffs at America's hands—the favoritism shown to England in the Jay treaty—the cold animosity of Pinckney and Marshall. "It was wished that they should come forward with some un-equivocal proof of their attachment to our cause: a cause which was but recently their own. Our finances at that time required us to sell a certain number of Batavian bonds . . . The Minister of Foreign Affairs gave them [the Americans] to understand that an offer made by them to buy up a quantity of these bonds would be regarded as a friendly act." He deprecated Messrs. X, Y, and Z as "intriguing politicians" who were "eager to intoxicate the Americans with the idea of their own importance," but who had no authority to speak for him. But as to the $240,000 cash payment which had been demanded, or of the blackmailing threat of bombardment, there was nothing to say except to deny knowledge of them, and this Talleyrand did. The pamphlet was published at once in Paris and somewhat later was translated into English and printed in London.

The fact was that Talleyrand had miscalculated; he had not expected America to put so high a valuation on national honor, or to be capable of unified action. The source of his error was identified in a letter written to the Directory by one of the more penetrating of the French diplomatic observers then in the United States, Louis-Guillaume Otto. "Our agents wished to see only two parties in the United States, the French party and the English party; but there is a middle party, much larger, composed of the most estimable men . . . the American party which loves its country above all and for whom preferences for France or for England are only accessory and often passing affections."

A gambler always, Talleyrand knew how to accept an adverse roll of the dice. To allow affairs to drift was unwise. A limited war, such as America contemplated, could exceed its limits overnight—and this at a time when France had no warships or soldiers to spare. Besides, a more amicable relation with America might soon prove important in another connection. Faltering Spain could never hold its Louisiana territory in the face of an American invasion. By careful manipulation, her North American colonies might be transferred to the French flag, and to this end the acquiescence of the United States was, if not essential, at least desirable. In any event, it was better not to stimulate any further expansion of the American army and navy.

President Adams had left a door open, hinting that he might after all negotiate if assured that his envoys would this time be received with respect, honor, and so forth. Why not? Nevertheless, it would not do to give the Americans too much encouragement all at once. Talleyrand's *amour-propre* demanded that he show resentment of the atrocious references to himself in the debates of the Congress. He sent for Gerry, whom he had kept in France against just such an emergency. The interview began with some histrionics—a little cursing, a little shouting, a little vituperation of America. To his surprise, little Gerry retorted with flashing eyes and biting words. Talleyrand instantly changed his tone. Ah, well, he said, it was all a mistake, an extraordinary misunderstanding. America should not assume that France was her enemy—on the contrary, the French government wanted only peace and friendship with the United States—would receive her ministers with good will. If Gerry would carry these thoughts to President Adams, passports would at once be provided for his return to Boston. The American accepted gladly, and was on his way.

Talleyrand knew, however, that Gerry, as a Republican and a discredited ambassador, was unlikely to have much influence on anyone in the Federalist administration except, perhaps, his friend the President. Another and sounder channel was needed. The American minister in Holland, William Vans Murray, was known to stand high in Adams's favor. Talleyrand sent off a note to the French minister at the Hague, Pichon, with detailed instructions for a message to be given to Murray for the President. Advances made by the United States for a negotiation with France, the message said, would be received by France in a friendly spirit.

The event justified the effort. Murray's letter to Adams arrived only a few days after Gerry had called on the President at his home in Quincy; and it corroborated Gerry's account of Talleyrand's change in attitude. Adams was at that time conferring with Pickering and others in his Cabinet on his next message to Congress, in which the quarrel with France was to be reviewed. Over their dismayed protest, he decided to include a sentence which carried a distinct implication of a desire for peace: "Whether we negotiate with her or not, vigorous preparations for war will be alike indispensable." There, however, he stopped. Before he would commit himself further, he wanted additional reassurance; for the message from Talleyrand, as Adams wrote to Murray, had after all come at second hand. In February 1799, Murray replied, enclosing an official dispatch from Talleyrand to Pichon. Any plenipotentiary whom the United States would send to France to settle their differences, wrote the Foreign Minister, "would positively be received with the regard due to the representative of a free, sovereign and powerful nation."

Adams's doubts were now sufficiently allayed so that he could proceed.

He had come to distrust Pickering and the others in his Cabinet as outright agents of Hamilton, so that he would no longer consult with them; and moving with a boldness reminiscent of his younger days, he sent a message to the Senate, nominating Murray to be minister to France.

9. *"Shocked and Grieved"*

Horror is not too strong a word to express the Federalist reaction. Hastily Secretary of State Pickering wrote to Hamilton: "We have all been shocked and grieved . . . I beg you to be assured that it is wholly *his* [the President's] *own* act, without any participation or communication with any of us . . ." A similar letter from Sedgwick, the Federalist senatorial leader, called Adams's action "false and insidious," embarrassing and ruinous. George Cabot, speaking with the voice of authority, considered the Murray appointment "impolitic, unjustifiable, dangerous and inconsistent," and a reason for opposing Adams's renomination for the presidency. Secretary of the Treasury Wolcott, writing to Cabot, went further: "If the strange and disastrous course taken . . . is to be pursued . . . a war with Great Britain is hardly avoidable." The President's pretense of "impartial and independent sentiments" was only a foundation for "an address to the latent animosities of our people against the English."

To Cabot and his friends negotiation with republican France automatically implied a rise of "anarchy" in America. His innermost thoughts in the matter came out in a letter to Hamilton, in which he warned that Adams was "but little attached to the support of the public credit and the rights of property." Further proof, if it was needed, of the President's iniquitous disregard for the rich and the well-born lay in the fact that he had just spared the life of a German-born Pennsylvania agitator named Fries, who had been sentenced to death by the courts for trying to organize resistance to federal tax collectors.

In their astonishment and confusion, the senatorial right-wing leaders made a move which, in the long run, was to be fatal to their hopes. If they had let the Murray nomination come to the floor of the Senate, it might have been defeated, but they wanted more: they wanted the President to withdraw it. To this purpose, five Federalist senators of the Foreign Relations Committee called in a body on Adams. The President faced them with a sharp rebuke: they were violating his Constitutional prerogative, he thought. Sedgwick, who was one of the group, admitted that their visit was irregular, and suggested that it be considered unofficial. To this the President agreed. But on no account, he said, would he withdraw the nomination, and if it was rejected by the Senate, he would propose another three-man mission to go to Paris, with Murray one of the three. Enraged, the senators retired to confer, and decided to accept the President's challenge by voting down the nomination. But before the issue reached the point of debate in the Senate, the President sent in another message, proposing the two additional names for the Paris mission: Oliver Ellsworth and Patrick Henry. The Federalist leaders instantly recognized that they had fallen into a trap of their own making. Murray alone they could have safely rejected, but hardly the Federalist Chief Justice of the Supreme Court, or the great Virginia conservative and patriot.

Hamilton's realistic advice to the senators was to accept the situation; it was, after all, one thing to send a mission, another to make peace. There could be many a slip. Meanwhile, "the mode must be accommodated with the President." The Federalists yielded, voted, and confirmed all three nominations. Subsequently, the aged Henry declined the appointment, and Governor William R. Davie of North Carolina went in his place.

Even so, the Hamiltonian faction did not admit total defeat. Pickering wrote to Murray that before the new envoys could sail Talleyrand would have to give formal and unequivocal assurance that their reception would accord with his earlier promise. Prodded by Murray, Talleyrand wrote the required letter, but could not restrain a remark or two about the "capricious and insincere" attitude of the American Government. This was all Pickering needed. As soon as he received Talleyrand's letter, he called the President's attention to its impertinent language. Adams's vanity was well known; Pickering expected indignation from him; but in this instance the President rose above personal pique. He simply instructed the Secretary of State to give Ellsworth and Davey their formal directives, and speed them on their way.

For five weeks more Pickering delayed, hoping for some development that would render the mission futile. The day arrived when he thought he had it. Sensational news had been received from France. The armies of the Second Coalition were driving the French before them. Russian troops under General Suvarov were master of North Italy. Talleyrand had resigned. There was a rumor that the Directory was about to fall, that the Bourbon monarchy would be restored. What purpose now in sending the mission?

Hamilton, directing the Federalist strategy as usual, felt that the moment called for a display of *force majeure*. Adams was then convalescing from a severe illness. He had left Philadelphia, for the seat of the government was being transferred to the new capital on the Potomac, Washington; but the presidential "Palace" had not yet been completed, and he had taken up residence in Trenton. The President's weakened condition did not deter Hamilton. With Pickering, Wolcott, and McHenry as his advance guard, he himself called uninvited at Adams's house, and as further reinforcement he brought with him the Chief Justice, Oliver Ellsworth, who although he had accepted a place on the mission, was generally in accord with Hamilton's views of foreign policy. All Hamilton's great powers of persuasion were exercised in the hope that the sick President would agree to delay the mission indefinitely, but Adams, keeping his temper, merely listened. When his unwelcome visitors left, dissatisfied, they had no notion of how deeply they had incensed him. With his New England dander up, he seized his pen, sent for a courier; and early the next morning Pickering, Wolcott, and McHenry found on their desks peremptory orders to issue the necessary papers, and instantly provide a frigate to carry Ellsworth and Davey to France. They had no choice but to resign or obey, and after consultation with Hamilton, they obeyed.

In later years, Adams was to refer to his decisions on the French mission as "the most disinterested and meritorious actions" of his life. "I desire no other inscription over my gravestone," he said, "than 'Here lies John Adams, who took upon himself the responsibility of peace with France.'"

10.   *The Hand of Bonaparte*

Secretary of State Pickering's obstruction of the new mission to France, and the resulting delay, came as an unexpected boon to Talleyrand. If the Americans had come early in 1799, they might have driven a hard bargain. France's military expectations were then collapsing with terrifying speed on the continent. Egypt was about to be lost. The French fleet was demoralized; even the tiny American navy had scored successes against it. In the Caribbean the French frigate *L'Insurgente* had been beaten and captured by America's *Constellation*, under Commodore Truxton, and scores of French privateers had been ignominiously hauled into American harbors as prizes of war. France had no ships or men to spare for transatlantic adventures. An American threat of war at that moment could have extracted many a concession from the tottering Directory.

Talleyrand's resignation from the Foreign Ministry was no more than a little jump to separate himself from the débâcle which he foresaw. He had faith in his catlike ability to land on his feet. The only question in his mind was, after Barras, who? Many persons of influence favored making the popular General Moreau dictator of France, or perhaps the spectacular young General Joubert. But to Talleyrand, whose nose for the future was always keen, the intrigues of Joseph and Lucien Bonaparte in the national legislature to give power to their absent brother, Napoleon, had the smell of success. Knowing the hero as he did, Talleyrand considered his early return from the fizzling Egyptian expedition a good possibility. Unfortunately, Bonaparte might well hold him partially to blame for having advised the

Egyptian venture in the first place. To offset this disadvantage, there was Talleyrand's scheme to acquire Louisiana from Spain without cost—a project which would be certain to appeal to Napoleon. And where could he find another Foreign Minister of so much experience and subtlety? The sensible procedure for a Talleyrand in such a confused situation was to shake off official responsibility, commit himself to no party, and keep on good terms with all, but especially with the Bonapartists. The shrewd pilot fish knows his sharks.

By the time the three American envoys arrived in Paris, in March 1800, the kaleidoscope had been shaken again. Russia had withdrawn from the war; Napoleon had made his spectacular re-entry into France, scored his *coup d'état*, and become First Consul and virtual dictator. More, he had got over his annoyance with Talleyrand, and appointed him again Foreign Minister—but with the understanding that he, Napoleon, would assume direct authority over the policies which Talleyrand was to execute. The American problem interested him. He had read and approved a memorandum from Talleyrand, stressing the desirability, at the moment, of American good will, while France put herself in position to acquire Louisiana. With the proper stimulation from France, Talleyrand asserted, America would become "a naval rival to Great Britain," and perhaps a decisive influence in the war.

However, his personal feelings about the United States were so bitter, after the XYZ affair, as to unfit him for negotiation with the new American mission, and Bonaparte assigned the responsibility for the American treaty to his brother Joseph, later to become, for a time, the King of Spain. Consequently, when the American envoys called at the French Foreign Office, Talleyrand hurried them to Napoleon, who pleased them by the warmth of his greeting, and impressed them by the force of his personality. At the news of George Washington's death, they learned, he had ordered black crêpe to be "draped on all the flags and field colors of the Republic for ten days," as a tribute to greatness. All this was hopeful enough, but as the Americans settled down to work with Joseph Bonaparte, an awkwardness appeared. Their instructions, which Pickering had drafted with his tongue in his cheek, and which Adams had felt obliged to sign, compelled them to say that their government insisted on a mutual renunciation of the treaties of 1778, and on an indemnity of $20,000,000 for ships and sailors seized by the French. From the standpoint of the new France, the treaties were of little consequence. But the money was another matter. Napoleon was not a man to pay out even a small sum if he could help it, let alone an unthinkable number of millions. The American demand was inadmissable, but before flatly saying so, Joseph Bonaparte waited for the outcome of the Italian campaign which his brother was then planning.

The news of the stunning victory over Austria at Marengo some weeks later produced a sharp rise in French morale and a corresponding weakening of America's bargaining position. Talleyrand now joined in the conference, and offered alternative propositions: either the old treaties, with their extraterritorial privileges and their obligations on America would be continued in force, and the indemnities would be settled by compromise; or there would be a new treaty, with no indemnities. Unless they chose to break off the negotiations, the Americans saw, they would have to depart from their instructions and make concessions. Finally they signed an agreement, the so-called Convention of 1800. Under it, the old treaties were to become inoperative, and together with the question of the indemnity were referred to future negotiation. Each nation undertook to restore all property captured from the other. Governmental and commercial debts owing on both sides were to be paid.

11. Boomerang

The arrival in Washington of the draft of the Convention with France precipitated a new crisis for President Adams. He was determined that come what might, the treaty would be signed, and to avoid sabotage from within his own Cabinet, he had ousted Pickering, and appointed John Marshall as Secretary of State. A new and cunning strategy was then conceived by the Hamiltonians to prevent ratification of the Convention—not to reject it outright—they had no satisfactory excuse for that—but by emasculating it, to compel the President himself to reject it. Accordingly, they declined to ratify unless Adams agreed to expunge the article which referred the question of the Treaties of 1778 and the indemnity to the future. But the grim President saw the trap and refused to fall into it. He simply signed the Convention without the disputed clause and sent it back to Paris.

The change made by the Senate did not bother Talleyrand and Bonaparte at all; but if one change, why not another? Napoleon promptly wrote in a proviso to the effect that the expunging of the article on the indemnity was to be taken as an abandonment of claims on both sides. Murray, Ellsworth, and Davie were distressed; it came to them that in the Convention as it now stood, the American government had given up all of its reasonable and just claims for indemnity, in order to get rid of two old and bedraggled treaties. The boomerang, however, was of America's own hurling. Once more the modified Convention crossed the Atlantic to the Senate, where, without fanfare, it was ratified and forgotten. Peace reigned again between the world's two great republics.

Secretary of the Treasury Wolcott wrote a sorrowing letter to George Cabot. "I cannot believe that the British government or their merchants will consider it for their interest to permit us to prosecute a free commerce with France; and if . . . our trade shall be interdicted, the United States will commence or retaliate hostilities." This prophecy, while it needed a dozen years for fulfillment, was of course exact.

CHAPTER FIVE

Witch Hunt

1. *Flank Attack from the Right*

The preservation of American neutrality was a moral triumph, perhaps the only real triumph of Adams's administration. But being only a moral triumph, it was unpopular. The public had been whipped into frothing expectation of war; and when there was no war, they felt somehow cheated. Right-wing Federalists were especially bitter. As men like Wolcott and Cabot could clearly see, the peace with France opened wider the way for the rise to power of Jefferson, who, in the cool shadows of the vice-presidency, had been quietly biding his time. The formidable Cabot especially was unwilling to sit back under so terrible a threat. He would rather have seen Lucifer in the Presidency than Jefferson. It was not only that the man was anti-British and anti-aristocratic. His imaginative, almost speculative approach to foreign affairs and domestic economy frightened Cabot, and his egalitarian beliefs promised innovations, the end of which could not be clearly foreseen. The right wing feared that a Jeffersonian revolution was in the making which would alter the entire relationship of the United States to England and cut away their own wealth and power.

Cabot could not forgive Adams's refusal to go to war against the Jacobins while an adequate pretext was at hand. Impatiently he dismissed the argument that America lacked the resources for war against a major antagonist. As he saw it, war would have stimulated business, and business would have stimulated an irresistible urge to victory. "Avarice," he wrote, "would have fought our battles . . . a love of glory would have grown upon the love of gain." Like Talleyrand, he was convinced that Americans would do anything for business.

The great fear in Cabot's mind was that as the cloud of a French war evaporated, the storm warnings would again point to England; for search and seizure of American ships by the British was a continuing scandal. Even more serious, impressment was a growing flame under public opinion as England sought to make up for her Navy's manpower shortage at America's expense. Reports filtering back to the United States told of violent removal of American sailors from their ships at the caprice of British officers, and of their physical abuse by men who regarded the cat-o'-nine-tails as a mild disciplinary tonic. The American people were not interested in the nice legalistic point that Jay's Treaty, by failing to mention impressment, had provided England with a color of justification for the seizure of seamen whom she suspected of being British subjects. All they knew was that Americans were being whipped by Englishmen. Every time a British frigate exerted its alleged rights over a helpless American merchantman, the national temperature rose another degree.

Could England be persuaded to moderate her aggressions on American commerce? Cabot put his ideas on the subject into writing for Wolcott, who was in close touch with important British officials. An appeal, he felt, should be made to England's commercial sense. "This country for half a century to come may be immensely valuable to Great Britian as a consuming customer, and this connection would be *at least* as beneficial to us as to them. Nothing but violence can interrupt this salutary intercourse . . . Great Britain ought to be made to see that we will not sacrifice our interests to our passions . . . that we are not the dupes of her rival . . . that we will never quarrel with her or embarrass the commercial intercourse with her while she regulates her own conduct with us by the rules of acknowledged justice."

But Cabot was not really hopeful that England would respond favorably. And what if she did not? Was there another way to silence Anglophobe propagandists of "anarchy"? It seemed to him essential that some way be found to gag the Jeffersonian opposition. As early as 1796, hints of this purpose were reflected in his correspondence with Hamilton and others; and subsequently the seething popular resentment generated by the XYZ sensation seemed to him to offer an unparalleled opportunity to establish a far-flung censorship of American opinion.

The Cabot coterie (known also as the Essex Junto, from the name of the Massachusetts county in which Cabot resided) was small. Fisher Ames, one of the inner group, once remarked that in the entire country not more than five hundred men were of his way of thinking. But what they lacked in numbers, they made up in wealth and influence. If Hamilton would stand with them, and throw his power into a drive to identify radical Republicans as subversives, the thing might be done.

As the leader of the entire Federalist party Hamilton had to adjust himself to the thinking of such moderates as Adams and Marshall, but in spirit he was far closer to Cabot. It has been cynically said that in his efforts to enlarge his own thin estate he gravitated more and more to the commercial magnates who could be most useful to him, and so became a tool of New England reaction. But there is little evidence for such an assertion. His convictions were his own, and he was never dollar-minded. His growing impatience with the Adams wing was almost certainly due to genuine alarm inspired in him by the rise of the Republicans, whom he, like Cabot, equated with social disorder and war against England. In New York, more and more

Republicans were calling themselves Democrats—a significant word. Hamilton did not seriously believe, as Cabot and Pickering did, that Jefferson was contemplating the confiscation of the great estates, and a social revolution going beyond even that of France, in which the country would be turned over to the "American Jacobins." Nevertheless, danger was in the air. There were too many poor. Farmers were having a hard time. The national credit was low, interest rates had risen to 8 per cent, prices were falling. Once people began to forget about XYZ, they would begin to remember their personal troubles, and to hold them against the government. To make matters worse, the country was feeling the impact of a new rush of immigrants from Ireland, where rebellion was being bloodily suppressed by the British. Many a newly arrived Irishman was finding ready American ears to listen to his tale of horrors endured at the hands of England's soldiers. Coupled with French propaganda, the Irish passion was bound to have a political effect.

In 1798, the leading Federalists felt that time was running out, that it was now or never. Enough Republicans were aligned with the Federalists in the House to give them the majority they needed to supplement their advantage in the Senate. Another year, another six months might be too late. Hamilton by nature was disinclined to curtailments of personal liberty, or of the freedom of the press, but the logic of the situation was inescapable. If Jay's Treaty was to continue in force, and peace with England be preserved, the government of the United States would have to remain passive under provocations to which the treaty gave implicit sanction, such as impressment. To this Jefferson as President would never consent; so that future relations with England, not to mention the social stability of America, would hinge on the election of 1800. A means, therefore, had to be found to block the Republican drive for votes. However objectionable a direct attack on freedom of the press and of speech might be in theory, it could not be avoided. Nothing must be allowed to destroy peace with England or interfere with the rights of property.

2. *"Let Us Not Be Cruel . . ."*

A burst of propaganda in New England heralded the new Federalist policy. Newspapers clamored that the diabolical French had vast numbers of agents in the country who were trying to divide the American people. Unless these aliens were jailed or deported the country would fall into such anarchy as France had experienced. State secrets were being given to the enemy, true patriots were being slandered. The drums of panic sounded louder and louder, they filled the ears of the country, until even Jeffersonians in Congress began to jig to the rhythm. Speech followed speech. The French had to go. The Irish immigration had to be stopped. The thousands of Irishmen who were taking up residence in New York and Boston had to be held back from the citizenship which would give them the right to vote for "anarchy." Federalists rose in the excited House of Representatives to propose that aliens be required to wait fourteen years to become American citizens, instead of five, as in the past; that the President be authorized, at his discretion, to order out of the country any alien "whom he shall judge dangerous," or "shall have reasonable ground to suspect" of endangering the public peace. And the House approved. The Senate went even farther, initiating a Sedition Bill which, among its clauses, made American citizens subject to heavy fine and long imprisonment if they dared "to combine . . . with intent to oppose any measures of the government of the United States," or "to intimidate . . . any person holding office under the government," or to organize meetings to oppose these measures, or to publish any writing against the Congress or the President "with intent to defame them."

Hamilton, Cabot, Ames, and other Federalist leaders subsequently tried to avoid personal identification with these bills, the far reach of which startled many of the Hamiltonians themselves. The Sedition Bill in particular caused much searching of consciences in Congress. As a remedy, it seemed more dangerous than the disease it was intended to cure. But most Federalists were then less interested in freedom of the press than in freedom from the press. Eager to put an end to the partisan mudslinging of Republican editors, who had recently gone to unprecedented lengths in bespattering the reputations of respectable opponents, they stood in a solid phalanx behind the Alien and Sedition Bills.

Jefferson issued an impassioned warning against dictatorship-in-the-making: "If this goes down, we shall immediately see attempted another act of Congress declaring that the President shall continue in office during life." But the Federalists, able to muster a majority in both Houses, trampled down the opposition. When a Republican congressman declared on the floor that the Alien Bill "would have disgraced the age of Gothic barbarity," Federalists arose to call his speech "evidence of seditious disposition." When Gallatin reminded the House that the people were devoted to the Constitution, and since the Whisky Rebellion had cheerfully submitted to the nation's laws, so that the Sedition Act was unwarranted, he was sneered at as "an alien Frenchman." It took a brave man to denounce the bills, knowing that, once they became law, he might be tarred forever as a subversive.

The dictatorial powers given to the President by the bills caused no qualms among the Federalist leaders. Washington privately supported them. Hamilton made a token show of concern—the bills, he thought, went somewhat too far—"let us not be cruel or violent"—"energy is a very different thing from violence." But he offered no serious criticism. The Federalist right wing, with support from defected Republicans, had the bit in its teeth, and XYZ had opened the road. Both bills were passed by Congress and went to the President.

The strength which Adams had shown in resisting the pressure toward war was absent now. Although he expressed misgivings about the bills, he allowed them to become law, for to have refused would have meant an open break with the strongest element in his party, and the certainty that he would be deprived of the second term on which he had set his heart. It was his belief that through temperate administration of the new laws he could prevent abuses while conciliating the Hamiltonians by a show of force. The implications of the Alien and Sedition Acts for the future of his party and his own place in history seem to have escaped him.

With the new laws in force, there was a wave of panic among recently arrived aliens. Hundreds of Frenchmen promptly left the country. In Boston, Irish immigrants were assaulted and abused on the streets. The Federalist press of 1799 burst into joyous doggerel:

> *Each factious alien shrinks with dread*
> *And hides his hemp-devoted head;*
> *While Slander's foul seditious crew*
> *With gnashing teeth retires from view.*

Old Dr. Joseph Priestley, scientist, friend of Franklin, freethinker and defender of the French Revolution, who had sought sanctuary in America from the British Government, was denounced as an atheist and a spy, and threatened with deportation. So were other noted liberals of foreign birth. Newspapers urged deportations of all aliens who expressed anti-British sentiments. Even Hamilton said that "the mass of them ought to be obliged to leave." But the President held to his policy of restraint. After a few months, the country realized that he had not sent a single alien out of the country, and he was accused by ardent Hamiltonians of pitiable weakness and folly.

But the Sedition Act produced somewhat more satisfactory results for its authors, producing for a time something like a reign of terror among Republican publicists. A noted South Carolinian, Aedanus Burke, subsequently wrote to Madison that the Sedition Act had "struck into the minds of men such a dread and panic in this city, there were not ten men to whom I dared speak my mind . . ." "The despotic insolence with which one part of our fellow citizens hunted down those who differed from them" had been, he said, the worst experience of his life. Twenty-five well-known Republican editors and writers were prosecuted under the act and ten were convicted, imprisoned, and fined. These convictions, few as they were, represented a significant proportion of the elite of Republican journalism.

The charges aired in court seemed to prove all the accusations of petty egotism which had been leveled against Adams. The guilt of one victim of the Sedition Act, Lyon of Vermont, a member of the House of Representatives, lay essentially in the fact that he had accused the President of an "unbounded thirst for ridiculous pomp, foolish adulation, and selfish avarice." Another was sentenced to six months in prison and a fine of four hundred dollars for saying that in 1797 Adams had hardly been "in the infancy of political mistakes," such as he made in signing the Alien and Sedition Acts. But the President also looked after the reputations of other Federalist leaders. One editor was imprisoned for declaring that Hamilton had tried to buy the famous Republican newspaper *Aurora* in order to suppress it. Adams took especial satisfaction in the jailing of Callender, a corrupt journalist who had for a time been subsidized by Jefferson, and who wielded one of the country's deadliest poison pens.

Under the influence of these examples, a distinct sobering in the prose of the Republican press was soon noticeable. The purple adjective gave way to the qualifying clause, the outright lie was supplanted by the rhetorical question. Federalist editors, on the other hand, indulged in an orgy of unpunished libels aimed primarily at Jefferson, Madison, and Monroe. In their first enthusiasm, some Federalists thought they stood on the threshold of a new era, from which would emerge an authoritarian, strongly centralized government, such as Hamilton had dreamed of from the beginning. When John Marshall, who was then running for Congress from Virginia, urged repeal of the Acts, his temerity brought down on him the wrath of New England's lords of reaction. He was said to have degraded himself. Newspapers proposed that he be read out of the party. George Cabot contemptuously remarked that Marshall had "much to learn on the subject of a practicable system of free government."

3. "A *Natural Right to Nullify* . . ."

Witch-hunting, while always an interesting pastime, is exhausting for any people, especially when many of them secretly agree with the witches. The color of Federalist success soon began to fade. Republican editors found subtle ways to avoid prosecution without ceasing to criticize, and the offensive laws rapidly became objects of popular detestation and ridicule. The main sites of opposition were the South and West. One day the Hamiltonians opened their newspapers to discover that the legislature of Kentucky had openly defied federal authority to enforce the Alien and Sedition Acts. Guided by Jefferson, it had adopted resolutions asserting the rights of the individual states to determine for themselves whether the federal government, in any law which it passed, had exceeded the powers which the states had granted to it. The wording of the resolutions had a challenging bluntness. "Where powers are assumed which have not been delegated, every state has a natural right to nullify . . ." Northern conservatives stood shocked. If the doctrine of nullification should prevail, how could secession be prevented in some future crisis?

Protests against Kentucky's action were sounded in many states and in the Congress, but almost at once another state emphasized the threat. The language of the Virginia Resolutions, written by Madison, was somewhat more temperate than that which Jefferson had given Kentucky, but it too described the Constitution as "the compact to which the states are parties," denied the right of the federal government to go beyond that compact, and insisted on their right "to interpose." Years later, when John Calhoun said that the principles of nullification were first taught in the Virginia and Kentucky resolutions, Madison issued a denial. Virginia's intention, he averred, had been to grant individual states the right not to resist federal laws by force, but only to test their constitutionality. The fact remained that the doctrine of nullification, which was to become a weapon of southern reaction, was brought into American history as a defense against northern reaction.

Although in their own time censure of the Kentucky and Virginia resolutions was widespread, they had the effect which Jefferson had intended: they made people think again. Was the country to risk disintegration for the sake of two laws which even many Federalists blushed to defend? More and more it was evident that the Alien and Sedition Acts were heavy liabilities to the Adams administration.

The President, however, with the dogged irritability that marked all of his works, stuck to the positions he had taken, antagonizing everyone, on the left, on the right. Whether the Jeffersonians liked it or not, the unpleasant laws would stand as threats to the opposition, but were to be enforced as little as possible. Whether the Hamiltonians liked it or not, negotiations for peace with France would continue. Whether anyone liked it or not, John Adams was John Adams.

CHAPTER SIX

The Pendulum Swings

1. *Prometheus Bound*

As the century came to its end, the President found himself increasingly lonely and estranged. His own party was crying out against him for refusing to go to war with France. The ground swell of popular resentment against the controversial laws was turning into a wave of indignation against him personally. Everything was awry. His only chance of vindication was to be re-elected. And that chance inevitably depended on the one man whom he had come to hate more than any other, Hamilton.

In the critical phase of Hamilton's life which opened with the presidential campaign of 1800, there was to be seen an almost perfect working out of Promethean doom. His last frantic clutch at power was like the climax of a play by Aeschylus, revealing the terrible beauty, the sad radiation, the final glowing of somber colors produced by the disintegration of greatness.

As the autumn of 1800 approached, the mastermind of the Federalists was appalled by the speed with which the country was forgetting Genêt, forgetting XYZ, sinking back into neutrality and Anglophobia. The blame he assigned largely to Adams. If the President had not balked him, the country would have been at war with France, allied to England, safe for Federalism. The painful fact remained that Adams, still popular in New England, was certain to be the major Federalist candidate in the election. The American people did not love him, but they gave him a kind of grudging respect; and he was, after all, the President.

For Hamilton, there was bitter irony in the fact that if he succeeded in bringing a Federalist majority to the electoral college, it would re-elect a man for whom he felt profound contempt. As for the second personality on the slate, C. C. Pinckney of the XYZ affair, he represented for Hamilton merely the usual Federalist sop to the South. As a practical politician, however, he was accustomed to working with such instruments as were at hand. His first task was to hold back the Jeffersonian onslaught in the popular voting for the state legislatures. New England was still safe for the Federalists, but the states between the Potomac and the Hudson showed signs of wavering. If the South's Republican phalanx was to be beaten, Federalism needed a majority of the electors from New York, New Jersey, and Pennsylvania.

Hamilton's first shock came when the early Pennsylvania election produced a Republican majority in the state legislature. To offset this disaster, he regarded an impressive victory in New York as absolutely essential. With enormous energy he sought to awaken the conservatives of the state to the peril in which he believed they stood. From questions of principle the level of the campaign soon descended to crude libels. The Republicans were still somewhat inhibited by the Sedition Act, but the Federalists felt no restraint. Wild rumors about Jefferson began to circulate, and if Hamilton did not himself spread them, he did nothing to check them. Jefferson, it was said, had embezzled from estates entrusted to his care, had robbed a widow, defrauded children. Thousands came to believe these falsehoods which Jefferson, except in letters to personal friends, chose proudly to ignore. In time, they burned themselves out, acridly, like rotten wood.

2. *Devices of Despair*

Hamilton could count on the votes of many upstate farmers, but New York City, with its already large immigrant population, would be decisive. There he was up against Aaron Burr, whose exceptional political talents Hamilton respected, and whose lack of scruple he feared. Burr's power was so great that in return for his support, the Jeffersonians had been compelled to back him for the Vice-Presidency. Through the Tammany Society of New York he had succeeded in organizing the city's Democrats with a thoroughness never before seen. In ward after ward, they could be counted on to turn out the vote, shouting "Burr and Tammany!" Burr's hold on the people was especially strong in the poorest and roughest sections of the city —so strong that Hamilton regarded him as the American Catiline, fully capable of inflaming the rabble and encouraging mob violence against the affluent citizenry, if it served his purpose. But Burr's power went beyond the riffraff. He was a gentleman, sought after in society, on pleasant terms with Hamilton himself; he was handsome, personable, witty; his opportunities to involve persons of influence in his fortunes were unlimited; and he could offer favors to many a local officeholder in return for aid in the elections. Dark and mysterious intrigues were rumored between him and officials of the city. He was the Captain MacHeath of American politics. Respectable newspapers were surprisingly gentle with him. His following was not like Jefferson's, not moved by instinctive feeling for greatness and good will, but it was formidable in its belief that Burr, given power, would deal generously with his supporters.

At the ward level of electioneering, Burr had no equal in his time. Hamilton's aristocratic outlook, intellectual mode of expression, and generalized view of politics would have unfitted him for the contest even if he had a popular political program, and he did not. He made speeches in the city, but to educated audiences; he wrote articles, but for thoughtful readers. What he said was eloquent and often compelling, but it left the mass of voters unmoved.

On Election Day, Tammany did all that Burr expected of it and piled up a huge majority in the city. Statewide returns showed that the new legislature would be controlled by the Democrats. Its delegation to the electoral college would be overwhelmingly for Burr and Jefferson. For Hamilton to lose his own state was bad enough; to lose it to a Burr sickened him. Desperation made him leap at an idea against which calm judgment would have warned him. Several die-hard Federalist congressmen called on him to insist that all was not lost, after all. John Jay was still governor of New York. If Hamilton were able to obtain the co-operation of his old friend, Burr might yet be undone.

The plan was based on the article in the federal Constitution dealing with the procedure for the election of the President, and which read, "Each State shall appoint, in such Manner as the Legislature thereof may direct, a Number of Electors . . ." The article did not specify, however, that this power adhered only to the legislature as constituted in the most recent state election. What if the new legislature had not yet been convened? Could it not be assumed that the power to dictate the manner of appointment of electors would still rest in the old legislature? And the old New York legislature, technically still in existence, had a Federalist majority. If Jay were to call a special session, its members could drive through, and Jay as Governor could sign, a law removing the power to choose the electors from the legislature. This power could be assigned instead to state voting districts, with each district to choose one elector. If these districts were shrewdly mapped out, the Democratic vote, concentrated in the city, would control comparatively few electors. The Federalists, on the other hand, would have the numerous, if sparsely populated upstate districts. Thus, regardless of the statewide popular vote, a heavy majority of Federalists would represent New York State in the electoral college; and the national election could still be won.

3. "Swift and Easy Is the Descent to Hell"

Genuine distrust of popular government, and fear that the Jeffersonians would lead the country into war with England were working in Hamilton; but so was the power-urge of a man unaccustomed to defeat. He knew that in taking up this proposal he was suggesting a bald-faced fraud upon the people of New York, and the circumvention of the Constitution of the United States under the cloak of a technicality. But it was no time to be overscrupulous, as he saw it.

To refuse a request from Hamilton was not easy for Jay, but he did not have to reflect very much. Unlike Hamilton, he was a justice of the law, accustomed to try to rid his mind of bias, and he was also a deeply religious man, for whom moral values were paramount. A fraud was not less a fraud in his eyes for being convenient, and he had no intention of jeopardizing his historical position by lending himself to chicane. Courteously but firmly he rebuffed the anxious party leader. It was an improper scheme; he could not consider it. With that word, the Federalist party which Hamilton had done so much to create began to crumble.

Hamilton was bitterly disappointed, but he was always resilient. A ray of hope had come suddenly from another direction. In South Carolina the people had shown their loyalty to the Pinckneys, and the state had remained Federalist. Hamilton, counting heads carefully, decided that if all the Carolina electors, as well as those elsewhere, would hew closely to the line of his instructions, his party might yet beat Jefferson and Burr either by a vote or two in the electoral college, or in the House of Representatives. He was gambling now with his last stake, and he put it on his ability to control his party. Even southerners, he calculated, would recognize that at such a crisis, sectional prejudice had to give way to the greater necessities of class security.

At that moment, chance dealt him a backhanded blow. Secretary of State Pickering's persistent attempts to prevent ratification of the treaty with France had just driven Adams to demand his resignation, together with that of McHenry, the Secretary of War. In a querulous outburst of indignation, the President made a provocative reference to "a British faction" led by Hamilton. These were inflammatory words to put before the American voter at such a time, and especially about his own party's leader. Instantly Hamilton wrote to the President to deny the charge; received no reply; wrote again; was still unanswered.

"*Facilis descensus Averni*"; Hamilton as a student had known his Virgil, but he could not resist the next temptation. Recalling his unsuccessful attempt of four years earlier, when he had tried to displace Adams with Thomas Pinckney, he wondered whether it was possible that the same strategy might now turn up the Presidency for C. C. Pinckney, and push Adams into the discard. From the beginning he had urged that every Federalist elector vote for both men, and only for both men, on the logical ground that a party victory against such odds as faced the Federalists could be achieved only by total unity. It was easy to translate this position into a new version of his former plot. Pinckney was to be given as many northern electoral votes as Adams, and far more southern votes.

But even so Hamilton was not content. The written word was his natural outlet, and the bubbling rancor in him spilled onto paper. He was captivated by the notion of revealing Adams as the petty, inconsistent, and foolish man that he believed him to be. Always a conscientious craftsman, he sought out the latest information derogatory to the President for the writing that was in his mind. The vindictive Pickering and McHenry gladly provided him with the facts at their disposal, but Hamilton was not satisfied. He wrote to Wolcott, who was still Secretary of the Treasury, for his contribution; and had it. Loyalty to the President was felt by few of the men around him.

A long letter, intended for publication, took shape under Hamilton's vitriolic pen. In it Adams stood exposed as a man so vain, pompous, uninformed, unreasonable, and incompetent as to be totally unfitted for the office which he held. Perhaps the clearest indication of what was happening to Hamilton was his refusal to put this inescapable conclusion into words. At the end of his philippic, he allowed it to disintegrate into an unblushing *non sequitur*, almost unbelievable in a writer of his talent. In spite of everything, he said, the public ought to re-elect Adams, rather than permit Jefferson to become President. Personal hatred on the one hand, and his sense of responsibility to his party on the other, had trapped him in a timid ambivalence which he had never revealed before.

Close friends of Hamilton, who knew that he was at work on this extraordinary diatribe, begged him to put it aside. He would not. In his own words, he was "in a very belligerent humor." However, to placate them, he agreed to confine distribution of the letter to his confidential circle. The electoral vote, he maintained, would not be affected.

The letter was given to a printer, on whose discretion he counted; but a whisper went abroad that it existed, and came to the ears of Aaron Burr, who heard everything in New York. Before a single copy of the little pamphlet had been sent out by Hamilton, Burr had obtained one, by means which only he knew. The next day the Democratic press had it. The public could hardly believe its eyes. Hamiltonians throughout the country froze into voiceless astonishment. They saw their leader as the party's Samson, blind, enchained, frenzied, pulling down the columns of Federalism in his last agony. Whatever hope of victory there had been for Adams, whatever chance that Hamilton might hold his party's electors in line, was now gone.

And that there had been a chance was suggested by the electoral vote. Although some northern Federalists refused to vote for Pinckney, and some southerners for Adams, the two Federalist candidates came very close to Jefferson and Burr, who tied with seventy-three votes each. Adams had sixty-five, Pinckney sixty-four. It was Adams's conviction to the end of his life that he would have been re-elected if Hamilton had not betrayed him.

4. "This . . . Shook Them"

Burr's success startled the country, shocked Jefferson, and surprised Burr himself. Corresponding Tammany societies which then existed in other cities besides New York had worked hard for him, but aiming always at the Vice-Presidency. Suddenly he found himself close to the fulfillment of his ambitions. The choice between him and Jefferson would now be thrown into the House of Representatives, with each state having a single vote. Jefferson could count with certainty only on a few states in the South. Burr could depend on almost as many in the North. Neither could win a majority without the support of states controlled by the Federalists. Here was a situation to Burr's liking. Jefferson could never bring himself to trade for election with the opposition party, but Burr could. The convictions and policies of his party meant nothing to him. He wanted to win, and the bulk of his supporters were as opportunistic as himself.

Jefferson, alarmed not only for his own hopes but for the future of American democracy, sought to appeal to an ethical sense which Burr did not have. In an urgent letter, he wrote to Burr that "the enemy would endeavor to . . . divide us and our friends. Every consideration satisfies me that you will be on guard against this, as I assure you I am strongly." By that time, Burr was already negotiating with the more venal elements among the Federalists in Congress. A promise here, a promise there, began to bring him the advantage he sought.

But to the Federalist right wing, which included the most influential Federalist senators and congressmen, one Republican was almost as bad as another. There was not enough to be had from Burr to justify the risks of a Republican administration, if it could be avoided. And now, to their delight, they saw that it might be avoided. All that the Federalists in the House had to do was withhold their votes. This would deprive the states which they controlled of a voice in the election. Neither candidate could then obtain a majority of the states.

The Constitution did not clearly provide for the contingency which they foresaw, and in which the country would be without a Chief Executive. However, it did say that in case of the death or resignation of both the President and the Vice-President, Congress could by law declare "what Officer shall then act as President." It was the belief of the Federalists that, under this clause, they could compel the Congress to name at their choosing the official who would become acting President, if the election proved fruitless. Jefferson understood this: he exposed their game in a letter written on December 15, 1800. "Several of the high-flying Federalists have expressed their determination . . . to prevent a choice by the House . . . and let the government devolve on . . . a President of the Senate *pro tem*, by what they say would be only *a stretch* of the Constitution." Another suggestion mooted among the Federalists was that the executive authority be given to the Chief Justice of the Supreme Court. This, they thought, would be John Jay, for he had just been renominated by Adams to this post, and had not yet declined.

For Jefferson, it was a time of almost intolerable anxiety. He made a last effort to appeal to morality and reason. Let a convention, he proposed, be called to amend the Constitution, and find a proper solution to the problem. He could hardly have been surprised when the Federalists shrugged away this suggestion, but he was angry. He had always believed that when, in the course of human events, it becomes necessary to oppose injustice, a decent respect for the opinions of mankind may require the use of force as a last resort. What his emissaries said to the Federalist leaders may be surmised from a letter in which at a later time he recounted the history of the crisis. "If they [the Federalists] could have been permitted . . . they would certainly have prevented an election. But we thought it best to declare openly and firmly, once for all, that the day such an act passed [giving executive power to the President *pro tem* of the Senate] the Middle States would arm, and that no such usurpation, even for a single day, would be submitted to. This . . . shook them."

The Federalists were shaken, in fact, to the point of permitting the election by the House to proceed. They knew that they lacked popular support, and violence was in the air. Republican extremists were rumored to have decided that any public officer who unconstitutionally accepted the executive power would be put to death. In a letter written long afterward, Albert Gallatin, who was Jefferson's chief agent in the House, said that bodies of armed men had been organized in Maryland and Virginia and stood ready to march on Washington. When alarmed Federalist congressmen appealed to the Governor of Pennsylvania for a militia force to protect the capital in the event of civil war, they found him understandably reluctant.

Gallatin's private talks with Federalist leaders made their position painfully clear to them. Under this threat of force, and knowing their unpopularity, they had to permit the election; and their hatred of Jefferson in consequence became hysterical. They felt that if they could keep him out of the Presidency, that in itself would be almost enough of a victory. Burr's advances had been well received by some of them; and meeting in conspiratorial groups, Federalist leaders laid plans to throw the election to him. Against such a development, the Jeffersonians had no recourse. They had demanded the election; they were about to get it.

5. The Final Incandescence

It was at this moment that Hamilton rediscovered in himself the integrated strength of mind that had given so much aid to Washington and that had won the admiration and respect even of his opponents. The "very belligerent mood" that had led him into the wild attack on Adams had passed. He ceased all at once to be the rabid partisan and the angry egotist. He was illuminated by the white-hot knowledge that he, and only he, could hold the country together. In the final test, he stood with the few great leaders against the many little connivers, regardless of party. He hated Jefferson, the arch-Republican and the friend of France, but it was a hatred in which there was no contempt. It was altogether different from his scorn of the cunning intriguers who wanted to steal the Presidency from Jefferson, or from his fear of the infinitely dangerous Burr. He knew in his heart that Jefferson, for all his talk of arms, was a respecter of law, a believer in fair play, who disliked violence, and was in most matters far more cautious than Hamilton himself.

He flung himself into the Congressional turmoil, the old irresistible Hamilton, moving his friends with entreaty, coercing them with logic, snaring them with hints of favor. A number of Federalists were turned away from Burr by the unmistakable sincerity that glowed through Hamilton's letters. "I beg of you, as you love your country, your friends and yourself, to reconsider dispassionately the opinion you have expressed in favor of Burr." "For Heaven's sake, my dear sir, exert yourself to the utmost to save our country from so great a calamity" [as the election of Burr]. If the Federalists supported Burr, he, Hamilton, could no longer "be of a party which will have disgraced itself and the country."

At the end, he concentrated his fire on four men, all of whom still favored Burr, and who happened to hold decisive votes—Delaware's only congressman, the influential James Bayard, one representative from Vermont, and two from Maryland. At first, he seemed to have failed. All of these men considered themselves pledged to Burr, and voted for him on the first ballot, when neither candidate won the necessary majority. Jefferson had eight states; Burr six; in two they were tied. In the long sessions which followed, thirty-four more ballots were taken, with the same result. There were rumors that several states were about to switch to Burr, seduced by his promises; but Hamilton's efforts did not cease. Bayard was persuaded to enter into secret conversations with Gallatin, and was given reassurance that he "might confide in the result," if Jefferson won. Hamilton wrote to Bayard in the same vein, saying that Jefferson was not "zealot enough to do anything . . . which will contravene his interest or his popularity. He is as likely as any man I know to temporize and calculate . . ." The established system, Hamilton assured Bayard, would be preserved under Jefferson because it "could not be overturned without danger to the man who did it."

This was enough for Bayard, who shared his thoughts with the Federalist representatives from Vermont and Maryland. A plan was conceived by which they could elect Jefferson without openly violating their commitments to Burr—merely by withholding their votes. On the next ballot, the thirty-sixth, their abstentions tipped the balance, and ten states went for Jefferson.

In this way, the Constitution of the United States was kept intact. Hamilton, who had inadvertently made Jefferson Vice-President, now consciously and deliberately had made him President. The election of 1800 was perhaps the world's first example of a peaceful revolution, of a fundamental reversal of national policy achieved by legal means, and without bloodshed. Its leading participants recognized the enormous social significance of Jefferson's victory. In the last minutes of Adams's presidency, the Federalists made a unique effort to leave their mark on the government by appointing their own people to every vacant post in the government—and to some created for the occasion. On March 3, the Senate stayed in session until midnight to confirm the President's nominations. At dawn the next day, having done all he could to hang Federalist millstones around Jefferson's neck, Adams drove moodily out of Washington on the road to Massachusetts, in order not to be present at the inauguration of his successor. His last constructive act as President had been the apppointment of John Marshall as Chief Justice of the United States.

CHAPTER SEVEN

A Time for Hope

1. *Deep Fog in London*

News of Jefferson's election came to William Pitt as one more increment of darkness in the deep gloom that enveloped England. The war on the Continent was lost. The Second Coalition which Grenville had created around Russia, and which had seemed to offer such promise, had dissolved after Marengo. At Luneville, Austria had signed a treaty of peace which was an abysmal capitulation. Spain, Portugal, Naples, the German states were all in a panic to make terms with the conqueror. Aside from England, the only countries still in the lists against France were Turkey, Naples, and Portugal. Austria, among other nations, had supinely pledged herself not to import merchandise from England. Victories of the Navy in the Mediterranean and the Atlantic, while impressive enough, were hardly adequate compensation for the vanished profits of business, and British merchants were loud and ever louder in protest.

France knew England's sensitive spots, and how to reach them. In India, her aid had encouraged Tipu Sahib's fierce rebellion, which, even though finally suppressed, had left the country in a state of extreme unrest, and had compelled the sending of reinforcements from England. French forces had backed the spectacular Wolfe Tone and other leaders of the Irish rebellion which still smoldered ominously, using up British tax money and military forces needed elsewhere. French influence had persuaded Czar Paul of Russia to join with the Kings of Prussia, Denmark, and Sweden in reviving Armed Neutrality to resist England's naval rules limiting their trade with France.

Nature was compounding England's man-made troubles. The harvest had failed. Riots in the West Country to protest food shortages and high prices had compelled the use of soldiery to suppress them. Business had slumped, Consols were down, so were stock company shares on the Royal Exchange. It was becoming harder and harder for Pitt to find money to prosecute the war. What, Englishmen were demanding, had they got in return for the millions of pounds which had been sent to Austria and Prussia and Russia to pay for the coalition armies? How long were they to continue to pour their gold into Europe's bottomless well? In the past ten years, the national debt had doubled, reaching the appalling figure of £227,000,000. The government's annual expenditures for the armed services were double the taxes which it was able to collect. The ingenious graduated income tax, the first of its kind in Anglo-Saxon history, had brought in new revenues, but at a heavy price in popularity. Parliament still stood with Pitt, it was true; but the irrepressible Charles James Fox never ceased to remind England of the amputation of her civil liberties, and a ground swell of Whiggism was rising again.

Even the King had no smiles for Pitt now. Aging and mentally unstable, George nevertheless had some fight left in him. It was Pitt's view that the time had come to settle the Irish troubles, and ease the wartime strain, by granting Ireland Parliamentary union with England and allowing Catholics full citizenship. To the Act of Union, passed by Parliament, the King at last discontentedly agreed, but at the thought that Catholics might be permitted to hold public office in England, the stubborn old man balked with all his Hanoverian doggedness. He could not or would not grasp Pitt's point that in a war with "Jacobin and atheistic France," Roman Catholics were bound to be England's staunchest allies. Since his signature was necessary before the Emancipation Act, as it was called, could become effective, they had swiftly reached a deadlock. The whole nation knew of the struggle between them, and divided on the issue.

2. Exit Pitt, Quietly

Even Grenville, on whom Pitt so greatly relied, now treated him with a certain reserve. The cloud between them had risen a few years earlier, in 1797, when word came from an agent in Paris that the Director Barras could be bribed to make peace with England, if enough money were offered. After careful investigation, Pitt became fully convinced that the bid was genuine, and wrote of it to King George, saying, "The sum he [Barras] names is a very large one, amouting to £450,000; but it seems not to be more than would be wisely employed if he can make good . . ." Subsequently, working through Boyd, a prominent British banker, Barras raised his price: Bonaparte's early victories encouraged him to demand £1,200,000 for a peace in which England would have Ceylon returned to her. Thereafter, Pitt on his own initiative sent off a messenger to Barras with a virtual acceptance of the offer. But not having consulted Grenville, he found it necessary to send him an apology: "the offer seemed . . . so tempting, and the time pressed so much to an hour . . ." Grenville answered in the style of glacial scorn which was natural to him, "I cannot deny to you that the whole of that transaction is so disagreeable to my mind that I am very glad to have been saved the necessity of deciding upon it . . . I shudder at what we are doing . . . It would be ten thousand times safer to face the storm . . ." He could not, he added, bear the thought of "*purchasing* our safety." His arguments, and the difficulties which Barras was then encountering in

Paris, made Pitt lose confidence in the negotiation, and it was dropped; but the relations between Pitt and Grenville, while always courteous, never had quite the same quality of mutual confidence as before.

To make matters worse for Pitt, after the expulsion of Barras from France her new master, Bonaparte, swiftly proved himself more than an original military strategist. His supervision of foreign policy, with the serpentine Talleyrand as his agent, showed distinct flair. An open letter dated Christmas Day 1799, to King George III, and pleading for peace, had moved Europe's unsophisticated masses: "Is there no means by which we can come to an understanding? . . . I beg your Majesty to believe that . . . it is my sincere desire to make a practical contribution . . . towards a general peace." Grenville's reply had of course been lordly and arrogant, and Bonaparte had known precisely how to use it to rekindle France's fighting spirit. "The First Consul has promised you peace," he immediately told the French people. "Should some misguided power still wish to tempt destiny . . . the First Consul himself will march forth to conquer it at the head of the warriors he has more than once led to victory." Having made good his words at Marengo, he had proceeded to reveal yet another facet of his personality, tricking the Americans into a treaty, the Paris Convention of 1800, by which they gave up a valid claim to millions, and received nothing in return.

The Americans! As if anything more had been needed to add to Pitt's worries, his reports from the new capital, Washington, told of democracy rampant, Jefferson triumphant, Hamilton retired to private life. America's mood was dangerously confident. It affected even Englishmen, such as Robert Liston, who represented England in Washington for a time after Hammond's departure and who warned that war with the United States "must bring with it extensive damage to our navigation, loss of Canada, and the *world* behind it."

It made Pitt uneasy to see British industry increasingly dependent on the American market and American raw materials. Nearly one fifth of British manufactured exports had been absorbed in the United States during 1800. Between 1794 and 1801, thanks to Whitney's cotton gin and Jay's treaty, British imports of American raw cotton had risen from almost nothing to over 20 million pounds annually. America's total export trade with the British empire had tripled in the same period. Should America become aggressive, the British economy would be vulnerable. The new President, it was true, seemed to have learned caution since the days of the Declaration of Independence. For a man who had indulged in so much violent denunciation of England, his first statements in office were unexpectedly mild. But Pitt never trusted any statesman's peaceful protestations. He knew from his own experience that national policy is not a

thing fixed and definite but an ever changing expression of the world complex; that time plays tricks with men's purposes, and that a pledge of peace,
even when sincere, is worth no more than a hope that all will go well.

But the British people were war-sick, they wanted peace, with America,
with France, with the world. Pitt did not believe that any treaty with victorious France could endure, but a truce, a breathing spell—there might be
justification for that. Unfortunately, neither he nor Grenville was the man
to negotiate with the enemy. The inference was inescapable: they had to
go. He was in any event weary to the bone from the long and desperate
struggle to win a war without employing a British army; and like Hamilton
in America, with whom he had much in common, he was painfully insol-
vent.

The immediate problem was to select the right issue on which to resign,
one which was weighty enough to justify his decision, yet would not impair
the nation's morale, or his own reputation. He chose the issue of Catholic
Emancipation; most Englishmen would approve his desire for a settlement
of the Irish troubles; in the public mind, the responsibility for his going
would thus rest on the unpopular King. Nor would it be as if, in resigning,
he was really giving up power. With a shrewdly chosen successor, someone
agreeably disposed to accept guidance, he could still provide the spirit,
if not the voice of the new government, until he was ready to resume office.
He thought he knew the right man for the interim—Henry Addington, who
for years had served him as Chancellor of the Exchequer—a well-meaning
mediocrity, a natural-born compromiser, with a sanguine disposition and
a good flow of pompous words. He had the additional qualifications of
being well-liked in Parliament, where he had been Speaker of the House;
he was versed in finance, and popular with the middle class from which
he came. Addington's father had been a doctor, and the son longed for a
peerage and the fellowship of the Lords—a characteristic which amused Pitt,
to whom titles were toys for other men.

In his own state of uncertainty, he could offer Addington only very general counsel on how to deal with France: "If we are firm, and our domestic
difficulties do not increase, we may secure creditable and adequate terms."
"The question of war or peace is not in itself so formidable as that of the
scarcity [of food] . . . for the evils and growing dangers of which I confess
I see no adequate remedy." Addington was unperturbed by such anxieties,
all eagerness to bring peace to England.

With tragedy in his heart, but calm exterior, Pitt made a suitable speech
in the House on the Catholic question and offered his resignation to the
King. At the last minute, the thought of what he was giving up was too
much for him, and he could not refrain from a suggestion that he might,
after all, continue in office if His Majesty insisted. But His Majesty did not

insist; on the contrary, he accepted a little too readily Pitt's nomination of
Addington to take his place. He was tired of brilliant, contentious ministers.
In the audience which he then gave to the fluttered Addington, he said
querulously: "My nerves are weak . . . Your father, Dr. Addington, said
twelve years ago that quiet was what I wanted, and that I must have."

3. A Passion for Peace

Hamilton had gone, Pitt had gone, Bonaparte had come. Years later,
Dostoyevski would say of this moment in history, "The former face of the
world was destined, at the end of the past century, to assume a new guise."
The main voice of destiny in Europe was that of Napoleon—the "arch-
accident"—while in America, Thomas Jefferson spoke for the new era. Both
appeared to represent the democratic impulse which was throbbing on either
side of the Atlantic, and one of them did.

In a spirit of grateful relief after all the stress of the election, Jefferson
moved into the stone "Palace" near the depressing mud flats of the Potomac (it would be restored and painted white after being burned by the
British in 1814). Much of his time had to be spent in receiving congratu-
lations—coupled often with requests for political jobs—from old-time
Republican zealots, many of them from the West. It was primarily to put
them at their ease that he began to affect the shabby and untidy clothes
which at first sight made foreign diplomats wrinkle their noses. He did not
mind appearing a little ridiculous to aristocrats if he could make the ordinary
American, the shy townsman, the inarticulate backwoodsman, feel understood and welcome. In addition, of course, the contrast of his informal
manner and dress with the dignified style of his Federalist predecessors
would not be lost on the country. Jefferson was the first President to recognize the political disadvantages of conspicuous dignity in America. He knew
that the American man in the street would forgive him, and even admire
him for knowing Greek, playing the violin, and designing buildings, but
would resent any pretension to fashion or grandeur in his personal life. He
was expected to be a democrat, and he was; his hospitality to all visitors,
regardless of status, was to help drain his fortune during the eight years
of his Presidency.

The reports from abroad, and especially Pitt's resignation, he found altogether encouraging. The end of the war was in sight. Yet he could see clearly
enough that the continuance of peace for America, over the past twenty
years, had been largely accidental. The country, living under the shadow of
swords, had been more fortunate than it realized. As he wrote to John
Adams long afterward, "we knew not how we rode through the storm with
heart and hand, and made a happy port." From the moment that the first
treaty with England had been signed in 1783, the new institution of

American sovereignty had pressed strongly against the confining walls of the British Empire. Again and again America's steely purpose had rasped on England's flinty sense of power, and each time it was events outside the control of the two governments which had extinguished the sparks of war before they kindled.

Now Bonaparte's shattering victories and peaceful gestures were having their effect. Britain's war spirit was ebbing fast. Its last flaring was embodied in excited reports which came to Jefferson from London and Copenhagen. Swedish and Danish participation with Russia in Armed Neutrality had been regarded in England as gravely menacing the British economy. With the submission of Holland and Hamburg to French domination, the Baltic nations had become a leading source of essential food imports for England, and her main channels of entry for trade with the continent. She could not afford to stand by while they linked themselves to Bonaparte. When warnings to Denmark proved futile, Grenville had insisted that a fleet be sent to intimidate the Danes, and Pitt, in the last days of his ministry, had perforce agreed. A declaration of war would have forced Russia and Prussia to take up arms against England, so there was none. Instead fifty warships sailed for Danish waters, with Horatio Nelson as second in command.

When the Danes proudly and emphatically rejected a British ultimatum, Nelson's squadrons entered the harbor of Copenhagen, and engaged its strong coastal batteries and defensive fleet. For a time, the battle seemed to go against him. His commander, Admiral Parker, at one point signaled him to withdraw, but Nelson, placing his telescope to his blind eye, declared that he could not see the signal, and persisted, until the Danes ceased fire and agreed to negotiate. As matters turned out, however, the entire action had been unnecessary. A few days before the battle, Czar Paul of Russia had been murdered, and his successor, Alexander I, had brushed off French advice, and agreed to compromise with England on the subject of maritime rights. Thereafter Armed Neutrality had once more dissolved.

As a demonstration of ruthless naval power, the Copenhagen enterprise was an unqualified success; but Jefferson felt with indignation that England's last pretense of a moral position had crumbled. How could she now claim to be leading the forces of righteousness against the terroristic French? In cannonading the ships of a neutral nation without a declaration of war, she had, as he saw it, testified to her own desperation and brutality.

Copenhagen aside, and with Pitt and Grenville out of the Cabinet, the chances of sustained peace seemed promising. The new man, Addington, was evidently earnest in seeking a treaty with France; and he also showed a comparatively friendly disposition toward the United States. Offenses of the British Navy against America were already becoming less frequent. If he would put an end to impressment, all might yet be well between the two nations. Rufus King in London had been instructed to deliver a message to the British Government: "The United States . . . requires positively that their seamen who are not British subjects, whether born in America or elsewhere, shall be exempt from impressment." A favorable response from Addington could go far to heal one of the worst of the festering sores in transatlantic diplomacy.

4. Peace, If . . .

The President felt able to write to his militant old friend, Thomas Paine, in the spring of 1801, "Determined as we are to avoid, if possible, wasting the energies of our people in war and destruction, we shall avoid implicating ourselves with the powers of Europe even in support of the principles which we mean to pursue. We believe we can enforce these principles . . . by peaceable means." What were these peaceable means? For another correspondent, at almost the same time, Jefferson developed the point: "Our commerce is so valuable to them [the European powers] that they will be glad to purchase it when the only price we ask is to do us justice. I believe we have in our hands the means of peaceable coercion . . ." This conception had for many years been the mainspring of his foreign policy. He saw it as possibly opening up to the world a new method of coping with international disputes. As early as 1794, he said in a letter, "I love peace, and I am anxious that we should give the world still another useful lesson, by showing to them other modes of punishing injuries than by war . . . I love, therefor . . . [the] proposition of cutting off all communications with the nation [England] which has conducted itself so atrociously. This, you will say, may bring on war. If it does, we will meet it like men; but it may not bring on war, and then the experiment will have been a happy one."

Peace, then—except perhaps in the Mediterranean, whence humiliating news had come. The Dey of Algiers had compelled an American man-of-war—the *George Washington*, of all names—to haul down its flag, fly the colors of Algiers, and carry an Algerian ambassador to Constantinople. The words of the Dey, on this occasion, were: "You pay me tribute, so you are my slaves." The insult could not be allowed to pass unchallenged; and now word had come that the Pasha of Tripoli, in order to express his dissatisfaction with the size of the American tribute, had declared war on the United States, and had cut down the flag at the house of the American consul there. Long ago, as minister to France, Jefferson had urged a concerted effort by the western powers to stamp out the Barbary pirates, but had been rebuffed by Vergennes. As President, he saw no choice for America but to undertake the task by herself. The decision troubled him deeply. It ran counter to Republican principles, which held a large navy to be politically undesirable, a tool of reaction, and economically wasteful, a sinkhole of public funds. But he knew better than to try to be consistent at the expense of the nation's self-respect and commerce. Warships would be built and sent to the North African coast, and American merchantmen would be given the freedom of the Mediterranean. With this exception, there could be peace.

No war, no serious war, not with England, not with France, not even with Spain. Jefferson thought it probable that in time the hard-pressed Spaniards would consent to sell Louisiana for a price, for their administrative costs far exceeded revenues from the colony. Looking to the future, the President had an inspiring vision of the United States in possession of all the Gulf provinces and the entire Mississippi and Missouri valleys. He had already discussed plans to explore the Missouri with his private secretary, Captain Meriwether Lewis, whom he considered fully qualified to head the expedition, when the time should be ripe.

There was, to be sure, a persistent rumor that Bonaparte had been beforehand with the Spaniards, that even while he was negotiating with the Murray mission for peace with America, he had signed a secret treaty with Charles IV of Spain under which Louisiana would come to France in exchange for an Italian province. Jefferson found this hard to credit. That France and Spain had explored the subject was likely enough, but surely Bonaparte and Talleyrand knew that America would regard such a transaction as an unfriendly act. The United States could not quietly accept a transfer of her southern border from a weak foreign power to a strong one. A move in this direction by Bonaparte might be enough to throw the United States into England's arms. To deter him in case he actually contemplated so aggressive an action, Jefferson turned to an old friend, the noted French economist, Pierre Samuel du Pont de Nemours, who was then planning to return from the United States to his native country. Du Pont had access to Bonaparte; and he was authorized to speak for the President, and review all the arguments against French possession of Louisiana.

5. "Let Us Unite . . ."

No war, and equally, no unnecessary partisan quarrels within the nation. It was to this end that Jefferson declared in his inaugural address: "Let us unite with one mind . . . We have gained little if we countenance . . . political intolerance . . . Every difference of opinion is not a difference of principle. We are all Republicans, we are all Federalists." He was a partisan, but he was distrustful of partisanship. He knew that wherever the democratic spirit is untrammeled, partisanship is likely to be at its most irrational. It was his belief that the way to keep the Republicans in power was to show moderation to opponents: in this spirit, he urged disappointed extremists of his own party not to press too soon for radical legislation—to see the wisdom of Solon's remark that "no more good must be attempted than the nation can bear." With the help of Albert Gallatin, his gifted Secretary of the Treasury, he counted on making most of the government's advances through reduction of costs and taxes. He intended "to reform the waste of public money, and drive away the vultures who prey upon it."

The Alien Laws were for practical purposes a dead letter, and the Sedition Act—"that libel on legislation"—had expired; the excise tax on whisky, toward which the western farmers felt such hatred, would be repealed; the Constitution would be amended in respect of the procedure for the election of the President and Vice-President. These things being done, the federal government could leave the rest to the states. The American people would soon recognize the falsehood of hysterical predictions by such men as George Cabot and Timothy Pickering that his election meant social upheaval on the French model. Everyone spoke of "a Republican revolution," but revolution in the conventional sense was far from his purpose or disposition. Thorough study of classical history had made him politically cautious. He knew that no party and no statesman is ever proved right in the long run, and that humility is the ultimate wisdom in a man of government. Change there would have to be in America, but it would come to meet evolving needs and by the will of the nation.

It took a long time to correct social injustice. Jefferson had a keen sense of fair play, and all his long life tyranny over the poor by the rich could fill him with a sense of outrage that was youthful in its intensity. But this did not mean that he would allow hot anger to be translated into national policy. Innovation, he was aware, is strong political medicine, and a little of it goes a long way. To many he seemed to be doctrinaire, but he was in fact an empiricist. He would toss out ideas to observe the public's and his own subsequent judgment of them, and he had no hesitation in changing them. The mood of the American multitude, he sensed, was frequently mutinous, but it was far from revolutionary. They followed him not for his theories, but because they trusted him, because they felt instinctively that he stood with them against the aristocrats and the magnates of business. The way of life that Hamiltonian government had given them was much to their liking; all that they objected to was the Hamiltonians.

Far from being in danger of a revolution, the nation actually faced the opposite peril—that changes in its laws and institutions would not be achieved in time to prevent calamity. Adams, in his last frenzy of frustration and pique, had invaded Jefferson's area of privilege when he appointed John Marshall to be Chief Justice. In its existing composition, the Supreme Court was bound to be hostile to almost any reformist legislation. Even more serious, Adams had created and filled a host of new federal judgeships,

many of them unjustified by need. "They [the Federalists] have retired
into the judiciary as into a stronghold," Jefferson wrote privately and with
bitterness. ". . . From that battery, all the works of Republicanism are to
be beaten down . . ." For a time, he considered asking his overwhelmingly
Republican Congress to amend the Constitution so as to limit judicial
tenure to a fixed term of years. But mature reflection prevented him from
promoting such an amendment, partly for fear that it might weaken the
authority of the Constitution in other areas of government, but mainly
because it was almost certain to be defeated.

In spite of the packed courts, the President saw little reason for pessimism.
The many evils of democracy—excessive partisanship, corruption, demagog-
uery, slowness of decision, frequent mediocrity in high places—were more
than compensated, he believed, by the energies which it awakened in the
people. At fifty-eight, he himself was full of vigor. And he had learned to
trust himself. Perhaps the chief difference between him and his predecessors
was that Washington and Adams regarded themselves primarily as rulers,
while Jefferson saw himself as a leader. His administration would help his
countrymen extend their individual liberties and opportunities, and correct
serious inequities in American life: he was sure of it. He was sure, too, that
his foreign policy would prove to the people that national self-respect and
peace are compatible.

6. The Guns Are Silent

His confidence in the future was further buoyed, when, not many months
after taking office, news came that preliminary articles of peace had been
agreed upon between France and England. Dispatches from Rufus King
in London and from Robert Livingston in Paris said that Bonaparte had
begun by rebuffing Addington's overtures, but that reverses to French arms
in Egypt and on the seas, and the collapse of Armed Neutrality in the north,
had subsequently softened him. Seeing that it was no longer possible for
France to hold Egypt, hoping to get something for it while there was still
time, he had sent an envoy to London for negotiations.

The definitive treaty was to be drawn later at Amiens, but its main terms
were already known. Their effect was to recognize the hegemony of Bonaparte over the numerous satellite republics and kingdoms which France
had established around her. But Addington's face, or at least some of his
features were saved. The French were to evacuate not only Egypt, but
Naples and Rome. And there was the usual bandying about of islands all
over the world. England was to retain Ceylon and Trinidad, which she
had occupied during the war, but she had to promise to return strategic
Malta to its former possessors, the Knights of St. John. The French also
prodded Addington into a few other sacrifices: to let the Cape of Good

Hugues would be involved

Hope become a free port; to modify the boundaries of Guiana in France's favor.

Livingston mentioned casually that the British had also agreed to interpose no obstacles to the sailing of a French army to Santo Domingo. A native revolt there, led by the remarkable negro patriot, Toussaint l'Ouverture and secretly supported by England and by President Adams, had wrested the island from the control of France. On the whole, Jefferson was inclined to see Santo Domingo returned to French rule, in order to weaken british influence in the West Indies, and to stimulate American trade. The news that the noted General Leclerc, Napoleon's brother-in-law, was in command of the French expeditionary force suggested that Bonaparte did not intend to leave the outcome to chance.

The first response of the English and French peoples to the peace, Jefferson read, was wildly enthusiastic. On that note of cheer, the year 1801 ended, and an unaccustomed stillness came over the western world. Gunfire might still be heard as British cruisers chased American smugglers in the Caribbean, as settlers in the Northwest Territory pushed embittered Indian tribes toward the Mississippi, as American frigates took revenge on Barbary pirates, but the armies and fleets of the great powers refrained from battle. A man of peace was President of the United States; a man of peace was Prime Minister of England; and a man who said that he wanted peace was First Consul of France. It was a time for hope.

PART FOUR

THE POUNDING SURF OF CRISIS
1802—1812

CHAPTER ONE

The Triggering of War

1. "L'Ambigu"

As the diplomatic shuttle flew between the capitals of the great powers, the crimson pattern of the Napoleonic era began to appear on the loom. One of its main threads was Bonaparte's estimate of England's intentions. After Pitt's resignation, he seems briefly to have believed in the possibility of a lasting peace—which is to say, he believed that England's will to fight had withered—at least, that she would no longer contest French pre-eminence on the continent, provided that some considerable part of her trade there remained to her.

This was for him a moment of high aspiration. He was struck quite seriously by a conception of himself as the giver of peace, prosperity, and republicanism to Europe, as Bonaparte the Good. And peace in Europe meant freedom to act elsewhere, to the greater glory of France. Her colonial empire was to be rebuilt in Louisiana. The revolt of Toussaint in Santo Domingo was to be put down by a veteran French army which could there-after be moved on to New Orleans, if it proved necessary to chastise the Americans. The flabby Spanish monarchy was to be forced to share its imperial privileges in South America with France. Naval cruisers and mer-chant vessels would carry the tricolor all over the world, as proudly as the ships of England, in the century past, had carried the Union Jack.

A fleeting vision, it was nevertheless enough to lead him irretrievably to disaster. Under its spell he committed France to transatlantic adventures which he was bitterly to regret. But months before the failure of his west-ward ambitions became clear, he had already begun to realize that the premise on which they were founded—England's desire for a long peace—was highly unreliable. He was never a man to ignore evidence, even if it was unwelcome, and the evidence from London, as it emerged, quickly disabused him of the notion that Pitt's departure from the government and the cessation of fighting signaled a fundamental alteration in British policy.

A hint of the future came to Bonaparte soon after Henry Addington was made Prime Minister. A little French newspaper called L'Ambigu was then being published in London. Its editor was a Frenchman, Jean Peltier; its readers were émigrés living in England; its content was largely gossip and, when gossip failed, outright fabrication. In the early days of 1802, while the definitive treaty of peace was being negotiated at Amiens, Peltier conceived the idea of filling his sheet with something that was sure to be popular: a compendium of all the scurrilities then being circulated in aristocratic circles about the lowborn Bonaparte and his Creole wife, Josephine, formerly married to the late guillotined Vicomte de Beauharnais. Napoleon was portrayed as "this little monkey of four feet," "an old Columbine, refuse of all the Clowns of the Revolution," pirouetting with the castoff mistress of Barras. Were the gentlemen of England to make terms with the false-hearted scum of Corsica?

A popular Tory newspaper, *The True Briton*, promptly followed Peltier's lead by publishing an English version, even cruder, of the same material. In due time, copies of these newspapers and others equally vicious found their way to the Foreign Ministry at Paris. Immediately an urgent message went by private channels to officials of the Foreign Office in London. The outrageous attacks had been seen by the First Consul, and had produced a very bad effect. Could not something be done with these irresponsible editors? "There needs to be a strong effort to close their mouths," wrote an informed Frenchman, Louis-Guillaume Otto, who had negotiated the preliminary treaty for France. Otherwise, the peace was not likely to endure. French newspapers, closely controlled by the government, had begun to respond with comparable assaults on the leaders of England.

These warnings reached Addington, as did also a note from one of his own trusted diplomats, then in Paris, about the "inconceivable damage done by inflammatory newspapers poisoning the public mind" on both sides of the Channel. He was somewhat disconcerted. What could he do? To antagonize the Tory press would be to cut his own political throat; and Peltier was the protégé of high French aristocrats who were intimately connected with the greatest lords of England. The Prime Minister put the matter aside until there came to Whitehall a secret emissary carrying direct authorization from Bonaparte, one Joseph Fiévée, who had been told to stress the gravity with which the First Consul viewed the British attacks on his character. Specifically, Fiévée urged that *L'Ambigu* be suppressed, Peltier punished, and the London papers generally made to exercise restraint. Even then the most that Addington would concede, and that only reluctantly, was the commencement of an insignificant prosecution of Peltier in the courts. As for the British press, he agreed only to write cautionary letters to the editor of *The True Briton* and one or two other newspapers. These missives turned out to be feebly reproachful. "I doubt whether it be possible even for you to be aware of the consequences produced by opprobrious observations, in papers of such established reputation as yours, on the proceedings of foreign governments and those who are at their head." "God forbid I should lay a finger on the liberty of the press, but . . ."

A few personal attempts to influence Tory journalists by bribery and persuasion left Fiévée discouraged, and his report to the First Consul was that not only the British press but the British Government was still essentially hostile to France. Addington, however, accustomed as he was to the excesses of a free press, saw little real importance in the episode. The gibes at himself in the French newspapers left him untroubled. Entirely lacking Bonaparte's sensitivity to the currents of propaganda, he could not conceive that for the Frenchman the only inference to be drawn from the libelous exchanges was the probability that war would soon be resumed.

The Prime Minister was, in fact, blandly optimistic. The British people seemed pleased with him. Business was improving. Consols were rising on the exchange. The country and the Parliament had enthusiastically welcomed his assurance that the right of habeas corpus would be restored, and that the unpopular income tax would be repealed. If all went well at Amiens, where the British and French envoys were meeting to draw up the definitive peace treaty, the way would be clear for steadily improving relations with France, perhaps even for a commercial agreement which would reopen the entire Continent to British merchants.

2. Lord Cornwallis Recommends

The man whom Addington selected to negotiate at Amiens had the confidence of the people: General Charles Cornwallis, the first Marquess Cornwallis. No one held against him any longer his unfortunate surrender to George Washington: it had been so long ago. Since then, he had maintained British dignity as Viceroy of Ireland—and it would have been unfair to blame him for the troubles there. Beyond question he was a staunch soldier; would he not therefore be a strong diplomat? In pitting him against the French, Addington felt, John Bull's character at its sterling best would be made a barrier to French cunning and trickery—and the choice would be popular in the press.

The Prime Minister believed that the Amiens treaty would be an easy elaboration of the preliminary articles already agreed upon. Twenty years earlier, when Shelburne had sent Oswald to Franklin, he had known that he could count on Franklin to appreciate the candor of his envoy without abusing it. But the selection of Cornwallis to deal with Bonaparte lacked any such rationale. It was like sending an amiable old hippopotamus to negotiate with a young lion. The thickness of his skin could not save him.

Cornwallis was instructed to go first to Paris, talk with Bonaparte himself, and try to arrive at an informal understanding before proceeding to Amiens. This was especially important since there were some important matters which had been omitted from the preliminary articles. A word from Bonaparte could greatly simplify the talks at Amiens. And at all hazards, an effort was to be made to prevent Talleyrand from being delegated as the French negotiator; for any treaty of which Talleyrand was coauthor would be suspect in England. The Marquess obediently avoided Talleyrand, obtained an audience with Bonaparte—and was painfully offended by his cold and patronizing reception. The First Consul, then in his early thirties, talked to him almost as to a schoolboy; and it was true that in his eyes English generals were merely elderly schoolboys in uniform. The preliminary articles of London, he said, spoke for themselves. There was no need for him to become personally involved in the final treaty. He would be represented at Amiens by his brother, Joseph Bonaparte, surely a sufficient proof of his regard for the importance of the meeting. So long as the British lived up to the preliminary articles, there need be no difficulties. And now, if the General would excuse him . . .

With this Cornwallis had to be content. At Amiens, he found himself facing brother Joseph, who was courteous enough, but whose instructions were to entrench himself behind the letter of the preliminary articles, and go no farther. Cornwallis manfully applied himself to his task. The most difficult problem, as he saw it, was to find ways of assuring that, after the transfer of Malta to the Knights of St. John, the island would remain neutral, with France, like England, unable to reoccupy it.

Joseph Bonaparte had a suggestion. Would not the best guarantee of neutrality be simply to demolish the forts on the island, and render it militarily indefensible? The idea struck the honest Cornwallis as entirely reasonable. That it might have been put out simply as a test of England's final purpose did not occur to him. Instead of quietly evading the suggestion, he offered to transmit it to Addington, with the recommendation that it be accepted, as an earnest of British good faith. Nothing could have been better calculated to give Bonaparte a glimpse of the real views of British authority on the peace. Addington had no more understanding of what the French were up to than Cornwallis. He discussed the matter with his Cabinet—and was startled by the violence of its objections. The Admiralty in particular stood aghast at the thought of reducing Malta to helplessness, when the island would soon be needed again to support the Navy in war. Against England's admirals and generals the Prime Minister dared not press the point, and the word went back to Cornwallis: the Maltese forts must stay intact.

Like spreading ripples in a lake, the consequences flowed. Cornwallis was compelled to tell Joseph Bonaparte that some other method of solving the problem would need to be found. Joseph, hardly surprised, sent this word on to his brother in Paris. It merely confirmed Napoleon's expectation. First L'Ambigu, now this. Pitt or no Pitt, the British Government aimed only at a truce, not at a peace.

3. "I Am Sanguine . . ."

The First Consul gave orders to Joseph to continue negotiations, to raise difficulties, to concede nothing of importance. It was evident to him that Addington was counting on the treaty to secure his political status, and would in consequence be a weak opponent. England, not France, would make the compromises. Meanwhile, under cover of the talks, the French position on the continent would be consolidated. There was nothing in the articles which had been signed in London to prevent Bonaparte from establishing a republic in North Italy, with himself as President. At a later time, there would be nothing, technically, to prevent Switzerland from similarly being brought under French "protection"—to the exclusion of British commercial interests there.

Englishmen in the ruling classes were infuriated by news of the formation of the Italian Republic, seeing in it proof that Bonaparte's appetite for conquest had not diminished. Nevertheless, the negotiation at Amiens proceeded on its higgling way. By a concession here and a concession there, authorized by the anxious Addington, Cornwallis finally extracted Joseph Bonaparte's signature on the treaty. Triumphantly, the Prime Minister announced the news in his uniquely pompous style. "I am sanguine. . . . that a system may be adopted, which, by keeping clear of the extreme of distrust on the one hand and of credulity and weakness on the other, will be suited to the temper, character and interest of both countries."

4. "A Fen of Stagnant Waters"

Crowds in London's streets cheered the first proclamation of the treaty, cheered again when it was reported that Bonaparte had declared a "festival of the peace" in France, cheered still louder when William Pitt himself advised ratification of the treaty by Parliament. They could not know that Pitt had just written a private letter stating his conviction that "no compact or covenant made with Bonaparte could be secure." For a while thereafter Addington enjoyed the illusion of success. He had listened to the crowds, and he really believed in his popularity. Even the debate on ratification in Parliament did not generate enough heat to dispel the rosy mist. Grenville, in the Lords, sneered at so much weakness in one piece of paper; in the Commons, Pitt's friends attacked the agreement on Malta, while Pitt himself sat in enigmatic silence; but both Houses gave Addington their votes.

Immediately after ratification, many members of Parliament eagerly journeyed to Paris, which had been closed to them for ten years, and where the gay life offered blessed relief from Hanoverian austerity. Among the visitors was the unreconstructed Whig, Charles James Fox, openly gloating over the treaty as a final blow to the hopes of the Bourbons. An old-time friend of French republicanism, he was presented to Bonaparte, who was himself feeling expansive, for the French Senate, like good puppets, had just urged him to become Consul for life. He gave Fox warm assurances of his good will toward the British people, and Fox carried back to England his feeling that Bonaparte, who had drunk his fill of glory on the battlefield, was now ready to devote himself to the prosperity of a France at peace. But the most significant moment of their talk had come when it turned to the subject of assassination. A complex plot to kill King George, which was headed by an Irish army officer with the singularly appropriate name of Despard, had not long before been uncovered in England. Despard was erroneously thought by many Englishmen to be an agent of Bonaparte; and this dishonoring accusation was in the Consul's mind as he remarked that an attempt to assassinate him some time earlier had been instigated by Pitt. As an Englishman, Fox felt that he had to deny the charge, but he could not fail to catch its implication. Bonaparte regarded Pitt as his sworn enemy. A return of Pitt to power in England would be taken as a warlike move.

This was also the view in England's best informed circles. In the great houses of British society, amused men made bets on how long "the Doctor," as Addington was dubbed, would remain as Prime Minister. The final authority in England then rested less in the cabinet than in a congeries of political-minded and articulate aristocrats from among whom every administration was virtually compelled to draw its members. These mighty men would sometimes grudgingly permit a talented commoner to set the pace for England if he was strong and able enough to persuade them, but they would never accept him merely because he would obey them. Although as a temporary expedient they had allowed Pitt to foist Addington on them, it was apparent that the man had soon to go.

For the ordinary Englishman, the dissatisfaction felt with Addington was not based on political grounds or on aristocratic prejudice. It was a felt lack of moral leadership. The country, as it watched its well-meaning Prime Minister, somehow seemed to be losing its self-respect. At a time when the ruler of France was the victor of Marengo and the President of the United States was the author of the Declaration of Independence, Addington seemed to stand for nothing in particular. There was no inspiration in the man, or in the country under his rule. William Wordsworth caught this feeling in the despairing poem in which he called England in 1802 "a fen of stagnant waters." Creative activity seemed to be at low tide. There was Europe, experiencing a surge of brilliant and original activity in the arts and sciences. It was the year when Gauss opened the gate to higher mathematics with his theory of numbers, when Cuvier broke new ground

in anatomical science, when Beethoven celebrated Bonaparte in the Eroica
Symphony, when Pestalozzi uncovered modern principles of child education. By contrast the best that England could show were further technical
improvements in the power machinery of Manchester's cotton mills.

5. Troubles of a Well-Intended Man

Not many persons had any idea of what was actually happening as the
Tory hierarchy decided on war. To paraphrase G. K. Chesterton, it was a
secret too important to be told to the government, an occult secret which
the political priestcraft kept for the privacy of its rituals in clubs and draw-
ing rooms. Addington, on the other hand, was making a mistake fatal to
public men, of not being private at all. Everyone knew his plans for peace,
and his enemies were prompt to blow them up in advance. He did not have
an inkling of the most terrible truth of politics—that peace is attractive only
in wartime. He had no idea of the extent to which an energetic nation
must continuously be stimulated, titillated, and kept occupied with hopeful
and creative work if it is to be content with peace. Because the war had
stopped, he thought that it had ended. Even the Admiralty's stand on Malta
he did not take very seriously; he still intended, in the summer of 1802,
to give up the island, as agreed.

No one had ever told the Prime Minister that while a statesman through
his own efforts can easily make things worse, a good deal of help from the
universe is required to make them better. There was no humility in him.
His powers seemed greater to him than they were. He really thought that
the authority of his high office would allow him to reshape British policy.
It was a shock to him to discover the strength of his enemies.

The opening salvo against his peace came from William Windham, a
member of Pitt's private circle. When the Amiens treaty was submitted to
Parliament, Windham made a speech so devastating, so comprehensively
critical, that even though it did not prevent ratification, it dispelled hope.
He was merely contemptuous of the weakness which had ceded the island
of Elba to France—which had adjusted the boundaries of Guiana—which
enabled the French and Spanish to trade on equal terms with England at
Cape Town; but the cession of Malta he found inconceivable and wicked.
He warned against the too rapid easing of restrictions on American trade
with the British West Indies, at the expense of British merchants. He could
see only blind folly in allowing Bonaparte to send an army to Santo Domingo, or to occupy Louisiana. Had the Prime Minister no regard for the
security of the British Empire? Were British interests to be forced out of
the Caribbean as they had been forced out of North Italy? Was France to
become a commercial rival of England in South America, and to absorb
the colonies of faltering Spain as they fell away?

The country was sobered by these questions. It listened also to another voice, that of the young, brilliant, and contentious George Canning, one of Pitt's foremost disciples, and a popular versifier. He made a little doggerel couplet that caught on:

> As London to Paddington
> So Pitt is to Addington.

A poem from his direct pen advised the country that if war came again, it "should turn to the pilot who weathered the storm." But his most telling blow was delivered a little later in Parliament. "I am no panegyrist of Bonaparte but I cannot shut my eyes to the ascendancy of his genius . . . To stand up against him . . . we want arms of the same kind . . . one great commanding spirit!" Whether he meant Pitt or himself was not altogether clear. In those days, every ambitious young politician secretly dreamed of himself as another Bonaparte, and in Canning, as his subsequent career showed, ambition was rampant. In any case, it was ludicrous to think of Addington as a "great commanding spirit."

Pitt continued cautious, maintained good personal relations with the Prime Minister, and gave advice when called upon. Nevertheless, it came to him as a surprise to discover that this creature, whom he had used for a specific purpose, now actually fancied himself as a statesman in his own right, and had no intention of stepping down from the seat of power. Pitt's feelings burst out when, after a talk with Addington in July 1802, he described him to friends as "the vainest man he had ever met with," and again as "a man of little mind, of consummate vanity, and of very slender abilities." He was particularly incensed by the Doctor's handling of the nation's finances. In his bid for popularity, Addington had grossly over-estimated the government's revenues, insanely cut away taxes, invited a dangerous deficit, and reflected on Pitt's own stern budgetary administration.

The pressure from Pitt's followers in Parliament was hard enough for Addington to bear, but all at once he was struck by a cannonade from a totally unexpected quarter. England's master of controversial prose, William Cobbett, had left America in disgust after the Republican victory (and after being successfully sued for libel) and on his return to England had founded a new and widely read journal, the *Political Register*. Late in 1802, a series of scathing open letters to Addington in this newspaper set London agog. Cobbett pointed out something that other British publicists were overlooking—the significance of the attitude of the United States to England's future. The Peace of Amiens, it was evident, meant French commercial supremacy on the continent. Where, then, were British merchants to turn for business? How was England, with its markets shrunken, to pay for the food imports on which its survival increasingly depended? As matters stood, the American market was not to be counted on, whereas American competition could be ruinous. And Addington, by suspending England's wartime restrictions on American trade, was encouraging that competition. "Be you assured, Sir," Cobbett wrote, "that one part of the plan of the rulers of France is *to make the interest of America coincide with the ruin of England*, and in the prosecution of this plan, nothing can be imagined more effectual than the granting to America, what she has so long and so anxiously sought for, those commercial concessions, which England will not, which England cannot grant her."

Bleakly, Cobbett followed his train of logic to its conclusion. If Addington maintained his American policy, England's favorable balance in trade with America would swiftly diminish. American industry was expanding. Soon the United States might be expected to adopt protective tariffs in order to keep out British imports. Continential trade therefore had to be assured at any cost. If it turned out that war with Bonaparte also meant war with Jefferson's America, even this was preferable to the certainty of economic collapse under the Addington peace. Prepare for war; lay the foundation for another European coalition against France, so that England would not have to fight alone; this was the final meaning of Cobbett's message.

The Parliamentary attacks on the Prime Minister fed on the *Political Register*. As the country's confidence wavered, business began to slump, prices on the Stock Exchange to fall; and those who had been warm to Addington turned cool. Pitt chose this time to break off relations with him, a sure sign that he intended to supersede him.

6. Victory Without War?

There was an unexpected streak of doggedness in Addington. Urgings that he resign at once in favor of Pitt left him hurt but unmoved. He ignored an ominous remark by King George, who had returned briefly to lucidity, that the peace was, after all, only "experimental." The Prime Minister was not, as his critics alleged, without a foreign policy. He did not rely on peace by ingemination. On the contrary, he counted on a very definite strategy to achieve his goal. And that goal was nothing less than victory without war—a peace which would restore the power and profits of British commerce in Europe and elsewhere.

Addington was often unwise, but he had sense enough to fear Bonaparte's designs. And it was because of this fear that he had so readily agreed to France's acquisition of Louisiana. Reports from America had convinced him that the United States would never peacefully permit the Mississippi Valley, on which her heart was set, to fall into French hands. The position of the shrewd permanent officials of the Foreign Office was that Addington should do everything in his power to encourage the movement of French troops across the Atlantic, for when France and America stood face to face in hostility, England could breathe easier. In this spirit, British ships were lent to Bonaparte to facilitate landings of his troops on Santo Domingo, and the retrocession of Louisiana to France by Spain was given every diplomatic encouragement.

Simultaneously, Addington looked for ways to inflame American opinion against the retrocession. Through the year 1801, ignoring widespread rumor, the French and Spanish governments had preserved the secrecy of the Treaty of San Ildefonso, at which Charles IV agreed to give up his troublesome colony of Louisiana, if France would augment the Italian possessions of his son-in-law, the Duke of Parma. England's first need was for indisputable evidence of the treaty's existence—evidence which would give President Jefferson firm ground on which to base a protest against it. With this purpose, the British Minister at Madrid, John Frere, was instructed to obtain a copy of the treaty by whatever means.

There was one man in Spain on whom Frere could pin his hopes—Manuel de Godoy, the proud Prime Minister and former lover of Queen Luisa, who had conferred on him no less a title than "Prince of Peace." Godoy hated and feared Bonaparte, and for months had been delaying the formal transfer of Louisiana on one pretext after another. Unlike King Charles, he believed that Spain's interests demanded close ties to England. It was easy for Frere to establish a friendly intimacy with him, with the result that early in November 1801, the Prince of Peace handed him a copy of the coveted treaty. It went to London by fast courier, and was promptly given to Rufus King, the American minister in London, who, on November 20, dispatched it to Secretary of State Madison.

7. "We Must Marry Ourselves to the British Fleet"

From the moment in January 1802, when President Jefferson read the Treaty of San Ildefonso, he realized that he and the Republican Party stood in the gravest political jeopardy. If Bonaparte were not prevented from obtaining control of New Orleans, the Federalists would have an overwhelming issue on which to return to power. Hamilton had wished in 1798 to lead an army against the Spaniards and make Louisiana part of the United States; and the crushing attacks that he would now be in a position to direct against Jefferson's pro-French policy would be as damaging as those of the XYZ affair. Even the western Republican vote might be lost, for the men of Kentucky, Tennessee, and Ohio would never forgive the party that allowed France to dominate the Mississippi.

As soon as news of the treaty became public, the Federalist press began its drumfire of criticism. The New York *Commercial Advertiser* recorded Hamilton's position. Either the United States would have to seize New Orleans by force or be prepared to lose her western states, since they would "join those who will be in possession of the navigation of the Mississippi . . . they cannot do without it." The way for the United States to get New Orleans, said the *Commercial Advertiser*, was by an alliance with England in war against France. This article appeared on March 12, 1802. A few weeks later, Jefferson boldly espoused almost identical views. In this reversal, he was motivated by much more than a desire to protect his party's position in the west. His own vision of America's future did not permit him to tolerate Bonaparte's plan. The President's writings of the period show that he felt in his blood the gigantic stirring of the young nation, and thrilled like a boy to the idea of distant explorations beyond the Mississippi. His dream of a great continental republic was being challenged as well as his conception of his own role in American history. Both were all at once in conflict with his avowed foreign policy. He had built his reputation as a friend of France, as an enemy of monarchical England, and as a stern opponent of what he had termed "entangling alliances" with Europe. At a single stroke, the Treaty of San Ildefonso had made these positions obsolete. Now, like every great statesman in time of crisis, he put reality before doctrine and followed his intuition at the expense of consistency.

His extraordinary capacity to adapt to new circumstances, and to sacrifice any theory which failed to prove itself in practice, expressed itself in a long and tempestuous letter to Robert Livingston in Paris, containing a message for Bonaparte. "We stand completely corrected of the error that either the Government or the nation of France has any remains of friendship for us . . . The cession of Louisiana . . . to France works most sorely on the United States. It will form a new epoch in our political course . . . There is on the globe one single spot, the possessor of which is our natural and habitual enemy. It is New Orleans through which the produce of three-eighths of our territory must pass to market . . . The day that France takes possession of New Orleans fixes the sentence which is to restrain her [the United States] forever within her low-water mark . . . From that moment, we must marry ourselves to the British fleet and nation." This from Jefferson!

To deliver this aggressive statement to Livingston he turned to Du Pont de Nemours, who was within a few days of sailing for France. To Du Pont the President wrote urging him to warn France of a war "perhaps not very long hence," one "which will annihilate her on the ocean." "If you can be the means of informing the wisdom of Bonaparte of all the consequences, you have deserved well of both countries."

Du Pont, however, was a loyal Frenchman, as well as a friend of Jefferson.

He considered the President's stand to be extreme and somewhat unfair, and he said so. Why offend Bonaparte's military pride, and thus make war certain? In a cogent letter, he asked the President to look at the matter from the French point of view. France and Spain both took it as certain that the United States, once in possession of New Orleans, would promptly begin to covet Mexico, especially the region north of the Rio Grande. "That your nation, Mr. President . . . think of conquering Mexico is not questionable." If these militaristic ambitions were indulged, the principles of democracy would be forgotten, and the American Republic would be corrupted forever. Why not, instead, approach the matter in a spirit of peace, and offer France a "liberal and generous" cash payment—which Bonaparte badly needed—for New Orleans?

This letter somewhat annoyed Jefferson, but at the same time it struck his imagination. He had thought of purchasing Louisiana from Spain; why not from France? The government's financial position had been greatly strengthened under Gallatin's shrewd guidance, so that the money might be found. The President talked with James Madison, and the Secretary of State promptly wrote to Livingston, asking him to explore with the French government the possibility of a sale of New Orleans. The Floridas also were to be discussed, for word had come that Bonaparte was pressing the Spaniards to yield Mobile and Pensacola.

8. Godoy Determined

Spaniards know how to hate, and in Madrid, Manuel de Godoy, the Prince of Peace, hating Bonaparte for a dozen personal, as well as for patriotic reasons, had become almost fanatical in his determination to thwart the French dictator. But how? He knew that King Charles needed better grounds than he had to delay further in carrying out the San Ildefonso treaty. Bonaparte had increased the size of the promised Italian territories to the point where the temptation was irresistible to the dynastic-minded Queen Luisa, whose pressure upon the wavering King was, in the final test, bound to be greater than Godoy's. His arguments in the council chamber could not suffice much longer to keep Louisiana out of Bonaparte's hands—and not only Louisiana, but West Florida and Mexico, for with French troops in New Orleans the adjacent provinces would be easy prey.

Godoy was something of a peacock, but there was in him a hard core of toughness and a considerable finesse in the use of diplomatic weapons. The possibilities of procrastination had not yet been fully exploited. Spain's envoy in Washington had reported that in American political circles a project to buy Louisiana from the French was much mooted. Here was a point on which King Charles could hardly fail to support a Spanish negative— and if France refused to heed it, the retrocession could again be postponed.

Following this line of thought, Godoy requested the French minister in Madrid, St. Cyr, to inform Talleyrand that the Treaty of San Ildefonso would be implemented only on condition that France pledge herself not to sell Louisiana to a third party.

A good effort, it nevertheless proved futile. In Talleyrand, Godoy was up against a man five times as clever and ten times as unscrupulous as himself. An official note from Paris promptly removed the difficulty. Spain's attitude "perfectly conforms with the intentions of the French Government," said the French Foreign Minister, and he avowed "in the name of the First Consul" that "France will never alienate" the reacquired territory.

But Godoy had another and stronger pretext for delay—the need to define the boundaries of Louisiana, and of the Italian lands to be given to Spain. Specifically, he had resolved—and obtained the King's agreement—that West Florida was definitely to be excluded from the retrocession. Here he felt that he had Bonaparte on the hip, for it was a point on which France could not lightly yield. If New Orleans was to be defended from the sea against possible blockade by the British fleet, it would be necessary for the French to prevent England from using Mobile and Pensacola as bases. Strategically, possession of West Florida was essential to the security of Louisiana—a fact which the First Consul could not ignore, and which promised to prolong indefinitely the bargaining over the retrocession.

With grim pleasure, Godoy informed Paris of the Spanish position on West Florida. The result might have been predicted. There arrived posthaste in Madrid a new French envoy, General de Beurnonville, with an offer designed to tempt the King and Queen beyond resistance. If Bonaparte could have the Floridas, he would create for the benefit of the Queen's relatives a new Italian kingdom, not just a dukedom, to include all of fertile Tuscany and wealthy Parma. But even for this powerful move Godoy had a counter. So far-reaching a rearrangement of Italian territory, he said, could hardly be undertaken without the consent of other interested European powers. With this excuse, he sent for John Frere, and with tongue in cheek, desired to know whether England would consent to Bonaparte's plan for the Floridas and Parma. Frere went through the correct motion of asking London for an opinion, and was soon able to give Godoy a formal answer—England would not consent. At the same time, a messenger went to St. Petersburg with the same question. This gave Czar Alexander an excuse to inform Spain that he was unalterably opposed to the cession of Parma to Spain; in his view, the estates of the duchy rightfully belonged to the King of Sardinia.

A diplomatic ring had been formed around France. With elation that he did not bother to conceal, Godoy summoned Beurnonville to a meeting, and told him (in words which the French envoy reported to Talleyrand) that "the British minister had declared to him . . . that his Britannic Majesty . . . could never consent that the two Floridas should become an acquisition of the Republic; that the United States of America were in this respect of one mind with the Court of London; and that Russia equally objected to France disposing of the estates of Parma in favor of Spain." Added Beurnonville, "In imparting to me this procedure of the British minister, the Prince had a satisfied air, which showed how much he wished that the exchange, almost agreed upon and so warmly desired by the Queen, should not take place."

Godoy had checked Bonaparte, but he was not foolish enough to think that he had achieved checkmate. He knew well enough that while Bonaparte preferred to have legal title to West Florida, it was not absolutely essential to his purposes. If he were to accept Louisiana on Spain's terms, he could certainly find an excuse to put troops into Mobile and Pensacola soon thereafter; and what could Spain do to stop him?

9. *Bonaparte Encouraged*

The First Consul meanwhile found himself in a quandary. If he did not soon occupy New Orleans, there was a real possibility that the wrathful Americans of the western states might decide to drive out the Spaniards by force, and so forestall him. The Spanish garrison at New Orleans was small, and whatever its loyalty to King Charles, it had none to France. Only the early presence of a substantial French army in Louisiana could assure a successful occupation. But Leclerc's troops, on which he had counted for the purpose, were being seriously delayed in Santo Domingo. It now appeared that suppression of the "slave republic" would not be easy. The voluntary surrender of Toussaint (who made the error of trusting to Bonaparte's honor, and so perished miserably in a French dungeon) had not broken the spirit of the rebellious Negroes, who, as Leclerc wrote, were "incredible fanatics" in their desire for independence. Terroristic methods, torture and lingering death could not break their spirit. The seventeen thousand men under his command, Leclerc told Napoleon in an early letter, would not be enough to blast the rebels out of their mountain fortresses, since at the same time he had to defend the coastal towns and plantations against native attacks. Trusting in his brother-in-law's judgment, Bonaparte in the spring of 1802 ordered an additional expeditionary force of ten thousand seasoned troops, accompanied by squadrons of the French fleet, to Santo Domingo. It was his thought that after the reconquest of the island, these troops, at least, could be moved on to New Orleans.

West Florida was a stumbling block; but suddenly in the summer of 1802, the splendid news came that Godoy had unaccountably changed his mind in the matter. A letter from Spain offered to carry through the retrocession of Louisiana without further delay, merely reserving the question of West Florida. If Bonaparte suspected an ulterior motive, he shrugged it aside. Louisiana was his at last; that was enough; the rest would follow.

10. *Addington Disturbed*

It seemed to Henry Addington that he stood close to one of the great diplomatic triumphs of British history. Reports from the West Indies said that the French army in Santo Domingo had run into unexpectedly strong native resistance. This was great news for England. By encouraging Bonaparte to extend himself across the Atlantic, the Prime Minister believed, he was draining the strength of France and preserving the peace of Europe. The news was heartening. Edward Thornton, the British chargé d'affaires in Washington, reported an increasing disposition on the part of the American Government to cultivate British friendship, and an evident determination not to yield control of the Mississippi to the French without a fight. "He [President Jefferson] reiterated to me with additional force the resolution of the country never to abandon the claim of free navigation . . . declaring that should they be obliged at last to resort to force, *they would throw away the scabbard.*" Frere in Madrid, in his own way was equally encouraging in his accounts of Godoy's position. The West Florida transaction appeared to have reached an impasse.

Time was working against Bonaparte, Addington thought. The United States was in an angry mood. France had pledged herself not to sell Louisiana. England's navy commanded the Caribbean. While Godoy held fast France could not get Mobile and control of the Gulf of Mexico. In Europe the strength of Austria and Prussia was reviving. Russia had taken a forbidding attitude toward Bonaparte. It seemed to the British Prime Minister that his diplomacy was about to triumph where the great Pitt's militancy had failed. England might even be able to hold on to Malta without war. The writing of the Maltese clause of the treaty had been slipshod, and technical reasons had been found for postponing the cession. As soon as Bonaparte's embarrassments sufficiently enmeshed him, a new treaty, reflecting the altered balance of power, could be initiated.

Then, all at once, the outlook darkened. To his concern and bewilderment, Addington learned that Godoy had come forward with an offer to carry out the retrocession of Louisiana immediately, that Bonaparte had instantly agreed, and that the matter was settled. Frere in Madrid was unable to explain Godoy's change of mind. It was a shock, it was a disappointment, it was a mystery.

11. "Very Secret"

Behind the mystery of Godoy's abrupt decision to give up Louisiana without further delay was an extraordinary chain of circumstance, which began with a letter from New Orleans dated July 1801. For months this letter had lain almost unnoticed in the office of Spain's Secretary of the Treasury, Soler. Written by the Intendant of Louisiana, the chief finance officer there, its burden was that America had been guilty of violations of the rules established by Pinckney's Treaty, under which the Spanish authorities in New Orleans regulated America's Mississippi commerce. These rules provided that goods arriving by river boats might be deposited in the city's warehouses, until they could be transshipped to ocean going vessels, and that goods imported from abroad for the American trade might be similarly stored pending the upriver haul. In both cases the Spanish authorities had the right to supervise the movement of the goods and to impose a tax of 6 per cent on their value.

The Intendant, who had charge of "the American deposit," wrote to Soler that he suspected some Kentucky boatmen of smuggling goods out of New Orleans without paying the required tax, and worse, of smuggling Spanish gold coinage, export of which was strictly forbidden. Soler did not get around to consideration of the problem until the spring of 1802, after the Peace of Amiens had been signed. Then it seemed to him an issue grave enough to require a decision at a higher level. For in the writing of Pinckney's Treaty in 1795, Godoy had insisted on authority to discontinue the right of deposit after three years, and Pinckney (against the advice of subordinates) had accepted the stipulation, in the conviction that Spain would not dare to act upon it. Spain therefore could, if she chose, legally close the deposit as a punishment and warning to lawbreaking Americans. However, the political consequences of such action could hardly fail to be very grave. The Mississippi trade had expanded enormously and become exceedingly profitable since 1795, paralleling the large increase of the American population in the valley towns. Treaty or no treaty, it was certain that the American government would regard closure of the deposit as a hostile act, conceivably justifying war. And the Creole population of New Orleans, which indirectly prospered greatly from Mississippi trade, might be expected to stand with the Americans.

Soler relieved himself of the burden of the affair by bringing it to the attention of Spain's Foreign Secretary, Pedro Cevallos—which meant to the attention of Godoy, for Cevallos was no more than his puppet. At that point, the problem coincided with the Prince's need to find some way out of his difficulties in connection with West Florida. Queen Luisa was pressing him hard from one side, General Beurnonville from the other, to meet Bonaparte's terms. Whether he liked it or not, the time was nearly at hand when the Treaty of San Ildefonso would be put into effect.

A question remained in his mind: since Louisiana had to go to France, could it at least be made so hot for Bonaparte as to burn his hands? It was in this connection that the letter from the Intendant of Louisiana struck his imagination. If King Charles would stand by him, the Frenchman might yet be taught a lesson.

Wheels turned within the Court, and presently Cevallos wrote a confidential note to Treasurer Soler. King Charles, he said, had authorized immediate discontinuance of the New Orleans deposit, and he enclosed a royal order, marked "Very Secret," to that effect. This was in July 1802. Simultaneously, Cevallos was instructed to notify Talleyrand that no further obstacles would be interposed to the retrocession of Louisiana. A trap had been baited for Bonaparte.

The royal order regarding the deposit, which Soler promptly dispatched to the Intendant of Louisiana, Juan Morales, contained an extraordinary caution. Under no circumstances was Morales to let it be known that such an order existed. The plan to close the deposit was to be concealed until the last moment not only from France and America, but even from other Spanish officials in Louisiana. The public would be told that Morales took the action on his own initiative, in accordance with the existing treaty between America and Spain, under which the right of deposit had long since expired.

12. Bonaparte Trapped

At last Louisiana belonged to France—on paper, at least—but the First Consul's mood of optimism did not last long. Within a few weeks, he received the first of a series of dream-shattering reports from Leclerc—reports which were to alter the trends of French, British, and American history. An epidemic of yellow fever had wrecked his hopes as all of Europe's generals and diplomats had not been able to do. Of 28,300 French soldiers in Santo Domingo, only 4000, wrote Leclerc, were fit for service. "The occupation of Santo Domingo has until now cost us 24,000 men, and we are not yet definitely masters of it." The story of the hosts of Sennacherib had been repeated. "My position," wrote Leclerc, who would himself soon be dead of the fever ". . . has become very bad . . . In order to be master of Santo Domingo, you must send me 12,000 men without losing a single day." Later, even before these 12,000 arrived, he asked for an additional 5000 men, and for over a million dollars in gold. Otherwise "St. Domingo will be forever lost to France."

Although Bonaparte's closest military advisers protested the sending of additional reinforcements, although he himself was enraged by the situation, he saw no choice. His entire transatlantic strategy, his hope of an American empire, hinged on the rapid reduction of Santo Domingo. Shipyards in the north of France, and even in Holland, began to work at a frenzied pace in order to build the additional naval vessels and troop transports required. Regiment after regiment of veteran soldiers was equipped for expeditionary duty in the Caribbean, until nearly 50,000 Frenchmen had been sent there to die.

As Bonaparte saw the situation in the autumn of 1802, the large number of troops in Santo Domingo made an early occupation of New Orleans more important than ever. It was only from a Louisiana in French hands that he could count on a dependable supply of food-stuffs for Santo Domingo over any considerable period. He envisaged American wheat moving to the French West Indies to feed his men; they meanwhile would subdue the island, and restore its exports of sugar and coffee to Europe. The resulting large profits would of course go into the treasury of France. Nothing was to be allowed to interfere with this purpose. Consequently, he was seriously disturbed by Jefferson's warning that the United States would not peacefully accept French possession of Louisiana. The immediate problem, he felt, was to allay American fears. When Robert Livingston asked whether France would consider the sale of New Orleans and the Floridas, Bonaparte gave him some encouragement, although privately he considered the notion ridiculous.

Subsequently, as the year 1802 approached its end, he instructed his man in Washington, Pichon, to give a pledge to President Jefferson that France, as owner of Louisiana, would preserve American rights in the free navigation of the Mississippi. But the hope that he had induced a softening of the American attitude was short-lived. The news from New Orleans of Spain's sudden and arbitrary revocation of America's right of deposit at the mouth of the Mississippi knocked the props out from under his strategy. At this moment, the assurances of French good will which he had sent to Jefferson became worthless. Pichon reported that the United States had exploded with anger. Even though France had not yet formally taken possession at New Orleans, it was assumed that Bonaparte, whose troops were expected there any day, was responsible for the provocative order. The American people, Pichon wrote unhappily, stood ready to fight side by side with England against what they considered to be a France bent on the conquest of their continent.

Godoy's trap had closed around Bonaparte. He could not go forward, he could not go back. His frustration burst out in oaths which startled his listeners, and showed which way the wind was beginning to blow: "Damn sugar, damn coffee, damn colonies!" To occupy Louisiana meant a war he dared not risk. With Santo Domingo devouring his finest troops, with the problem of supplying them from France daily becoming more difficult and costly, with England's navy able at any time to cut his supply routes, he was frantic.

13. *The Wrong Inference*

News of the closing of the New Orleans deposit reached Washington in the middle of November 1802. By that time, the American West was roaring with rage at the unexpected assault upon its established ways and its prosperity. Although the withdrawal of the right of deposit did not deny to the United States the free navigation of the Mississippi, it materially cut away the benefits of navigational rights. Without warehouses, the huge Mississippi flatboats would have to remain loaded in the river until their cargoes could be transferred directly to ocean-going vessels—an intolerable nuisance. Soon, in the popular mind, the idea grew that Spain had closed the river itself to American boats. Secretary of State Madison sent a somber note to Madrid stressing the gravity of the crisis as seen by the rivermen: "The Mississippi is to them everything. It is the Hudson, the Delaware, the Potomac, and all the navigable rivers of the Atlantic States, formed into one stream." Caustic reproof by Jefferson to the Spanish minister in Washington, Irujo, so alarmed him that he demanded instant revocation of the order from New Orleans, for he did not know of its origin in Madrid; and he sent a screaming protest of his own to Godoy.

A rash of violent denunciations of Spain broke out in the press. Kentucky's leading newspaper, the *Palladium* of Frankfort, stated that if the President would go to war for the Mississippi, Kentucky alone would contribute twenty-six thousand militiamen, and eleven thousand rifles. In New York, Aaron Burr, writing under the name of Coriolanus, published inflammatory newspaper articles urging the westerners to secede from the union if necessary, and conquer New Orleans themselves. Congress authorized the President to call on the governors of the states for eighty thousand militiamen. But only a few days after the country learned of the closing of the deposit, word came from Paris that King Charles had yielded to Bonaparte, and that France would soon take formal possession of Louisiana. Public opinion immediately shifted. Now the French were seen as the true villains of the piece. Within a few weeks, all America believed that the New Orleans order was a gauntlet flung at Jefferson's feet by the First Consul. The President himself came to this mistaken conclusion. His first diplomatic retort was to generate rumors that America would shortly enter into formal alliance with England. At various functions where Pichon, the French chargé, was present, Jefferson made it a point to be seen in confidential conversation with England's Thornton. Gloomily, Pichon reported to

Talleyrand that he feared the worst. "I noticed at his [Jefferson's] table that he redoubled his civilities and attentions to the British chargé." "I cannot help seeing that there is a tendency toward adopting an irrevocably hostile system."

For all this play acting, which he enjoyed for its own sportive quality, Jefferson was still intent on the preservation of peace. And not only for humanitarian reasons. He saw war as an invitation to political reaction and the return of the Hamiltonians to power. Already arch-Federalists like Timothy Pickering and Fisher Ames were reportedly trafficking with Burr to promote the secession of the West, and create an independent empire which would absorb Spain's vast dominions in the Americas. The war fever, Jefferson realized, needed to be reduced, not inflamed. In his annual message to Congress, delivered in December 1802, the President carefully subordinated the Louisiana crisis. Bellicose western congressmen and British observers were equally disappointed. Edward Thornton wrote to London that the message was "a very foolish thing."

To calm the West, and so gain time to negotiate the Mississippi crisis, Jefferson turned to a recourse on which every President relies when he does not know what else to do—the introduction of a fresh note of hope into the situation, in the shape of a new and popular personality. The obvious man in this instance was James Monroe—respected in the West, where he owned large tracts of land—esteemed in France, where he had done obeisance to the Republic—acclaimed in the Republican party, for the future leadership of which he was already contending. Early in 1803, Jefferson named and the Senate confirmed Monroe as a special envoy to go to Paris and assist Livingston in persuading the French to the sale of New Orleans. "On the event of this mission," Jefferson told the Senate, "depend the future destinies of this Republic." National considerations aside, he saw the effort as a means to make the westerners feel that their interests were being fully considered by the government, and of detaching them from the dangerous plots of Aaron Burr.

It was Jefferson's impression, drawn from diplomatic dispatches and news reports, that France had acquired the Floridas, as well as Louisiana. Not knowing the full extent of Bonaparte's desperation, he thought America would be miraculously fortunate if the First Consul would consent to part with the city of New Orleans, and perhaps the Floridas. The vast remainder of Louisiana west of the Mississippi he could see no way of dislodging from French hands. Monroe was told that he and Livingston might offer $10,000,000 for New Orleans and the Floridas; and that if the negotiation failed—as Jefferson expected it to fail—they were to go to London, and lay the groundwork for an alliance with England.

14. *The Cutting of the Knot*

Weeks before Monroe sailed for France, the indignant letters written by Irujo to Godoy, warning that the American West was ready to march on New Orleans, had borne fruit. The Prince of Peace felt it advisable to tempt the fates no further. He had done his utmost to harm Bonaparte, but it might be months before France assumed control in New Orleans, and if meanwhile the hotheaded Americans were to attack, Spain would become involved in an unnecessary and disastrous war. By the middle of April 1803, a royal authorization was in the hands of Irujo, empowering him to instruct Intendant Morales in New Orleans to reopen the deposit immediately. Without a moment's delay, he informed the American government of Godoy's new order, and the President promptly published the news for the country to read. The crisis, so far as Spain was concerned, was thus dispelled.

There remained the great question—how would Bonaparte respond to Monroe's offer? It was answered, in the way of such things, by events beyond the control of both men. Shortly before Monroe arrived in France, Addington had been confronted by a major Parliamentary crisis. Reports of bristling activity in the French-controlled shipyards of Holland were setting all England astir with fear of invasion. Under questioning, the French assured Addington that their new program of ship construction was designed solely for the reinforcement of the army in Santo Domingo and the transport of troops to Louisiana. The new vessels, they pointed out, were of the ocean-going type, and included no flat-bottomed boats such as would have been required for a cross-channel assault on England. The only reason why the completed ships had not already sailed for the West Indies was the extraordinary ferocity of the winter, which had sealed Holland's harbors with ice. Addington himself was inclined to accept this explanation as true—and it was—but he was totally unable to control the situation. The initial spark of concern over invasion was deliberately fanned into a blaze of fear by leading officials of the War Office and Admiralty, who had come to the conclusion that with Bonaparte so deeply committed across the Atlantic the opportunity to strike at France ought not to be missed. A Parliamentary resolution calling on the Prime Minister to take action was acclaimed on all sides, until Addington realized that he and his peace policy were sliding to disaster. The issue was obvious: if he insisted on peace, he would be forced to resign. His choice was to remain in office. To forestall his enemies, overnight he became an advocate of preventive war, and drafted a message from the King to Parliament, urging immediate measures to protect England from invasion.

News of the King's message came as a shock to Bonaparte, who perfectly understood what lay behind. Holding an audience at the Tuileries, he publicly challenged the British ambassador, Lord Whitworth, "And so you are determined to go to war!" When Whitworth formally denied any such intention on England's part, the Consul bitterly attacked the British for seeking pretexts for war, and for refusing to give up Malta as promised. "Woe to those who do not respect treaties! They shall answer for it to all Europe!"

Now it was unmistakable to him that the Louisiana project had to be liquidated, once and for all. The unforseeable—the fanaticism of Santo Domingo's Negroes, the *aedes aegypti* mosquito, Godoy's closure of the New Orleans deposit, and the icy winter of 1802–1803, among other chances —had forced his hand. In this crisis, his pledge to Spain that France "would not alienate" Louisiana became, in his mind, a scrap of paper not worth two thoughts. If the Americans would pay enough—and France needed money for the imminent war—why not let them have their New Orleans? Contemplating the prospect of armies and battlefields, his state of fury at the perversity of circumstance gave way to calm determination. He would renounce his transatlantic ambitions, he would turn instead on his enemies in Europe, and destroy them. Instead of having to wage an overseas war for Louisiana, he could use the colony to bind the United States to him in good will forever. Not France, but England in the years ahead would be regarded as America's enemy. As always, no sooner did he know what necessity required him to do, than he had a complete rationalization ready to explain why he chose to do it.

Many of those around him who had shared his dream of reviving France's ancient colonial glories could not give it up as readily as he. To brothers Joseph and Lucien, who came to remonstrate with him as he lay in his bath, he responded with curt admonitions to mind their own business—and to make sure they understood, splashed them with the bath water. On Talleyrand, who opposed the sale, he turned a cold and fishy eye—for after all, it was the Foreign Minister who had seduced him into the Louisiana adventure in the first place. April 11, 1803, two days before Monroe reached Paris, was the crucial day. The First Consul sent for his Minister of Finance, Barbé-Marbois, and made the extraordinary statement which Marbois later recorded in his *History of Louisiana:* "Irresolution and deliberation are no longer tolerable. I renounce Louisiana. It is not only New Orleans that I will sell, but the entire colony, without reservation. I know the value of what I renounce . . . I renounce it with utmost regret. It would be foolish obstinacy to try to hold it. I direct you to negotiate this affair . . . Do not wait even for Mr. Monroe's arrival; have an interview this very day with Mr. Livingston . . ."

Within a few minutes, word of Bonaparte's decision came to Talleyrand,

and he reacted characteristically. Sloughing off his own convictions as easily as a snake sheds a skin, he adopted those of his master. Since Louisiana was to be sold, he would restore his own prestige by taking the lead in the matter. The ambitious Barbé-Marbois had to be shunted aside. In such a situation, minutes could be precious, and an urgent message went to Robert Livingston requesting an immediate conference at the Foreign Ministry. When the American entered Talleyrand's office, he was startled by a sharp and instant question: what would the United States offer for New Orleans and all Louisiana? Livingston, who was somewhat deaf, asked to have the question repeated, while he caught his breath. It was necessary for him to temporize—his instructions applied only to New Orleans and the Floridas —but he recognized that an event of monumental importance was about to unfold. He had worked hard to persuade France in the matter, and it seemed to him unfair that Monroe, who had not yet arrived, should share the credit. He rushed back to his office, wrote a lengthy letter to Jefferson, describing the new development, and sent it off by fast boat.

15. "The Noblest Work . . ."

Two days later, Monroe, whose confidence in himself was always majestic, brought to the negotiation the measure of reassurance which Livingston needed. This was not the time, they agreed, to stick to the letter of their instructions. Bonaparte was impatient. A week later, after concentrated haggling, a figure was reached—$15,000,000 for New Orleans and all of Spain's former possessions west of the Mississippi and north of Mexico. Three fourths of this amount was to be paid in the form of bonds bearing 6 per cent interest; for the remainder, the United States was to assume debts owed to her citizens by France. It was a transaction for which neither the President nor the Congress was prepared, but the two Americans unhesitatingly took responsibility for it on themselves. "We have lived long," said Livingston, after signing the treaty of purchase, "but this is the noblest work of our lives." Bonaparte, a little later, explained his decision to France: "Henceforth, Louisiana will be associated with the independence of the United States of America. We shall always keep friends there who . . . will be devoted to our welfare . . . The United States owe their independence to France; henceforth they will owe us their growth and their greatness."

For the first time since the XYZ affair, Talleyrand smiled at an American. "You have made a fine bargain for yourselves, and I suppose you will make the most of it." He was referring to a question from Livingston about the extent of the territory involved; although the treaty of purchase did not speak of the Floridas, Livingston wondered whether they had not been included in the retrocession by Spain. And what of the area called Texas, north of the Rio Grande? Talleyrand, who knew precisely what the

Spaniards had ceded to Napoleon, pretended ignorance. "I do not know . . . I can give you no direction," he said. Still seeking clarification, Livingston and Monroe sent a message to Bonaparte, but without learning anything more. It was the First Consul's hope that confusion over the boundaries might yet embroil America with Spain, to his later advantage. Barbé-Marbois quotes him as saying, "If an obscurity did not exist, it would perhaps be a good policy to put one there." This was shrewd; not only the anti-Spanish but the anti-British war spirit of the next decade in America would be fanned strongly by desire for the Floridas.

There still remained for Talleyrand a diplomatic chore—to explain to King Charles of Spain why the French Government had departed from its pledged word not to resell Louisiana. What followed was in its way a brilliant piece of work. Spain, not France, had been responsible for the sale, Talleyrand averred. If the deposit at New Orleans had not been closed, the United States would not have threatened war against France and an alliance with England, just as a new European crisis loomed. And thereafter, Spain's reversal of policy, in reopening the deposit, had virtually conceded America's permanent rights in New Orleans, and cut deeply into France's sovereign powers there. The French Government had been left with no alternative but to sell the entire colony. This was Talleyrand at his Mephistophelian best, seldom truthful, but always plausible.

Events now moved rapidly to the denouement. Lord Whitworth presented Talleyrand with an ultimatum requiring the French to abandon their naval preparations in Holland; it was rejected with contempt; on May 16, 1803, a few days after extricating himself from the Louisiana trap, Bonaparte declared war on England. Europe's most spectacular military adventure was about to begin. Napoleon, who had begun as a creature of the Republic, would now emulate Caesar. As de Tocqueville remarked, instead of Liberty, Fraternity, and Equality, the French Revolution had produced Infantry, Artillery, and Cavalry.

CHAPTER TWO

The Heady Wine of Empire

1. *The* Real-Politik *of Thomas Jefferson*

The diplomatic stage for the War of 1812 was now set, with all the actors in the wings. No one then living could have foretraced the tortuous path of historical circumstance about to open before the United States. At first, England accepted the accomplished fact of the Louisiana Purchase without serious misgivings. In fact, she profited thereby, a fact which tended to reconcile her to the transaction. No American bank had resources or credit large enough to assume responsibility for the redemption of American bonds deposited with Bonaparte as security for Louisiana. The supranational financial traditions of the time, which had come down from the days of the Fuggers, enabled the United States to employ for the purpose a leading banker of London, Alexander Baring. In this Baring had the blessing of the Foreign Office; so that the British government facilitated payments which Bonaparte would soon use in a genuine attempt to mount an invasion against England's shores.

The only serious protest against the transfer of Louisiana to American hands came from Spain. Minister Irujo, speaking for his government, indignantly pointed out to Secretary of State Madison that America had placed herself in the position of a receiver of stolen goods. In selling Louisiana against her pledged word, and without making good the promised transfer to Spain of the Italian provinces, France, said Irujo, had forfeited title to Louisiana. More, Bonaparte had violated the French Constitution by disposing of the colony without permission of the Chamber of Deputies and the Senate of France. The United States, so Irujo alleged, had no claim to Louisiana under any recognized body of international law. If the territory were to be sold, Spain, not France, had the only right to dispose of it.

This was perfectly true, perfectly obvious; it was also perfectly meaningless. As usual, the President, who loved to theorize, completely ignored theory when confronted by crisis, and like any sensible politician dealt with hard facts as they emerged. The question in his mind was not whether the United States was morally justified in occupying Louisiana, but only when. Impatiently he waited for word that the ships carrying Bonaparte's representatives had eluded the British fleet and arrived at New Orleans, so that the transfer from Spain to France and thereafter from France to America, might be promptly carried through. Meanwhile, Spain's anguish left him indifferent.

With a cool ruthlessness that Bonaparte himself might have envied, Jefferson set about to complete the collapse of the Spanish empire in North America by adding West Florida to the United States. "We have some claims," he wrote to Senator Breckenridge of Kentucky, "to extend on the sea-coast . . . eastwardly to the Rio Perdido, between Mobile and Pensacola, the ancient boundary of Louisiana. These claims will be a subject of negotiation with Spain; and if as soon as she is at war we push them strongly with the one hand, holding out a price with the other, we shall certainly obtain the Floridas, and all in good time."

A little later, "some claims" became "our right." A letter to Madison asserted that "our right" to West Florida was "substantial." Talk of payment ceased. James Monroe, then America's minister to Spain, was instructed to demand West Florida as "a *sine qua non,* and no price to be given for it." The "right" to which the President referred rested essentially on the fact that France had once owned West Florida as well as Louisiana. But this, as Irujo retorted, did not mean that the retrocession of the one automatically signified the retrocession of the other. At no point in the transaction with France had Spain yielded her authority over the Floridas. But by now the American public was convinced that West Florida was properly part of the Louisiana bargain. Southern landowners were determined to waste no time in taking possession of the rich Gulf lands. Although Jefferson in his heart recognized the dubious character of America's claim, he gave his blessing to firebrands in Congress as they tried to force the issue with Spain. Their leader was the bold young Virginia orator, John Randolph. At his urging, Congress accepted a bill, the notorious Mobile Act, which calmly annexed West Florida to the United States, and asserted the right to establish laws for the territory. When Irujo heard of this invasion of Spanish sovereignty, he refused at first to believe it. The news seemed to him, as he wrote to Madison, simply a journalistic libel on the character of the American Government. Was it possible that the United States had so far abandoned legality and respect for the rights of others? Jefferson's signature on the bill, early in 1804, left no room for doubt. Spain swiftly retaliated. Orders went out from Madrid to Spanish warships to seize American merchant vessels carrying English cargoes. Spanish troops raided into the United States from West Florida, capturing a number of American citizens. The Foreign Minister at Madrid passionately told an American envoy, George Erving, "You may choose either peace or war . . . I advise you to go to war now if you think that is best for you."

The President had been against the Federalists when they sought to rally the nation for an attack on New Orleans, but he was for the Republicans as they prepared to take up arms against West Florida. With native caution, however, he decided to wait until his new minister to France, General John Armstrong, could report on Bonaparte's attitude. "What," Armstrong asked Talleyrand, "would be the course of this government [France] in the event of a rupture between us and Spain?" When the blunt answer came back, "We must take part with Spain," Jefferson quickly muffled the drums. Spain's fighting capacity was one thing, France's another. American policy underwent a sudden change. Jefferson's next annual message to Congress piously assured the world that Spain had "misunderstood" the Mobile Act; the United States, he insisted, was not contemplating aggression.

A new plan was taking shape in his mind—to make a secret treaty with England. In return for an American declaration of war against Spain— which, for practical purposes, meant also against France—England was to be asked to assure American possession of West Florida. But at the very moment when the proposal to London was being drafted, news came that British warships had resumed seizures of American vessels trading with the French West Indies. To tie the United States to England under these circumstances was unthinkable. The President took in sail again and tacked. This time he proposed "that we should address ourselves to France . . . and offer to *her*, or through her, a sum of money for . . . the Floridas." Instead of war with Spain, he was now advocating bribery of France.

Because it seemed almost as if he was obsessed with desire for the Floridas, Jefferson was in his time accused of being a greedy imperialist, held back from open war only by timidity. It has since become evident, however, that he was motivated less by the desire for new territory than by concern for the nation's security and future peace. In his view, it was certain that if America did not occupy the Gulf lands, sooner or later England or France would wrest them from Spain, and America would then be compelled to fight a great power; and his shifty maneuvers were specifically calculated to avoid this danger. And there were other considerations. He was, of course, an expansionist, but in more than the ordinary, territorial sense of the word. By expanding America's boundaries, he felt, he was also expanding the horizon of human freedom. The Declaration of Independence was still his passion and his creed. He believed that the American system of government was qualified to bring benefits to men everywhere—that the expulsion of the tyrannical Spanish government from the American mainland would be a triumph for mankind as well as a national gain.

His goals were definite; it was only his methods that were confused. Trying an experiment here, an experiment there, he put the American Government in the anomalous position of having added West Florida to its dominions by act of Congress, while carrying on a complex international intrigue aimed at persuading France to accept money for Spain's colony. The entire problem finally reduced itself to a single point: how would Bonaparte react if offered a few million dollars for the Floridas? He had just crowned himself Emperor Napoleon I, he was preparing for war on a titanic scale, and it was difficult to predict his response to the American advances. Jefferson wrote Robert Livingston, who was still in Paris, to urge "cultivating the disposition of the French government to take our side of the question." For this purpose, the President realized, he would have to make it plain that his recent display of friendship for England had been only a mask.

2. Jefferson as a Hamiltonian

Mingled with his diplomatic motives for challenging England was another perhaps stronger—the need to put the New England Federalists on the defensive in the coming presidential election. By presenting England once more to the American people as the enemy, he could seriously embarrass the pro-British Federalist opposition.

His anxiety to strike at the Federalists was the greater because they had found a mortifying chink in his armor. There he was, the great advocate of strict construction of the Constitution, and of states' rights. Yet, without any sanction from the Constitution or states, or even from the Congress, he had paid out millions in federal monies for a territory whose acquisition would reshape the future of the American people. The Federalists did not precisely reject the idea of the Louisiana Purchase. Rather, they exploited it to reveal the President as a man whose avowed principles could not be trusted—as a political trickster, a shallow opportunist.

As the author of the Kentucky Resolutions of 1798, Jefferson had some explaining to do to the country, as well as to himself. At first, he thought he would have to ask Congress and the states "for an additional article to the Constitution, approving and confirming an act which the nation had not previously authorized." But between the lines of the letter in which he made this suggestion there were almost audible sighs. The truth was that he wanted desperately to avoid a constitutional debate just then. Bonaparte was waiting impatiently for his money. Who knew when he might change his mind, and sell Louisiana to another buyer; or, if he were to be beaten in the new war, whether his successors would abide by his agreements? It was not a time for argument and delay.

His efforts to rationalize his position for the record led him into some appalling lapses in logic—which he himself preferred to call "metaphysical subtleties." In a letter to a supporter, Senator Nicholas of Virginia, he twisted and turned like a fox pursued by hounds. "Our peculiar security is in the possession of a written constitution. Let us not make it a blank paper by construction . . . The grant of the treaty-making power [is not] boundless. If it is, then we have no Constitution." Therefore he saw virtue, he said, in asking the states to grant an enlargement of the federal powers in the instance of Louisiana. On the other hand, he would really be very pleased if Congress decided to do nothing of the kind. "If, however, our friends shall think differently, certainly I shall acquiesce with satisfaction." That is to say, he would "acquiesce with satisfaction" if his party chose to make "blank paper" of the Constitution in what he believed to be a good cause.

As usual when an old doctrine blocked the road to a new opportunity, it was the doctrine that the President threw aside. To carry through the Louisiana transaction, he had to make an extraordinary about-face—to become, for practical purposes, a Hamiltonian, an advocate of paternalism in government. A letter which he wrote to his friend Senator Breckenridge admitted as much. "It is the case of a guardian, investing the money of his ward in purchasing an important adjacent territory; and saying to him when of age, I did this for your good."

The fact was that Jefferson, knowing the sincerity of his democratic convictions, felt that he could in good conscience take liberties with the Constitution; but he did not intend to see anyone else try it. In the end, he fell back on the sense of history and innate mysticism which were the real foundations of his statesmanship. In high politics, he knew, things seldom turn out the way they are planned. Many a statesman, like Columbus, "sets out for the golden Indies and winds up in Cuba." The world panorama changes too rapidly for the human mind to maintain a grasp on the complex whole. There are always some factors in the equation which the planner has missed—so that in a sense every governmental plan is obsolescent from the moment it is applied. As with all great national leaders, feeling was more important to Jefferson than plan. The conception of a loose union of states federated under a central government with very limited powers had seemed hopeful to him in the 1780s; he used it for partisan purposes in the 1790s; but in the 1800s he recognized its impracticability. But this does not mean that he lost sight of his principles.

His essential principle of government, like Ben Franklin's, was that its only valid test is human welfare. When the right of people to life, liberty, and the pursuit of happiness was concerned Jefferson never hesitated. It was in support of this right that he held firmly to his pacifism and to his belief in representative government. His domestic and foreign strategy and tactics were those of a cautious opportunist, but only a man of powerful conviction could have maintained his central policies.

What had to be done would be done. The entire country cheered at the long-awaited news that in December 1803 Governor W. C. C. Claiborne had assumed authority over Louisiana, and the Stars and Stripes had risen over New Orleans. For a year afterward, Americans continued to drain their whisky glasses to the man who had made their country an empire, "the immortal Jefferson." When Federalists assailed the President for paying out "a stack of silver dollars three miles high" for "an enormous desert," they were answered by crushing arithmetic: America had bought a million square miles (actually 828,000) at less than three cents an acre. When Jefferson was accused of trampling on the Constitution, his critics were reminded that no drop of American blood had been shed for the acquisition of all Louisiana, and that a few years earlier Hamilton had been prepared to go to war with Spain and France in order to seize New Orleans alone. As Jefferson had guessed, his political tergiversations bothered the people not at all. Like himself, they sensed that Louisiana was part of the American destiny, and they did not much care how they got it.

3. Misadventures of Anthony Merry

In England, everyone agreed that Henry Addington had to go, everyone except Addington. For almost a year after his "victory without war" proved to be illusory, he clung precariously to his pinnacle, while Canning, Windham, and Grenville tugged at his legs. In an effort to prove himself a war leader, he donned a military uniform, but quickly took it off again after Richard Brinsley Sheridan called him "a sheep in wolf's clothing" and set England snickering. Possibly the last self-expressive act of his administration, before he yielded the reins of government to Pitt, was the selection of a new minister to the United States. The amiable young man who was given the appointment, Anthony Merry, was by disposition and conviction well-disposed to America, and eager to be an instrument of enduring peace across the Atlantic. When Addington chose him in preference to more experienced and more aggressive candidates for the post, he indulged the instinctive preference for conciliation which in all other respects had been thwarted.

Late in 1803, Merry, accompanied by his wife, came to Washington with his head full of glowing anticipations, derived from Thornton's reports, of an Anglo-American alliance against Bonaparte. He was speedily disillusioned. From the very first moment of his arrival, he was made to feel, if not unwanted, at least inconsequential. When he was presented by Secretary of State Madison to the President, he was startled to see Jefferson appear in old clothes and moccasins, which made Merry think him at first to be only some slovenly servant. At his first diplomatic dinner, he found himself and Mrs. Merry seated below the Spanish minister and his wife—a breach of protocol which greatly mortified the British couple. Merry wondered whether the treatment accorded him was a calculated insult to

England. A few days later, the question was answered. Secretary of State Madison and his famous wife, Dolly, gave a dinner at which they went to considerable lengths to ignore Mrs. Merry. This may not have been altogether a matter of policy, for the lady was something less than a social delight; Jefferson himself commented, in a letter to Monroe, that she was an undesirable and pushing character who had "disturbed our harmony extremely," and thereafter "must eat her soup at home."

Merry's bitterness grew; and it was to have painfully distorting effects on Anglo-American diplomacy. "I have now but too much reason to fear," he wrote to the Foreign Office, "what I did not at first suspect, that the marked inattention toward me of the present administration of this country has been a part of their unfriendly disposition toward his Majesty and toward the nation which I have the honor to represent." He became even more convinced of America's enmity when Madison held an official meeting with him, regarding a treaty to establish a definite boundary between Canada and the United States. A draft of the treaty had been signed by Rufus King in London, and Merry regarded the matter as nearly settled. He learned otherwise. The Senate, Madison informed him, had flatly rejected the treaty on the ground that the boundaries which it sought to establish in the West might conflict with those of the Louisiana Purchase. In his next letter to London Merry wrote that he suspected the American government of having "ideas of encroachment on his Majesty's just rights" in Canada.

Just before the year's end, Madison opened a diplomatic attack on England from another direction, by officially informing Congress that impressment of American seamen by British naval vessels had not ceased. In 1803, there had been forty-three such impressments, and twelve of the men seized had carried proof of American citizenship. Congress thereupon began to debate the possibility of protecting American sailors by force, if necessary. This worrisome news Merry sent on to London, but he had hardly done so when he was given still graver matters to write about. The United States had decided to challenge once more England's authority to set wartime rules for American commerce.

Specifically, Madison urged that, since the commercial clauses of Jay's treaty had recently expired, a new treaty be negotiated, under which the right of search-and-seizure would be sharply restricted, impressment discontinued, and American ships allowed to trade freely between the West Indies and France. Merry gave the Secretary no encouragement. That this suggestion would even be considered by his government was altogether unlikely, he said; and in a letter to London he stated his conviction that America was establishing a diplomatic basis for war with England.

To the Foreign Office, beset as it was by the cares arising from the onset of war with France, the abrupt change in America's policy was extremely disturbing. A special report prepared on Merry's dispatches viewed the outlook with foreboding. It concluded, "Everything . . . now depends on our firmness. If we yield an iota . . . we are lost."

4. Merry Conspires

In the conviction, deep-dyed by personal animosity, that war was inevitable and imminent, Merry involved his country in two major conspiracies designed to crack the American union and to leave the United States helpless against British power. At that time, early in 1804, the Cabot coterie was in a state of great agitation. In their eyes, the Louisiana purchase was a threat to the national future—by which they meant their own political influence. Jefferson's tremendous popularity was bad enough; but worse were the implications of the policy which he had established for the rule of Louisiana. It was easy to foresee that if he were not checked the vast territory would presently spawn a number of agrarian states, which would weight Congress heavily on the Republican side and reduce mercantile New England and Federalism to political impotence.

The first effort of the right-wing Federalists, when they found they could not prevent the Louisiana Purchase, had been to deny future statehood to the new regions. Since the Constitution did not provide for the rule of territories acquired by purchase, they held that Louisiana must be regarded as a colony in the European sense. Congressional approval of such a policy would have allowed Louisiana to be exploited by private interests outside the framework of federal law. But under Jefferson's tutelage, Congress put into effect a system of territorial government that gave power to governors appointed by himself, and aimed at the conversion of the territory into states section by section, as it became heavily populated.

Men like Cabot and Timothy Pickering saw only one hope of saving Federalism—secession. If Jefferson was re-elected—and they saw little hope of defeating him—let New England become a separate nation, in alliance with old England. Although Hamilton disagreed, Cabot, on February 14, 1804, wrote to Pickering that he expected such a move to be made "at some period not very remote," especially if Jefferson were to provoke war with Great Britain. A month later, the plot had advanced so far that it could no longer be kept secret. Gideon Edwards, one of Jefferson's Connecticut supporters, told the President that "Our leading Federalists are all royalist . . . If they cannot effect a change in the Administration they are resolved to divide the Union." Merry wrote to London of his hopes that the New England states would "go forward rapidly in the steps which they have already commenced toward a separation from the Southern part of the Union . . . Their plans and calculations respecting the event have

been long seriously resolved. They think . . . it will happen suddenly, yet
with quietness and the universal concurrence of the people . . . They
naturally look forward to Great Britain for support and assistance . . ."

The intrigue took on larger dimensions when, in the summer of 1804,
the state elections made it certain that Jefferson would be overwhelmingly
re-elected, with George Clinton replacing Aaron Burr as Vice-President.
Burr, then seeking to succeed Clinton as Governor of New York, was defeated, in part through Hamilton's vigorous attacks on him. The setback
was a mortal blow to his ambition. For some time he had been in secret
correspondence with Pickering and other Federalist leaders with the purpose of linking New York to New England in the secessionist conspiracy.
It was after his hopes in this respect were thwarted that he carried his rage
at Hamilton to the dueling ground, and killed him. Soon thereafter a message of startling import came to Anthony Merry, and he transmitted it to
the Foreign Office in these words: "I have just received an offer from
Mr. Burr, the actual Vice-President of the United States . . . to lend his
assistance to his Majesty's government . . . in endeavoring to effect a
separation of the western part of the United States . . ." Later he passed
along a request from Burr, who was trying to raise a private army in the
West, for the support of a British naval squadron at New Orleans and a
loan of half a million dollars. "He certainly possesses," wrote Merry, "all
the talents, energy, intrepidity and firmness which are required for such an
enterprise."

5. Pressures on Pitt

For the first time, the United States was actually engaging in power
politics under a leader of extraordinary suppleness, tenacity, and patience.
But all that Merry could see or wanted London to see for America was the
probability of secession and disaster. There is no mention in his dispatches
of the chief facts of American life in the early 1800s—the astonishing growth
of her population and her productivity. Yet these were the facts which were
rapidly changing America's role in international affairs, especially vis-à-vis
England. A quarter of a century earlier, the population of Great Britain
(excluding Ireland) had been less than eight millions in an area of roughly
90,000 square miles; that of the colonies about three millions on an Atlantic coastal strip of about 300,000 square miles. Driven by the pressures
of the industrial revolution, Great Britain's population had since risen by
25 per cent to ten million. But in the same period, America's population
had more than doubled, while her continuous land area had quintupled
and her production of wheat, corn, pork, and cattle had climbed prodi-
giously. Her merchant marine was now second only to England's, and had

in fact become the largest factor in the carrying trade of the North Atlantic. Her national psychology from being that of a colonial people was rapidly becoming imperialist.

The implications of all this for England were clear enough for those who chose to see. The increase in the economic importance of the United States had sharply altered the world's balance of power; and the foresight of Benjamin Franklin and Lord Shelburne in warning against British attempts to restrict American growth had been vindicated. Those attempts had merely produced estrangement without compensatory benefit to England. Facing a hostile France, which numbered more than twice as many inhabitants as themselves, and was self-sustaining as England was not, the British people found that in alienating American friendship they had put themselves in grave jeopardy. Their prosperity and perhaps their national survival now demanded sustained trade with a young nation which for a generation had bathed almost daily in resentment of British attitudes and practices. Only the usefulness of the two nations to each other in the face of the danger from France had thus far enabled the peace to hold in the teeth of adverse chance. Many men on both sides of the water feared, with reason, that sooner or later some unfortunate combination of circumstances would touch off an Anglo-American war, unless England voluntarily modified the arbitrary rules under which she dominated the seas.

When in 1804 William Pitt resumed his old place at the head of the British Government and shouldered the burdens of war with France, a struggle over American policy was more than he could face. Middle-aged, tired, and suffering from disorders which would soon kill him, he was only a fraction of the man he had been. To rid himself of the problem, he assigned the decision on America to the Foreign Office, as he had done in the old days. But this time he could not fall back on a Grenville, who, however haughty and stern, was an imaginative and capable diplomat. Disapproving of much that he saw in the new Pitt, and ambitious to lead the nation in his own right, Grenville had refused to serve with him again. The Prime Minister, under great pressure, allowed England's foreign affairs to be entrusted to the mediocre Lord Harrowby, who was as aggressive as Grenville but far less intelligent.

Confronted by the American question, Harrowby, who had neither knowledge nor intuition of America, fell back on Merry's reports. From these he gathered that Pickering's or Burr's conspiracy would soon split the United States, and that the Mobile Act would put her at war with Spain and France over West Florida. The trend of events, it seemed to him, made America highly vulnerable. Jefferson, in his desire for West Florida, had turned against England; then let him pay the price for his error. There would never be a better time, Harrowby thought, to challenge the United States on all issues in which her interests conflicted with England's. This was no time for delicate diplomacy. The motto of the British *Naval Register,*

> *The winds and seas are Britain's wide domain,*
> *And not a sail, but by permission, spreads,*

fully expressed Harrowby's policy. England was struggling for her life, and America would either conform to her needs or be chastised. Although on the surface Anglo-American relations in the spring of 1804 were comparatively calm, actually they stood on a point of crisis.

CHAPTER THREE

"War in Disguise"

1. *The British Case*

The impressment issue provided the first test of Anglo-American relations under Pitt. Through James Monroe, who was in London, Secretary of State Madison addressed a memorial to Harrowby on the subject, recapitulating America's many and serious grievances. His main point was that the American flag protected all sailors on American ships, regardless of their national origin. While he did not flatly deny England's right to reclaim deserters from her navy, he demanded that she desist from her search-and-seizure policy. Where the presence of British deserters on an American vessel was suspected, the matter could be settled by "a certified list of the crew," or citizenship papers, or "such other evidence . . . as would be satisfactory in a court of judication."

Despite the strong tone of this note, both Madison and Monroe recognized that England had certain strongly felt complaints which would have to be dealt with before the matter could be settled by treaty. American citizenship papers meant little. British sailors who managed to reach American ports needed only an hour to find an American ship captain looking for experienced hands, and a dollar or two would buy the deserter witnesses who would swear that he had been in America for decades. Evidence to the contrary was obligingly overlooked by the courts. One professional witness in this trade, a woman, kept a man-sized cradle in her home, and insisted on putting the citizen-to-be into it, in order to be able to swear truthfully that she had known him "from the cradle." All this was common knowledge, and the sea captains of England could hardly be blamed for maintaining that a British, Scottish, or Irish voice was a better test of actual citizenship than an official document issued by an American court. Albert Gallatin admitted that of the four thousand new hands annually absorbed by the American merchant marine, more than half were British-born, and a great many of them deserters.

To avoid the irksome question of the authenticity of papers, the British simply fell back on the ancient Roman doctrine, *nemo potest exuere patriam*, which they expressed as "Once an Englishman, always an Englishman." Under this ruling any sailor on an American vessel who was, had been, or might conceivably be English became fair game. That individual cases of injustice were frequent the British did not deny. Many a genuine

American was handed away to the terrors of England's "floating hells" on no more evidence than blue eyes or a florid complexion, and was thereafter flogged into obedience to his Majesty's officers.

The essential fact was that the contrast between a British fo'castle, British food, and the incessant cat-o'-nine-tails on the one hand, and the high wages and comparatively reasonable discipline of American vessels on the other, had created a dangerous manpower shortage in England's navy. "Dollars for shillings" was the seductive slogan of the Yankee shipowners. Some British ships that touched American ports sailed away so short of hands that they foundered because they were unable to lower sail rapidly in a storm. During 1804, an entire squadron of His Majesty's Navy, which had put into Norfolk harbor (as it was entitled to do under the Jay treaty) was unable to sail because of desertions; and its officers were deeply mortified when the erstwhile crewmen jeered at them in the streets. Lord Nelson, according to Harrowby, averred that in the years prior to 1802, no fewer than forty-two thousand sailors had illegally left His Majesty's service for American ships.

England, engaged in a mortal war, simply could not afford to let matters stand at this point. Not impressment was the root of the trouble, Harrowby told Monroe, but American refusal to aid in returning deserters. Impressment, in the Foreign Secretary's view, was simply a way of redressing a wrong which threatened England's survival. Moreover, it was a time-honored practice. For more than four hundred years England had been impressing neutral sailors in wartime. What was legality in international affairs, if not a prescriptive right established by long and undisputed usage? To ask England to give up the right of impressment was to challenge her most precious tradition, that of mastery of the seas.

Here was a conflict difficult to negotiate, but not necessarily beyond negotiation. It was thinkable that America might find ways to aid England in checking desertions if the British in turn would establish impressment rules that exempted Americans of genuine citizenship. Lord Harrowby, however, replied to Madison's overture in such a way as to rule out the possibility of fruitful discussion. His manner toward Monroe was barely short of a prolonged sneer. He harshly criticized the United States Senate for "mutilating" treaties after they had been signed, and went out of his way to convey his contempt for Madison's diplomacy, which he termed "acrimonious." In effect he said that there was nothing to negotiate.

Monroe promptly reported to Madison his belief that British policy toward America was about to change for the worse. "My most earnest advice is to look to the possibility of such a change," he wrote. Shortly thereafter, Harrowby put his official position into writing. Its essence lay in two sentences. "The pretension advanced by Mr. Madison that the American flag should protect every individual sailing under it on board a merchant vessel is too extravagant to require any serious refutation. In the exercise of the right [of impressment] . . . irregularities must undoubtedly frequently occur; but the utmost solicitude has been uniformly manifested by his Majesty's government to prevent them . . ." The most that Harrowby would concede was a meaningless promise to order British naval officers "to observe the utmost lenity in visiting ships on the high seas, and to refrain from impressments in the ports of the United States."

With this note, the impressment issue began to mushroom to its full growth, poisoning the future relations of the two nations.

2. *"Ban the Broken Voyage!"*

Pitt's central strategy, as before, was to keep the French continually pouring their blood and wealth into continental wars, without expending British lives, and while cutting off France's sea communications. Since the French merchant flag had been almost driven from the seas by English warships, trade between France and her transatlantic colonies had fallen into American hands. To stifle that trade was part of England's grand war plan. The problem was to take the necessary action without provoking American reprisals damaging to British commerce and revenues.

It was an urgent problem, and for more than wartime reasons. In the twelve years between 1790 and 1802, the number of American merchant vessels in transatlantic commerce had tripled, rising to over 1000, representing nearly 250,000 tons. It was Albert Gallatin's estimate that after 1803 the average rate of increase in American shipping was 70,000 tons per year, or 300 vessels. Meanwhile comparable British shipping had actually declined. The Stars and Stripes had become familiar in every part of the globe at the masthead of merchant vessels which were swifter, more capacious, and more daringly handled than those built in British shipyards. Restively, the mighty East India Company had watched the increase of American shipping in its waters until over 70% of India's foreign trade was carried in American bottoms. Was England to wage war against France and Spain only to let neutral America usurp her place in commerce? To stunt the growth of the American merchant marine, it seemed to many Englishmen, was essential to their future prosperity.

The most disturbing feature of the situation, from England's standpoint, was that her maritime laws were no longer effective in regulating American trade with France. Although the Rule of 1756, which had once more been put into effect, forbade American ships from making direct voyages from the French West Indies to France, there was nothing in the rule to prevent a so-called broken voyage. Without contravening the letter of the rule, an American ship could carry a West Indian cargo to an American port, un-

load it, and take on another cargo, of the same kind, which, if non-contraband, could safely be carried to France. Soon American shipowners reached
a point of confidence at which they did not even bother to unload the West
Indian cargo in a home port. Instead, the captain would be handed new
bills of lading, invoices, clearances, and passports purporting to show that
the cargo had been taken on in the United States; he would discharge any
members of the crew on whose tongues he could not rely; in their place,
he would hire new men without knowledge of the cargo's origin; and within
a few hours, he could set sail for a European port, comfortable in the
knowledge that no British cruiser had legitimate cause to seize his vessel.
The loss of time occasioned by the need to sail west before sailing east was
not a serious deterrent to this practice. In many instances, a single cargo of
West Indian sugar, sold at the high prices then prevailing on the continent,
brought the American shipowner enough profit to enable him to buy another ship.

By 1804, the so-called doctrine of the broken voyage had become the
bugaboo of the British Admiralty. Like bees to honey, the Americans
were swarming into West Indian waters. Equally aggravating to the British
was the fact that many a French and Spanish vessel, unable to sail under
their own flags, hastily became "American" by means of taking on an American captain and crew equipped with proper certificates, and hoisting the
Stars and Stripes. Napoleon was happy to encourage this arrangement; and
in spite of England's command of the seas, the French felt no shortage of
imported commodities.

For the British West Indies, the capture of the European market by
French sugar transported in American vessels was a catastrophe. The American demand for British sugar was negligible. The islands were consequently
left with only one important customer—England—for their main product—
and this at a time when they were producing the largest sugar crops in their
history. As the full magnitude of the disaster came home, officials and
planters hastily took ship for England, to lodge hot protests with Pitt's
government. Their cry was, "Ban the broken voyage!" But they were too
late. By the summer of 1804, London's warehouses were crammed with
unsalable sugar, and further shipments from the West Indies had to be
sharply curtailed; while members of Parliament who had made fortunes
in the Islands screamed their pain.

3. The Privateering Interest Speaks

British manufacturers, whose exports were suffering from the decline of
buying power in the West Indies, promptly joined in the outcry against
the broken voyage. So did shipowners whose vessels had been deprived of
profitable traffic. They reasoned that if the British colonies could not take

their goods, then war or no war, an effort had to be made to share in the French West Indian trade which the Americans were monopolizing. For this purpose, they urged Pitt, and he agreed, to establish a number of free ports in England's Caribbean colonies, where British manufactured exports could be exchanged for the sugar, molasses, and rum of the French Indies, and for American wheat and lumber, in triangular trade.

Although from Pitt's standpoint the plan was a success, to the sugar growers of Jamaica and the Bahamas the free ports were the last straws on the sagging back of their economy. For now French crops had been put into direct competition for the British market; the price of sugar collapsed to the lowest level ever seen, and a wave of bankruptcies struck the islands.

At first, Pitt showed comparatively little interest in the abject plight of the sugar planters, but there were sources nearer to him which he could not ignore. One of the mighty components of political power in England was the so-called privateering interest, which included the high command of the Royal Navy. If the West Indians had their reasons for resenting American evasions of the Rule of 1756, so did the braided admirals of England. The broken voyage, legalizing as it did the transatlantic crossings of American vessels, had cut deeply into their incomes. Where now were the scores of merchant-prizes which once had been brought in by British men-of-war or privateers, and which, when sold at auction, had brought generous rewards to the fortunate commanders of the captor ships? Many a sea lord of England had grown rich in the 1790s by hawking after American merchantmen, or by taking shares in privateers; and after the Peace of Amiens foundered, the Admiralty had naturally expected to renew the profitable pastime. And the eagerness went far beyond the uniformed officers. Rich men in all walks of life owned stock in privateering companies. England's greatest aristocrats and the King himself had speculated with success in this congenial business. To have the doctrine of the broken voyage stand between them and their proper perquisites seemed an intolerable injustice. When in the autumn of 1804 the Admiralty addressed Pitt in favor of strong measures against American trade with France, it was thinking of much more than wartime strategy.

Standing against the West Indian and privateering interests, and for good relations with the United States, was a strong group of moderates, including William Grenville and Charles James Fox. Under their caustic criticism, Pitt had to proceed carefully. To denounce the broken voyage out of hand would have stirred up a political storm. But what government cannot do in one way, it can generally do in another. Pitt's problem was solved for him when the courts of England came to his aid.

Some months earlier, an American merchant vessel, the *Essex*, had been taken into port by a British privateer. Its captain pleaded his rights under the doctrine of the broken voyage, and the case was brought before Admiralty court. In July 1805 one of England's foremost jurists, Sir William Scott, pronounced judgment on the *Essex*. Although in a previous case he had indicated that an American customhouse receipt for payment of duties was sufficient proof that the voyage had actually been broken, now he was of another mind. Customs receipts in themselves, he held, were not after all adequate proof that the owner of the ship had unloaded the West Indian cargo in an American port. The receipts generally in use showed only that the American importer of the cargo from the West Indies had posted bond to cover payment of duties at the port of entry. Such bonds might very well be fraudulent in intent, mere devices to make it appear that the ship had unloaded cargo. Unless the customs receipt showed that the duties at unloading had been paid in cash, it could not be accepted as evidence of a broken voyage. The *Essex* was accordingly confiscated.

Here was a legal cord with which to trip the Americans. With the *Essex* precedent, the majority of American vessels in the transatlantic trade became lawful prize. Long before the ominous news could reach the United States, joyful British cruisers moved in on scores of American merchantmen then heading for European ports, inspected their custom-house receipts, and put prize crews aboard them.

England roared approval. But this bold stroke, far from satisfying the anti-American elements in England, merely whetted their appetites for more. As Cobbett pointed out in the *Political Register*, Sir William Scott had not actually ruled American commerce out of European waters. What, after all, was the loss of a hundred wooden ships to America, whose shipyards could replace them in a few months? The *Essex* decision had merely required neutral shipowners to carry a different form of custom-house receipt. Presumably, if no more than this were done, Yankee ingenuity would soon be able to devise fraudulent documents which met the new requirements, and thereafter American ships would continue their trade with France. The Rule of 1756, according to Cobbett, would no longer serve England's need. What was wanted was a complete cessation of American commerce with France. If this meant war, let it be so.

4. *The Book That Shook England*

The argument over American policy had thus far been confined largely to the cabinet, courts, and Parliament. Aside from Cobbett, British journalists and their readers paid little attention to the complicated problem of the broken voyage. All at once, however, the issue became a subject of heated public discussion. The change was brought about largely by the publication in London, in July 1805, of a pamphlet of over two hundred pages, under the title of *War in Disguise, or The Frauds of the Neutral*

Flags. Seldom has the potency of the book as a factor in political history been so clearly revealed as in this instance. The author, James Stephen, was a lawyer, experienced in Admiralty work in the West Indies. He could cite many examples of cases in which American vessels had evaded the Rule of 1756 through the subterfuge of the broken voyage. More, he had scandalous evidence that powerful British interests were winking at frauds against England's interest. French ships sailing under neutral flags could, he said, insure themselves with Lloyd's against seizure, and Lloyd's, for a special fee, would secretly agree "not to dispute the neutrality of the property or avail themselves of any sentence pronouncing it to be hostile."

Stephen reminded his readers that the economic collapse of the British West Indies touched their own pocketbooks. "Mortgages and other creditors in the mother country are entitled to receive a large part of the annual returns of a West Indian plantation." The blame for the situation he placed squarely on American transgressions. Why should England hesitate to make open war on American commerce, when the United States, by the use of fraudulent papers, was waging disguised war on England? With fanatical intensity, he urged that British navigation rules be changed to eliminate the broken voyage. All movements of neutral ships between West Indian and French ports should, he held, be regarded as continuous and hence illegal voyages, regardless of the route taken. The effect of such a ruling, should it be adopted by the British Government, would be to make most of America's ocean shipping lawful prize for England's sea lords.

Stephen had facts, he wrote clearly, he hammered away at his single theme, and his book caught on. In a few months three large editions had been printed, and literate England buzzed with excited talk on the subject. The Tory press made the book its bible of policy. Other pamphlets took up the same battlecry. A leading sugar merchant, Charles Bosanquet, urged England "to avail itself of the fortunate opportunity of going to war with America—of doing that now which, sooner or later, must be done." Popular opinion, from being apathetic, began to sway heavily toward the side of the Admiralty and the West Indian interests. In Parliament speakers quoted from Stephen until the phrase "war in disguise" was as familiar as the words "cold war" were to become in the next century. Even in the United States the book had a vogue among the apologists for England. Its impact on the Congress was strong enough to cause James Madison to write a long critique in reply, and have a copy put on the desk of each senator and representative. It was a tedious piece of work, which when all was said, made a single telling point—that America must "be permitted to judge for itself" the law of the sea. "No minister . . . nor prince . . . must dictate to the Parliament of the United States."

Stephen's blunt anti-American stand at first met some opposition in England, especially from the textile industry, and Whig members of Parliament questioned whether British sea power was great enough to master both France and America. News of Nelson's great victory at Trafalgar, however, convinced most Englishmen that the last serious challenge to British might at sea had been removed. In the resulting surge of optimism, Pitt was urged not only to cut off American trade with Europe, but also to compel the European neutrals, especially Denmark, to buy British sugar, for the sake of the West Indies.

Pitt hesitated; why push all the remaining neutrals into war against England at the same time? It seemed to him advisable to await the reaction of the United States to the *Essex* decision and the subsequent ship seizures. It was possible, as he told his Cabinet, that Jefferson might declare war, in which event England could postpone action against the European neutrals while chastising the Americans.

5. *"This Is Very Embarrassing"*

In that crucial summer of 1805, of all unfortunate times, Jefferson's intelligence from England was at its most meager. Prior to the *Essex* decision, Monroe had left London on a mission to Spain, and the President's knowledge of events in England was confined to scanty clippings from the British press, mailed from London by a legation clerk. His main concern continued to be the obstinate attitude of Spain and France in the Florida matter. He was so exasperated at the French and so far from having an inkling of the new British policy that he again wrote Madison to raise the possibility of an alliance with England, "to come into force whenever a war shall take place with Spain or France." A few days later he wrote again: "I consider the cavalier conduct of Spain as evidence that France is to settle with us for her . . . and that if she can keep us insulated till peace, she [France] means to enforce by arms her will . . . We should not permit ourselves to be found off our guard and friendless." And yet again: "I think it important that England should receive an overture as early as possible, as it might prevent her from listening to terms of peace [with France]."

This, however, was a short-lived notion, killed by a new move in Paris. Early in September the President received an encouraging dispatch from John Armstrong, saying that Talleyrand had suddenly taken a new tack in the Florida matter, suggesting that the United States begin to negotiate for the territory with Napoleon, ignoring Spain. "The more you refer the decision to the Emperor," the French Foreign Minister had said, "the more certain and the easier will be the settlement." At this word, Jefferson immediately pigeonholed the project of a British alliance. Instead, he asked Congress for a secret fund, to be expended at his discretion, for the purchase of West Florida from France.

It was then that he was shaken by news of the *Essex* decision and its aftermath. His mind was so concentrated on Florida that his first concern was not how to retaliate against England, but the probable effect of the British action on Napoleon: now that there was no chance of an Anglo-American alliance, would France still consider the sale of the Floridas? He quickly learned the answer. The Emperor had just sent a new minister to the United States, the flamboyant General Louis-Marie Turreau; and Turreau shrugged the Florida matter aside. France, he said, expected that America, under this new provocation from England, would forego territorial adventures and manfully stand up to her enemy. When the President hesitated, the Frenchman was indignant at what seemed to him sheer cowardice. Jefferson was all words and no action, he wrote to Talleyrand. Sarcastically, he quoted the President's words: "We have *principles* from which we shall never depart; our people trade everywhere, and our neutrality shall be respected everywhere . . . On the other hand, we do not want war—and all this is very embarrassing."

In a talk with Madison, Turreau made another effort to promote war between America and England. "I took occasion to express to Mr. Madison," he reported to Talleyrand, "my astonishment that the schemes of aggrandizement which the United States appeared to have, should be always directed toward the south, while there were still in the north important and convenient territories such as Canada, Nova Scotia, etc. 'Doubtless!' replied the secretary, 'but the moment has not yet come. When the pear is ripe it will fall of itself!' "

Turreau drew the inference: America was willing to fight weak Spain for the Floridas, if France would not intervene; but she would not fight mighty England for Canada. Let the Emperor therefore continue to support Spain, and the Americans would not dare to strike in the Floridas or Texas. At the same time, they could hardly now resume negotiations for a British alliance. As Turreau saw it, the United States had been isolated; Jefferson had worked himself into a tight diplomatic corner, threatened on one side by England, on the other by France, and unable to come to terms with either.

6. *The President Is Affable*

The winter of 1805 brought with it further provocation from England. British frigates appeared off the American coast, so many as to suggest a blockade, and began to stop and search every merchantman within gun range, seizing many as being in violation of the *Essex* decision. American merchants rushed to protest to the President; congressmen bayed their indignation; newspapers demanded redress. The Salem *Register* voiced the prevailing sentiment when it said: "Never will neutrals be perfectly safe till free goods make free ships, or till England loses two or three great naval battles." But how the United States was to win those battles the *Register* did not say.

Although the President could not ignore the public clamor, he was determined not to yield to it. America was in no position to fight England—and an alliance with the British navy might yet turn out to be essential to America's security. Accordingly, Jefferson decided to give the appearance of resisting England, while actually preserving his freedom of maneuver. At his request, Congress passed a Non-Importation Act, barring English goods from American ports; but he insisted on suspending operation of the act for nine months, until he could observe the trend of events. The country, to its astonishment, saw that not a sword, not even a whip, but an olive branch was in the President's hand. Calling in the suspicious Anthony Merry for a talk, he dazed the Englishman by his affability. Incredulously, Merry wrote to London that Jefferson had said nothing about the ship seizures, or the British cruisers outside of New York Harbor. On the contrary, he seemed to have in mind some form of co-operation with the British Navy in the event of French landings in the Floridas.

The Floridas, always the Floridas. Members of Congress, like Merry, found it hard to comprehend Jefferson's preoccupation with Spanish territory, with British cruisers seizing ships and impressing sailors a few miles off shore. When he insisted on having two million dollars with which to negotiate with Napoleon, some representatives, led by John Randolph, protested the move as dishonorable; for had not Congress's earlier law already claimed the Floridas as part of the United States? A new outcry against his "lack of principle" left the President unmoved. There was nothing he enjoyed so much as an interesting combination on the diplomatic chessboard. With a wink to Pitt and a nod to Napoleon, he was trying to establish a bargaining position with both sides.

The first sixty days of 1806 brought news which, as Jefferson's supporters saw it, justified all his backing and filling. At Ulm and Austerlitz, the Third Coalition had collapsed. Napoleon was master of Europe. The news had broken Pitt's fragile health, and with "the Austerlitz look" on his gray face he had declined to his death a few weeks thereafter. Grenville was the new Prime Minister, supported by a comparatively liberal coalition of Whigs and Tories. Napoleon's friend, Charles James Fox, had become Foreign Secretary. With this abrupt change, there opened up once more the prospect of a peaceful settlement between England and America.

CHAPTER FOUR

Passive Resistance

1. "Highly for the Interest of Our Country . . ."

James Monroe, in 1806, was not a happy man. His diplomatic career in the past two years had been a long series of rebuffs, from England, from France, from Spain. He was hungry for a resounding success, not only because America needed it, but perhaps even more because he needed it. This was no time for him to be overlooked or disregarded by his countrymen. Another presidential election was only two years away; Jefferson was unlikely to run again, and Madison, although the President's heir-presumptive, was far from being an inspiring figure. Monroe's own popularity in the South and West was considerable. Although his was a rather flat and mediocre mind, it was coupled with extraordinary energy and determination, and average men were attracted to him far more than to the more intellectual Madison. If he could come back to the United States bearing a triumph, who could foresee how the popular vote would go in 1808? Even the Federalists would vote for the man who brought them peaceful trade with England.

The only foundation on which this dream might materialize was a new treaty with England—and not another Jay's treaty, but one which gave due recognition to America's increased maritime importance. Was such a treaty possible? The advent of Fox to the Foreign Office raised Monroe's hopes, and he wrote to Madison that the new minister "put me more at my ease than . . . any person in office since I have been in England."

A negotiation for a new treaty slowly took shape. Its difficulties were multiplied for Monroe by instructions from Madison which suggested that the Secretary of State was well aware of Monroe's presidential ambitions, and was anxious to eliminate a rival. The conditions imposed by Madison for a treaty were such as England, even with the well-disposed Fox as negotiator, could never accept. Monroe was told that the British government must give up the practice of impressment, restore American trade with the British West Indies, and pay indemnity for ship seizures subsequent to the *Essex* decision. More, he was not to be allowed to conduct the negotiation single-handed. The rising lawyer and statesman, William Pinkney of Maryland, was designated to join Monroe in London. Credit for a treaty, if there were to be one, would be shared.

With the cards stacked against them, Monroe and Pinkney nevertheless plunged hopefully into the game. They felt that, in the final test, the President would allow them far more discretion than Madison's instructions suggested. Unless a serviceable treaty could be made with England, America was bound to suffer heavily. Already her ships were being denied access to European ports. At Napoleon's orders, Prussia had closed her coast to British imports, and England had retaliated by establishing a partial blockade of France. Maritime insurance rates were soaring, and many American businessmen were refusing to risk shipments abroad until their neutral rights at sea were clarified. New England was especially hard hit by declining trade, and the federal Treasury was losing revenue. In these circumstances, Jefferson was bound to want a treaty: so the two envoys believed.

Their hopes were nearly, but not quite dashed when in early autumn Fox suddenly died, and his place was taken by Lord Howick, capable enough, but a harder man. Where Fox had given some encouragement on the matter of impressment, Howick flatly insisted that it be excluded from the treaty. He would consent to nothing more than a separate memorandum, promising that the British Government would exercise great care not to impress American citizens. As for Madison's other conditions, they were even more flatly rejected. England refused to consider payment of indemnities for ship seizures; and in Howick's draft of the treaty, American trade with the West Indies became almost wholly subject to England's will.

Monroe and Pinkney realized that if they signed such a treaty its chances of ratification were slight. But what, they must have asked themselves, had they to lose by signing? In terms of American politics, their status would be improved if they put the onus of rejection on the President instead of taking it on themselves. In this spirit, early in December they affixed their signatures to the discouraging document. Years later Monroe explained that under the circumstances "it seemed to me to be highly for the interest of our country . . . to get out of the general scrape on the best terms we could . . . The treaty was an honorable and advantageous adjustment with England."

2. A Nudge from Napoleon

Long before the Monroe-Pinkney treaty reached America, it was obsolete, wrecked by a curious turn of events centering in Germany. Prior to Austerlitz, in a pretty stroke of diplomacy, Napoleon had persuaded the Hohenzollerns of Prussia to remain out of the coalition against him by giving them, among other benefits, the Electorate of Hanover, long a fief of the British crown, and which his troops had occupied. The loss weighed heavily on the minds of Whitehall, but they knew a trick or two of their own. A strict blockade of Hanover was imposed; but thereafter, an informal hint went to Napoleon from his old friend Fox to the effect that a general peace might be possible if Hanover were restored to England. Interested, Napoleon explored the possibility, and secret notes on the subject were exchanged. Fox's death knocked the props out from under this flimsy negotiation; the Emperor lost hope that British diplomacy would compromise, and went on to blazing victory under the sun of Austerlitz. But the consequences of the abortive bid for peace had only begun to reveal themselves. Grenville, an old hand at the great game, saw that he could gain a tactical advantage by letting Prussia know what Napoleon had been up to. Events quickly verified his judgment. When reports of the secret negotiation for Hanover came to Frederick William III of Prussia, he concluded that France intended to take back her bribe, and dispatched an indignant protest to Paris. At first, Napoleon took the matter rather lightly. Even word that Prussia was conscripting troops for her strong army did not seriously disturb him. A diplomatic warning to Berlin, he felt, would suffice to bring Frederick William to his senses. To Talleyrand he wrote, "Prussia must disarm in a mood of . . . reassurance touched by fear. That is the only language she understands." Soon afterward, however, he learned that Grenville had agreed to send a large sum of gold to Prussia on condition that she join in the next assault on France. The Emperor waited no longer. In September 1806 he poised his armies in the Rhineland; early in October he overran Germany; on October 12, he gave Frederick William a last chance to avoid disaster; on October 13, he wrote to the Empress Josephine, "The poor King of Prussia . . . I am sorry for him—he is a good fellow"; on October 15, at Jena, as he himself put it, he "executed some remarkable maneuvers . . . and brought off a great victory." A few days later, his triumphant army was in Berlin.

His military operations had not prevented him from closely following events in Hanover and London. The British blockade was causing serious discontent in northwest Germany, and reports of the progress of the Anglo-American talks made disagreeable reading. The Emperor feared that England, by assurances of trade, might yet be able to inveigle the United States into some form of alliance, to the detriment of France's strategic position. During his Berlin sojourn, he considered ways and means to get in the first blow and damage Anglo-American relations beyond hope of a treaty, while replying at the same time to the blockade. These lines of thought linked to a larger conception then taking form in his mind of an all-European economic system which, by totally excluding England's ships and merchandise, would bring the British to their knees. The device on which he finally decided was the terse document known as the Berlin Decree, promulgated in November 1806, and which read: "The British Isles are declared to be in a state of blockade. All commerce or intercourse with the said Isles is strictly forbidden . . . All the manufactures of that country, or its colonies, wherever found, are to be regarded as lawful prizes."

Although Napoleon could not enforce this "paper blockade" at sea, it struck at the very roots of America's position as a neutral. The entire north coast of Germany was by then under French control, as well as the Netherlands and Spain. Napoleon was saying to America and other neutrals that if their ships dared to trade with England, and subsequently entered continental ports between Seville and Hamburg, they would be liable to seizure.

For Grenville, the Berlin Decree was a shock, creating an ugly problem. On the one hand, there was something to be said for the Monroe treaty. Next to England, the United States had become the most important commercial nation in the world. A large proportion of British exports to the continent was then being carried by American vessels, and a treaty tying the two nations closer together had obvious advantages for England. On the other hand, it would not do to permit neutrals, including America, to accept the Berlin Decree and bypass England for trade with France. Failure by England to retaliate in kind against the Berlin Decree, regardless of the effect on neutrals, would be considered everywhere to be a sign of weakness.

Preferring to be gored by the smaller horn of the dilemma, Grenville promptly advised Monroe that while the new treaty would be signed, it would not be ratified unless Jefferson repudiated the Berlin Decree. This being said, the Prime Minister did not even wait for a reply from Washington. A few days later, the British Cabinet revived the old mechanism of the Order in Council, and on the ground that Napoleon's action had given England "an unquestionable right of retaliation," announced that no neutral vessel "shall be permitted to trade from one port to another" on coasts in the possession of France and her allies. This was in January 1807.

Monroe was appalled. Under this ruling, the American merchant could no longer put down part of his cargo at one place, part in another, or take advantage of variations in price between different localities. Every cargo brought to a single French-controlled port would require a separate transatlantic crossing. Not many shippers could hope to profit in the face of doubled transportation costs. As the Essex decision a year earlier had enabled Pitt to seize a great many neutral ships—over a hundred—so Grenville's Order in Council would trap additional scores of American vessels then heading unawares for Europe. As Napoleon had foreseen, England, in striking against Napoleon, had done a much greater injury to America and had made a dead letter of the Monroe treaty.

3. *The Press Is Confused*

In February 1807 newspapers in New York and Boston were freely predicting that the Monroe-Pinkney treaty, upon its arrival, would be submitted to the Senate and ratified. Even impressment was not regarded as an insuperable obstacle. British seizures of American seamen would certainly not become more numerous as the result of a treaty, and they might be lessened; so why should this issue be allowed to block an agreement on other points? The optimism of the pro-British element rose further with the first reports of the Berlin Decree. To many, an American rapprochement with England seemed the only possible answer to Napoleon. The rumor was widespread that Jefferson had finally turned his back on France, for the Emperor's refusal to agree to the sale of West Florida had made the President look a little foolish. He had got the Congress to grant millions for the purchase; to please Napoleon he had gone so far as to suspend American trade with the republic of Santo Domingo—an action which had no excuse in justice or economics, and which warped American policy out of its independent pattern—only to have the Florida negotiation wither on the diplomatic vine. Washington noted that the President was displaying marked coolness toward the Emperor's envoy, General Turreau, and for the second time, was showering attentions on a British minister. This was the easier for him, since the unfortunate Merry had been recalled and the man who had replaced him, David Montague Erskine, was agreeable, friendly, and liberal by conviction.

The arrival of the Monroe-Pinkney treaty brought matters to a head. Erskine received his copy before the ship carrying the official script made port; and he rushed hopefully with it to Madison's office. To his amazement, the Secretary was cool and indifferent; and that same night Jefferson startled the country by saying that, since the treaty failed to deal with impressment, he would not call the Senate to consider it. The first howl of Federalist protest had hardly been voiced, when another ship arrived with news of the British Order in Council. Jefferson's position now appeared to be wholly justified. If France had violated the rights of the United States, so had England. There was no more reason to make a treaty with one than with the other.

Now confused journalists expected that the President would put the suspended Non-Importation Act into effect, as a reprisal against England. But here again they were wrong. He still hoped, Jefferson somewhat vaguely told the country, for good relations with the British. And this in spite of the fact that the relatively well-disposed Grenville-Howick ministry had fallen, and been replaced by a group of Tories who were known to accept Stephen's "war in disguise" as the basis of their American policy. The dominant man of the government was the wealthy lawyer Spencer Perceval, arch-representative of the landed gentry, and a man whose mind was as narrow as it was tough; while the proud, gifted, intractable George Canning controlled foreign affairs.

Perceval's selection, one of the last acts of George III before his collapse into permanent insanity, promised nothing but trouble for America. He had hardly taken office when a leading Tory newspaper, London's *Morning Post* openly urged war with the United States, on the ground that "a war of a very few months, without creating to us the expense of a single additional ship, would be sufficient to convince her of her folly by a necessary chastisement of her insolence and audacity." This was duly reported to the President by Monroe, with the comment that England's "shipowners, the navy, the East and West India merchants and certain political characters of great consideration in the State" were seeking a war with the United States. "So powerful is this combination," Monroe added, that no concession was to be hoped for from them, except "what may be extorted by necessity."

4. "According to the Customs . . . of Civilized Nations"

If there was any doubt as to the meaning for America of the change in the British attitude, it was speedily dispelled. In March, 1807, officers of British men-of-war at anchor in Chesapeake Bay were incensed by an unparalleled wave of desertions among their crews, and even more by a report that four of the deserters had enlisted on an American frigate, *Chesapeake*, which was about to sail for the Mediterranean. A report went northward to Halifax, Nova Scotia, where the admiral in command of England's western fleet, George Berkeley, had his command station. Within a few weeks, the fifty-two gun frigate *Leopard* appeared off Norfolk, carrying orders for all British warships in American waters: find the *Chesapeake*, "show the captain of her this order . . . search his ship for the deserters . . . according to the customs and usage of civilized nations."

With reasonable luck, the *Chesapeake*, carrying forty guns, and then being fitted out for a year's voyage, would have been far out in the Atlantic before the *Leopard* arrived off Hampton Roads, but a month-long delay in the navy yard had prevented her from hoisting sail. Later courts-martial even brought out a suspicion that the incredible inefficiency of the navy yard personnel may not have been entirely accidental. However this may have been, on June 22, 1807, the ship was finally on its way, with a sunny day and a fresh wind. Her crew numbered 375; and on board her was the commodore of the squadron to which she was attached, Captain James Barron. When he sat down to his midday meal, he noticed that the *Leopard* was tacking in his wake, a mile away, but saw no reason for alarm.

Later that afternoon, the British frigate came in close enough to hail Barron, and her commander, Captain Humphreys, called that she had dispatches for him. Barron noticed that the gun ports of the *Leopard* were open, but attributed this to the heat of the day. To call his crew to stations, as navy rules required under such circumstances, seemed absurd. When he gave the order to heave to and accept a boarding party, he was prepared to extend every courtesy to officers of the *Leopard*. To his astonishment, a junior British officer handed him a note requesting him to deliver to the *Leopard* deserters from British warships believed to be among his crew.

That there were Americans on board who had deserted from the British Navy, Barron was aware; and also one deserter of British citizenship. There was no precedent, however, for taking deserters from American men-of-war; only merchant ships had been subjected to this indignity. Barron did not expect a search to be made. Taking advantage of a technicality in the British note, he wrote in reply an equivocal denial that he had the men in question with him. His hope was that the *Leopard* would not press the matter, but when the British party left he became uneasy and ordered the *Chesapeake*'s gun crew to their stations. Everything now depended on the time at his disposal. Although the *Leopard* carried the greater number of guns, the *Chesapeake*'s were heavier, and in a state of equal readiness she would have been nearly a match for the British frigate. But she was given no chance to prepare. Humphreys called over to Barron that "you must be aware of the necessity I am under," and Barron could see the *Leopard*'s crew take up battle stations at their ready guns. Trying to delay the action, he shouted through his trumpet "I do not understand what you say," but the only reply was a cannon ball across his bow. Then, courtesies dispensed with, the *Leopard* fired her broadside of solid shot and grape point-blank into the *Chesapeake* at a distance of less than two hundred feet, making a shambles of her deck.

The *Chesapeake*'s crew worked desperately at their guns, but deficiencies in training and equipment, and especially the lack of firing matches, put them at a hopeless disadvantage. Two more broadsides were poured in on them without a return of fire, killing three men, wounding eighteen, and shattering the ship's masts. Barron, who kept his head in spite of a bad wound, realized that he had to surrender or be sunk, and as a reasonable human being, he struck his colors. It was at this moment, while the flag was being hauled down, that Third Lieutenant Allen of the *Chesapeake* found a place in history. Rushing to ship's galley, he picked up a live coal in his bare hands, carried it to a loaded gun, and managed to get off a single shot which struck the *Leopard*'s hull—the only shot fired by the Americans in the entire battle.

When the British sent over a search party which seized three American deserters, and the one Englishman to whom they might legitimately have laid claim, Barron had the presence of mind to try at once to establish the diplomatic status of the assault. A note from him to the British captain offered to surrender the *Chesapeake* as a prize of war. But Humphreys was equally astute; in a formal reply he conveyed that there was no question of war; he had merely carried out his instructions; he could not consider the American frigate as his prize.

With rage in the heart of every man on board, the *Chesapeake* crept back to Norfolk. Her arrival marked the beginning of an almost irresistible call to the President from the people to take up arms for the nation's honor. "Vengeance!" was the cry of the press. "Such a thirst for revenge," wrote the Washington *Federalist*, had never been witnessed before. The South and West saw scenes of violence as men organized militia forces for expected action against England. New England was more cautious, but even in Boston explosive mass meetings forced Federalist leaders to pledge co-operation to Jefferson if war should come. Only the unshakable Essex Junto, Cabot, Pickering, and their friends, dared to voice the opinion that Admiral Berkeley's order to take deserters from the *Chesapeake* had been justified.

Heartened by the nation's unusual unity, the President said with satisfaction that the British had "touched a chord which vibrates in every heart." "Now then is the time to settle the old and the new." This sounded militant enough, but his official attitude, when he finally expressed it, was so mild as to shock the country. In a cautious proclamation, he told the people that "honorable reparation of the wrong that had been done" would be demanded from England, and that British warships would be denied the hospitality of American harbors. Monroe had been instructed to insist on official disavowal of the *Leopard*'s action, on the return of the Americans taken from the *Chesapeake*, and on the recall and punishment of Admiral Berkeley. Beyond these steps, another demand would be made on England to abandon the policy of impressment.

These merely diplomatic gestures failed to satisfy many of Jefferson's own followers. What was a mere proclamation in the face of *Leopard*'s guns? Surely anything less than ultimatum was weak and dishonorable. The rising young Tennessee soldier and politician, Andrew Jackson, who had viewed with disgust the recent trial of Aaron Burr on charges of high treason, denounced the Administration to a cheering crowd, with the satirical cry: "Millions to persecute an American; not a cent to resist England!" Even members of Jefferson's Cabinet prodded him toward war, notably Albert Gallatin, and the Secretary of the Navy, Robert Smith. Without result. While seeming to move with the tide of belligerence, the President was actually treading water in the opposite direction. It soon became clear that no overt reprisals would be taken until a reply arrived from Monroe.

5. A Hint from Copenhagen

In London, Monroe, with his customary optimism and energy, set about to obtain the required "honorable reparation" from the Tory ministry. At first he found the Secretary for Foreign Affairs, George Canning, surprisingly reasonable. "If the British officers should prove to have been culpable," said Canning, "the most prompt and effectual reparation shall be afforded to the government of the United States." Admiral Berkeley would be recalled from Halifax. A special envoy would be sent to America to discuss the problem of reparation. In a second talk, however, the Foreign Secretary's tone roughened. Although he was not at all convinced that the fault of the unfortunate *Chesapeake* affair lay with the *Leopard,* the question of reparation would be explored. But he could not comprehend why Jefferson had linked the question of impressment to his demand for reparation, thus befogging the central issue. Monroe was equally baffled. It did not occur to either of them that obfuscation may have been the President's purpose. A simple demand for reparation, he feared, would bring only a haughty British rejection, and so war. He conveyed as much to David Erskine, who eventually reported to Canning "that if the point of honor was to be taken into consideration by itself, he [Jefferson] foresaw greater difficulties in the way of an amicable adjustment of it." By introducing the demand for a cessation of impressment, with all its ramifications, Jefferson provided Canning with a reason to negotiate; and to gain time was his own objective.

The President had no expectation that England would yield on the impressment issue. That the forcible enlistment of American citizens into England's navy was unjust was evident enough; but he was far too experienced to expect a great power voluntarily to sacrifice its interests for the sake of an abstract conception of justice. He realized, too, that a weak nation which is always determined to fight for what it considers its just rights is likely to be continuously at war, and soon ruined—that without a supranational authority to decide where coercion leaves off and justice begins, fair play among the nations would always be a rarity. It made no difference that England's desertion problem was not actually America's fault—that it grew fundamentally out of an inhuman tradition of naval discipline and pay. To expect the British to change these conditions overnight, and especially in a time of war crisis, would have been totally unrealistic. Although American diplomacy could not afford to accept the principle of impressment, neither could it intelligently insist that embattled England let the navy on which she depended for survival go to rot. What Jefferson sought was not a surrender by England on impressment, but some indication of willingness to adjust the controversy.

But even this modest hope was quickly exploded. The first British reply
to his note of protest came not by way of the Foreign Office, but through
the London newspapers of early September 1807. A report from the Admiralty gave the world an example of what America might expect if she
irritated England too far. The city of Copenhagen had been shattered by
the British Navy. The reason? Simply the determination of England not to
let Napoleon dominate Danish trade. The Emperor, through the treaty of
Tilsit with Czar Alexander, had managed to close the ports of Russia to
English ships, so that the only significant coast left open for British trade
in northern Europe was the Danish peninsula. Napoleon's strategy now
demanded that Denmark be linked to his continental system. Not believing that England could forestall him, he relied upon an ultimatum to
compel the helpless Prince Regent of Denmark to give up his neutrality:
"Denmark must declare war upon her [England] or I will declare war on
Denmark." Just as the Prince seemed ready to yield, a mighty British
fleet appeared off Copenhagen, for the second time in six years. A contemptuous British diplomat sought out the Prince Regent in his palace and
carefully insulted him in order to eliminate any possibility of compromise;
troops and cannon were put ashore, and a bombardment of the helpless
city began by land and sea. Four days later, half of Copenhagen was a
smoking ruin, with two thousand dead. The surrender of the Danish fleet
followed, and the Prince's resistance to British policy collapsed. Napoleon
had delayed too long. The episode, as Spencer Perceval happily told Parliament, was "regrettable" but "unavoidable."

The implications of the sudden and brutal assault on a neutral country
were not lost on Jefferson. America's navy and coastal batteries were no
more a match for England than Denmark's had been. After Copenhagen,
the word "war" opened up visions of the destruction of New York, Philadelphia, Washington. No city on the American seaboard would be safe if the
British navy should be given its way.

Jefferson remained quiescent, hoping that the thundercloud of the
Chesapeake affair would dissipate without lightning. And it did. The rage
in American hearts gradually spent itself in words, and was replaced by a
feeling of disgusted resignation. In retrospect, the insult to the *Chesapeake*,
like that of the XYZ affair, did not seem to justify a war.

6. A Matter of Honor

Europeans accustomed to monarchs quick to cover blots on their
'scutcheons with the blood of their peoples were incredulous at the cheek-
turning of Jefferson and his countrymen. America, they thought, made a
sorry spectacle of crass materialism and dishonorable meekness. General
Turreau wrote to Talleyrand that the United States was so corrupted by

"sordid avarice" that it would "endure every kind of humiliation." Even American newspapers formerly friendly to the President reproached him for failure to restore the nation's honor. Jefferson remained unmoved. As a student of history and of philosophy, he knew that the definition of honor poses a delicate metaphysical problem. In statesmanship, especially, it is not easy to decide where the honor of a nation, for which a leader may conceivably be justified in asking men to lay down their lives, begins, and where the needs of a passing administration, for which few would die if they knew what they were doing, leaves off. The President's own experience had taught him that pious talk about the nation's honor is often only a shining mask for a rusty partisan policy. As a party leader, he himself had urged George Washington and Congress to reject Jay's Treaty for the sake of honor, even at the price of war. It was not an episode of which he could in retrospect be proud.

Struggling young America could not afford the luxury of sensitive pride; and the President knew how rapidly wounded honor can heal with time. During the XYZ affair, a single Frenchman's offensive behavior, magnified by the Federalist press, had been taken by many Americans as challenging their honor to the point of war. But ten years later most citizens could hardly remember what the trouble had been about. With this precedent, Jefferson felt secure in refusing to allow the popular sentiments of the day to define honor for him. Not that he was cynical. He understood well that honor, in terms of genuine self-respect, must be defended; that a sense of civic disgrace makes life less satisfying, less worth living for everyone with a feeling for his country. But he made a distinction between self-respect and pride; and he did not believe that a nation was disgraced by testing every possibility for the preservation of peace. If the war had been for national survival, he would have felt no hesitation in calling on Americans to fight and die, if necessary. Survival, however, was not in question. He did not think himself justified in subjecting his young and democratic country to a destructive war in order to preserve an old and essentially monarchical concept of national honor. Screams for "revenge" from feckless journalists eager to excite their readers struck him as childish. The affair of the *Chesapeake* was only a sympton of an underlying international disorder which most Americans did not even begin to comprehend. Without a more compelling reason, it was better, the President thought, to let the people feel temporarily humiliated, than to submit them to death, mutilation, and sorrow. Knowing as he did that the question of honor is essentially a moral question, and that international diplomacy, underneath its pretenses, is a thoroughly amoral business, he could only decide for peace. He preferred to be accused of cowardice than to see the nation hurt in an avoidable war. He did not have to prove his courage to himself at the people's expense. It was his opinion that in the long run most Americans would not think the worse of him for trying again, and yet again, to preserve peace.

Beyond the question of honor, the President believed that a weak America at peace in 1807 promised a strong America capable of victory against any opponent in the future. "For twenty years to come," he wrote to Du Pont de Nemours, "we should consider peace as the *summum bonum* of our country. At the end of that time we shall be twenty millions in number and forty in energy, when enountering the starved and rickety paupers and dwarfs of English workshops." Time favored America; it was "the most precious of all things to us."

7. *The Canning Style*

Most Americans in 1807 believed that George Canning was intent on provoking and humiliating the United States. This was a misconception. Canning, like James Stephen, genuinely believed that for more than a decade Americans had been taking an unfair advantage of England's distress. He was in consequence disposed to make no concessions to the former colonials, and he took pleasure in exercising his literary style, which was dagger-sharp, at their expense. It was never easy for him to resist a brilliant thrust, even when it was certain to make trouble. For all that, he was no warmonger. Younger than most of the men around him—he was then thirty-seven—Canning showed subtlety in restraining anti-Americans of the tough Perceval-Sheffield-Cobbett school. The caustic phrases which he constantly coined and which annoyed Americans—"*Republican* and *fool* are synonymous"—were a factor in his power to keep England's superpatriots in check. Under the cover of his flashing verbal attack, the actual content of his diplomacy was essentially peaceable. He acted as a brake on right-wing Tories and showed himself unmistakably for peace when he retained the soft-spoken David Erskine as his minister in Washington. Erskine was known to share the opinions of his father, Lord Erskine, a noted Whig leader who had made friendship with America the keystone of his policy. Yet Canning prevented Perceval from pushing young Erskine aside for a Tory fist-pounder. For all his sarcastic style, the Foreign Secretary knew the significance of tone in word-of-mouth diplomacy; and he had a genuine belief in the power of competent diplomacy to avert war. Considering the obstacles in his way, he succeeded remarkably well in keeping Anglo-American relations in a fluid state, against all the pressures then tending to crystallize them into a declaration of war.

The slightest move on his part to conciliate the Americans brought a storm on his head. His promise to Monroe that Admiral Berkeley would be recalled proved especially dangerous to him. The Tory press rose in its wrath, and the *Morning Post*, then the most influential newspaper in the kingdom, demanded that he flatly refuse reparation of any kind to the Americans, and not suffer England's "proud sovereignty of the ocean to be mutilated by any invasion of its just rights." Under heavy attack, Canning had no choice but to resign or concede something to Tory sentiment. While he would not change his stand on the recall of Berkeley, the impressment issue provided an opportunity to prove his patriotism, and gave the British lion a chance to roar. James Monroe was then about to return to the United States, leaving William Pinkney in his place. Calling Monroe to the Foreign Office, Canning asked him to inform the President that impressment could not be discussed in conjunction with the *Chesapeake*. Immediately thereafter he prepared a proclamation, which King George signed, and which instructed naval officers to intensify the search for, and seizure of natural-born British subjects serving on foreign merchant vessels. In case the foreign ship refused to give up the men in question, the matter was to be pursued through diplomatic channels. The British people took this order to be in some sense a retroactive justification of Admiral Berkeley, and Canning's popularity rose again. It was still further enhanced when he did not oppose the views of the Admiralty on a suitable punishment for the Admiral. Berkeley was simply assigned to another command—which turned out to be more important than the one he had left. Tory politicians, smacking their thighs over this rebuff to Jefferson, joyfully predicted that still stronger measures would soon be taken against the Americans, who were obviously afraid to fight. Too many American ships were still trading with Europe, in spite of the British blockade; others were actively supplying the French West Indies; had not the time come to drive them altogether from the seas?

8. Experiment in Peace-Diplomacy

Early in December 1807, before he knew of the new British proclamation and Berkeley's promotion, Jefferson received word from William Pinkney that Canning's special envoy, George Rose, would soon arrive in America. The chances of extracting a suitable agreement from Rose, the President felt, would be greatly strengthened by an intimation of America's firmness of purpose. The moment had come to make use of the Non-Importation Act which Congress had passed and suspended at his request a year earlier. At a signal from Jefferson, on December 14, 1807, the act went into effect. It would be a body blow, he thought, to British exporters of textiles, clothing, leather, silk, glassware, whisky, and many another product; and the President hoped that American businessmen would be encouraged to set up factories for such products, thus making the economy of the United States less dependent on England.

He had no sooner taken this step than news came of the King's proclamation on impressment of sailors from neutral warships. There was no way for him to know that the British move had been made largely for home consumption, to save Canning's political skin. It seemed to him to call for stern reprisal; but having already put the Non-Importation Act into effect, he was in the position of a soldier who has used the last bullet in his belt.

At this moment, Monroe arrived, with clippings from British newspapers predicting a new Order in Council by England to cut off American commerce with France and her colonies. Jefferson realized that such an order, if it resulted in the seizure of more American shipping, would almost certainly compel the war which he desperately wished to avoid. Without delay, he called a special meeting of his Cabinet, and put a question to them: what step should be recommended to the Congress to serve both as an answer to the impressment proclamation and as a safeguard for American shipping? He himself had no doubt of the right move—an embargo, which would prohibit the export of any goods to a foreign country from the United States, by land or by sea. He saw this action as yielding two major benefits. It would inflict heavy punishment on England, whose textile mills had become increasingly dependent on American cotton, and whose West Indian colonies needed American foodstuffs and lumber. It would prevent the seizure of America's merchant ships under the expected new Order in Council. The central purpose of the measure, as Jefferson later wrote, was "to avoid a war with England, unless forced by a situation more losing than war itself . . . I did believe we could coerce her to justice by peaceable means."

There was, Jefferson pointed out to the Cabinet, an encouraging precedent. When war had threatened with England in 1794, Congress had imposed an embargo for thirty days; and the war had been averted. This time, however, the President made no mention of a time limit, a fact which greatly alarmed one member of his Cabinet, and the most acute, Albert Gallatin. In a sharp and memorable letter to Jefferson, Gallatin expressed serious doubts that the embargo would succeed, and said that he thought a war would be better. "Government prohibitions do always more mischief than had been calculated." It was hazardous, he warned, for a statesman "to regulate the concerns of individuals, as if he could do it better than themselves." The embargo he described as "a doubtful policy, and hastily adopted." England would not treat America better because of it. Put it into effect if you must, he conveyed, but only for a short time, and leave the way open for a retraction.

But the President was by now all eagerness to try what he felt would be a great experiment in peace-diplomacy. Rejecting Gallatin's advice, he urged Congress to pass the required legislation without delay. "Our merchandise, our vessels and our seamen are threatened on the high seas . . . I deem it my duty to recommend . . . an immediate inhibition of the departure of our vessels from the ports of the United States." Congress, in secret session, became the scene of violent debate, as mercantile interests in New England and New York frantically fought the embargo, while the South and West, as usual, strongly supported Jefferson. In the end, large majorities in both houses constituted an extraordinary personal triumph for the President. He was, in fact, at the apogee of his power. Even Federalist Senator John Quincy Adams, of Massachusetts, son of the former President, voted for the embargo, solely on the ground that the President wished it. Through sheer force of personality, Jefferson was able to flatten American foreign policy to the shape of peaceful coercion, as in the West Florida matter he had pressed it into an imperialistic mold.

Part of Jefferson's hold on the Congress at this critical moment stemmed from the common feeling that he was unique among statesmen. When he spoke of his "passion for peace," people realized, he was not merely expressing a pious sentiment, to which most politicians gave lip service. With him the preservation of peace was more than a vision of the Holy Grail; it was a firm policy. He not only wanted peace, but he believed that he knew how to get it. His idea of peace through embargo startled and impressed Americans in his day much as Mahatma Gandhi's conception of passive resistance through boycott touched India's imagination in the next century. With both men, passivity went only so far as a rejection of physical violence as an element of resistance. In economic and propagandistic terms, both were highly aggressive in opposing the enemy, believing that shrewd application of economic penalties could dampen England's warlike spirit faster than gunfire.

CHAPTER FIVE

"Ograbme"

1. The President Is Praised

Spencer Perceval, England's Chancellor of the Exchequer and the voice of right-wing Toryism, was a man of few ideas, but when he had one, he fought for it. His great idea, as the year 1807 neared its end, was to make James Stephen's "war in disguise" the basis of British policy toward America. In the late autumn of 1807, before the embargo, he determined to compel the Americans to submit once and for all to British power, if not through war, then through militant diplomacy. After consulting with Stephen, and with committees of British merchants and ship owners, he decided on an Order in Council remarkable for its impudent and shrugging rejection of the former principles of British policy. Perceval proposed nothing less than a scheme under which American ships could trade with Europe only as licensed by the British government. This was the order of which Monroe had heard vague rumors before he sailed for America, and which Jefferson had anticipated in the embargo.

The coast of Europe, Perceval's order stated, was declared to be in a state of blockade from Trieste to Copenhagen. No neutral ship might enter a port within Napoleon's empire unless it had cleared from a British port, and had received an official permit, after paying a fee of sixteen guineas per ship. Any vessel attempting to violate the order would be regarded as lawful prize for British warships and privateers.

Previous British orders had made some obeisance to tradition, as embodied in the Rule of 1756, or in the ancient rights of wartime blockade. Perceval, however, dispensed with precedent. The message to America implicit in his order was: fight, or yield us a share of your profits in trade with the enemy. George Canning, reluctant to associate himself with so obvious a piece of diplomatic blackmail, was careful to make it clear that the order was not his work, but he did not oppose it, and in November 1807, it was put into effect.

When news of the order reached Napoleon, who was then in Milan, far from being disturbed, he was pleased. For some months he had been wrestling with the knotty problem of neutral shipping. It was common knowledge that American ships were carrying British goods into European ports in spite of his Berlin Decree, and jeopardizing his Continental System. He had to be a little careful with the Americans, if he was eventually to

bring them to his side against England; but now, under the guise of retaliation for the new licensing order, he could bear down heavily and at will on
American shipping in trade with England.

His riposte to Perceval was a masterpiece of its kind, vigorous and cunning. The Milan Decree began with expressions of horror at the licensing
order, as an unparalleled example of British tyranny on the seas. Then the
Emperor promptly went farther than even Perceval had thought to go. Any
neutral ship, he declared, which allowed itself to be searched by a British
vessel, or which paid duty in, visited, or intended to visit a British port was
thereafter lawful prize for the warships and harbor authorities of France
and her allies; and this decree would remain in effect until England
"returned to the principles of international law."

News of these two strangling edicts, one British and one French, reached
America early in 1808. Their first effect was to strengthen Jefferson's hold
on the country. Even those who doubted the wisdom of the embargo had
to admit that it had saved many American ships from seizure. In February,
American newspapers were giving the President credit for a kind of diplomatic clairvoyance. But now many expected him to rescind what they
assumed was a temporary measure. It was taken for granted that with the
embargo lifted, American ingenuity would soon find ways of evading British
and French rules, as it had always managed to do in the past. With a following wind, a little luck, suitable papers, and enough money to bribe coastal
officials, Yankee ship captains had always shown themselves able to go anywhere. If the British wanted their sixteen guineas a ship, let them have it.
If French and Spanish port authorities needed a little financial persuasion
to close their eyes when looking at an American ship's papers, what of it?
Profits were large enough to take care of such contingencies. Many confident
shipowners who had been growing rich on the soaring profits of neutral
trade quietly ignored the embargo in its early weeks; and a stream of vessels
sailed illegally from Boston and New York for England and France. Before
they arrived, their owners believed, the embargo would have been lifted.

2. The President Is Damned

A month passed, and another month, and still the embargo remained the
law of the land. It had become the fulcrum of the President's entire program. He seemed to be absorbed in a dream of an America permanently,
contentedly and peacefully isolated from the rest of the world. Away with
imports; away with shipping; "we should encourage manufactures of everything of which we raise the raw material." As he expressed it, "surpluses of
revenue" were to be "appropriated to the improvement of roads, canals,
rivers, education, and other great foundations of prosperity and union."
When Congress asked, "What surpluses?" the President had no answer. The
truth was, as Gallatin's reports showed, that the loss of revenue and cost of

enforcement of the embargo was forcing the government into debt. As Jefferson later admitted, the embargo was more costly to the country than war would have been. The financial-minded Gallatin repeatedly urged the President to let the nation fight rather than be pauperized. To no avail. Although Jefferson had always professed to consider a national debt a terrible threat to the nation, and had often challenged Hamilton on this ground, now the prospect of governmental borrowings left him indifferent.

It was as if he had chosen to stake his entire career on the success of the embargo. Far from rescinding it, he insisted that it be strengthened by a succession of supplementary acts. Coasting and fishing vessels were put under heavy bond to prevent them from taking cargoes to foreign ports. No sea-going vessel was permitted to take on a cargo except in the presence of a revenue officer. Any unusually large stocks of merchandise which might conceivably be intended for foreign shipment were to be seized and held until their owners gave bond that they would not be exported. The President alone was given power to license a ship to sail abroad. Lake, river, and bay shipping were placed under close restriction. Commerce across the Canadian border was so strictly interdicted as to make a New York congressman, Barent Gardenier, cry out to heaven against Jefferson's dictatorial methods. "All our surplus produce will rot on our own hands! . . . God knows what all this means! I cannot understand it . . . Darkness and mystery overshadow this House and the whole nation. We know nothing; we are permitted to know nothing. We sit here as mere automata . . ." If this was the way to peace, Gardenier and many another felt, then let there be war! But the President kept urging the country "to give the present experiment so fair a trial that on future occasions our legislators may know how far they may count on it as an engine for national purposes."

As the year 1808 unfolded, the concern of the people gave way to anger, and anger to rage. For the President to experiment was all very well, but how much did he expect the people to endure before he was convinced of the result? By April, Jefferson's popularity was dwindling fast. Up and down the Atlantic coast, the embargo struck like the hand of doom. Hundreds of stark-masted and barnacled ships, their timbers rotting, their crews dispersed, cluttered once busy harbors. A New York cartoonist caught the national fancy when he reversed "embargo" to "O-grab-me," and depicted it as a huge snapping turtle, biting savagely at the backside of the American shipowner. John Lambert, a British traveler and writer of the period, wrote vividly of the effects of the embargo. "When I arrived in New York in November [1807] the port was filled with shipping and the wharves were crowded with commodities of every description . . . The coffee-house slip and the corners of Wall and Pearl streets were jammed . . . But on my return . . . the following April, what a contrast . . . ! The port was indeed full of shipping, but they were dismantled and laid up . . . The streets near the waterside were almost deserted, the grass had begun to grow on the wharves . . . So desolating were the effects of the embargo which in the short space of five months had deprived the first commercial city in the states of all its life . . . ; caused above one hundred and forty-five bankruptcies; and completely annihilated its foreign commerce."

Southern ports were no better off. Sailors out of work in Baltimore became so numerous and desperate that city authorities had to double the police force to put down riots. In Charlestown, hundreds of deserters from the British Navy decided that they preferred the cat-o'-nine-tails to starvation. Lambert entered in his notes the fact that "upwards of one thousand" sailors in that city, "destitute of lodging and food," had begun to riot. "The English consul advertising that British seamen might have a free passage home in the British ships that were going to Europe, upwards of four hundred availed themselves of the offer, and sailed for England." In Connecticut a leading Hartford paper, the *Courant*, quoted a conversation overheard in the streets between two sailors, heading for Halifax, "for there's no standing this *dambargo* any longer." The British press took delight in reproducing such reports, and mockingly praised Jefferson for at last having found a means better than impressment for ending desertions from England's navy.

3. New England Resists

The South was in grave trouble. Cotton was allowed to rot in the fields for want of warehouse space in the ports. In Virginia, tobacco was given away for a cent a pound, for nothing. But slaves had to be fed and clothed, plantations maintained. The landed gentry of Virginia were shattered by the sudden cessation of income. Jefferson's own fortune, centered on tobacco lands, was irretrievably lost during this period. Nevertheless, since it was the great Jefferson who wished the embargo, open opposition to it in the South and West was surprisingly mild. It was in New England that resentment found full expression. Boston newspapers told readers day after day that Jefferson was "cutting the nation's throat to cure the nosebleed." Madison was blamed with the President, and so was Gallatin, whose opposition to the measure was not generally known. The government was being run, snarled a Boston wit, "by two Virginians and a Frenchman." Another said that Virginia had declared war on Massachusetts. From New Hampshire came a bitter little song:

> Our ships all in motion once whitened the ocean;
> They sailed and returned with a cargo.
> Now doomed to decay they are fallen a prey
> To Jefferson, worms and EMBARGO.

Wealthy Boston merchants and bankers quietly began to transfer their specie to Montreal for protection against worse to come. Soon a shortage of currency, as well as of manufactured goods, began to drive prices upward, aggravating the pangs of unemployment. Depression spread inland from the coast like a plague. Jefferson's hope that American entrepreneurs would quickly fill the gap left by the cessation of British imports quickly foundered when banks declined to lend money for such dubious ventures. Although in Connecticut some vigorous spirits, taking advantage of high prices for woven textiles and the glut of raw cotton in the South, hastily erected small spinning and weaving mills with American machinery, this and other domestic manufactures were regarded at the time as meager compensation for the suffering caused by the embargo.

Vermont went to the length of open defiance of the President. A vast smuggling trade was carried on across Lake Champlain with enormous rafts, guarded by armed riflemen, carrying New England produce daily to the Canadian border. From there it was taken to ports in the St. Lawrence for shipment to England. Revenue officers were helpless to stop the illicit trade. One raft built by the smugglers to carry Vermont's export surplus was said to be over half a mile in length, and to have at its center a bulletproof fort defended by several hundred men. When a company of militia tried to capture it, the soldiers were beaten back with loss of life. Upstate New York soon joined in the profitable game, which made profiting Canadian merchants and British shipowners chortle at the idiocy of the American government.

4. "Punqua Wingchong"

The aggravation of merchants was increased by rumors of a shady deal between the Administration and one of its wealthiest supporters, John Jacob Astor of New York. The noted fur trader, who was a close personal friend of Gallatin, had benefited from a curious exception in the rules of the embargo and the Non-Importation Act. The purchase of furs from Canada was not at first interdicted. On the contrary, the Governor of Canada, Sir James Craig, was permitted to send a mission to Washington to negotiate for the delivery of furs to Astor's company after the embargo went into effect. The fact was that Astor's position entitled him to some special consideration. He had built up a thriving trade with China—furs, gunpowder, and cannon in exchange for tea and silk—and he was understandably reluctant to see it ruined by a law which was, after all, intended only to injure the European belligerents. The elaborate plot which followed did credit to his imagination. Early in 1808 there appeared in New York a handsomely dressed Chinese mandarin, with the musical name of Punqua Wingchong, and with great funds at his disposal. Speaking through an interpreter, and showing high diplomatic credentials in Chinese, he asked authorities for permission to engage a vessel to take him back to China; and he proposed to carry with him merchandise which had been shipped to him "prior to December 22, 1807." Suitable representations were made in Washington, and Jefferson, Madison, and Gallatin all agreed that the mandarin should be allowed to take out of the country merchandise or specie to the value of $45,000. Philadelphia shippers got wind of the affair, and protested to Gallatin that the so-called Punqua Wingchong was an imposter, a wandering Chinese whom Astor had picked up in the streets, and who had been coached to play a part. Gallatin observed propriety by informing the President of the protest, but in the upshot the mandarin was permitted to sail under diplomatic immunity on Astor's ship *Beaver*—which the next year returned with a profit of $200,000 to show for the voyage.

Enlarged by gossip, the story of Punqua Wingchong became a damaging piece of anti-Jefferson propaganda. The Administration finally stopped Astor's fur trade with Canada, but not before many had come to believe that Jefferson was making political capital out of the nation's distress. It was true that his measures to enforce the embargo struck hardest in the region where his foes were strongest, Federalist New England. He instructed Governor Sullivan of Massachusetts to cut down imports of grain into the state "that we may not unnecessarily administer facilities to the evasion of the embargo laws." Nantucket and Cape Cod were patrolled by gunboats at the President's express order, and Secretary of the Navy Robert Smith was told that enforcement of the embargo was "not to be measured by money." When Gallatin expressed anxiety over the shrinking revenues of the Treasury, and spoke of needed enforcement acts as "arbitrary powers . . . dangerous and odious," the President replied sharply, "this law ought to be enforced at any expense *which may not exceed our appropriations.*" "I do not wish a single citizen to be deprived of a meal of bread, but I set down the exercise of commerce merely for profit as nothing when it carries with it the danger of defeating the embargo." "If . . . a continuance of the embargo is preferred to war, which sentiment is universal here," he wrote in August 1808, "Congress must legalize *all* means which may be necessary to obtain its *end.*"

That end, as Jefferson saw it, was the collapse of the British economy, and a withdrawal of the Orders in Council. The hollowness of this expectation was soon made clear to him.

5. *England Jeers*

It was Jefferson's belief that England could not much longer stand the strain of simultaneous cessation of manufactured exports to America and of raw material imports from America. He estimated that between Napoleon's Continental System and the embargo, England would have lost more than 50 per cent of her prewar market; and that she could not adequately feed her population without American grain. On these cheerful assumptions, Congress in the spring of 1808 passed a law authorizing him to suspend or modify the embargo if either England or France made reasonable adjustments in their measures affecting neutral commerce. Immediately he wrote to William Pinkney in London, instructing him to approach Canning with a proposal that the embargo and the Orders in Council be simultaneously rescinded.

Loyal to Jefferson as he was, Pinkney was deeply disturbed when this letter came to him, for he knew, as the President did not, that England was not to be "peacefully coerced." Jefferson's calculation had gone wrong on two counts. One was the unforeseen bumper harvests in England in 1807 and 1808, which had greatly eased the wheat shortage. The other was the unexpected laxity of Napoleon's vaunted Continental System, which had not prevented a flood of British manufactures from entering Europe. Although England's manufactured exports to America and the West Indies, which had run about $40,000,000 in 1806, fell away, her total exports in each of the years 1807–8 stood at nearly $200,000,000, so that the loss could be sustained. Moreover, there were compensations. Her shipping trade experienced a revival, and she recovered thousands of her seamen. Beyond this, her economy was being strongly buoyed by a huge increase in American smuggling. In spite of all that Gallatin's enforcement officers could do, British manufactures continued to pour over the Canadian border and American ships continued to trade with the West Indies. This process Spencer Perceval had deliberately encouraged by another Order in Council, which virtually promised immunity from seizure to ships which would smuggle wanted American raw materials. Some thought that the Anglo-American smuggling trade in 1808 approximated as much as one half of the legal trade two years earlier.

Such suffering as the embargo had inflicted on the British, Pinkney knew, had tended to inflame her spirit of determination rather than to break it. When Englishmen found the price of wheat nearly doubled, in spite of good harvests, they cursed Jefferson and his money-grubbing Yankees. When textile mills in the Midlands closed for lack of the American export market, when five thousand worker families were pauperized and some starved to death, it was Jefferson who was blamed, and not England's Poor Laws. Riots of unemployed men in Yorkshire and of famine-crazed Negroes in Jamaica were of America's making. The invective heaped on Jefferson in the British press was equal to anything the Federalists had ever perpetrated. His name was hissed in public places. He was assailed as a coward and despot. A pamphlet hinting that he ought to be assassinated was widely distributed.

From Pinkney's standpoint, the time was especially unfortunate for talk of compromise, for England was just then drunk with the dream of final victory over Napoleon. The myth of French invincibility on land had at last been exploded. In Spain, British and Spanish troops under General Wellesley had defeated a French army commanded by General Junot. British statesmen were predicting the imminent disintegration of Napoleon's empire. Given the temper of the moment, Jefferson's instructions to negotiate placed Pinkney in a highly disagreeable position. John Jay had been little worse off in 1782, when he was told to offer the Mississippi to Spain in exchange for a loan. An insulting rebuff was inevitable.

But he had no choice. A note embodying Jefferson's suggestion went to Canning, and presently the reply came back. England, said the Foreign Secretary, would make no move which could even mistakenly be construed into concession. His Majesty, however, in the kindness of his heart would be glad to see the embargo removed, since it was obviously "a measure of inconvenient restriction upon the American people."

Against this satirical stab there was little Pinkney could do except reply with dignity, and he did, at the same time urging Jefferson to save America's face by keeping the embargo in force.

6. The Good Neighbor Policy of Napoleon I

If matters went badly for Jefferson in London, they went worse in Paris. Napoleon was in trouble, and at such times there were no limits to his audacity. Months before Junot's defeat in Spain, an enemy stronger than General Wellesley had cast a shadow over Paris—money-lack. France was nearly bankrupt. One reason was that through Italy, Holland, and the German ports the continent's wealth was being drained to pay for a flood of British goods that the Emperor had not been able to check. He was caught in a circle of frustration. The more money that went from Europe to England, the less there was to be extracted from Europe to pay for Napoleon's armies, which were needed to keep Europe in subjection so that British goods could not enter Europe.

Controls in European ports were breaking down. Although members of his family, then ensconced on various European thrones, shivered at the bitter little notes that he wrote them on the subject, they appeared helpless to exert the necessary measures. His agents reported large stocks of British goods here, there, everywhere. Prince Eugene Beauharnais, Viceroy of Italy, was told "English merchandise is crossing Italy . . . This must cease . . . Arrange to have all English goods confiscated . . . throughout my Kingdom of Italy . . . War without respite on British merchandise—it is the only avenue to peace." Still sharper was the rebuke to brother Louis, King of Holland. "At the last Rotterdam fair, all the shops were overflowing with British goods. None of it was seized. I warn you that unless English merchandise is prohibited and seized, especially close to my frontiers, I shall send troops . . ." But the impersonal economic forces at work in Europe were too strong even for Napoleon. Europe needed more manufactured goods than France and her satellites could supply; England had those goods; and the distance between them was short. The Continental System grew steadily weaker from month to month, until the Emperor found himself in urgent need of new expedients.

Reports from all over western Europe told him that there were an extraordinary number of American ships then in ports under his control—ships which had evaded both the embargo and the British fleet to bring supplies to France. To seize these ships and their cargoes without payment was an immense temptation, especially since France's own shipbuilding program was badly handicapped by lack of funds. He certainly did not want to drive the Americans to the point of an open break with France, yet should he permit diplomatic niceties to deprive him of so ripe a plum? All that stood in the way of action was lack of a suitable pretext, and this his ingenuity quickly supplied. From Bayonne, in the southwest corner of France, came a decree which made professional European diplomats smile ironically. All American vessels in Spain, Italy, France, and the German ports were to be confiscated and French privateers were authorized to bring in others, whether or not they stood in violation of earlier French decrees. The reason? Nothing less than the Emperor's friendship for the United States. Since the embargo had prohibited sailings from American ports, such vessels must be either British ships in disguise, or had "denationalized" themselves by paying license money to England. To rid America of these troublemakers was the least that a friendly power could do.

To this bland hypocrisy, it was difficult to reply. John Armstrong's vehement protest was politely rejected. Two hundred and thirty ships, with an estimated value of ten million dollars, were lost to America. A little later, Napoleon expressed himself seriously on the subject to Robert Livingston, who approached him at the President's request. "England has made your ships tributary to her" (through Perceval's licensing order). "This I will not endure. Tell the President from me, that if he can make a treaty with England, preserving his maritime rights, it will be agreeable to me; but that I will make war upon the universe, should it support her [England's] unjust pretensions."

Jefferson had not yet heard of this action when he sent John Armstrong instructions similar to those issued to Pinkney—to ask France to end her decrees against neutral shipping, in return for the repeal of the embargo.

Napoleon, serenely contemplating the handsome returns from the Bayonne Decree, was content to be gently sardonic. Why should he wish to have the embargo lifted? Its adverse effects on France were small, and his West Indian colonies were being supplied by smuggled goods. He saw the embargo as "a generous decision" on the part of the United States "to renounce all commerce rather than acknowledge the domination of the tyrant of the sea." To the extent that the embargo injured England, it was an aid to France; therefor let it remain; his Bayonne Decree had been only a neighborly way of supporting it. Armstrong was compelled to report to Jefferson that "we have somewhat overrated our means of coercing the two great belligerents. The embargo is a measure calculated above any other to keep us at peace, but beyond this you must not count upon it. Here it is not felt, and in England it is forgotten."

7. One More Effort

The apparent indifference of the British and French to the embargo put Jefferson's administration in a jaundiced light. New England Federalists took savage pleasure in pointing to the decline of American prestige, and praised Perceval's licensing order as a logical retort to the embargo; while Republicans asserted that Napoleon had been justified in confiscating vessels which paid a tax to England. The country was torn with dissension and anxiety. When the talks on reparation for the *Chesapeake* incident failed, and Canning's envoy, Rose, returned to England, morale reached low ebb.

John Armstrong urged the President to re-establish America's position in the world by declaring war both on England and France. "Our war with France would be but nominal, while with England it would take a character of seriousness . . . Union is our greatest desideratum . . . A war with either of these powers exclusively would paralyze half your energies, whereas a war with both would put into motion every drop of American blood." The advice was rejected. The President's heart was still set on the embargo; the great experiment in peace-diplomacy had to be given its full trial. Even a message from Napoleon offering to give America the much coveted Floridas in return for an alliance was brushed aside.

In the spring of 1808, the citizens of the United States began to express their feelings at the polls. Elections in New York brought a large Federalist gain in the state legislature, and Massachusetts, which had gone for Jefferson in 1804, reverted to Federalism. Feeling against the embargo there was so intense that even so respectable a Federalist as John Quincy Adams was defeated for re-election to the Senate because of his support of the measure. In June, Gallatin told the President that the Republicans might well lose the Presidential election in the autumn if the embargo remained in force. "Vermont is lost; New Hampshire is a bad neighborhood; and Pennsylvania is extremely doubtful." By August he was even more disturbed. "At this moment the Western States, Virginia, South Carolina and perhaps Georgia are the only sound states and . . . we will have a doubtful contest in every other." Madison, on whom the President had conferred his mantle, was alarmed by the steady decline in his prospects. After all his service to the government, from its very beginning, was he now to be cheated of his reward by Jefferson's obstinacy? C. C. Pinckney of South Carolina, whom the Federalists had chosen as their candidate, suddenly loomed very strong. The President, however, remained unconcerned. Contrary to his advisers, he believed that most Americans, in spite of all recent disappointments, would vote for the man of his choosing.

When the election was held, and Madison was elected by a satisfactory majority, the President felt that his work was almost done. But not quite. The embargo was tottering—could he still push it back into place? If so, it would stand as a monument to his statesmanship, the hope of peace. With only a few months more of office remaining to him, he girded himself for a final effort. The Congress was asked to pass an Enforcement Act so far-reaching as to put the entire economy of the country under the strict control of government officials. Any merchandise anywhere, or any specie suspected of being intended for export could be seized by a collector of revenue, transferred at his will to another place, and held until a large bond was posted to guarantee that it would not be shipped out of the country. Collectors were to be immune to prosecution, and were to have the support of the Army, Navy, and militia in their enforcement activities. The Congress groaned, protests were loud and agonized, but so great was Jefferson's power that both Houses gave him resounding majorities. With his signature, on January 9, 1809, the Enforcement Act became law. Its effect was to impose on America a rigid economic dictatorship, exerting its controls not at the stage of production, but at the point of transportation.

8. The Pickering Conspiracy

Gallatin, as much as Jefferson, was active in promoting the Enforcement Act, but his motive was almost diametrically opposed to that of the President. He expected the new powers of the Executive to raise such a storm in the country that the embargo would be reduced to absurdity. He was right. On every side the political skies darkened and the lightning flashed. "How much longer," raged the Washington *Federalist*, "are we to pant under the pestiferous breath of this poisonous dragon?" In New England, men did more than write and talk. A drive toward secession gathered head with far more power than in the past, for this time it expressed not the ambitions of a few wealthy men, but the passions of the people. Timothy Pickering, the former Secretary of State, and now a United States senator, was the prime mover; but behind the scenes George Cabot lent the weight of his wealth and connections to the project. Both men were in secret correspondence with high officials in England. Pickering had convinced himself that "Jefferson stands pledged to Bonaparte to maintain the embargo." This delusion, to which he clung with all the desperation of paranoia, became the justification for his plot. If the President had sold out to France, then any patriot had the right—indeed, the duty—to join with England. A secret agent sent by the Governor of Canada, Sir John Craig, was admitted to the Federalist councils, and this man, John Henry, wrote enthusiastically to Craig of the effect of the embargo on the Boston magnates. "In a few months more of suffering . . . the people of New England will be ready to . . . establish a separate government . . . For a measure of this sort the men of talents and property are now ready . . ."

With the Pickerings and the Cabots the President could have dealt, but the ordinary people of New England, in their newspapers and their town meetings, were another matter. As reports poured in upon him, he saw that he could not persist longer in the embargo without risking civil violence on a large scale. The Enforcement Act had touched off an explosion of popular wrath. The Baltimore *Evening Post* quoted a circular distributed in Newburyport, Massachusetts, and which urged the people to "nerve your arms with vengeance against the Despot who would wrest the inestimable germ of your independence from you." Jefferson himself later described the situation: "I felt the foundations of the government shaken under my feet by the New England townships."

That the embargo could not last much longer, Jefferson finally had to admit. He hoped, however, to keep it on the statute books at least until he retired from the Presidency on March 4, 1809. The rest would be the responsibility of the Congress and President-elect Madison. A policy with respect to the embargo had already been decided by Madison and Gallatin. They planned to get rid of it simply by asking Congress, in late spring, for an ultimatum to England. The British would be told that unless they rescinded or suitably modified their Orders in Council, America would declare war. It was Madison's belief that America had been placed in so untenable a diplomatic position that war, with all its perils, had become the only way to maintain the nation's self-respect. And in the resulting excitement, the embargo would slide out of history with a minimum of criticism of its sponsors.

9. "A Mere Subterfuge to Extricate Themselves"

Congress was by now so full of rebels, Republicans as well as Federalists, that neither the House nor the Senate was willing to delay the death of the hated act out of consideration for Presidential feelings. February was the decisive month. As Jefferson wrote in a letter to his son-in-law, Thomas Randolph, the plan for "continuing their embargo till June, and then war" was rejected in a series of angry debates. "A sudden and unaccountable revolution of opinion took place the last week, chiefly among the New England and New York members . . . I believe it is perfectly certain that the embargo will be taken off."

Even within a few days of retirement, and relatively unpopular as he had become, Jefferson's influence on the Congress was still very much alive, and stronger than Madison's. It was the general feeling that while he did not openly wish to oppose the President-elect, nevertheless he was out of sympathy with the proposal to go to war. The bill introduced by the Republicans to kill the embargo was commonly believed to reflect Jefferson's preference, for it retained, in words at least, some semblance of his policy. "Pacific non-intercourse," the people were told, would replace embargo. The Non-Intercourse Bill excluded French and English ships from American ports, and prohibited all trade with the belligerent nations, while repealing the embargo with respect to the rest of the world. But as David Erskine said in a letter to Canning: "The intention . . . is undoubtedly to leave open as many places for their commerce as they can, consistently with keeping up an appearance of resistance . . . but it is thoroughly understood that the whole measure is a mere subterfuge to extricate themselves from the embarrassments of the embargo system, and is never intended to be enforced." It was common gossip in every port that smuggling was to be the order of the day.

Perhaps the most important feature of the Non-Intercourse Bill was a clause giving the President the power to reopen by proclamation trade with either belligerent, if one or the other country should rescind its restrictions on neutral commerce. Congress was offering American trade to the highest bidder. A weak bill, detested even by most of the congressmen who voted for it, nevertheless it seemed to them a lesser evil than either embargo or war. On February 28, it was passed by large majority in both houses, and Jefferson signed it at once. He had been spared the ignominy of ending his term with the embargo flatly repealed; and the war which he had so desperately tried to avoid was still not yet upon the country. One of his enemies, Josiah Quincy, representative from Massachusetts, summed up the prevailing sentiment. "Jefferson has triumphed. His intrigues have prevailed."

10. Failure?

A few days later Jefferson left Washington for Monticello. To many, he seemed to have failed, but not to himself. He had dared greatly for peace —and whatever else had happened, he had kept the peace. In a world at war, the nation had gained precious years without war. The embargo had hurt some Americans—but had it hurt America? Under its pressure, new factories had sprung up here and there with American capital and American labor. The seed of American industrialization, the key to economic independence, had been planted. As for popularity, he knew its vagaries too well to be greatly distressed by the loss of his own. Republican though he was, he had never allowed his highest decisions to be shaped by public opinion. In the final test, it was his private and highly individual opinion that determined his most important measures. The notion of being guided in statecraft by a public opinion poll would have made him scoff. He had achieved popularity not because he yielded to public clamor, but rather because his intuitions of the public need were generally valid, and came to be so recognized.

The embargo had sprung directly from his personal view that war would work great evil in American life. It would have been far easier for him to ask the Congress and the people to follow him to war. There was nothing heroic about peaceful coercion. Jefferson was accused of timidity, of abasing the nation before its enemies; but his critics failed to perceive the moral courage that he displayed in recommending his pallid economic expedients. The popular course, the easy course, would have been to whip up the emotions of the American people and the cantankerous Congress for a fight.

The people sensed the significance and sincerity of the President's purpose, and even when they were shocked by the painful result, they did not turn away from Jefferson. The embargo made men angry with him, but it was the anger of a loving wife with a husband who loses the family savings. She may tear her hair, but she does not want to divorce him. So the generality of the people with Jefferson. As later in the case of another crafty politician, Abraham Lincoln, they accepted his mistakes even while they bemoaned them. Like Lincoln, Jefferson was bitterly hated and attacked by a fringe of frightened conservatives, but the people—the real owners of America—were always on his side. They never doubted his zeal and selflessness in striving for what he conceived to be their security. He put the preservation and full development of the individual life at the core of his policy, and modified every other conviction that ran counter to it. The ideas incessantly churned up by his creative mind were recognized as a sign of vitality. He was Emerson's "endless seeker" personified, a man who knew that new problems demanded original solutions, and who never stopped trying to find them; and in spite of all that went wrong, the totality of his administration was a popular success. His personality engraved itself on his party, and his party became for a time almost identical with the nation, scoring overwhelmingly at the polls for the next sixteen years, while he was still alive. For between him and the ordinary men and women of the United

States there was a deep and felt bond of tacit understanding. With a healthy instinct for greatness, recognizing the essential purity of his character, they trusted him as they have trusted only a few Presidents in history. He was cautious, scheming, and inconsistent; but this did not prevent him from being a great and good human being.

It is fair to say that he could not have been great and good, or human, if he had not been sometimes inconsistent. In a very real sense, Jefferson's inconsistency was a sign of the humility in which he found his strength. He never pretended to the godlike righteousness of a John Adams. He was always ready to listen, and to be guided by those who had knowledge that he lacked. Jefferson felt the majestic uncertainty and mystery of the universe; he liked men and he loved women; and he drew his power in statecraft from these fundamental feelings. Moderate, cautious, patient, humorous, imaginative, he had the attributes needed to work for peace among the terrors of the international jungle. With his passing from the Presidency, something went out of it that could not be measured in terms of laws and diplomacy—inspiration.

Like George Washington, Jefferson understood that the chief function of the President of the United States is not specified in the Constitution— that it is to lift the eyes and thoughts of the people above the levels of the past. He knew how to make ordinary Americans feel part of the government, sharing in the decisions of the statesman. He warmed their hearts, and so they forgave him his failures. Ten years after he left office, they had forgotten the embargo, and remembered only Jefferson's great deeds. He wrote the Declaration from which America sprang to independence. He fought for the rights of the ordinary man against the gluttons of privilege. More than any other man, he reshaped the American republic into a democracy. And he kept the peace.

CHAPTER SIX

The Erskine Fiasco

1. *"On These Conditions"*

Englishmen were compelled, in the winter of 1808–09, to hold their breath and suspend their judgments in the face of the unpredictable. For the time was again dark with anxiety. Reports from Spain, where for the first time a large British army had been committed against Napoleon's forces, told of alternate victory and retreat, hope and dread. At home, a depression had gripped trade and manufacturing, and to account for it men pointed with anger to the pinch of the American embargo.

Just before Christmas, Foreign Secretary George Canning was stirred by a series of letters from David Erskine in Washington. On the basis of conversations with American leaders, Erskine reported that the United States would declare war on England if the recent Orders in Council were not revoked; but that if they were revoked, she was willing to remove the embargo. The Foreign Secretary perceived at once that simultaneous withdrawal of the 1807 Orders in Council and the embargo would leave England in an advantageous position, for the old Rule of 1756 and the impressment policy would still be in effect. For fifteen years his country had been trying to persuade the Americans to accept these conditions in their trade with Europe. If Erskine was correct, the moment was at hand; for the sake of peace, Jefferson and Madison were prepared to yield. Canning thought it possible that to assure the revival of British exports to America and increased imports of grain, Spencer Perceval might be persuaded to recall the recent Orders in Council. He had no way of knowing that pressures on Jefferson would soon cause the embargo to be lifted without any concession by England. There seemed every reason to take seriously both Erskine's hint of possible compromise and his alarming talk of war. The Foreign Secretary was well aware of Erskine's liking for the United States—for one thing, the young man had married an American—but he thought him too level-headed to let his judgment be influenced by sentiment. He concluded that at least some small diplomatic gesture toward America was justified, that mild conciliation was the indicated tactic. In this mood, he sent for the American minister, William Pinkney, and in a friendly meeting, hinted that the British Government was amenable to an adjustment of differences, knowing that Pinkney would so report to Washington.

Thereafter, he composed two dispatches to Erskine. The first outlined his views on an acceptable compromise of the long-standing *Chesapeake* dispute. The second and much longer dispatch went to the heart of the problem of Anglo-American commerce. Three main points were made. To begin, Canning said that he had gathered from Erskine's reports, that "the American government is prepared, in the event of His Majesty's consenting to withdraw the Orders in Council . . . to withdraw contemporaneously on its part the interdiction of its harbors to ships of war, and all non-intercourse and non-importation acts, as far as respects Great Britain, leaving them in force with respect to France . . .

"Secondly, . . . that America is willing to renounce . . . the pretension of carrying on in time of war all trade with the enemy's colonies from which she was excluded during peace.

"Thirdly, Great Britain . . . is to be considered as being at liberty to capture all such American vessels as may be found attempting to trade with the ports of any of those [enemy] powers . . .

"On these conditions, His Majesty would consent to withdraw the Orders in Council of January and November, 1807 . . ."

Canning then added a sentence which was to prove of great importance: "I flatter myself that there will be no difficulty in obtaining a distinct and official recognition of these conditions from the American government." Now it was up to Erskine to make good the promise of his letters.

2. *Madison Adds a Paragraph*

By the time that Erskine received Canning's dispatches the embargo had been lifted, the weak Non-Intercourse Act had been put in its place, and James Madison was President. It was perfectly clear to the British envoy that Canning's instructions, if rigidly adhered to, ruled out any hope of a settlement of the Anglo-American troubles. Yet the chances of a settlement, Erskine believed, were better at that moment than they had been for years. The United States had not forgiven Napoleon for the ship seizures under the Bayonne Decree. Popular sentiment had shifted toward England. The people were eager for an expansion of trade. The new Secretary of State, Robert Smith, formerly Secretary of the Navy, was far better disposed toward England than Jefferson, Madison, or Gallatin. Perhaps even more important, he was the brother of Samuel Smith, one of the most influential members of the American Senate. It was an open secret that Senator Smith and his followers had compelled Madison to put brother Robert in charge of the State Department instead of Gallatin, who had been the President's preference.

Early in April, Erskine was ready to act. In a talk with Robert Smith, he made it clear that he was anxious to heal, once and for all, the running sore of the *Chesapeake* controversy, and so open the gate to a solution of the commericial problem. Smith was surprised and delighted. Like all the American officials, he liked Erskine for his friendly and modest style, and his earnestness. In a very short time, they worked out an agreement. England was to make monetary payments to the widows or orphans of the men killed on the *Chesapeake*, and to release the American sailors taken from the ship. The United States was to withdraw its demand for the court-martial of Admiral Berkeley. Erskine then wrote a note disavowing Berkeley's action and offering reparation on behalf of His Majesty; and Smith in reply wrote America's acceptance.

When the Secretary took his draft of the note to the President, Madison found himself in an annoying position. There was a considerable coolness between him and his Secretary of State. He resented the manner in which Smith had been forced on him by the Senate, and he considered him inadequately qualified for diplomacy; and he would have had to be more than human not to be piqued by the fact that Smith was about to get credit for a large and unearned diplomatic coup. Madison, "Little Jemmy," as his party affectionately called him, at this time of his life had lost something of his early vitality. He had come to prefer solitary work at his desk, reading and writing reports, to the give-and-take of personal discussion. As the French minister, Turreau, reported to Napoleon, there was in the President something a little dry and pedantic, a little dusty-bookish. But this did not mean that he had mastered his ego. On the contrary, after his long subordination to Jefferson's fame and power, it clamored for nourishment. To let Smith handle this affair by himself, without some assertion of his own authority, was more than he was ready to concede; and perhaps, too, as he later said, he questioned Smith's capacity.

Not that he considered rejecting Erskine's proposition. The British note on the *Chesapeake* went far in conciliation, and Smith's draft reply was generally adequate. But the President could not resist adding his personal touch, and he wrote in a paragraph which according to Smith's subsequent account, made the Secretary's hair rise. He did not, the President said, insist on further punishment for Admiral Berkeley, but he felt that such punishment "would best comport with what is due from His Britannic Majesty to his own honor." Recognizing the danger of so gratuitous a rebuke to sensitive England, Smith objected (if his story is to be credited) but he had to give way to Presidential insistence. The note went to Erskine with the added paragraph, was accepted, and dispatched to Canning.

3. "I Have Adhered to the Spirit . . ."

As Erskine and Smith settled down to the next and crucial stage of their talks, the British envoy was confronted by a serious practical problem: should he show Smith the instructions from his government? That Canning expected him to do so seemed clear enough, from his remark about "obtaining a distinct and official recognition of these conditions." However, Erskine believed that he would be granted latitude in this respect, that it would be enough if he put forward the three points made by the Foreign Secretary not as unalterable premises, but rather as matter for discussion. Accordingly, he said nothing of Canning's dispatch.

Smith was delighted by England's readiness, as reflected by Erskine, to go more than halfway toward an agreement, and so was Madison, when he heard of the progress made. Neither seems to have thought to ask Erskine whether he was expressing his government's orders. In accordance with Canning's outline, Erskine asked first that America remove her restrictions against British commerce, while enforcing them against France. Smith pointed out that the Non-Intercourse Act had been passed by the Congress, and that its repeal in whole or in part was the prerogative of the Congress. The President could not constitutionally take this responsibility upon himself. A compromise was quickly reached: if England undertook to revoke the Orders in Council, the President would exercise the powers given him by the Non-Intercourse Act, to her benefit; and Congress would then be asked to pass a law formalizing the changed commercial relations of the two countries.

So far, so good. Erskine next raised Canning's second point, which in effect required America to accept the Rule of 1756. Smith's reply evaded a direct negative. The Non-Intercourse Act, he said, if enforced so as to rule out trade with France or her dependencies, would make recourse to the Rule of 1756 unnecessary. This was true enough, and Erskine agreed, and went on. Would America consent to allow the British fleet to enforce non-intercourse with France by seizing American vessels which violated the President's ruling? Here Smith protested with some vigor that America, as a sovereign power, could not consent to the execution of her laws by Great Britain. But what had England to gain by insisting on such a right? Once non-intercourse was put into effect against Napoleon, any American ship trading with France or her colonies would be violating American law. If the British navy seized such a ship, America could not very well present a claim against England.

All this struck Erskine as reasonable and convincing. He could see no logical ground on which Canning could demur. Within a day or two, he and Smith exchanged formal notes covering their arrangements. A date was established for withdrawal of the Orders in Council—June 10. On that same date, it was understood, the Orders in Council would be withdrawn, and intercourse with Great Britain, but not with France, would be renewed by the United States.

Erskine faced up squarely to the fact that he had gone beyond his instructions. Reporting the agreement to Canning, he said, "It became my duty to consider whether the Spirit of your instructions would be accomplished . . . or whether it was incumbent on me to forbear from making any Proposition, as I could not obtain a Compliance with the exact letter of your Instructions . . . I therefore rest my Vindication upon the Reasons detailed . . . for believing that I have adhered to the Spirit . . ."

4. *Slightly Premature*

On April 19, 1809, the date on which the exchange of letters between Erskine and Smith was completed, the agreement was no longer a White House secret; and among those who had been taken into the confidence of the administration was Senator Samuel Smith. Now the Senator, in private life, was a Baltimore merchant, whose firm, Smith and Buchanan, had made a fortune out of trade with Europe. It had been his large contribution to Republican campaign funds that had launched both him and brother Robert on their political careers.

No practical businessman in his position could fail to take into account that ships leaving the United States at once would reach England just in time for the revoking of the Orders in Council on June 10, and that those which arrived first would profit most. He was far too experienced, however, to take advantage of his inside knowledge, and so throw suspicion of undercover favoritism on his brother. At the same time, neither he nor the President could doubt that word of the Erskine agreement would soon reach other merchants, who would certainly be less considerate of the administration than Smith and Buchanan. How to put all American shipowners and shippers on an equal footing with respect to the imminent resumption of trade with England was a serious problem; and Madison thought it best not to wait for June 10 before publishing the Erskine agreement, but to release it to the press at once. He may well have been influenced, too, by awareness that the political value of the announcement would be greatly enhanced by surprise.

On April 20, the *National Intelligencer* carried the text of the Erskine-Smith letters, together with a proclamation by the President revoking nonintercourse with respect to England, as of June 10. The country was electrified. Hosannahs were heard up and down the Atlantic seaboard. Cargoes were rushed on board merchant ships, and crowds at the wharves cheered as their sails unfurled for England. Business improved overnight. Federalists long resentful of Madison suddenly saw him through new lenses. Here was no Jefferson, no Francophile, but a man who clearly understood the need for re-establishing ties with England, and fighting Napoleon if need be. Speaking for New England, Representative Dana of Connecticut rose in the House to praise Madison. "The reproaches of party . . . have been hushed;

industry is revived; mutual gratulations have succeeded to the voice of reproach . . . Can there be named any one act of any chief magistrate of the
United States which has produced a greater change than this?" The New
York press compared Madison to George Washington. Federalists announced that June 10 would be celebrated as a day of national rejoicing.

There was almost no dissent in the country. Even Madison's worst enemies gave him grudging credit. Some finicking critics did indeed assert
that the President's proclamation was, on the face of it, premature. But
captious comment of this kind was brushed aside in the general rejoicing.
So, too, were doubts which presently arose here and there as to ratification
of the agreement by the British Government. When men asked whether
the several hundred ships which had sailed for England would be safe from
seizure, Congressman John Randolph reassured the country in a widely
quoted speech. "Trade with Great Britain is unshackled . . . trade with
France is forbidden . . . Now, in the name of common sense, what more
could Mr. Canning himself want?"

5. Explosion in Whitehall

Mr. Canning could, and did, want a great deal more. There is a legend
in the British Foreign Office that when Erskine's dispatch on the *Chesapeake*
agreement came to him, and he saw Madison's reference to "his Majesty's
honor," he rose from his chair with a burst of profanity that was heard
throughout the building, and sent clerks scurrying from their desks in fright.
The agreement in other respects fell short of his instructions to Erskine,
but his attention was fixed on what seemed to him a deliberate offense to
the dignity of his government. Since when had Americans a claim to decide
what was due to the honor of an English monarch?

Thereafter, he read the text of the commercial agreement. By this time
he was calm, if prejudiced against whatever it might contain. Weeks earlier,
he had learned that the American embargo had been lifted, and that the
Non-Intercourse Act was not likely to prevent large-scale trade by the States
with Canada and the West Indies. This served his purpose excellently. So
long as England was supplied, a triangular trade was even better than a
direct trade, for it would give British shipping interests a monopoly of
the freightage of American goods from the colonies to England. Already
American cargoes carried in British bottoms had arrived in Liverpool from
Halifax. Any suggestion that this traffic revert to American vessels was
bound to be strongly resisted. Nor, under the circumstances, was there
reason for England to repeal the licensing system which brought her revenue
from American trade with France. It had to be considered, too, that the
Non-Intercourse Act assured a large number of smuggling American vessels

in the Atlantic, and many of these were sure to become the prizes of deserving officers of England's navy.

The new agreement could not be allowed to stand. That its repudiation would inevitably destroy Erskine in his ministerial capacity Canning regretted; but it was not to be helped. Erskine, by his overoptimism, had unwittingly played into the hands of Spencer Perceval. For years, Perceval had been urging Canning to replace Erskine by a sound Tory, and specifically by one of England's boldest exemplars of the mailed fist in diplomacy, the notorious Francis James Jackson. It was Jackson who had delivered the British ultimatum to Denmark prior to the bombardment of Copenhagen. His conduct to the Danish Prince Regent on that occasion had been so offensive that even George III expressed astonishment that the Prince had not kicked him out of his palace. Canning had resisted Perceval's pressure on the ground that selection of "Copenhagen Jackson" to replace the mild Erskine would be a slap in the face for Jefferson. But now a slap was indicated for Madison and Jackson was the man to give it.

On July 20, 1809, Canning informed the British press that the draft arrangement with the American Government had been repudiated, and Erskine recalled. A few days later, Francis Jackson took ship for America, with an impressive retinue of retainers—secretaries, a cook, and coachmen and servants in colorful livery. His secret instructions from Canning suited his imperious nature. As a pretext for repudiating the Erskine agreement, he was to charge the American Government with fraud in its negotiation, and with trickery in publishing the letters before their ratification. "The American government," wrote Canning to Jackson, "cannot have believed that such an arrangement as Mr. Erskine consented to accept was conformable to his instructions." As for the *Chesapeake* note, England would accede to their conditions only if the United States first recalled the proclamation barring British warships from her ports. The Orders in Council would not be modified or withdrawn unless the United States first prohibited all trade with France and her colonies. In any event, the Rule of 1756 would continue to be enforced by British warships, either with or without the consent of the American Government.

Yet there is an indication that even now Canning wished to avoid war with the United States, for he persuaded Perceval to one important concession. American merchant ships which had set to sea for England under Madison's unwarranted proclamation of April would be allowed to complete their round trips unmolested.

6. Pain in High Places

British notes containing word that the Erskine agreement was a dead letter and that Jackson would be sent to Washington did not reach President

Madison until late in July. They had the sound of doom. There was nothing for him to do but recall his April proclamation and re-establish non-intercourse for England. At this news, the nation stood aghast. Bewildered men gathered in the streets of the cities to ask each other whether war had come; and the President's popularity went down like a falling tree, as the disillusioned Federalist press broke out in a clamor against him.

In Washington, the feeling of terrified uncertainty rose when Erskine sadly took his leave. Madison and Robert Smith could not know what to expect from Jackson, but they feared the worst, and they were right. In his first meeting with Smith, early in October, the new British minister made no attempt to explain Canning's action. He had been instructed, he said coldly, to await new proposals from the United States; he had none to make for England. To his pleasure, his aggressiveness staggered Smith. "It was some time," Jackson complacently reported to Canning, "before he could recollect himself sufficiently to give me any answer at all." A second interview was even more calamitous. Upon Smith's strongly demanding an explanation of Canning's reasons, Jackson retorted that Canning had himself spoken on the subject with William Pinkney; and this would have to suffice.

When Smith's report to the President made it clear that there was no hope in Jackson, Madison decided that the time had come to build up a justifying dossier against an imminent declaration of war. He wrote out a note, which the Secretary signed, telling Jackson that it was deemed expedient to carry on all further discussions in writing. This picador's dart enraged the bull. In a furious reply, Jackson wrote to Smith there did not exist in the annals of diplomacy a precedent for cutting off verbal communications so abruptly. But he was equipped for a written as well as for an oral duel. As he saw it, Canning's instructions authorized him to insult the American Government, and long experience had made him a master of insults, bald and veiled. In his next letter, he said that Erskine, in making his first proposals to Smith, had for practical purposes communicated Canning's conditions orally; the American Government, he implied, knew from the beginning that Canning would never approve the agreement; it had taken advantage of a young and too eager diplomat.

Madison countered with restrained indignation. Jackson's letter surprised him, he said. If Canning's instructions to Erskine "had been communicated . . . the arrangement would not have been made." Here was the opening which Jackson awaited, and he lunged. The instructions, he insisted, "were, at the time, in substance made known to you." They did not contemplate the terms which Erskine was "actually induced to accept," and which "were substituted by you in lieu of those originally prepared." The President knew an insult when he saw one. His reply sharply rebuked "several irrelevant and improper allusions" in the minister's letter. "Such insinuations are in-admissible."

Jackson's retort did not yield an inch. Any insinuation in his notes, he said, could be "supported by incontrovertible evidence"; but he made no attempt to state what the evidence was. A reply promptly came back from Smith. "Sir . . . You have used a language . . . reiterating and even aggra-vating the same gross insinuation . . . no further communications will be received from you . . ." On the same day, Madison wrote Pinkney, in-structing him to ask Canning for Jackson's recall.

America's shattered state of mind was indicated by the atmosphere of Jackson's departure from Washington. When a resolution was introduced into Congress supporting the President's action in ousting the envoy, it was bitterly opposed by every Federalist in the House, on the ground that Jackson had not insulted the President, and ought not to have been cen-sured. A significant vote was taken, which showed that the country was again splitting, not only on partisan but on regional lines; for of forty-one Federalist votes against the resolution, almost all were from the North. In the coastal cities pro-British sentiment was at a new peak. After leaving Washington, Jackson stopped in Baltimore, Philadelphia, and New York, to be lionized by leading citizens, while the Massachusetts legislature by a large majority voted a resolution condemning the President's stand. The English envoy left the country convinced that although "the mob" might be against him, "the respectability" was on his side. War he considered improbable—the Cabots and the Pickerings would never permit it. Since this was precisely the belief of most British Tories, Jackson's report to the Cabinet went far to confirm Spencer Perceval in his policy of indifference to American protests. Canning was criticized for having allowed the Whig Erskine to remain so long in Washington. For the next two years of crisis England would be represented in Washington only by a chargé, John Morier, whose reports to the Foreign Office were too unperceptive to be of much use as a basis for decisions, and who did nothing to check the steady deterioration of Anglo-American relations.

CHAPTER SEVEN

The Cadore Letter

1. *Sympathy from Napoleon*

The spring and summer months of 1809, during which the Erskine agreement was made and repudiated, tested all the moral and military resources of Napoleon Bonaparte and France. An army under the first significant British general to appear in a generation, Arthur Wellesley, had opened a second front in Spain and compelled the diversion of large French forces southward, while Austria, revived by British gold, had mobilized for yet another test in the east.

Yet even at the moment of greatest danger to his army, that immensely active and logical mind never lost sight of the international diplomatic scene. An anguished report of the Erskine agreement from Turreau in Washington infuriated the Emperor. It seemed to presage an overt alliance between England and America—something to be avoided at all costs. The first need was to beat an orderly diplomatic retreat. America must be given no pretext to discriminate against France. Napoleon had dispensed with Talleyrand, whom he correctly suspected of conspiring against him with the Austrians, and he kept a close supervisory eye on his new Minister of Foreign Affairs, Champagny, afterward the Duc de Cadore. On June 10, the day when the Erskine agreement was supposed to go into effect, he wrote from the eastern front to Champagny instructing him to inform the American minister Armstrong that since the United States had caused Great Britain to revoke her Orders in Council, France also would modify her restrictions on neutral commerce; the Milan Decree would be revoked. But before America could learn of this decision, news came to the Emperor of Canning's repudiation of Erskine. Instantly, he reversed himself; no need now to conciliate; everything stood as before. Sensing that President Madison must be badly bruised, he did not miss the opportunity to salt the wound with sympathy. In a letter to the President, he asked, what, after all, could one expect from the British? "There is nothing astonishing in all this. It is a fine specimen of modern diplomacy."

In July, the Emperor's costly and difficult campaign against Austria bore fruit in the triumph of Wagram, and his prestige rose again like a released balloon. The crushed Austrians were forced to pay a badly needed indemnity into the French treasury. When thereafter Europe learned that the British expeditionary force in Spain had come to grief, and would be lucky to escape capture, rebels everywhere scurried to cover and ambassadors from neutral nations flocked to bend the knee. Far from making concessions to America now, the Emperor pressed his advantage. In Vienna, early in August, he drafted a stern decree ordering the seizure of all American ships in European waters so long as non-intercourse remained in force for France. A few days later, however, a letter came to him from John Armstrong, hinting that the United States might soon go to war against England if Canning persisted in his policy. This was too good a chance to waste. Napoleon decided that the Vienna Decree, not yet published, was to be kept secret; meanwhile he would find a better diplomatic basis for justifying seizures of American ships.

2. *The Emperor Outwits Himself*

Napoleon was marking time, and he was never at his best when he marked time. Money was his great concern. Reports coming to him from the port towns of Holland, Germany, and Italy told of sharply falling tax revenues. But without foreign trade, how could he collect taxes from people who lived by it? Deputations of desperate merchants from the satellite countries never ceased to beg him, however timidly, to relax his restrictions against their commerce with England and America. In the autumn of 1809, Napoleon came to an impulsive decision which, as much as any foreign army, was to wreck his empire. He yielded to the demands of the tradesmen and the urgencies of his treasury. At the very moment when England's military hopes had collapsed and England's economy was at its lowest ebb, he abruptly and voluntarily opened a breach in his continental wall. A new decree authorized "trade by exception"—an imitation of Perceval's licensing system. Permits would be sold authorizing ships flying neutral flags to put out from European ports under French control with food to be sold to the British at high prices, and to be paid for in specie. In this way, he hoped—vainly—to drain England of hard money, and produce a financial crisis that would speed her capitulation while strengthening his own treasury. A crop of strange flags never seen before or since on ships promptly blossomed in the North Sea and the English Channel. Little German principalities of the interior—Pappenberg, Kniphausen, Tönningen, Varel —which had never owned a ship, but which were technically neutral, suddenly found themselves the nominal possessors of a merchant marine.

It was Napoleon's belief that he could stop licensing whenever he chose. In this he failed to reckon with the momentum of trade, once it is established. In the year which followed his "trade by exception" decree, eighteen thousand licenses were issued to neutral ships—a development which, French historians have held, saved England from starvation, collapse, and defeat in 1810. Even more serious was the effect on Napoleon's military position, for "trade by exception," as much as anything, cost him his alliance with Russia. The year before, Napoleon had presented himself to Czar Alexander as a man of principle, fighting for the integrity of the European continent against British commercial aggression. Partly on this ground, he had won Alexander's support. Despite a falling off of Russian trade and complaints from his people, Alexander had tried to uphold the pledges given to Napoleon at Tilsit; but when he learned that the Emperor himself had betrayed the Continental System, his patience gave way. If France traded with England by way of neutral vessels, why should needy Russia suffer any longer? From this point on, Alexander insisted on reopening Russian ports to neutral ships, and the cloud of war between Russia and France rose on the eastern horizon.

To Napoleon, who for a time did not sense the full force of Alexander's resentment, his new policy in its early months seemed a success, for British money was coming into Europe in agreeable quantities. So far as the United States was concerned, he made no concessions. However neutral, she was not to share in the profits of the new trade with England. It amused him to hear that, with the announcement of "trade by exception," scores of American vessels had sailed for ports under his jurisdiction. Canning, in a similar situation, had permitted American vessels which had rushed to England during the Erskine affair to return. But the Emperor was in no mood for diplomatic niceties. Orders went out to the satellite nations: seize the American ships. A letter to the Prussian government left no doubt of his attitude: "Let them enter the ports and arrest them afterward. Deliver the cargoes to me and I will take them as part payment on the Prussian debt."

3. *"The Open and Loyal Policy of His Majesty"*

Ruthless though he was in diplomacy, Napoleon preferred when feasible to give at least lip service to the sanctions of usage and his former declarations. It was all very well to confiscate American vessels, but some justification was needed. When John Armstrong demanded to know the reason for the ship seizures, he found difficulty in replying. Early in January 1810, he wrote to Champagny, "Have several conferences if necessary, with the American minister . . . Let me know your opinion on the measures proper to be taken to get out of the position we are in." A month later Champagny thought he had an answer. It was all the fault of the Americans. He told Armstrong: "His Majesty could place no reliance on the policies of the United States," for although America had "no ground of complaint against France," nevertheless she had penalized the French along with the British in the Non-Intercourse Act. "He considered himself bound to order reprisals on American shipping . . . American vessels have been seized because Americans have seized French vessels."

This, however, was too patently false to survive a diplomatic test. Armstrong wrote a hot reply, demolishing Champagny's accusations, denying American aggression against French commerce, and detailing injuries inflicted on the United States by France. He concluded on a note of angry satire. "The confidence I feel in the open and loyal policy of his Majesty altogether excludes the idea that the rule was merely found for the occasion, and made to justify seizures not otherwise justifiable."

By the spring of 1810, over two hundred American vessels and cargoes had been taken, with a value of ten million dollars, and Napoleon tried again to build up his diplomatic position. A new decree, issued from Rambouillet, was international faking at its least inhibited. It now appeared that, after all, the disputed American ships and cargoes had not actually been confiscated. True, they had been sold, but the resulting moneys had been deposited in "a sinking fund." Let American shipowners not despair; the seizures might yet be the subject of adjudication and reimbursement. At last the Emperor felt that he was on solid ground. When Armstrong next complained, he could be told to file suit in any instance of improper seizure, and the French courts would decide. What could be fairer than that?

4. *The Private Emotions of Samuel Smith*

Now the American people knew the worst. Canning had insulted them, Napoleon had betrayed them. Non-intercourse, like embargo, had failed. In a report to the Congress, Albert Gallatin warned that it was "inefficient and altogether inapplicable to existing circumstances . . . Exportation by land [to Canada] is not forbidden . . . Ships sail daily for British ports." He concluded that "all the restrictions [affecting] . . . the commerce and navigation of the United States ought to be removed."

Was peaceful coercion therefore ended as a policy? Not quite yet. There arose in the House of Representatives one of its elder statesmen, the former Speaker, Nathaniel Macon, to introduce a bill to replace non-intercourse. Answering Gallatin's call to remove all restrictions on the country's ships, Macon's bill proposed at the same time to exclude British and French vessels from the nation's harbors. Importations from England and France were to be made only in American bottoms. The way was left open, nevertheless, to restore normal trade relations with England and France if they would lift their restrictions on American commerce.

It was a self-respecting bill, most congressmen agreed, and urgently needed. At that very time, hundreds of British smuggling vessels were hovering off the American coast waiting to pick up cargoes deposited for them at secret rendezvous by American suppliers. The profits of this illegal trade, with its freedom from government supervision and taxes, were making lawbreaking merchants rich. Something had to be done. Although most Federalists objected to the Macon bill, on the ground that it would damage England much more than France, some joined the Republicans in voting for it. Seventy-three to fifty-two, the House supported Macon; and the bill then went to the Senate.

There too the Republicans had a majority, if only a narrow one. It depended, however, on a group headed by Samuel Smith, and Smith on this issue was prepared to break with the administration. It was his guiding principle that any measure urged by Gallatin, "the foreigner," had to be opposed. A more bitter personal enmity did not exist in Washington. When Robert Smith gave a dinner for Thomas Jefferson, and invited the Gallatins, the invitation was ignored, and an explanation refused. It was an open secret that Gallatin believed Samuel Smith to have profited by inside knowledge of his brother's plans, and by illegal trade with England. He had openly charged that during Robert Smith's tenure as Secretary of the Navy the Baltimore firm of Smith and Buchanan obtained naval funds to which it was not entitled; and he never withdrew these charges, although the written evidence in the matter seemed to exonerate the Smiths.

Besides Gallatin's backing of Macon's bill, Samuel Smith almost certainly had more concrete reasons for wanting it defeated. The Senator, it appears, was then deeply committed, through Smith and Buchanan, to contracts to supply English purchasers with American produce—a fact which, if true, could hardly have failed to influence his judgment. When the Macon bill came before the Senate, he rose and moved to amend it before a conference could be held with House leaders. The reading of his amendment stunned the chamber. Of the entire bill he proposed to leave only one clause—that which excluded French and British warships from American ports. For the rest, there were to be no restrictions whatever on foreign vessels. A vote was held; a cynical coalition of Federalists and Smith Republicans voted for the amendment; it passed, although barely; and the battered corpse of the bill went back to the House. There, in an outburst of indignation, the Smith amendment was rejected. Once more the original bill was delivered to the Senate, together with an urgent request from Madison that it be passed.

By this time the attention of the nation was riveted on the contest between President and Senator over a law which might mean the difference between war and peace. Washington boiled with curiosity as to how Smith would reply to Madison, for any attack on the administration was certain to react upon his brother Robert. His speech was long and confused, but ingenious. The Macon bill, he felt, would cause England to retaliate on American commerce by barring American ships from her ports. It was therefore only an indirect way of restoring the embargo. Although he himself had supported Jefferson's embargo, that, he contended, had been an open measure, while this was a deception. "I will never agree . . . in this side way to carry into execution a great national measure."

He knew precisely what he had done. The Macon bill was dead, and the administration had nothing else to offer. At the end of his speech, he turned to an approving Senator in the next seat and said, "I have pleased you and my constituents, but I have killed Robert Smith." From this moment on, he felt sure that brother Robert would be ousted from the State Department; the only question was, when.

5. "I Am For Resistance by the Sword"

Desperately Nathaniel Macon tried to help Madison salvage something from the wreck of peaceful coercion. For with the defeat of the Macon bill, war talk was rapidly gaining head. In the Senate a lanky thirty-three-year-old Kentucky lawyer named Henry Clay rose to say that he had not liked the bill, it was "a crazy vessel, shattered and leaky," but he had voted for it because it afforded "some shelter, bad as it was." At least, it represented resistance—"the peaceful resistance of the law. When this is abandoned without effect, I am for resistance by the sword." Many influential men were inclined to agree. In Congress the great question was whether anyone could devise a bill which Samuel Smith would accept. The proposal that emerged in May 1810, was so feeble that even Macon, who as chairman of the responsible committee had to present it, was ashamed of it. Macon's Bill No. 2, as it came to be called, removed all restrictions not only on American but also on British and French merchant shipping. Its only pretense of resistance to foreign aggression lay in a clause excluding the warships of the belligerents from American waters and in raising duties on foreign imports by 50 per cent. Finally, it sought to bribe either England or France—no matter which—to treat the United States more kindly. If France should repeal her restrictive decrees on American trade before March 3, 1811, then intercourse with England would be broken off; and vice versa. Congressmen rose to denounce the bill as weak, naïve, dangerous—but no one was able to devise another that had a chance of acceptance. Macon No. 2 was passed by the House, and with one amendment, by the Senate. This amendment, however, was significant. Introduced by the Smith faction, it struck out of the bill its only useful provision—the increase in duties. Gallatin's treasury was not to benefit at the expense of Smith and Buchanan.

Madison was in a grim, fatalistic mood as he signed the bill. He knew that it lowered the nation's diplomatic guard; he knew that his enemies, England, the Federalists, and Samuel Smith had triumphed; but with non-intercourse repealed, even Macon No. 2, he thought, was better than no legislation at all. The Republican press growled its disappointment and resentment. Was the policy of sovereign America merely this: that if one of the great powers would agree to cease to harm us, we would undertake to resent the outrages inflicted on us by the other? Many a congressman began to worry about the reaction of his constituents. A Kentucky representative, Richard M. Johnson, later to be a Vice-President of the United States, expressed his disgust with the Congress. "My hopes . . . rest upon the people . . . We may disgrace ourselves, but the people will rise in the majesty of their strength, and the world will be interested in the spectacle."

In Whitehall, news of Macon No. 2 was received with glee. Francis Jackson wrote that Congress "has completed my triumph by repealing, without any concession on our part, the famous Non-intercourse Law . . . for the repeal of which Erskine last year had agreed to sacrifice our Orders in Council . . . They have covered themselves with ridicule and disgrace." Canning, while equally pleased, took a broader view. It seemed to him that the United States, by opening her ports to British commerce, had virtually declared war on France.

6. The Emperor Reacts

The Macon law struck at the heart of Napoleon's economic strategy, by affording England ample supplies from across the Atlantic. Speaking in Parliament, Canning predicted that reprisals by France against the United States would not be long in coming. The unexpected, however, was Napoleon's specialty.

The Macon law acted on him like a high-voltage shock. No sooner had Armstrong sent him a copy of the new act, than with immense energy he set about to shore up the tottering walls of his Continental System. An effort was made to put a stop to "trade by exception," by forbidding the issuance of further licenses. Denmark and Prussia were told that if they failed in strict enforcement of his anti-British and anti-American measures, they would have to reckon with his army. Brother Louis, King of Holland received a letter saying, "I learn that in defiance of my will, you calmly permit your ports to remain open to English trade . . . I shall be compelled to forget that you are my brother . . ." Shortly thereafter, French troops entered Holland and occupied the customs, and Louis abdicated. Sweden, whose new Prince Regent, Charles XIV, was Napoleon's former Marshal, Bernadotte, was threatened with war if the blockade of England was not enforced. To Czar Alexander in St. Petersburg went a letter strongly urging him to use the Russian fleet to seize six hundred merchant vessels, most of them neutrals, then known to be in the Baltic. "There are no neutrals," wrote Napoleon. "They are all English, disguised under various flags . . . They must be confiscated. This will destroy England." When Alexander refused, and referred to Napoleon's own recent scheme of "trade by exception," the French Emperor gave secret orders to his staff to prepare for war with Russia.

War with Russia—yes. But war with the United States? How could that benefit France? Studying the Macon law, Napoleon realized that it offered him an extraordinary opportunity. Superficially, its relaxation of restraints seemed to give England a monopoly of American trade, since France, without an effective navy, had no way to convoy merchant vessels to the United States. Actually, however, its fourth section contained a phrase so loose as to leave an opening for a Napoleonic coup. "In case either Great Britain or France shall . . . revoke or modify her edicts . . ." the President was to announce the fact by proclamation.

For Napoleon to revoke his decrees was unthinkable: such an action would admit the failure of the Continental System and play into British hands. But to appear to revoke them—that was another matter. With skill and luck, he might yet induce the United States to break off intercourse with England. A proclamation such as that contemplated by the Macon law might even in the end produce an Anglo-American war. If so, the British would have fewer naval and land forces available for fighting in Europe, and he would be in less danger of invasion from the west when the moment came to invade Russia. Could Madison be induced to proclaim that France had revoked her restrictive decrees? After all, he had announced the restoration of intercourse with England on no greater authority than Erskine's note. A similar move on France's behalf might be worth an entire army corps to France.

Much depended on the attitude of the American Armstrong. If he did not create obstacles, Napoleon would have a clear avenue to the President. Success or failure then would hinge on Madison's interpretation of the Macon law—on how much proof he would require that the revocation of the French decrees was bona fide, before issuing a proclamation against England. Napoleon was accustomed to taking long chances and he saw nothing to be lost by trying. On August 5, 1810, the Emperor called to his side Champagny, now the Duc de Cadore, and dictated a letter to Armstrong.

7. The Big Lie

This celebrated letter, signed by Cadore, was to put more strain on Anglo-American relations than even the *Chesapeake* incident or the repudiation of Erskine. It began with the bland statement that the Emperor regarded the new American law with the kindest feelings—as an act of friendliness toward France. The preceding Non-Intercourse Act, he said, had been a wicked, an injurious law; but now Congress had wisely retraced their steps. "The ports of America are open to French commerce, and France is no longer interdicted to the Americans. In short, Congress engages to oppose that one of the belligerent powers which shall refuse to acknowledge the rights of neutrals. In this new state of affairs, I am authorized to declare to you, sir, that the decrees of Berlin and Milan are revoked, and that after the first of November [1810] they will cease to have effect; it being understood that in consequence of this declaration, the English shall revoke their Orders in Council . . . or that the United States, in accordance with the act which you have just communicated, shall cause their rights to be respected by the English."

And finally, a touch of the sentimental flattery to which, Napoleon was convinced, Americans were always susceptible. "It is with the most particular satisfaction, sir, that I make known to you this determination of the Emperor. His Majesty loves the Americans . . . The independence of America is one of France's chief claims to glory . . . That which can contribute to the independence, to the prosperity and to the liberty of the Americans the Emperor considers to be in accord with the interests of his empire."

That same night, which he spent at the Trianon, Napoleon issued a secret order to his ministers. All American vessels and cargoes in the ports of France not subject to seizure under previous decrees were now to be confiscated and sold. Other American vessels wishing to enter French ports should be allowed to do so, but might not depart without special permission. America knew nothing of the Trianon order until 1821, the year of Napoleon's death on St. Helena. Albert Gallatin, then minister to France, accidentally uncovered the decree in a file of old documents, and sent it to the White House with an interesting comment: "No one can suppose that if it had been communicated or published at the same time [as the Cadore letter] the United States would . . . have taken that ground which ultimately led to the war with Great Britain."

When Cadore's letter came to John Armstrong, on August 6, 1810, it found him in a low mood. For months his dispatches had been repeating monotonously that Napoleon showed no intention of returning the seized ships or modifying his decrees. Armstrong's warnings of America's "high indignation" had left the French Government unmoved. The Emperor did not much care for him, and at one time, in fact, made a move to have him recalled. A long diet of futility and frustration had left his ego hungry for approval. Now into his gloom came a bright and unexpected ray of hope, the Cadore letter. Taken at its face value, it was everything for which Armstrong had been working. The thought of ending his mission in Paris on so majestic a triumph may well have weakened his native skepticism. The question whether there had actually been an imperial order revoking the Berlin and Milan decrees could not have failed to occur to him. But was this a time to look gift letters in the motive? If demands were to be made on the Emperor to prove his words, let them come from Madison, not himself.

His decision was to send Cadore's letter to the President, without comment, and at the same time to notify Pinkney, in London, of the substance of the letter. These dispatches were not long on their way when a disturbing note came from Robert Smith. It instructed Armstrong to warn France that she must restore confiscated American property and show "indisputable evidence" of a change in her policy before her relations with America could improve. Misgivings now smote him, and he wrote an urgent letter to the French Foreign Office. It centered on a single question: now that the Berlin and Milan decrees were revoked, was France prepared to negotiate compensation for cargoes seized and sold under subsequent decrees? The reply was a flat negative. "The merchandise . . . having been confiscated as a measure of reprisal, the principle of reprisal must be the law in the affair."

This was ominous, it threw grave doubt on the Cadore letter, but the time had passed for Armstrong to ask for "indisputable evidence" of the revocation order. His work in France, he felt, was done, and he took ship for America, leaving the American legation in the charge of his chief aide, Jonathan Russell.

8. *The Fog of Power*

Madison's personality now became the key to American policy; and it is interesting to note how shrewdly Napoleon had gauged it. The principles of government of which the President had nobly written in the great days of America's beginnings had lost something of their meaning for him. The warming glow of life in the inspired world of Franklin, Washington, and young Jefferson had vanished, and there was a chill in the political air. Madison remained a conscientious Republican, and upheld humanitarian ideals, but without heat. His mind had once been excited by ideas, philosophy had been his preoccupation; now he used his wide legal knowledge to serve strictly partisan ends. Unlike Jefferson, who even at his most inconsistent never lost his passionate devotion to peace, Madison was not passionate about anything. His remarks about war were always detached and cool.

In years of bachelorhood, with few if any women in his life, his manner had become solemn, humorless, and suspicious. The private virtues for which those who knew him best gave him credit were those of self-control: he was always kind to slaves and servants (but he never took a stand against slavery); he was temperate in his habits; his domestic life was a model of decorum. A late marriage did not break the crust which had grown around his emotions. If his childlessness ever gnawed at him, he did not say so; he had few close friends, outside of politics. It was difficult for him to unbend with anyone. He left the social side of his life in the hands of his wife Dolly, and the impression they made was caught by Washington Irving in a letter: Dolly "a fine, portly, buxom dame, who has a smile and a pleasant word for everyone . . . but as to Jemmy Madison—oh! poor Jemmy! He is but a withered little apple-John."

In dealing with Napoleon in the Cadore affair the President was at the disadvantage of having no guidance from Armstrong. The letter declaring that the Berlin and Milan decrees would be lifted on November 1 reached him five weeks before that date. The implication that he drew from Armstrong's failure to comment on it was that his minister considered it to be valid. Nevertheless, Madison's own reaction was one of distrust. His notes to Armstrong, whom he imagined to be still in Paris, show that the flaws in the letter did not escape the President's practiced eye. Cadore offered no proof whatever that the decrees had been repealed, and his wording was ambiguous. Was the phrase "in consequence of this declaration" to be taken to mean that the French decrees had been revoked, effective November 1, or merely that they would be revoked, if . . . ?

9. *The Calculation*

Although Madison never made a plain statement of the motives which led to his notorious proclamation in the Cadore affair, significant clues in the evidence strongly suggest the direction of his thinking. He seems actually to have believed that acceptance of the Cadore letter at its face value might stimulate England to lift her Orders in Council. For why, after all, would even so rigid a Tory as Perceval wish to let America drop into the open arms of France? And with the British orders removed, even if Napoleon had not previously revoked his own decrees, the Emperor would have no excuse for holding back any longer. Thus, so long as Napoleon lifted his decrees, regardless of whether he did so before or after the American proclamation, there was a chance that the affair would end with the United States freed from the worst of the restrictions on her trade, and at peace with both belligerents.

In calculating the British reaction to his contemplated proclamation, the President was encouraged by dispatches from Pinkney. Dogged was the word for Britain's mood, not confident. Personal rivalries in the Tory government had caused the sharp-toothed Canning to resign, and the new Foreign Secretary, Lord Wellesley, brother to the great general, was conducting his business in a quiet and unprovocative style. England was undergoing a serious economic, as well as military crisis, and pressure on Perceval's government from manufacturers and merchants to make some concessions to America was increasing from day to day. Following receipt of the Cadore letter, Pinkney reported, he had obtained an interview with Wellesley, and had told him Armstrong's news. The answer had been courteous and definite. "Whenever the repeal of the French decrees shall have actually taken effect, and the commerce of neutrals shall have been restored . . . his Majesty will feel the highest satisfaction in relinquishing a system which the conduct of the enemy compelled him to adopt."

Into this remark Madison may well have read hope that if America proclaimed the revocation of the French decrees, and threatened England with a resumption of non-intercourse, Wellesley might make at least some concession. It would be a gain, for example, even if he only sent a minister to the United States for serious negotiation. Since the Jackson episode, America had been denied the presence of a British envoy plenipotentiary. But if the British remained hostile and the result of the proclamation turned out to be war—at least, it would be with one country only, and that the ancient enemy. Two weeks before issuing the proclamation, the President wrote to Jefferson of "the advantage at least of having but one contest on our hands at a time."

10. *Toward Florida, via Cadore*

Madison could not fail to consider that if he issued his proclamation, and it proved to be without foundation, he would be called cheat or *naïf*. As an experienced politician, however, he was prepared to shrug off criticism that did not actually eat into his power. So far as popularity was concerned, the Cadore letter, even if it were a Napoleonic trick, might indirectly gain more than it lost. It struck him that adroit use of the moment might enable him to fulfill at last Jefferson's dream of acquiring the Floridas. For years, the chief deterrent to seizure of Mobile had been the threat of Napoleonic vengeance. Acceptance of the Cadore letter, however, constituted in effect the diplomatic alignment of America with France against England. This, to Napoleon, had become far more important than the Floridas; under the circumstances he might let them slip into American hands without much protest. As for the Spaniards, there was little reason to worry about their resistance. In West Florida especially, the Spanish government was in desperate straits. It did not know whether the mother country should be considered as allied to France through submission to Napoleon, or to England through revolutionary upsurge. The Spanish governor at Mobile, unable to find money to pay his starving troops, was in no position to offer a serious contest to American invaders. Sooner or later, Madison reasoned, the Floridas would be part of the United States; why not sooner? For pretext, it could be plausibly alleged that British naval forces, if not forestalled, might seize Mobile; and that many Florida Spaniards themselves sought American aid against their decayed government. In the context of the Cadore affair, a move into the Floridas was indicated.

Although, as the President wrote to Jefferson, he had "serious questions as to the authority of the executive" to take action in the matter without specific Congressional sanction, he would not let this deter him. He felt an urgent need to strengthen his personal hold on the country, and especially on his own party. The past three years had seen his political position steadily deteriorate. A strong move was being launched under cover to pit James Monroe against him for the Republican nomination in 1812. One of Monroe's vote-getting appeals was his reiterated conviction that the Floridas should be seized without delay. Another was that a compromise with England could and should be worked out. The first position made him popular with Republican expansionists, the second with Federalists. By moving into the Floridas at once Madison would pre-empt one of Monroe's sources of advantage; by bringing the British controversy to a head, he might dampen the rest of his political ammunition.

Not, therefore, one, but two proclamations were called for. The first was issued by the President on October 27, 1810. It stated that the Governor of the Orleans territory, W. C. C. Claiborne, was authorized to take possession of West Florida, although that region would "not cease to be a subject of fair and friendly negotiation." At the word, men throughout the south and west whooped with joy. A week later, they doubled their shouts in praise of the President, when they read his second proclamation. The French decrees had been revoked. England was put on notice of a revival of non-intercourse, in three months, unless that country followed France's example.

Gasping Federalists immediately formed their own ideas about the meaning of the two proclamations—a deal between Madison and Napoleon—the Floridas in exchange for war with England. The existing evidence, however, points the other way. Madison's letters of the period strongly suggest his feeling that, in the Florida seizure, he was overreaching Napoleon. To Jefferson he wrote his expectation that England, France, and Spain would all "resent our occupancy of West Florida," which might even bring on "a quadrangular contest."

Voices were raised in Congress, asking for proof that Napoleon meant what he said in the Cadore letter. How, lacking proof, could a President who had suffered from the Erskine affair risk another such folly? That Madison should feel some uneasiness over what he had done was natural enough. Not knowing that Armstrong was on his way home, and badly wanting clarification of the Cadore letter, he had Robert Smith write to Paris on the day of the proclamation in words through which anxiety unmistakably burned. "You will let the French government understand . . . [that the proclamation has been issued] on the ground that the repeal of these decrees does involve an extinguishment of all the edicts of France actually violating our neutral rights." "In issuing the proclamation it has been presumed . . . [that America's claims] on the subject of the sequestered property will have been satisfied." In a word, the American government, having proclaimed the revocation, was expressing doubts of France's good faith, and trying to leave escape holes for the President.

11. *Winter of Suspense*

Dispatches coming to the President from his level-headed chargé in Paris, Jonathan Russell, soon threw a murky light on the Cadore letter. Russell saw no reason to believe that the Berlin and Milan decrees had been revoked. On the contrary, a new seizure of an American ship under those decrees had just been announced in France. Disapppointed, the President nevertheless did not lose all hope. Napoleon had recalled General Turreau, and a new minister, Sérurier, was on his way to Washington. Perhaps he bore some proof of the revocation? This prospect too turned out to be a mirage. When Sérurier presented his credentials, and Robert Smith eagerly asked him about the status of the supposed revocation decree, the new envoy merely replied that he had no instructions in the matter. The implication was clear.

The news from Pinkney too was grave. Wellesley had gone into a profound silence. In response to a request for action on the President's proclamation, the Foreign Secretary would say only that he had been unable to obtain authentic evidence of the repeal of the French decrees. Pinkney then addressed several strong notes to his lordship, one of which was almost an ultimatum: it asserted that friendly relations could not exist between the two countries so long as England continued to restrict neutral trade. Still the Foreign Office gave no sign of interest. Finally the frustrated American announced his intention to return home, on the ground that England continued to be represented at Washington only by a chargé d'affaires. Urbanely, Wellesley opposed no obstacle to Pinkney's return. He agreed to send a minister to Washington; but there was no suggestion that the new envoy, Augustus Foster, would be empowered to negotiate concessions for England.

For Madison, that winter of 1810–11 was full of dark portents. His commitment to the Cadore letter was turning out to have large implications for his domestic as well as for his foreign policy. It played a part, for example, in the effort of Republican extremists in Congress to get rid of the Bank of the United States by declining to renew its expiring charter. Gallatin, with Madison's approval, was privately trying to save the bank, for since Hamilton's time, he had changed his mind about its value. Whatever its defects, it had with the years become an integral part of the financial structure of the federal government; and he feared the consequences if the Treasury was forced to rely for financing on greedy state banks. But when

Gallatin urged Madison to use his influence openly to save the bank, the President drew back. Its antagonists included the West's most powerful politicians, headed by Henry Clay; and Clay had linked his position to the President's proclaimed stand toward England. A large part of the bank's stock was held by Englishmen; were foreigners and potential enemies to be allowed to dictate the nation's fiscal policies? "All history," Clay declaimed in his ringing voice, "warns us that republics ought to guard against foreign influence." Had the influence of the British stockholders "released from galling and ignominious bondage one solitary American seaman?" To vote for the bank, he made it understood, would be to vote for the British Government and its Orders in Council, and against Madison's proclamation. Everyone remembered, too, that Madison himself had once sternly opposed Hamilton on the issue of the bank. Now, with his foreign policy in the balance, and an election approaching, he dare not take the risks involved in the bank's defense. Silence was his refuge. Although Gallatin warned him that the death of the bank would make chaos of the national credit at home and abroad, the President remained aloof while his own party ran roughshod over his favorite Secretary; and as a result of his silence, the bank was defeated in the Senate by a single vote, cast by the Vice-President, George Clinton.

Even the most popular element of the President's policy, his plan for the Floridas, generated problems for him. A strident quarrel had broken out in West Florida between Governor Claiborne's forces and American squatters in the territory, who were prepared to do battle to preserve rights which they felt they had established. The President saw the need to move with caution, but he was being pushed farther and faster than he had expected. Western expansionists in Congress had begun to insist that he seize East Florida as well as West, regardless of legal claim. "Retrieve the lost honor of the nation," urged Henry Clay. "British influence" should not be allowed to deprive the United States of "peaceful possession of the country [Florida] to which we are fairly entitled." "I am not, sir, in favor of cherishing the passion of conquest"—but he thought the United States should include West Florida, East Florida, "and some of the territories to the north of us also." The country's approval of this speech of Clay's made Madison cock an attentive ear, and he adjusted to his policy accordingly. East Florida, he decided, should be invested before British forces could go to the aid of the Spaniards there, and early in 1811, he asked Congress for a secret authorization "to take temporary possession of the said territory."

But it was the Cadore affair itself that filled Madison's mind. As February 2 approached, the date on which non-intercourse against England was to go into effect, Federalists in Congress made a major attack on his position by seeking to repeal Macon's law, an act which would automatically have revoked the proclamation; and they nearly succeeded. Assertions that he had been the dupe of Napoleon, and had become the vassal of France, were heard on all sides. His relations with Napoleon were described by John Randolph as "a bargain which credulity and imbecility enter into with cunning and power," while Senator Pickering hinted again at a secession of the New England states, in the event of war with England.

12. *Tightening the Knot*

The trend of the long Congressional debate on British policy threatened what was left of Madison's reputation as a statesman. Retreat, he felt, would be fatal, so instead he mustered his forces for attack. The Congress insisted on proof that the French decrees had been revoked, before they would declare non-intercourse against England. Something had to be put in their hands, so the President gave them the only relevant documents that he had—two letters written by French ministers and transmitted by Russell. The sense of these letters was that the government of France regarded the Berlin and Milan decrees as temporarily and conditionally suspended—very far from the action required by Macon's law. But Madison was caught in a vicious spiral, and sliding fast. The French letters provided at least a diversion—a new ingredient which went into the Congressional pot, and caused it to boil again.

This time, Republicans loyal to Madison proposed a bill affirming non-intercourse with England, in accordance with the President's proclamation. Instantly the extreme anti-British faction proposed an amendment, under which trade with England would remain closed until and unless she should cease to impress American sailors. That this was a *non sequitur*, and full of danger, was pointed out, but the Administration, believing that the amendment would aid the bill's chance of passage, did not oppose it. Late in February, and only a few days before adjournment, the amended bill went to the House for a vote. In desperation, the Federalists attempted what is said to have been the first filibuster in Congressional history, until Congress, repeatedly obliged to remain in session until three o'clock in the morning, became a scene of flaring tempers and challenges to duels. Finally, however, the Republican majority mastered the opposition by violating the procedural rules of the House; and at five o'clock in the morning of February 28 the bill was passed. A day or two later the Senate concurred. Congress had vindicated the President's position. But in so doing, it had sharply tightened the knot of Anglo-American relations by making a resumption of trade conditional not only on repeal of the Orders in Council but on an even more unlikely change in England's impressment policy.

The Congressional session ended with Madison breathing more easily. The bank had perished, government finances were topsy-turvy, loss of revenues from British trade promised to cut tax revenues by one half; but Congress had made an honest President out of him, by accepting the Cadore letter, and had given him the authorization that he needed in order to seize the Floridas. If, by lending himself to the Napoleonic strategy, he had brought the threat of war with England to a new peak, at least, he thought, the country would soon be able to show some concrete territorial gains to compensate for its anxiety.

His trouble now was that, having encouraged the expansionists and ultra-nationalists in Congress by ignoring the sanctions of law in the Cadore affair and the Florida issue, he could not easily curb them. To many hot-blooded southerners and westerners especially, Madison still seemed too cautious, too timid. There was much talk of a surge southward into Texas, Mexico, and South America, to support anticipated revolutions against Spain. The proponents of this plan, most of whom wore Republican cloaks over imperialistic hearts, wanted a bold leader, and their eyes were on Monroe. He had just been elected governor of Virginia, and it was widely agreed that he would be the strongest possible candidate for the party in the election just ahead. The only other serious contender, De Witt Clinton, Mayor of New York City, Madison feared much less; for Clinton, although his impatience for war satisfied the most belligerent, suffered in the eyes of the south from his northern origin.

The thought of losing his second term was as intolerable to Madison as it had been to John Adams. He recalled only too clearly the heavy sacrifice that Adams had made on the altar of peace, when he had refused to capitulate to the war-minded Federalists who held the power of yea or nay over his political future. Madison had then applauded the moral courage of the crotchety New Englander, but he had no intention of following in his steps. To say that whatever had to be done to hold the presidency, that he would do, hardly exaggerates the impression that the President had begun to make on his contemporaries.

13. "The Little Belt"

During the early months of 1811, a possible course of action took shape in Madison's mind—action which would solve not merely one problem, but two. Gallatin, infuriated by the incessant senatorial goading of Samuel Smith, had threatened to resign if Robert Smith remained in the Administration, on the ground that the Secretary of State was privately sabotaging the Administration's policy. Smith would have to go, the President hastily agreed, but the choice of a successor was still open. He waited until Congress had adjourned, and then, through a friendly senator, inquired of Monroe whether he would accept the post, if it should be offered to him. There was a strong implication that the move, if consummated, would put him in the same position of heir-apparent that Madison had held relative to Jefferson. Monroe was tempted. Confronted with a choice between the uncertainty of a fight for the presidency in 1812, and the virtual assurance of success in 1816, he saw much to gain by acceptance. However, he was cautious. Would he be given a free reign to pursue his project of peace with England? Madison gave every promise required of him.

All that remained was to get rid of Robert Smith. The President first tried to avoid an open breach by offering the Secretary the post of minister to Russia. Bewildered, Smith was for a time inclined to accept, but when he awoke to the insulting nature of the proposal, became indignant. Madison then coldly demanded his resignation on the ground of incompetence. Smith, who had been in Jefferson's Cabinet for eight years, who had served Madison through three years of strain, and who thought he had established a harmonious relationship with his chief, was crushed. Following his resignation, he tried to defend himself against Madison's imputations; the trouble, he asserted, had come from his efforts to save the nation from the consequences of the President's pro-French bias. But, as the city of Washington knew, no grapes are so sour as those in the mouths of men out of office; and Smith went into the political discard with a badly tarnished reputation. His experience provided a vivid demonstration of the truism that Presidents seldom become angry over the inadequacy of their appointees until after the political pressures which caused them to be appointed have been removed.

The President's luck seemed to have turned for the better. Early in May, an action took place at sea which strongly suggested the attack on the *Chesapeake* in reverse. This time it was an American frigate, the forty-four-gun *President,* which fought a British corvette of far inferior gun power, the *Little Belt*. British and American versions of how the incident occurred differed sharply. But the essential fact was that the powerful *President* was under orders to search for the British frigate *Guerriére,* which had been reported near Sandy Hook, seizing American vessels and impressing American sailors. If found, the *Guerriére* was to be required to return the impressed men; and few on board the *President* doubted that this would be their chance to avenge the *Chesapeake.* In the distorting dusk of a North Atlantic evening, the *President* overtook the *Little Belt* and hailed her. Receiving no answer, her captain believed the British vessel to be the *Guerriére.* As to who fired the first shot, some uncertainty persisted; but the *President* was as ready with her broadside as the *Leopard* had been four years earlier. After a few minutes, the *Little Belt* was out of action, with thirty-two men killed and wounded. The news sent patriotic America into raptures and was a political godsend for Madison. The public naturally, if irrationally, felt that the nation's honor, battered with the *Chesapeake,* had been restored by the *President.* By association, Madison received credit. Even the name of the victorious frigate redounded to his advantage.

Thus, in the spring of the year 1811, the President's political position had been considerably improved. Yet he had not absolutely committed himself to a fight with England. Federalist anxiety abated when he made it plain that Congress would not be asked to prepare the country for war. Concrete evidence of his gain came from Massachusetts, where an election ousted Senator Pickering, and showed that even in the heartland of Federalism the people had rallied behind Madison's diplomatic challenge to England.

CHAPTER EIGHT

Voices of the Frontier

1. *Lord Castlereagh Cautions*

England's Secretary for War, Lord Castlereagh, was one of those who felt that a war with the United States would be a useless drain on his country's strength at a time when she needed all her resources for the death grapple with Napoleon. Especially he was concerned over the strategic weakness of Canada, which he considered almost indefensible against a determined invasion. All his information from Sir James Craig indicated that such an invasion was the common hope of the Americans. At the time of the *Chesapeake* affair, Jefferson himself was known to have seriously considered an attack on Canada in reprisal. Since then the danger had increased. Castlereagh inquired of Craig, a famous soldier who had fought in the American Revolution, as to his plans for defense, in the event of an invasion. Craig had a definite reply: in order to hold out until reinforcements could arrive from England, it would be necessary to make use of Indian tribes against the Americans. "If we do not use them," wrote Craig, "there cannot be a moment's doubt that they will be employed against us." With this Castlereagh agreed, but he was cautious: Craig, he advised, should not go too fast in his approach to the Indians, lest he inadvertently touch off a war. "We are to consider not so much their use as allies as their Destructiveness if enemies," was the key sentence of the Secretary's instructions.

Craig thereupon ordered an effort to win over the Indians on the American border "without any particular allusion at the present to any possible state of hostilities." The British minister in Washington was urged to reassure the American government that Canada had no desire to foment trouble between the Indians and the United States. Meanwhile the advance British post of Fort Amherstberg, near Detroit, became the center of negotiation with the tribes. On the other side of the border, however, most men assumed that England was planning to launch an Indian war against America, as in the days of Little Turtle. The Governor of the recently established Territory of Indiana, General William Henry Harrison, wrote to the War Department in Washington to expect war: "The Chippeways, Ottawa, and part of the Pottawattomies only wait for the signal from the British Indian agents to commence the attack." From 1807 to 1811, this was the gist of American opinion all along the frontier.

2. *The Shawnee Prophet*

Harrison was well aware that much more than British intrigue lay behind Indian unrest. It was a specific policy of the American Government that the Indians were seeking to resist. That policy had been expressed by Thomas Jefferson (who regarded himself as a friend of the Indians) as early as 1803 in a letter to Harrison remarkable for its frankness: "Push our trading houses, and be glad to see the good and influential citizens among them [the Indians] in debt; because we observe that when these debts get beyond what the individual can pay, they become willing to lop them off by a cession of lands." Harrison dutifully carried out this policy, primarily by encouraging traders to sell demoralizing quantities of cheap whisky which quickly reduced the Indiana tribes to poverty and decay. It became the habit of chiefs who had fallen heavily into debt to tradesmen to cede tribal lands, which did not belong to them, to the Indiana territorial government, which in turn sold them to speculators and reimbursed the tradesmen out of the proceeds. Eventually, the lands came into the possession of pioneering farmers. On the American side, no one from the President down seems to have been aware that this procedure might be considered something less than virtuous. One treaty after another signed by Harrison and the chiefs of individual tribes systematically pushed the Indians ever northward and westward.

The chief of the Shawnees, Tecumseh, determined to try to stem the white tide by peaceful measures. His method was realistic and practical. Instead of permitting the Americans to make treaties with single, defenseless, and incompetent Indian tribes, he proposed to organize all of the tribes of the region into a federation, inculcate discipline and habits of temperance among the braves, and insist that future treaties for land be made only between the American Government and himself, as the spokesman and leader of a sovereign people. Although this intelligent demand evoked Harrison's respect, he was unable to grant it. Tension increased. White settlers, recalling the days of Little Turtle, began to fear that if Tecumseh's federation took shape, they would be massacred. Land speculators and traders did their best to generate an atmosphere of panic, in the hope of pushing Harrison into "preventive" military action.

Chief propagandist for Tecumseh among the Indians was his brother, Tenskwatawa, a fanatical mystic known as "the Prophet" because of supposed clairvoyance. His emotional appeals to old racial memories and to common sense rapidly brought one tribe after another into Tecumseh's federation. By 1806 the frontier was a ferment of anxiety. The only strategy open to Harrison, so far as he could see, was a counterappeal to the Indians. Selecting one of the largest and best disposed tribes, the Delawares, he addressed a letter to them, in which he attempted to expose the emptiness of the Prophet's pretensions. "My children, tread back the steps you have taken and endeavor to regain the right road . . . Who is this pretended Prophet? . . . Demand of him some proofs . . . some miracles . . . If he is really a prophet, ask him to cause the sun to stand still . . . No longer be imposed on by the arts of an imposter . . ."

This letter, entrusted to an Indian, fell into the hands of the British. Which imaginative officer among them was versed in astronomy and saw its possibilities is not recorded, but there seems little doubt that information went to the Prophet that on June 16, 1806, a total eclipse of the sun would be visible to his people. He was not a man to question Fate. Soon all the tribes of the Northwest heard that on the designated day and hour, the Prophet, as proof of his miraculous powers, would cause the sun to disappear. When the day came, and the earth was covered by the moon's shadow, thousands of frenzied Indians put aside any doubts they may have had and acknowledged the Prophet as a true voice of the Master of Life.

Formal federation of the Seven Nations under Tecumseh followed. Almost at the same time, he heard of the attack on the *Chesapeake*. Observing the bellicose American reaction, anticipating an early war between England and the United States, he was determined that the Indian interest should be protected. Since the Americans would not consent to treat with him as the spokesman for the Seven Nations, he would turn to the British.

3. *Tecumseh Warns*

In the spring of 1808, a grand council of the Seven Nations was held at Fort Amherstberg. According to the diary of Colonel William Claus, the British officer in command there, the American Government was notified that the purpose of the meeting was simply to encourage trade. But General Craig himself came from his capital of York to address the chiefs, and to bring them lavish presents; and after dances and games in his honor and exchanges of gifts, he spoke for two hours. Stand fast against the Americans, he urged, entertain no more proposals to sell your lands, but refrain from hostilities. The chiefs on their part agreed that Americans were "always telling them lies and taking their country away from them," and that they must defend themselves. Craig described the success of this meeting for Castlereagh, adding dryly, "In America, fortunately, the system of gratifying these people is not much in vogue."

The Amherstberg meeting, as reported in the American press, created a fresh wave of alarm. One of Kentucky's leading newspapers summarized what was being said and concluded: "The prevailing opinion . . . is that there will be a war," in which America would have to deal with "2,000 Indians, almost exclusively warriors . . . armed and supported at the expense of the British." Harrison wrote to the War Department that the federation of the Seven Nations "was produced by British intrigue in anticipation of war." Reports that Craig had distributed new British rifles among the tribes especially chafed the American frontiersmen at a tender spot, and their aggressiveness increased with their irritation. Now more than ever they were determined to drive the British out of Canada. Craig himself began to have doubts of the wisdom of his policy, for he wrote to Castlereagh of his efforts to restrain the tribes, lest they bring war on England. "A war so near our own frontiers would be very inconvenient . . . and would expose us to suspicion . . . which would sooner or later involve ourselves."

Unlike his fire-breathing brother, the statesmanlike Tecumseh had no illusions about the outcome of a war fought against America by the Indians without Canada's aid. The warriors of all of the Seven Nations numbered fewer than three thousand, while the whites in Ohio alone, where there was a population of over two hundred thousand, could if necessary put an army of ten thousand and more into the field. Tecumseh thought, however, that he had created a situation in which he might expect British backing if he were forced to fight. Holding back the tempestuous Prophet, he awaited the moment when a new crisis between the two white nations would lend itself to his purposes.

In 1810, he thought that the moment had come. After the Erskine repudiation, rumors that the British signal for an Indian attack was about to be given became so general that Harrison sent for Tecumseh, and in a tense meeting sought to persuade him to a treaty of peace on American terms. The chief declined, in a reply that amounted to an ultimatum: if the Americans would restore lands unfairly extracted from the Indians and thereafter pledge themselves to negotiate for land only with Tecumseh's federation, he would be their ally; but otherwise he would be against them in their war with England.

At once Harrison began intensive recruiting for an Indian war—but not a war of defense. One of the strong appeals made for volunteers in the region was based on a description of fertile lands lying north of the Great Lakes, and which the enterprising invaders might hope to claim for themselves. Men from Ohio, Indiana, and Kentucky who might otherwise have hesitated to leave their occupations and expose their scalps were tempted by the prospect of broad Canadian fields to be had for the fighting. Greed was supplemented by the fact that many pioneer farmers, having staked out what they believed to be ample land for their needs, were discovering that their crops were too small to be profitable. Largely because of primitive methods of agriculture and lack of fertilizers, large acreage was required to yield enough produce to support a family, and farms were quickly exhausted. Even farmers with more land than they could cultivate ruefully realized that the time would come when they would have to add new tracts to their domains, or move on. In spite of enormous unpopulated expanses, land hunger was already prevalent. And the Indiana frontiersmen hesitated to move west. There were rumors of ferocious Indian tribes in the Illinois prairies and the plains across the Mississippi; drinking water and timber for construction were reputed to be scarce there; and the few rivers known were considered unsuitable for navigation and mill runs. For the typical speculator or land-poor American of the period, lower Canada was far more tempting than Illinois.

In the summer of 1811, Harrison had gone so far toward open hostilities that President Madison found it necessary to caution him. "I have been particularly instructed by the President," wrote Secretary of War William Eustis, "to communicate . . . his earnest desire that peace may, if possible, be preserved with the Indians." This being said, however, Harrison was allowed to position his forces as he saw fit; and he determined to use them in the way which, he knew, would best please the angry and ambitious men of the frontier. In the northern part of Indiana, on the Tippecanoe River, a strong force of Indian braves under the personal command of the Prophet had established headquarters and moved southward into new hunting grounds on land claimed by white speculators. They appeared peacefully disposed, but the common consensus of the Indiana government was that they had to be dislodged. President or no President, Harrison was determined to march on Tippecanoe before the year was out.

4. "No Man . . . Wants Peace More Than I"

One of the men most active in urging Harrison on was Henry Clay of Kentucky. As early as 1810 he was marked by the country's knowing politicians as a man who would make history; he knew it, and was eager to begin. Using his golden eloquence and his homespun charm with shrewd control, as tools to a purpose, he rapidly made Washington feel his personal force. People had no doubt where he stood. He was openly contemptuous of the diplomatic mind, with its delicate balancing of values and its qualified judgments. Unlike Madison, unlike Monroe, his position was clearly defined. He was for war, "demanded by the honor and independence of the country." War with England, war if need be with France, but war. It was as simple as that. Behind this apparent simplicity, however, was a broad and sure understanding of the road to political power. He spoke for the frontier, and the frontier had begun to assert itself in Washington as never before. The forests and valleys west of the Alleghenies were no longer a mere backyard for the nation, ruled by eastern wealth and policy. Everywhere in the west towns were springing up, roads were being built, new farm lands were being opened. The center of population of the country was shifting ever westward. The census of 1810 showed that out of a total national population of 7,240,000 the recently admitted states of Ohio, Kentucky, and Tennessee already comprised almost a million, and this did not include the towns and settlements of the Louisiana and Indiana territories.

The frontier was vigorous and unsophisticated; it thought in simple, direct terms, in terms of personal experience; if a man's honor was challenged, he fought, or he was less than a man; if a nation's honor was challenged, it ought to fight, whatever the odds, or it was less than a nation. American seamen had been impressed by British warships? Then fight. The *Chesapeake* had been unfairly attacked? Then fight. But Clay's mind operated on a considerably more advanced level. Young as he was, he knew the difficulty of separating the honor of the nation from the advantage of the party and the ambition of the leader. He inveighed against eastern materialism and "the low groveling parsimony of the counting room," but for all that it was the practical interest of the frontier, more than the sentiment of patriotism, that had determined his position.

A new question had arisen in American politics—could the agrarian West, by linking itself to the South, dominate the mercantile East? The foreign policy of the nation would hinge on the answer. The issue was sharply drawn. Despite the Orders in Council, the export trade of the coastal cities was centered largely on England and on trade with the Baltic countries through the British licensing system. Eastern merchants, estimating that even if only one cargo in three escaped seizure and was sold either in England or on the Continent they made enough profit to justify the risk, saw peaceful compromise of differences with England as essential to their security. Precisely the opposite influences operated in the West. Most of its trade had always moved through New Orleans to the West Indies, and to France and Spain. British blockade and peaceful coercion had wrecked this commerce. Western exports of grain and lumber had fallen so far since the embargo that Mississippi River traffic in 1810–11 was said to be smaller than at any time since the Louisiana Purchase. All over the country there was a crisis in agriculture, but it was worst west of the Alleghenies.

The frontier had been willing to back Jefferson in a costly experiment, but it felt no such obligation to Madison. When the repeal of non-intercourse did not produce a revival of their trade, the frontiersmen could see no way of getting rid of frustrating blockades except by war. That the war should be against England they had no doubt whatever, for France was their best potential customer. And there were other factors. The West knew little and cared less about British contributions to America's development, but it did know what an Indian massacre was like. Too many scalps had been taken by braves with knives made in England. The entire Mississippi Valley was influenced, too, by the strong pro-French feelings of New Orleans, which served as its cultural metropolis as well as its port; and by the dramatic and positive personality of Napoleon. Reports of his enormous conquests excited and attracted the frontiersmen: this was a soldier, a leader of men, no shilly-shallying Madison, no high-toned, looking-down-the nose George Canning. The one reason for war against France to which the West had ever given weight was Napoleon's hold on the long coveted Floridas, but now even that reason had vanished. With England acting as self-appointed protector of the disintegrating Spanish empire, it was only from her navy, no longer from France, that serious physical resistance might come to an American drive southward.

Clay and the men whom he led saw a war with England as productive of nothing but good for the West. Their minds were filled with a dream of war in which the Floridas and Texas would be seized to the south, Canada to the north; there would be glory; there would be gain; there would be new states added to the Union under the aegis of the Republican party; and the political power of the western leaders who gave the country such a victory would be unshakable. It was in this conviction that Clay, soon after his appearance in the Senate, took a Cato-like stand from which he never thereafter deviated. England must be whipped again, as she had been whipped in the great days of the founding fathers. "No man in the nation wants peace more than I do, but I prefer the troubled ocean of war . . . with all its calamities and desolation, to the tranquil and putrescent pool of ignominious peace." The discovery that chauvinistic oratory, introduced by a little pious lip service to peace, could open the road to power tempted him to ever more eloquent promises. "The conquest of Canada is in your power . . . The militia of Kentucky are alone competent to place Montreal . . . at your feet." Some senators found his charismatic style distasteful, and on a number of occasions the raised eyebrows and faint smiles of elder statesmen when the young man spoke were noted by the press. The atmosphere of rebuke around him was a factor in the decision reached by Clay, early in 1810, that his influence would be greater in the House, with its "accustomed turbulence" than in "the solemn stillness of the Senate." Running without opposition, he was elected that summer as Kentucky's leading representative in the fateful Twelfth Congress of the United States.

5. Hawks of War

The South, too, was restive and angry, convinced that war in defense of the national honor was overdue. And in defense, too, of the price of cotton. Baltimore and Charleston merchants might prefer peace, but the planters of the interior could not forgive England for screwdriving dictation of the amounts of cotton that America might ship abroad, and the prices to be paid for it. But the chief appeal of the thought of fighting England lay in the fact that war was considered a short cut to seizure of the Floridas and Texas. The South's impatience for these territories was uncontrollable. Cotton plantings were on the increase; and the wasteful plantation system, using up land at a tremendous rate, was compelling landless men to look elsewhere for their livelihood at the same time that the landed were seeking to add to their properties. Rich or poor, the typical southerner had his heart set on conquest of the rich Gulf lands. And since feeble Spain, owning these lands, was under British protection, the fight would have to be with England. The only question that remained was how to persuade the rest of the country to declare the war that the South wanted. The answer lay in Canada; this was the bait with which the northern states were to be tempted from peace.

There was also a more subtle force, not yet clearly expressed, but which had begun to generate hatred of England. A few years earlier, Parliament, in a humanitarian mood, had forbidden Englishmen and English ships to engage in the slave traffic. The American government had followed with a similar ban, leaving the market to Yankee smugglers and Spanish traders. In the three years after 1807, the price of slaves had increased about 25%. And now it was reported that many Englishmen, influenced by the radical William Wilberforce, were demanding that slavery itself be abolished throughout the British empire. Already this pernicious way of thought had taken root in New England, where too many men had become outspoken against slavery in America. Foresighted southerners asked themselves whether, if this doctrine were to prevail in the heavily populated North, with its financial power, they would be able to remain in the Union. From this question, it was but a step to the conclusion that to protect their most sacrosanct institution against northern attacks the prestige and influence of England in America had to be cut away.

As the West had found a voice in Henry Clay, so the South discovered its most effective spokesman in young John Calhoun. Tremendously energetic, gifted with a penetrating and logical mind, educated at Yale, married to a landed heiress, he, like Clay, was earmarked for success. When, in the spring of 1811, he was elected to the House of Representatives from South Carolina, veteran congressmen made way for him, as for Clay of Kentucky. For election returns from all over the country had confirmed the power of these two, as the most effective advocates of war with England. The American people were weary of uncertainty. Years of economic frustrations, maritime humiliations, Indian massacres, and anti-British preachments had finally begun to prevail over commercial caution and the human desire for peace. Revolt at the polls in the West and South against "submission men" had swept away nearly half of the former members of the House of Repre-

sentatives. The men who replaced them were young, hot-blooded Republicans of the Clay-Calhoun stamp, if without their genius—"pepperpot
politicians," "buckskin boys," as their enemies called them; "War Hawks,"
as they proudly called themselves.

Madison's problem was thus complicated by a new difficulty: could he
control the War Hawks in the next Congress? Political falconry had never
been his forte. Although his party was solidly in power, with all but seven
seats in the Senate, and a four to one majority in the House, he sensed that
his own political future was again in jeopardy. With war sentiment rampant,
his re-election to the presidency could be assured only in one of two ways.
Either the British would have to concede enough to make it appear that he
had triumphed without war—in which event, he could keep the War Hawks
on leash; or to prevent them from turning on him with claws and beak he
would have to submit to their tugging, and let them soar.

CHAPTER NINE

Scruple and Inhibition

1. *"The Americans Grow Warm"*

The discouragement of the President grew when the new British minister, Augustus Foster, arrived in Washington, for although he had all the marks of a thoroughly qualified diplomat, his instructions were to yield nothing on any major point of dispute. Only in one matter—the *Chesapeake*—was he authorized to make an offer of settlement. The reparation proposed was as meager as it was tardy, but Madison felt that the attack on the *Little Belt* would justify him in the country's eyes if he accepted. This hope too was disappointed. The moment it was known that the settlement had been reached, Republican papers from Kentucky to New York berated the Administration. The Lexington *Reporter* said the Cheapeake agreement was "only a sop, to stop the mouth of Congress." "Like restoring a hair after fracturing the skull," jeered the Baltimore *Whig*. The New York *Evening Post* saw the President's action as "DECEPTION . . . exactly what we expected . . . Good God—Reparation!!!!"

Unable to reduce the mounting war fever, Madison and Monroe made a concentrated effort to convince Foster that England's last chance for peace depended on repeal of the Orders in Council, and their earnestness broke through his shell of skepticism. After he had been in the country only a few weeks, his dispatches to Wellesley began to reflect America's actual state of mind with more accuracy than had been found for a long while in reports to the British Cabinet. Writing on the *Little Belt* affair, he described the willingness of the American Government "to settle this, with every other difference, in the most amicable manner, provided his Majesty's Orders in Council are revoked; otherwise, to make use of it, together with all other topics of irritation, for the purpose of fomenting a spirit of hatred toward England, and thereby strengthening their party."

Foster's notes carried conviction and produced an effect. The British administration, which had lost no previous opportunity to fan popular indignation against America, became suddenly cautious in the matter of the *Little Belt*. This affair, which a little earlier would have touched off hysterical British demands for war, in 1811 received astonishingly little notice in England's press. One newspaper complained that the government had "knuckled down to the Yankees" in the *Chesapeake* settlement; another insisted on large redress for the *Little Belt*; but the prevailing tone was surprisingly calm. When the government proposed to send a special envoy to America to negotiate reparation, the entire incident quickly dropped out of notice.

While the serious Foster was generating concern in the British Government, the clever and effervescent French minister, Sérurier, was having the opposite effect on Napoleon. In the summer of 1811 he enthusiastically reported to Paris that "the Americans grow warm very slowly, but at last they are heated; and at any moment the least spark can light up a conflagration from the Gulf of Mexico to Canada." Madison's indignation at Napoleon's double-dealing made little impression on Sérurier. He reported it to Paris merely as an interesting sidelight on the situation. "The revocation of the Decrees of Milan and Berlin has become a personal affair with Mr. Madison." But that any change was required in the Emperor's disposition toward the United States, he never even remotely suggested.

2. *Monroe Thinks Again*

Napoleon could only conclude that his cynical American policy was succeeding, and that it should be maintained at full strength. In this, as generally in his estimates of Madison's attitudes, he was right. The President's anger at France, which he expressed to Sérurier and often paraded in his cabinet, was not deeply felt. While his official notes to Joel Barlow in Paris fulminated against the Emperor's disregard of pledges given, and even warned of "hostile conditions between France and America," his private communications showed that where Napoleon was concerned all could be forgiven. A letter to Jefferson, written in March 1811, indicates his real attitude: it was difficult, he said "to understand the meaning of Bonaparte toward us. There is little doubt that his want of money and ignorance of commerce have had a material influence . . . In all this his folly is obvious . . ." To excuse Napoleon's aggressions and deceptions on the ground of "ignorance" and "folly" was sufficiently grotesque, but Madison went farther in his misreading of Napoleon's mind. The Emperor's failure to carry out the Cadore "agreement," he thought, was due to his lack of faith in America's promise to break off intercourse with England! Like Jefferson before him, the President was disposed to tolerate from France offenses which, coming from the British, brought out his righteous wrath. To say that he had at this stage decided on war, however, would be an exaggeration. So vigorous a decision was beyond him. His letters to Jefferson and others give the impression of a man confused, always coming from some place, but never going anywhere. It was as if the abrasive events of his presidency had rubbed away his Jeffersonian idealism and left him barren of resources for peace. He seems to have regarded himself as an American Sisyphus rolling the stone of peace upward but knowing all the time that it would not reach the top. In this spirit, he had allowed American policy to be sapped of its power of initiative; it could only totter as pushed. Jefferson's "peaceful coercion" had given way to Madison's dazed opportunism.

The President's pro-French bias was generally recognized, and it put James Monroe in an annoying position. On him fell the requirement to reproach Sérurier for Napoleon's defaults, and to demand that his promises be fulfilled. But Sérurier knew perfectly well, and Monroe knew that he knew, that the American people had ceased to worry very much about the Cadore letter, and that there was nothing that the President could do about it. To compound his embarrassment, the Secretary of State was forced to tell Foster the precisely opposite story: that England had no reason to delay the repeal of her orders, for the French decrees were no longer in effect. Monroe lacked zest for this empty little game. His hope of working out a diplomatic compromise with England, he now saw, was altogether illusory, so long as he lacked presidential support. Madison's espousal of the new Non-Intercourse Act against England had created a situation that no Secretary of State could alter. The road to peace was now blocked not merely by a diplomatic muddle, but by a law which pushed diplomacy to the sidelines—which required a virtual British surrender, on impressment as well as on the Orders in Council, before trade could be resumed.

3. "After This, Will Any Doubt?"

The President, motivated largely by his desire to please the hotspurs, had convened Congress one month earlier than usual. When the House assembled on November 4, 1811, he became instantly aware that the prevailing wind was from the West—and no mere breeze, but a gale. The administration had supposed that one of the veteran Republicans of the House would be made Speaker, but on the first ballot, in defiance of all precedent, the freshman representative, Clay of Kentucky, was elected to the post by a tremendous majority. At that moment the young man became the second most powerful political figure in the United States. As he sat in the Speaker's chair on the rostrum, reporters observed that his unofficial title, Chief of the War Hawks, was fittingly symbolized by the enormous stone eagle, with outspread wings and claws, high above his head in the chamber. With remarkable skill Clay threw himself into the task of reorganizing the House committees in the same image. Calhoun was put on the powerful Foreign Affairs Committee, where he soon became acting chairman. They could see no obstacle on their road to war. Using his gavel with a force and mastery that inhibited opposition, Clay was able to dominate the House in spite of fretfulness at his steam-roller tactics. "The boy dictator," John Randolph called him. "Mark my words, sir," he told a friend, "we shall have war before the end of the session."

The President's message to the Congress, read on November 5 seemed deliberately to play into Clay's hands. Unblushingly, Madison maintained the fiction that France had revoked her objectionable decrees, although he admitted that no proof had yet been given "of an intention to repair the other wrongs done to the United States." Toward England, however, he showed himself openly hostile, blaming the troubles between her and the United States solely on British refusal to repeal the Orders in Council. He went on to invite—but indirectly, always indirectly—a declaration of war by the Congress. The period had arrived, he said, "for more ample provisions" to maintain the nation's rights. "Congress will feel the duty of putting the United States into an armor and an attitude demanded by the crisis, and corresponding with the national spirit and expectation."

One hope of peace, and only one, was implicitly conveyed by the President. It was observed that he spoke not a word about impressment. For Augustus Foster this was a significant omission. Was the President saying that if the Orders in Council were repealed, war might be avoided even if the impressment issue were not immediately settled? His letter on this point was noted in Whitehall. But for the rest, Madison's message was as aggressive against England as his nature permitted.

If the War Hawks needed anything more, it was some new shedding of American blood for which the British could be held accountable, and even this was not denied them. A week after Congress had convened, news came from Indiana of the expected fight at Tippecanoe. It was hardly more than a frontier skirmish between a force of about five hundred Indians, and an American "army" of nine hundred, led by General Harrison; and later accounts disclosed that the victory of the Americans was dubious, Harrison's generalship had been mediocre, and that the battle had resulted largely from his provocative actions. At the time, however, all that mattered was that scores of Americans, including some Kentucky volunteers, had been killed and wounded by Indians armed with new British rifles and knives. The resulting outcry in the nation released many in Congress from their last Jeffersonian scruples. Here, surely, was provocation enough to put an end, once and for all, to passive resistance. "British-Savage War! The Blow Is Struck!" The frontier press shrieked its rage and blood lust. "The war on the Wabash is purely British," asserted Kentucky's editors. Tennessee, through the mouth of the commander of her militia, Andrew Jackson, roared that "the blood of our murdered heroes must be revenged!" Pennsylvania's leading newspaper asked, "After this, will any doubt? . . . Will Congress treat the citizens of the Western Country as they have treated the seamen of the United States?"

4. *The Inward Search*

Underneath all the furore, however, there seemed to be some hidden inhibitions at work in the government. The Foreign Affairs Committee of the House was surprisingly dilatory in its deliberations. Impatiently the House waited, and at last the committee reported a resolution "in favor of actual war, at a given period." Fifty thousand volunteers were to be recruited, merchantmen were to be armed, warships refitted for active service, privateers encouraged. "It is the sacred duty of Congress," solemnly the committee gave assurance, "to call forth the patriotism and resources of the country . . . to procure that redress which has been sought for by justice, by remonstrance and by forbearance in vain."

The war, then, was to be for redress? This was not quite satisfactory to some congressmen. Searching their consciences, they could not fail to see that if the war was to be waged on this ground, it should be against France, as much as against England. As the House proceeded to debate the war bill, other reasons for fighting were set forth. The veteran Macon of Carolina preferred to think that the country was about to fight for justice—"for the right to export our native produce." A prominent War Hawk encouraged dubious legislators by reminding them that the United States in war could destroy British fisheries and British West Indian trade, while conquering Canada, and that all this would not, after all, cost very much. "By carrying on such a war at the public expense on land, and individual enterprise at sea, we should be able in a short time to remunerate ourselves ten-fold for all the spoliations she [England] has committed against our commerce." Here was a solid, if tough, reason for sending fellow Americans into battle, but more sensitive congressmen were somewhat dismayed by so much frank materialism. A young representative from Tennessee, a Jeffersonian known for his integrity, Judge Felix Grundy, whose former stand against war was well known, searched his heart for the benefit of the House. War was always a danger to liberty—they were "about to ascertain by actual experiment how far out republican institutions are calculated to stand the shock of war." He was not entirely sure that the nation could subsequently "again assume our peaceful attitude." If it had been wrong, as Jeffersonians held, to go to war in 1799 against France, was it right to fight England in 1812? Despite all this, Grundy thought that perhaps the Republican party would be justified in reversing its policy, in order to "resist by force the attempt . . . to subject our maritime rights to the arbitrary and capricious rule of her [England's] will." But here, too, he had to admit a difficulty. If Orders in Council and impressment, if even the *Chesapeake* incident, had not been considered sufficient reason for war in 1807, what had happened in five years to make them causes now? Grundy avoided having to answer the embarrassing question by falling back hurriedly on the fight at Tippecanoe to account for his change of mind. The war, he thought, had "already begun." By this time, however, Tippecanoe was some weeks in the past, and there was no evidence, nor ever would be, that the British were responsible for the battle. More and more the attack on Harrison's force appeared as a desperate Indian attempt to stop the American invasion of tribal lands

As the Congressional debate went on, the weakness of the moral position of the War Hawks became the center of argument. Soon they found it necessary to fall back on the unanswerable mystique of imperialism. Canada and the Floridas—all North America—had to become part of the United States—it was so written in the stars—the national honor could be satisfied with nothing less. Declamations to this effect were made so frequently as to produce profound irritation among thoughtful congressmen. To retort, there arose on the floor of the House John Randolph, the "madcap Virginian," long a lone wolf of the Republican party, shrill, baretoothed, many thought a little deranged, but enormously effective in polemic. With satire, jeers, and sneers at those who invoked honor without understanding the meaning of the word, he bore down on the War Hawks' real purpose. The war legislation he saw simply as "a scuffle and scramble for plunder" by agrarian interests. For the splashing patriotism of the West he had nothing but contempt. It was but a cover, he thought, for a landgrab. "Ever since the report of the Committee on Foreign Relations came into the House, we have heard but one word—like the whippoorwill, but one monotonous tone—Canada, Canada, Canada!" Let the nation beware, he warned, for the conquest of Canada would give anti-slavery elements a new accession of strength which in the end would force the South to secede.

Southerners, shaken by Randolph, were reassured by young John Calhoun. "The real spirit of union," he confidently asserted, would be increased, not diminished by war. To those who hesitated to fight England lest they give economic advantage to special interests, Calhoun flatly declared that "protection and patriotism are reciprocal," that it was the duty of the nation "to protect every citizen in the lawful pursuit of his business." Calhoun was effective, but the uneasiness of the House grew as it groped to explain its own bellicosity. One congressman justified his position by asserting that he was against war, but for the war legislation; and as legislators have done since the days of ancient Rome, he quoted the hoary fallacy that the best way to prevent war is to prepare for it. Finally, voices were raised to beg that the debate be shortened. Was it not absurd, one congressman asked, to put the enemy on notice of the country's intentions by open discussion of what should have been a secret plan? England was being given far too much opportunity to reinforce Canada.

In time, the Congress grew tired of talking and voted on the so-called war resolutions, which were carried by huge majorities in the House and Senate. It was noted that a number of prominent Federalists crossed party lines to vote with the War Hawks. Their motive, however, was peculiarly their own. With their eyes on the election of 1812, Federalist leaders were now willing to gamble on the chance of a short, undecisive, unpopular war in order to recapture the government. In dispatches to Wellesley, Augustus Foster reported that some Federalists in Congress "make no scruple of telling me that they mean to give their votes for war . . . that war will turn out the Administration, and they will have their own way, and make a solid peace with Great Britain." The Federalists, he said again, were "pushing for measures so decisive as to leave him [Madison] no retreat. It has been told me in confidence . . . that if the Orders in Council are not revoked he must eventually be ruined in the opinion of the nation." Therefore, urged the Federalists, let England by all means retain her orders until after the election. Foster himself found this line of reasoning unsatisfactory. He reiterated to Wellesley that England would have to revoke the orders if war was to be prevented.

Many Americans believed that the vote on the resolutions actually meant war. It did not dawn on the people for some time that Congress had done no more than to instruct itself to prepare for war by appropriate legislation, which now had to be created and passed. Nevertheless, the President was pleased to have Congress thus take the initiative, and relieve him of responsibility. He was encouraged, too, by word that Thomas Jefferson himself had publicly spoken for war out of his retirement. "We are to have war, then? I believe so, and that it is necessary . . . War or abject submission are the only alternatives left to us. I am forced from my hobby, peace."

5. A Talk on New Year's Day

At the year's end, not many people outside the administration realized how difficult it was for Madison to give open aid to the War Hawks. The fact was that he could see no way to ask outright for war on England unless he was willing also to urge war on France. Reports had arrived telling of heavy depredations by Napoleon against American ships, not only in the ports of Europe, but on the high seas. The Emperor had managed to get a squadron of French warships past the English fleet and into the Baltic. There they had systematically captured a large number of American merchantmen engaged in trade with Russia. Other American ships trading with England had been burned and sunk. "His Majesty loves the Americans," the Cadore letter had said: the contrast between word and deed would make Madison more than ever seem the dupe of France, if under these conditions he were to seek a declaration of war on England. One of the President's strongest Congressional supporters, Nathaniel Macon, wrote in a private letter that "the Devil himself could not tell which government, England or France, is the more wicked."

Madison's internal discomfort was further increased by knowledge, not yet given to the American people, that from the beginning of 1807 to the end of 1811, French seizures of American ships had substantially exceeded those of England. The most popular of New York's newspapers, the *Evening Post*, never ceased to remind its readers that the French as well as the British had mistreated American sailors, who had been "robbed and manacled . . . and marched without shoes to their feet or clothing on their backs in the most inclement weather some hundreds of miles; lashed along the highway like slaves, treated with every possible indignity, and then immured in the infernal dungeons of Arras or Verdun." A Massachusetts rhymester caught the weakness of the administration's position in a caustic verse:

> If England look askance, we boil with rage;
> And blood, blood only can the wound assuage;
> Yet whipt, robbed, kicked and spit upon by France,
> We treat her with the greater complaisance.

This was the psychological background against which, on New Year's Eve, the President read a report come from Savannah that sailors off French privateersmen had engaged in a fight with American sailors. Knives had been drawn and men killed on both sides; after which a mob had set fire to the French ships and destroyed them. That the French minister, Sérurier would cry out was a foregone conclusion. An urgent request from him for a meeting with the President was promptly granted, and on New Year's Day he called at the Executive Mansion, vigorously protested the Savannah incident, and demanded reparation. This was a little too much even for the mild Madison. He retorted (as Sérurier wrote to Paris) that "it was not less distressing to learn what was passing every day in the Baltic," and accused the French Government of "hostilities as pronounced as were those of England."

The same day, Sérurier was privately given to understand by Monroe that until the French Government modified its policy, the administration could not press Congress for a declaration of war on England, and he hastily sent a report of this conversation to Napoleon.

6. And Still No War

As time moved into January 1812, and the Congress struggled to create and pay for a suitable army and navy, the President's failure to urge them on made many wonder. He was accused of wishing to see Congress take full responsibility, so that if the war should prove unpopular, he himself would not be too deeply committed when he had to go before the voters in the autumn. Representatives and senators fumed and boggled at the unpleasant tasks before them. Lacking presidential leadership, they were unable all through January to arrive at a suitable plan for financing the war. Only with great difficulty was Congress able to squeeze out of itself even a law authorizing the President to accept volunteers for war service. Meanwhile, a letter from Gallatin told the House that the financing of war would require sharp increases in taxation on whisky, on salt and other commodities, and a rise in duties on imports. Here was news sure to dampen the patriotic fervor of many congressmen's constituents. The West resented the tax on whisky, the South thought the tax on salt unjustified, the East was mortified by Gallatin's proposed new tariffs. His failure to say all this at the beginning of the session was sharply criticized, and a protracted debate on war finances followed. By February, so much of the war spirit had oozed away that a bill proposing to build thirty-two new warships at a cost of $7,500,000 was defeated in the House. The majority of the Congress were ready to vote for a declaration of war, if the President had asked for one; but in four months they had not voted for a single practical measure designed to win the war if it should come.

The country, sensing the indecision in Washington, began to think that the war cloud was lifting. On February 28, 1812, John Jacob Astor, who was in close touch with Gallatin, wrote with glee and in his own inimitable orthography to a Canadian correspondent that "We are happy in the hope of Peace & have not the smalest idia of a war with england."

CHAPTER TEN

The Crillon Comedy

1. *The Gentleman from Paris*

In the middle of January 1812, there appeared in Washington a handsome Frenchman who bore the distinguished title of Count Edward de Crillon, whose manner, decorations, and letters of introduction would have been enough to assure a good reception even to a man without ancient and noble lineage. He called first on Sérurier, and after presenting his credentials, entranced the minister with a story so remarkable, and of such large implications for the American administration, that Sérurier unhesitatingly gave him an introduction to Monroe. The Secretary of State was similarly impressed. Within a few days of his arrival, Crillon was seated in Madison's office, enthralling the President.

Some years earlier, Crillon said, he had unfortunately incurred the Emperor's displeasure, and had thought it best to leave France. England had received him, not as a traitor to France, but simply as a private gentleman and aristocrat, down on his luck; and in London, he had met a young Irishman, Captain John Henry. This was the man whom the Governor General of Canada, Sir James Craig, had a few years earlier sent to Boston as a secret agent. In that capacity, Henry had come into the possession of information in the form of letters showing the readiness of prominent Federalists to side with England in the event of war. It seemed to him that in return for his patriotic service the British government ought to pay him more than Craig had paid, and he was able to obtain some encouragement in this direction from Francis Jackson. In 1810, therefore, he traveled to England to solicit a just reward, which he estimated at no less than £32,000, but after more than a year his hopes were still unfulfilled. Whitehall had its own methods for such cases; Henry was shuttled from office to dusty office in a dreary passage of time, until finally the light dawned. He then quitted England in a bad humor and took ship for Boston.

Through a coincidence, so Crillon said, he himself had independently decided to visit the United States, and elected to travel on the Boston packet. During the long voyage the two unfortunates became close friends and confided in each other. The young Englishman felt that he had been badly treated by England—a country which he had never been taught to love—and would be justified in disposing of his letters to a more appreciative buyer—for example to the government of the United States. He could not be sure, however, how far the American Government would trust a confessed British agent or how generously it would deal with him. Here Crillon had a suggestion. His own connections were of the best; he at least would be assured of a hearing. It would be his pleasure to serve his new friend by approaching the French minister, Sérurier, who, he felt sure, would receive him in spite of his slight contretemps with the Emperor. And he had still another suggestion. Henry was a man of refinement, of civilized tastes, of sensibility. Upon being rewarded by the American Government, he could not very well stay in the United States, where his letters if published would incur the enmity of prominent citizens. Nor could he go back to England. Why not, then, France, and a life of ease and pleasure? Crillion could solve this problem also. He himself, while short of ready cash, was agreeably rich in land and châteaux. One of his estates, at St. Martial near the Spanish border, yielded a fine income, but he himself now had little benefit from it. Well, then? Henry was excited by the prospect of life among the French *noblesse* and they made a written covenant: if, following Crillon's efforts, Henry was suitably rewarded by the American government, he would pay the sum of $50,000 to Crillon out of the proceeds, in return for title to St. Martial. A fair purchase price for the letters, Crillon agreed, would be $125,000.

2. *The John Henry Papers*

President Madison, impressed by Crillon's frank story and charmed by his personality, asked his wife to give a dinner for him, and for several weeks thereafter the young Frenchman was lionized by Washington hostesses. Sérurier, seeing in him a valuable instrument for French policy, gave him financial assistance and spoke enthusiastically of his "conduct and language" in letters to the French foreign office. Meanwhile, a messenger was sent to Henry in Boston, with instructions to bring him to the President under conditions of absolute secrecy.

Early in February, Madison held in his hands the allegedly explosive letters. He must have felt some disappointment. Most of them were copies or paraphrases of letters which Henry himself had written two years earlier to Sir James Craig, telling of his talks with prominent New England Federalists. To be sure, Henry drew some controversial conclusions from these talks, such as that America's chances of avoiding defeat by England were negligible. "A war," he insisted to Craig, "would produce an incurable alienation of the eastern states, and bring the whole country in subordination to the interests of England." But such statements, however disturbing, were not actual evidence of Federalist treason. One document struck the President as perhaps more useful than the others—Henry's original instructions from Sir James Craig. Considered in conjunction with Henry's letters, it could be regarded as evidence that the British Government had sought to foment dissension and secession in the United States by the use of a secret agent.

The President's mind, at that moment, was focused on two practical objectives: to push Congress into adopting Gallatin's wartime tax measures, and to aid the Republican-Democrats in the spring elections for the state legislatures. The John Henry papers might not be in themselves significant, but shrewdly presented, they could advance the interest of the President and his party. The question remained, how much were the papers worth to the Treasury of the United States? The $125,000 asked by Henry was out of the question. How much then? Monroe, who handled the monetary transaction, offered $50,000, which he could find in a discretionary fund which Congress had placed at the President's disposal to deal with unforeseen contingencies in foreign affairs. The figure left Henry a little blue; it was no more than would pay for the estate at St. Martial. After talking with Crillon, however, he decided to accept; for the revenues from St. Martial, he learned, would repay him in a year or two. Crillon solved the problem of immediate funds for him by providing drafts on a friend in Paris who served as his banker. The deal was struck; on February 10, 1812, Monroe gave the money to Crillon, who then handed to Henry the title deeds to the estate at St. Martial.

From the President's standpoint, it was desirable to have Henry out of the country and on his way to France before the great day of the exposure. He had determined on a device which he felt certain would make publication of the letters doubly effective. Recalling vividly the effect produced by John Adams when he substituted the letters X, Y, and Z for the names of Talleyrand's agents, Madison permitted Henry to keep the names of his Federalist friends out of the letters, and to substitute rows of enigmatic asterisks. The actual names would be the President's secret, not to be shared with Congress; and hence a dark threat over the heads of the Essex Junto.

Henry was rushed from Washington to New York, and put on board an American warship to insure his safe arrival in France. Joyously, Sérurier reported to the Foreign Ministry in Paris that the great day was about to dawn. "The Administration has decided to publish Henry's documents . . . Much is expected of this exposé. The conduct of M. Crillon since his arrival here has never ceased to be consistent and thoroughly French . . . I hope that the service he has just rendered . . . will earn him the indulgence of the Emperor and the return of his favor." To a request from Monroe that nothing be said of the way in which the President had obtained the letters, Sérurier readily agreed.

As Adams had sent the XYZ papers to Congress, so now did Madison with the John Henry papers. A covering letter charged England with "fomenting disaffection to the constituted authorities of the nation," and of plotting to destroy the union, "forming the eastern part thereof into a political connection with Great Britain." For all his partisan purpose, however, the President did not forget his duties as statesman. A curt note went to Augustus Foster, saying that he hoped publication of the Henry letters might "produce a good effect by bringing matters in a more peremptory manner before his Majesty's government."

The first result of the John Henry disclosure was all that the President had hoped for. The Republican press instantly beat drums and sounded trumpets. "The Plot to Dismember the Union" was a typical headline; England was accused of trying to blast "the holy bond" of American unity. Henry Clay expressed his delight. The letters, he felt, would "accelerate a declaration of war." Macon said that he was "struck with horror" and called for war without delay. Reporters noted that when the letters were read to the House, many a New England Federalist "began to kick and squirm"—"looked pale"—"wiped away great drops of sweat."

The John Henry papers were on everyone's tongue. "Henryism" became the derisive word to describe pro-British leanings. Overnight, however, Federalist panic gave way to sober reflection. What actual proof had the President offered of the party's involvement? The letters were not written to Henry, after all, but only by him; and they were not originals, merely copies or paraphrases. In fact, close reading made it possible to say that the papers, instead of implicating New England Federalists in a treasonable intrigue, actually exonerated them of complicity. For it was plain from Henry's statements that his unnamed informants had never realized that he was a British agent, and so could hardly have conspired with him. As for the proof that the British Government employed secret agents and *provocateurs*, was this surprising, or justification for war? At that very time, as the Congress knew, raiders subsidized by the administration were in East Florida, ostensibly to aid a mythical revolution against the Spanish government there. Was the President less culpable, critics asked, than Sir James Craig? The question, which was repeated again and again, became so embarrassing to Madison that he had finally to protect himself against it. With obvious discomfort Monroe disavowed the Florida raiders. Their leader, General Matthews, was told that he had "mistaken the President's wishes"; and his loud protests were ignored.

Federalist leaders quickly decided that the President, in publishing the Henry papers, had harmed them less than he had himself. When they demanded a Congressional investigation, his party did not feel safe in refusing it; and in consequence the administration was soon badgered with more awkward questions. How had the President dared to spend $50,000 of the taxpayers' money for papers which were merely an unsupported libel on a political party? How had he got them? Who had received the money? Madison's insistence that the letters must speak for themselves satisfied no one. Even Republicans felt that if the President knew more than he was telling, having gone so far, he was obliged to share the rest of his information with the people. A Congressional resolution was passed, calling on him to reveal the names of Americans who had conspired with Craig; and Monroe had to reply that the administration did not have such information. Then, Federalists retorted, what purpose were the letters supposed to serve? Merely that of partisan politics?

The star witness called by the investigating committee was the Count de Crillon himself. Always correct, dignified, charming, and before an audience filled with feminine admirers, the Count told his story with engaging frankness, withholding only Sérurier's part in the affair. Of the letters themselves, he professed ignorance. A few days later, his prestige undamaged, he took ship for France with the avowed intention of begging Napoleon's forgiveness and the right to serve in the advance guard of the army then being mobilized for the war with Russia. In his pocket were warm letters of recommendation from Monroe to Barlow, and from Sérurier to the Emperor.

3. *"At What a Moment!"*

For about two weeks, the President remained hopeful that in spite of difficulties the Henry papers had strengthened his position. Then on March 23, news came that French warships had seized and burned two American merchantmen loaded with grain, which they had been licensed to carry to British troops in Spain. Overnight the Henry affair was dropped by the press. So the President still believed that the French decrees had been repealed? Republicans as well as Federalists vented their fury at Napoleon, and as the tide of public opinion turned, Madison found himself once more the butt of attack as a mere dupe and errand boy for the Emperor. Monroe sent in haste for Sérurier, and spoke to him in words of astonishing frankness, which the French minister reported to Paris:

"Well, sir, it is evident that we are to receive nothing but outrages from France! And at what a moment! At the very instant when we were going to war against her enemies . . . We have made use of Henry's letters to uplift the nation and the Congress . . . within a week we were going to propose . . . the declaration of war . . . It is at such a moment that your frigates burn our ships, destroy all our work, and put the Administration in the most false and terrible position in which a government can find itself."

Instantly Augustus Foster took advantage of the situation by demanding, once again to see the official French document which revoked the Napoleonic decrees, and which alone could justify the American demand for repeal of the Orders in Council. Monroe and Madison squirmed. The only reply they could make was that "the case of the two American ships which were burned could not be said to come under the Berlin and Milan decrees." It was a defense so feeble and meretricious that even the administration's friends in Congress could not stomach it, and sat in silence under the Federalist attack.

So much strategy, so little result! The war with England once more seemed remote.

4. Thirty, Sixty or Ninety Days

Having exhausted his own resources, the President listened to the opinions of Henry Clay. It was Clay's view that the country would never prepare adequately until it found itself at war. Declare war first, prepare later, he advised. But before the declaration, let an embargo be placed on all shipping for thirty days. American merchantmen would thus be off the high seas and protected from seizure when war began. The President agreed in principle, but characteristically thought thirty days too short a time. As a measure of precaution, the embargo ought to be laid for sixty days, he suggested: the additional month would provide greater flexibility for the administration. Clay, while not pleased, made no serious protest; to him the important fact was that at last Madison had come to a decision. That night, March 15, the Kentuckian bluntly told Senator James Bayard of Delaware that there would be war.

The new measure was proposed in a secret message to Congress and debated behind closed doors, on April 1, 1812. Although few opposed the idea of an embargo, the question of its duration became a matter of hot debate. Prominent congressmen openly stated their belief that England should be given a chance to react to the embargo before war was declared. It seemed not impossible that England might yet make concessions in order to avoid the stoppage of American grain shipments to the British army in Spain. Her economic condition, by all reports, was worsening, and her political attitude softening. George III had at last been declared insane, and his son, the Prince Regent, the former friend of Charles Fox, was steeped in Whig ideas, one of them the desirability of peace with America. At the opening of Parliament in the preceding January, American newspapers reported, the Prince had been extremely temperate in his remarks about the United States. Some congressmen even saw hope in the fact that Lord Wellesley had resigned as Foreign Minister, and his place had been given to Castlereagh, who was comparatively well-regarded in America, if for no other reason than because he had fought a duel with Canning and had wounded him slightly. From all this, moderates in the Congress reasoned that time was working for peace, and that its chances would improve if only the War Hawks were not allowed to carry all before them. Hearkening to this argument, Congress concluded that the embargo should remain in force not for sixty, but for ninety days. In the same spirit, a number of representatives began to press for an early adjournment which would make a declaration of war impossible until Congress reconvened in special session. The narrow margin by which this move was blocked by Clay revealed the declining influence of the War Hawks.

5. Madison Agonistes

Suddenly everything was going wrong for the President. The Massachusetts election resulted in a worrying Federalist victory: so much for the effect of the John Henry letters. New York elected a Federalist Assembly. There was open talk that either Mayor De Witt Clinton of New York or Monroe might replace Madison as his party's nominee in the autumn. Ardent patriots in the South were turning against him, for with his disavowal of General Matthews his scheme to subsidize an American-led "revolution" in East Florida had collapsed. As for the embargo, public disapproval of it was growing from day to day. Port conditions had begun to resemble those of 1807. Finances too were a constant worry. An attempt by Gallatin to float a national loan in order to finance the expected war failed miserably when the banks of leading states refused co-operation. Out of $11,000,000 of "government stock" offered, only $6,000,000 was taken.

What had happened to the war fever? Sérurier gloomily reported to Paris in May that "this cooling of the national pulse . . . adds to its [the administration's] embarrassment and hesitation." To discourage the French minister further, the country learned that Madison had been unable to obtain any further information on the Berlin and Milan decrees from the French government. "On this news," he reported to Paris, "the furious declamations of the Federalists, of the commercial interests, and of the numerous friends of England were redoubled; the Republicans, deceived in their hopes, joined in the outcry . . . nothing was heard but a general cry for war against France and England at once."

The nadir of the administration's prestige was reached when a dispatch arrived from Joel Barlow that gave everyone in Washington, outside of the President's immediate circle, the best laugh of the decade. The Count de Crillon, said Barlow, was a fraud. He was not a member of the famous Crillon family. No one had ever heard of him or of the alleged estate of St. Martial. The person on whom he had drawn funds in Henry's behalf had long been dead. Sérurier informed Paris that "the President . . . and all the secretaries . . . are a little ashamed of the eagerness shown him [Crillon] and all the money they gave him . . . On my part . . . I have little to regret . . . I have constantly refused to connect myself with his affairs . . . The papers have been published and have produced an effect injurious to

England without . . . a single *denier* from the Imperial treasury." What Sérurier did not know was that Crillon was an agent of Fouché, head of Napoleon's secret police.

As the Crillon comedy came to its end, the Federalists pressed their advantage. Anti-war proposals began to emanate from the Congress. The President was urged to appoint a strong minister to England, where there had been no qualified American envoy for a year. Petitions for the repeal of the embargo were circulated. John Randolph shook even the War Hawks by a speech on the nation's unpreparedness. "I know that we are on the brink of some dreadful scourge . . . some awful visitation from that Power whom, I am afraid, we have as yet in our national capacity taken no pains to conciliate . . . Go to war without money, without men, without a navy! Go to war when we have not the courage, while your lips utter war, to lay war taxes! . . . The people will not believe it!"

Among other troubles, Madison's administration suffered from the fatal defect of dullness. He never seemed to grasp the point that in order to make government effective, it is first necessary to make it interesting. People generally, and Americans especially, have never been willing to submit themselves to colorless authority. To make men agree to alter their established ways or put up with protracted pain in the hope of a later good, there must be inspiration in the air, a feeling of faith in the future. It is enough for the success of a Secretary of State if he is able to extract agreement from the few, but a successful President in time of crisis has to be able to inspire enthusiasm in the hearts of the many. In Madison's time, both the enthusiasm and the agreement were lacking. The public refused to follow him when he went forward to meet issues. For him, the only path open was that of least resistance, where the pitfalls are always deepest.

By mid-spring the President had almost lost hope that the War Hawks would be able to push the Congress into war. When a group of prominent moderates from both parties urged him to send a mission to England to negotiate peace, he seized on the idea as a tired swimmer grasps at a floating log. Senator Worthington of Ohio reported to friends that the mission, to be headed by Senator Bayard of Delaware, was settled. To prepare the way for it, the Washington *National Intelligencer*, which Madison used as his sounding board, published an editorial asserting that the embargo "is not war, nor does it inevitably lead to war." Amazed, the country realized that the discouraged President no longer had a policy; he was frankly groping for a way out of his dilemma, without war, and without losing the presidency.

CHAPTER ELEVEN

The Bullet of Chance

1. *The Practical Man*

The guiding principle of British policy toward America, up to the spring of 1812, had been the conviction that the United States would not fight. It was a conviction instilled in the mind of Prime Minister Perceval by "War in Disguise" Stephen, "Copenhagen" Jackson, and John Henry, who had many a letter from New England Federalists to support their thesis. Even Foster's dispatches, flatly warning of war in the near future if the Orders in Council remained in force, did not shake Perceval. He was one of those men who are so anxious to feel certain that they never take time to find out. It was his view that the United States really had no right to complain. Nevertheless, since she did complain, England would be understanding and gentle. In a speech to Parliament in late February, the Prime Minister deprecated the suggestion that England was in any way hostile to the United States. His country, he said piously, "could bear more from America for peace's sake than from any Power on earth."

His righteous confidence seemed able to withstand every strain. A formidable test came when riots linked to the Orders in Council broke out in the northern countries. The textile industry had once more become badly depressed by loss of the American market. Unemployed and starving workers, however, found it easier and more gratifying to vent their feelings on a visible and immediate cause—the spinning and weaving machines which had displaced much hand labor. They entered mills and smashed machinery, until the scale of the riots soon became so wide as to suggest an organized conspiracy. Troops had to be called out to suppress the Luddites (a name taken by the rioters in memory of a worker named Ludd, who had been the first to smash a weaving frame as an act of defiance). Although the breaking of spinning and weaving frames was made a capital offense, and men were hanged for it, the trouble grew until there was talk throughout England of another Wat Tyler rebellion.

Martial law, stern suppression by force, and wholesale executions of workers was Perceval's answer to the Luddites. He paid little heed to angry Whigs in Parliament who pointed to the Orders in Council as the real root of the insurrection, and demanded their repeal and the restoration of the American market. He shrugged at petitions for repeal from textile manufacturers, who were not comforted by knowing that fellow Britons owning

? check out this point —

ships sailing under neutral flags were reaping rich rewards from the orders. If there had to be a choice, he was for shipping, as more essential to England's welfare. As for the unemployed men and women who were exciting sympathy on the streets of London by their pinched faces, tattered clothes, and Hogarthian misery—their lot was of course to be regretted, but such was the way of the world.

2. *Perceval Stands Fast*

Late in March, however, heavy pressure against the orders began to come from sources that Perceval could not ignore. The Russian ambassador, in the name of Czar Alexander, made strong representations against permitting the orders to generate an Anglo-American war. The Czar, having managed to end his war with the Turks, was rallying all his forces for defense against Napoleon. It was his hope that while Napoleon's army was approaching Russia, England would seize the opportunity to land troops in the Netherlands. If the British Government now allowed itself to be diverted into an American war, both Russia's outlook and England's would be darkened.

The Russian view that the Orders in Council ought to be repealed promptly for the sake of peace with the United States found strong support even in Perceval's Cabinet. Richard Wellesley's resignation as Foreign Secretary had involved this issue, for he feared that a transatlantic war would increase the difficulty of supplying his brother's army in Spain, then heavily dependent on American grain. So prevalent was desire for peace with the United States that Perceval had found the greatest difficulty in replacing Wellesley with a qualified Tory who would support the orders. A number of the most prominent men in his party had refused to serve under him, and Castlereagh, the former Secretary of War, who had finally accepted the Foreign Office, was known to have reservations on the subject. More than once Perceval himself had to rise in Parliament to defend the orders against punishing attack. His speeches in their defense were monotonously consistent. He made no pretense that the orders were founded on justice or morality. The principle underlying them, he said in his characteristic style, was simply "to secure to the natives of England that trade by means of licenses, the profits of which without them would devolve to the hands of aliens." In other words, it was a matter of business—and let the Whigs attack business, if they dared.

In spite of all that he could say, Parliament would not let go of the question. Early in March, the Marquess of Lansdowne, son of the late Earl of Shelburne, followed in his father's footsteps as a champion of peace with America by urging the House of Lords to form a committee for consideration of the Orders in Council; and he was supported by Wellesley and Grenville. The eloquent young Whig, Henry Brougham, made a similar motion in the Commons. A sharp debate followed, in which the dangers of Perceval's policy were fully exposed. It reached its climax when George Canning took the floor. Commonly regarded, if without much ground, as coauthor of the orders, he was expected to support Perceval. Instead, he turned on him. It was his view, he said, that the orders no longer served to injure France, but now "operated solely to the injury of the neutrals," and were thus no longer justifiable.

Parliament was intensely excited as the motion to review the orders came to a vote. When the Tory majority held and the Commons rejected Brougham's motion, Perceval did not wait to assert his triumph. Determined to foreclose the issue, he instructed Castlereagh to draft a dispatch to Foster in Washington, reaffirming the British Government's policy. The resulting document made no more attempt to defend the principle of the orders than had Perceval in the House. Instead it took a position on one of the narrow legalisms dear to his heart. England, wrote Castlereagh, stood ready to rescind the orders as soon as France revoked her decrees. But even if France were to issue a decree of revocation, if that decree applied only to America and not to the other neutrals England could not regard it as justification for a similar action on its part. The British Government had never engaged to repeal its orders "as affecting America alone." To do so would be "the grossest unjustice to her allies and to all other neutral nations." This was casuistry carried to new heights, even for Perceval.

3. Perceval Yields

Despite his outward self-assurance, the Prime Minister knew that his political position had been badly weakened by the controversy over the orders. The next attack might be fatal, might force him to choose between resignation and capitulation, unless he could quickly strengthen his ministry with influential figures. Where to find new blood for the Cabinet? By this time, hardly a politician in England was willing to link his fortune to Perceval's, on Perceval's terms. Desperately, he turned at last to a man for whom he had always expressed contempt, the man responsible for the Peace of Amiens, Henry Addington, now Lord Sidmouth. When even Sidmouth would not accept a cabinet post unless the Orders in Council were reconsidered, Perceval reluctantly yielded to his stipulation. The administration, he said, would no longer oppose Parliamentary action on the orders.

Instantly a change was perceptible in the government's attitude toward America. The Prince Regent, on April 21, issued a formal statement which in tone distinctly foreshadowed repeal of the orders, although still making it conditional on revocation of the French decrees. Opponents of the orders, men like Lansdowne and Brougham, called on the people to express themselves. Petitions for repeal, signed by hundreds of prominent men, poured in on Parliament. Hearings before Parliamentary committees showed that the orders had been largely responsible for the blight that had fallen on the British economy. The drift of the House was steadily away from Perceval. Right-wing Tories did their best for him, but early in May some British newspapers were predicting repeal and Perceval's resignation.

4. *A Man Named Bellingham*

The American legation in London, at that time, was under the charge of Jonathan Russell, who had been transferred from Paris a few months earlier. His state of mind was badly depressed. The British Government, now that it had sent Foster to Washington, was irked by failure of President Madison to appoint a ranking minister in Pinkney's place, and it paid little attention to Russell. With his acquaintance in British political circles exceedingly limited, and knowing little of Parliamentary politics and personalities, he could not easily form independent judgments of the trend of national sentiment. The British press, which was habitually insulting to the United States, and official documents received from the Foreign Office were his chief reliance for information. With these as a basis, he early came to the dispirited conclusion that Perceval's majority in Parliament was large and solid, and that the orders would not be repealed. From the American standpoint, he reported to Monroe in March 1812, the situation was hopeless; and he repeated this early in April. Over the next month, the President heard nothing from him to indicate the large and growing pressure on Perceval to recall the orders.

On May 11, however, Russell had at last something of consequence to report. The city was suddenly alive with horrified excitement. That morning, entering the House of Commons, the Prime Minister had been approached by an unknown man, who had pulled out a pistol and without a word shot him through the heart. For a brief time it was believed that the assassination was politically motivated. One newspaper even alleged that the assassin was an American. But inquiry soon revealed that the tragedy sprang only from the deranged mind of a sick and unfortunate Englishman named Bellingham, who had never met Perceval, but had fixed on him as the author of his troubles. Somehow Bellingham had obtained a pistol, and the rest followed, leading, as the London *Times* sorrowfully said, to the death of "a thoroughly honest politician, whose private character was above all reproach or suspicion."

The political implications of Perceval's death for America were obvious to Russell. Eagerly now he awaited developments in Parliament. It was his hope and belief, as he wrote to Monroe, that a new government would quickly be formed, and would repeal the orders without delay. Almost at the same time, Russell received from Monroe a note announcing the ninety-days' embargo. Calling on Castlereagh to present it formally, he directed attention to the date on which the embargo had taken effect, April 4. On July 4 it would expire. The implication could not be missed: England had until then to avert America's "second war of independence" by repealing the Orders in Council. Much now depended on a prompt choice of the next Prime Minister and on his ability to organize a Parliamentary majority. But the Prince Regent, hoping for a coalition Tory and Whig ministry, found that Whigs like Grenville and Gray would not serve under Tories like Wellesley and Canning, and vice versa. Week after week of hectic political jockeying passed until a precious month had gone by; and still the British administration was without a head, and no significant action could be taken.

5. The Emperor Obliges

The new French Minister of Foreign Affairs, Hugues Maret, Duc de Bassano, was a far more positive personality than Cadore, who had been abruptly ousted by Napoleon a year earlier for being insufficiently enthusiastic about the Russian war. News of the American embargo, sent by Sérurier, reached Paris in the early days of May, quickly followed by a dispatch quoting Monroe as saying that "imminent war with England . . . was inevitable if the news expected from France answered to the hopes they [the American Government] had formed." To Bassano's thinking, Sérurier's dispatches came at an excellent time; they would make an excellent parting gift for the Emperor, as he prepared to leave for the Russian frontier. There was only one danger—that if France failed to make some responsive gesture toward America, the Congress might yet insist on including her in any declaration of war. Ever since his arrival in Paris, the American Joel Barlow had been hounding Bassano with wearisome demands for proof that the Emperor had actually revoked his decrees, and for redress in the matter of ships subsequently seized or burned. A strong note, dated May 1, 1812, had stressed the danger of delay. No one had to tell Bassano that Madison's political fate in the next election might depend on the desired proof.

Napoleon was then extremely busy with military preparations, but he recognized the importance of the papers which Bassano put in his hands. To set the Americans finally at England's throat and to re-elect the impressionable Madison were goals worth a little effort. On May 10, 1812—one day after the Emperor had left for the Russian frontier—Bassano calmly handed Barlow a decree which the American, by his own account, stared at with incredulity. It was dated at St. Cloud, April 28, 1811; it was signed by the Emperor; and it stated that previous decrees would cease to apply to American shipping, as of November 1, 1811—exactly one year after the date of the Cadore promise.

The St. Cloud Decree was a piece of audacious mockery characteristically Napoleonic. That it was concocted for the occasion, Barlow strongly suspected; otherwise, surely, it would have been produced long since. But the essential point was that, while ostensibly supporting Madison's contention that France had revoked her decrees, at the same time it contemptuously announced to the world that he had either been completely hoodwinked by the Cadore letter, or had chosen to serve as Napoleon's henchman. The revocation, if the St. Cloud Decree could be believed, had taken place only months after the United States had broken off intercourse with England; it was merely a payment for services rendered.

What was Barlow to do? Accuse the Emperor and Bassano of fraud? Cautiously, he asked Bassano whether the St. Cloud Decree had been published. The Foreign Secretary had evidently been expecting the question. Without turning a hair he replied that although the decree had not been published, it had been communicated to the former American chargé in Paris, M. Russell, and also to Sérurier in Washington. Barlow thought it extraordinary, then, that the news had not previously reached the President. Doubtless, came the ready explanation, the dispatches had been lost because of some mishap at sea. Barlow tried again. How did it happen that the decree was never submitted to the French Senate? As to that, said Bassano, the Emperor did not wish other neutral nations, and especially Russia, to know that America was being favored.

There was nothing for Barlow to do except send copies of the St. Cloud Decree to Madison and to Jonathan Russell in London. Bassano took care of Sérurier, in a letter which insisted with a straight face on the fiction of copies lost at sea. "I have learned from M. Barlow that he is not acquainted with the Decree of April 28, 1811 . . . You yourself, sir, have never acknowledged its reception . . . This silence makes me fear that . . . [it] did not reach you, and I think it proper to enclose here a new copy."

6. England Concedes

The St. Cloud Decree, transmitted by Jonathan Russell to Castlereagh in the middle of May, was a serious embarrassment to the still headless British Government. Only a month earlier, Castlereagh himself, writing for Perceval, had taken the position that the Orders in Council could not be repealed until the French decrees had been revoked—and revoked for all neutrals, not merely for America alone. And here was an ostensible act of revocation designed to apply exclusively to the United States! It is understandable that Castlereagh heatedly called the St. Cloud Decree "a disgraceful trick;" Napoleon had put him in a position where he could not endorse repeal of the orders without reversing the position which he had taken a month earlier.

To the Foreign Office it was perfectly obvious that Napoleon was seeking to prevent repeal, that he was counting on the orders to assure war between England and America. The decision as to how to proceed had to await the selection of a new Prime Minister. More precious days passed; then, early in June, the Prince Regent gave up his notion of a coalition, and called on Lord Liverpool, a capable man, who had seen service as Foreign Secretary, to form an all-Tory cabinet. By June 8 Liverpool had picked his men and obtained Parliamentary approval. Almost his first act was to announce his intention to deal with the Orders in Council. Four days later the Cabinet discussed the matter. A way around the problem was proposed: instead of letting Parliament force repeal of the orders, why not voluntarily suspend them, without explanation? So it was arranged. On June 16, when Broughham rose in Parliament to move for repeal, he was answered by Castlereagh with the somewhat embarrassed announcement that the Orders in Council had just been suspended on the initiative of Lord Liverpool.

England, with the exception of her shipowners, breathed a deep sigh of relief. The Tory press changed its mind overnight, ceased to defend the orders, and even expressed indignation that they had been permitted to survive so long. "We are most surprised," sternly said the London *Times*, which had staunchly supported Perceval, "that such acts could ever have received the sanction of the Ministry when so little was offered in their defence." The remaining question in the minds of Englishmen—and of Jonathan Russell, as he sent the good news to Washington by fast boat—was whether it could reach Madison in time. If war came, ruefully said the *Times*, it would be the most unpopular war ever known. "Everyone would say that with happier talents it might have been avoided."

CHAPTER TWELVE

"Chaff Before the Wind"

1. *Clay's Ultimatum*

On April 9, 1812, President Madison was preparing to send a peace mission to London to negotiate for repeal of the Orders in Council. On June 18, two days after England had bowed to American pressure by suspending the orders, the United States declared war on England. The written evidence of the intervening seventy days reveals the sequence of events that made up the President's unhappy mind for him, putting an end to what Sérurier called his "perpetual oscillations."

The propulsive touch that launched Madison toward his final decision came from Henry Clay. A diary kept by Senator Thomas Worthington of Ohio records that on April 12 or 13—the precise date is uncertain—a group of "hot-headed violent men" headed by Clay called at the Executive Mansion. Officially they represented the Republican-Democratic caucus of congressmen on whose vote the nomination for the presidency would depend. According to the diary, Clay told Madison that "nothing less than open and direct war with England would satisfy that committee," and that "they would forsake him and be opposed to him" if he persisted in his peace overture to England. Subsequently Madison informed Worthington "that his friends had waited upon him," and that he considered himself "bound to comply with their wishes."

This, at least, was what Worthington wrote; and while historians have sought to throw doubt on the authenticity of his story, it is difficult to believe that he invented it for the purposes of a private and unpublished diary. He was, however, a strong advocate of peace and in attributing overt threats to Clay, he may have distorted the Kentuckian's tone in the affair. The relationship between the President and Clay had always been, and continued to be pleasant and unconstrained—which is not likely to have been the fact if the Speaker had browbeaten Madison in the presence of others. Clay had nothing to gain and much to lose by challenging Madison's dignity and self-respect. There was no reason for him to do so. It was easy for a man of his persuasive talents to put the case for war in terms of the nation's security, and to let the rest be tacit. All that was necessary was to quote the Republican newspapers of the period on the trend of events in Europe. The prevailing belief of the party was that Napoleon would soon conquer Russia, and thereafter beat England to her knees. Little weight was given to the fact that, in such an eventuality, despotism would have conquered constitutional government. The desire to be on the winning side was strong in the country, and few stopped to remember that in most wars the winning side can seldom be chosen with certainty until after the fight is over, and not always then. The treatment which Napoleon's former ally, Spain, had received at his hands did not shake the conviction of many War Hawks that a wartime alliance with the victorious Emperor would give America a subsequent claim on his good will.

Even those who were less sanguine of Napoleon's success could find a rationale to justify war against England. If one assumed that the French had not enough strength to master England, there was all the more reason for the United States to aid them; otherwise she might later have to face British might by herself. Madison's incessant correspondence with Jefferson shows that this plausible, if superficial reasoning carried weight with him.

It is hard for a statesman and impossible for anyone else to distinguish between his motives of public policy and his motives of private satisfaction. In Clay's eloquent mouth the argument that it was safer to fight at once than later could have provided the President with respectable reasons for saving his political skin, and not much need have been said about the nomination. Nevertheless, when Federalist Congressman Josiah Quincy of Massachusetts rose on the floor of the House to assert that "plunging into a war with Great Britain was among the conditions on which support for the Presidency was made contingent," not a single Republican rose to defend Madison against the charge. With superfluities boiled away, the residual fact emerges that Clay delivered an ultimatum to the President, and Madison yielded to it.

2. "The More Immediate Impulse"

On April 14, the administration's chief organ, the *National Intelligencer*, came out with an editorial completely reversing its pacific stand of five days earlier. No talk of peace missions now. Two sentences told all: "Let war therefore be forthwith proclaimed against England . . . Any further discussion, any new attempt at negotiation, would be as fruitless as it would be dishonorable."

There is convincing evidence that the editorial was written by James Monroe, possibly at the instigation of Madison himself, but at the time its style was thought to resemble Clay's. Washington took its authorship for granted, and Federalists said that Madison was being driven by Clay "like chaff before the wind." The elation of the War Hawks was unconcealed. On April 18, Calhoun wrote that "war is now seriously determined on." A week later, when the House rejected a Senate move to recess on the ground that war would be declared before the embargo had run its course, the Republican press roared its approval. As to the contention of the Federalists that England would soon repeal her orders, it was brushed aside. The main reason for war, according to the War Hawk leaders, was not the orders, but impressment. "Accursed be the American government, and every individual of it who . . . shall agree to make peace with Great Britain, until ample provision shall be made for our impressed seamen, and security shall be given for the prevention of such abominable outrages in future." Thus the leading Republican magazine, *Niles' Weekly Register*, a few days after Madison's capitulation to Clay.

Yet a shade of doubt of the President's intentions still remained in the minds of the War Hawks. The Republican-Democratic caucus had been expected to convene in April, but Clay, who had power to fix its date, showed himself in no hurry. Soon a rumor spread which Augustus Foster hastily communicated to London: "The reason why there has been no nomination made in caucus yet, by the Democratic members, of Mr. Madison as candidate for the Presidency is, as I am assured in confidence, because the war party have suspected him not to have been serious in his late hostile measures, and wish previously to ascertain his real sentiments." To take advantage of this situation, the British envoy conceived a remarkable idea: nothing less than to persuade Federalist leaders to promise Madison their support, and so make him independent of the War Hawks, if he would forego a declaration of war. Here, however, Foster ran up against the hard fact that most Federalists would have none of Madison on any terms.

By the middle of May, the caucus could no longer be postponed. The War Hawks held to their bargain, and Madison was unanimously renominated. He could not yet be easy, however. Disturbing news soon came from New York—that Federalist leaders there had struck a malodorous bargain with the dissident Democratic Governor of New York, De Witt Clinton. In return for Federalist support, Clinton, who firmly controlled New York State, had agreed to seek peace with England if he should be elected President. What made this development particularly ominous was that letters reaching Madison from unofficial sources in England strongly suggested that a pacific change in British policy was imminent. If it came, it would greatly strengthen Clinton's chances. The President's quandary was reshaping itself around him. With Clinton standing for peace, defiance of England was the only possible campaign position left open to himself. But if he was to justify a declaration of war, he needed fresh evidence of England's hostility to put before Congress without delay—a reason for war that did not apply as much to France as to England. It must have been an enormous relief to him when, late in May, Lord Castlereagh's dispatch of April 10 arrived, setting forth the inflexible Perceval policy. Years later,

Madison insisted that "the more immediate impulse" to war had been given by this dispatch. Coming when it did, it enabled him to tell the Congress that England had given America a choice only between war and base submission. A few days later, on June 1, 1812, he called the Congress into secret session to hear his war message.

3. Pretext and Reality

The internal evidence of the President's message shows that it had been in preparation for weeks. Like all Madison's state papers, it tried to make up by thoroughness what it lacked in inspiration. His problem was to rally the country's partisans to a semblance of unity in the face of danger. To this end, he began by reciting the long and mortifying list of abuses which the United States had suffered at England's hands over the years. Then he went on to summarize his reasons for a declaration of war. First among these reasons he put impressment. Here he was secure—few Americans denied that the forcible seizure of American sailors was an outrage warranting war. Even though over twenty years some of the heat had gone out of the issue, it could still be depended on to excite patriotic fervor.

By emphasizing impressment, the President safeguarded his position against expected concessions by England on the Orders in Council. He needed a reason for war which English diplomacy was not likely to remove. It did not trouble him that the British and his political adversaries could say, with some justice, that in thus pushing impressment to the fore he was ruthlessly misleading the American people. For more than two years, impressment had been distinctly subordinate in the President's negotiations with Foster, and repeal of the Orders in Council had been almost the sole demand made by the United States on the British Government. To cite impressment as the chief justification for war was like blaming one's grandfather for one's troubles. The impressment problem was actually much less acute in 1812 than it had been in preceding years. Whigs in England's Parliament had been hotly criticizing their government in the matter, and for the first time, British naval officers were making a serious effort to distinguish between real and pretended American citizens. Early in 1811 Castlereagh had been compelled to supply Parliament with figures on the number of impressed Americans in the British Navy. Thirty-five hundred sailors, he found, claimed American citizenship, and there was reason to believe that about half might be telling the truth. This was a grave admission; but against it had to be put the fact that approximately fifty thousand deserters from the British Navy were estimated to be serving on American vessels, and the American government had done nothing to end the traffic in illegal citizenship and forged papers. For a decade, Gallatin estimated, desertions had cost England an average of about twenty-five hundred men per year; while the annual toll of impressments was about five hundred—of whom about one fourth were actual American citizens. If the American government had not long since offered more resistance to the British impressment policy, the reason lay partly in the fact that, in terms of manpower, the advantage of the existing situation was overwhelmingly with the United States. The same factor was influential in preventing compromise. It is significant that up to this time the American government had never offered, as it was soon to offer under the adversities of war, to exclude native Englishmen from U.S. vessels if England would give up the right of impressment. In the days of Charles James Fox, England had been ready to discuss such an offer. The entire history of the impressment controversy reveals Madison as much less than candid in making it, in 1812, the main pretext for a declaration of war.

Besides impressment, the President told Congress, three other provocations by England justified military retaliation—the harassing of merchantmen off the American coast, the imposition of paper blockades of Europe's coast, and last, the Orders in Council. All of these were serious grievances; what Madison did not say was that Augustus Foster, within the previous fortnight, had indicated the readiness of the British government to negotiate on all three counts.

The realities of Madison's position were not to be found in his message. His diplomacy had reached a dead end; he was weary and devoid of new ideas; his political situation made him susceptible to pressures toward war; and he held two dangerously wrong convictions—that Canada could be easily conquered; and that after Napoleon defeated Russia, England would be at France's mercy. A complex of depression, ambition, and misconception had brought him to war, more than England's crimes.

His avowed reason for selecting that particular moment for war was equally based on fallacy. The President read Castlereagh's note of April 10 as making further delay useless. Yet he knew that strong elements in the British Parliament were fighting hard for repeal of the Orders in Council. Apparently he had no intuition of their success, or if he did, he kept silent. Meanwhile Congress acted on the assumption that England had put an end to negotiation.

4. "Throw Forward the Flag!"

The President's effort to bridge partisan differences by whipping up a sense of national outrage against England proved unavailing. From the first, the Congress was bitterly divided. On June 3, the House Committee on Foreign Affairs asserted that the United States must fight "or submit to the most shameful degradation," and a bill calling for war was introduced by Calhoun. Now came a ticklish moment; Federalists asked that the debate be made public, saying not unreasonably that in a matter of such transcendent importance as war the people had a right to know how their representatives voted, and why. Clay, however, was in no mood to take risks. Open debate might have proved fatal to his hopes. Exercising the extraordinary powers of the Speaker, he ran over the opposition, and the session continued in secrecy. Debate dried up when Federalist leaders silenced their party, rather than accept his ruling. When a vote was taken, it revealed that the House had split not only along partisan but also along regional lines. Approximately three fourths of the Republicans voted for Calhoun's bill, and all of the Federalists against it. Of the 79 affirmative votes, 48 were from the south and west, 14 from Pennsylvania, and 17 scattering. Of the 49 votes against war, 34 were from the New England, New York and New Jersey, with 15 scattering.

The Senate, too, considered the war measure in secrecy, but there the debate lasted two weeks. The vote, held on June 18, showed 19 for war, 13 against. Some whispered that Madison had counted on the Senate to defeat the war measure. Foster noted that on the night before the final vote, the President "looked ghastly pale." It is understandable. With the passage of the war bill, he found himself compelled to enter the struggle with the wealthiest and most productive section of the country aggressively pulling the other way.

Shortly after the declaration left the Senate, he had signed it. Dispatches to military and naval officers, authorizing them to commence hostilities against the enemy, went out the same day. The degree of disorganization in the War Department is suggested by the fact that John Jacob Astor's agents on the Canadian border knew that war had been declared, and had taken steps to safeguard fur shipments, before the news reached most of the American commanders. Suspicion of having shown unfair favoritism to Astor subsequently fell on his friend Gallatin, but apparently Astor's advantage derived more from his remarkable private express system than from official connivance.

The President, painfully aware of the country's lack of preparedness, declared that he had decided to "throw forward the flag of the country, sure that the people would press onward and defend it." This was an optimistic assumption, as Congress proved at once, when the question of financing the war arose. Opposition to new excise taxes was so strong that none were imposed. The Treasury was permitted to borrow five million dollars, and with this great contribution to the war effort, Congress adjourned.

Wealthy Federalists promptly let it be known that they would continue to refuse participation in war loans. Some of them went so far as to tell Foster, as he left the country for Canada, that if the British Government stood firm, the United States would be forced to back down. Belief that the war would fizzle out within a few weeks grew when a copy of Napoleon's St. Cloud Decree reached Washington shortly after the declaration. A glance at its date was all that was needed to shatter once and for all Madison's frayed hope of the Emperor's good faith. It was evident to all that he had allowed the country to be swindled. Feeling against France rose still more when news came that her men-of-war had seized American merchant ships even since Bassano had handed the St. Cloud Decree to Barlow. Given this proof of Napoleon's contemptuous double-dealing, many in Madison's own party felt that he could not in reason maintain his war against England unless he were prepared to fight France as well.

5. No Armistice

Advocates of an early truce were still further heartened by the arrival, early in July, of news that the Orders in Council had been suspended before America's declaration of war. The same word came to Augustus Foster, then safe in Halifax. Working with Canadian authorities, he swiftly completed arrangement for an armistice between British and American forces in the east. The American commander at New York, General Dearborn, who had been Jefferson's Secretary of War, was so sure of the propriety of an armistice that he signed an order suspending hostilities without even waiting to hear from the President.

He did not, however, know his Madison. The President did not for a moment permit his war commitment to waver. Recruiting sergeants were beating their drums, newspapers calling for volunteers, and detachments from Kentucky and Tennessee, from the Carolinas and Virginia, from Maryland and Pennsylvania, were trickling toward the Canadian border. If the rising flame of patriotism were to be stifled now, it might prove impossible to rekindle it later. In a letter to Jefferson, Madison contended that acceptance of an armistice "would have a bad effect on patriotic ardor." With much groaning and creaking, the rickety American machine of war had begun to move. In July a small army under General William Hull made a foray into Canada from Detroit; another, in the Niagara region, prepared to march on Montreal. The President could not afford to let external events take his war away from him, especially with the election still four months away, and with Henry Clay looking over his shoulder. A letter went from the President to Jonathan Russell in London: he was to accept an armistice only if the British first agreed to renounce the practice of impressment and the right of blockade. These conditions, difficult at best for England to accept, were phrased so peremptorily as to make plain America's intention to fight. As for Dearborn, he was flatly told to resume hostilities. The President could not, he explained, agree to an armistice arranged by merely "local authorities."

In October, the Canadian government again proposed an armistice, with the formal approval of the British Cabinet. Now the President insisted on proof that impressments had ceased before he would consent to stop hostilities. Impressment had become the one weapon he could count on to torpedo talk of peace.

CHAPTER THIRTEEN

"Greatest of all the Lessons"

1. *Narrow Squeak for Madison*

"Perhaps," says Herbert Butterfield, in his *The Whig Interpretation of History*, "the greatest of all the lessons of history is the demonstration of the complexity of human change and the unpredictable character of the ultimate consequences of any given act or decision of men." The sorry, dreary, and inglorious war dragged its way onward, creating problems greater than any it would solve. That summer of 1812, the easy optimism of the West vanished. General Hull was forced to retreat first to Detroit, and finally to surrender, with the result that British troops and their Indian allies overran American territory as far south as the Wabash. Disgrace was compounded in the East. Near Niagara an American invading force was outmaneuvered by Canada's General Brock and compelled to surrender while a large body of New York State militia, watching the battle from the American side of the river, refused to go to their aid. Subsequent investigation disclosed that the militia had decided to stand on their constitutional rights. They were not, after all, required to serve outside the borders of the United States. Their officers, moreover, knew the sentiments of New York's De Witt Clinton, who regarded every defeat of the American Army as improving his chances in the election.

Demoralization in the economic life of the country paralleled that of the military. The war did not even have the small virtue of most wars, which is to cause the people, at least at the outset, to stand together in a common purpose. In the Federalist strongholds of New England and New York, men disappointed by the failure of an armistice to materialize promptly established their private truce with England. The embargo on trade with the West Indies and Canada was so widely disregarded that customs officers threw up their hands. It was said that in the summer of 1812 there was as much trade on the Canadian border as in any normal season, war or no war. In Georgia, too, smuggling reappeared as a full time occupation for hundreds.

The administration could give the people no inspiration, because it had none itself; no guidance, because it did not know where it was going. For a people who had been assured by Jefferson and Clay that Canada was theirs for the plucking, the defeats of 1812 were hard to bear. By midsummer, wherever the President looked he saw humiliation and dereliction. Fortunately for him, the losses at Detroit and Niagara were soon thereafter compensated by equally unexpected successes at sea. If America was shaken by the loss of Detroit, England was amazed at the defeat of her famous frigate *Guerriére* by the guns of the *Constitution*. "The truth is," confessed the London *Courier*, "nobody ever supposed that one of our best frigates would not be a match for the American." America's ecstasy over the *Constitution* grew when, soon afterward, the British warship *Java* surrendered to her. But the chief strategic importance of such victories did not lie merely in England's loss of a few ships of her tremendous navy. The significant point, not then realized by the American people, was that the triumphant *Constitution* and her sister ships were clearing the seas for a swarm of privateers. Armed American vessels equipped with letters of marque and sent out as speculative business enterprises had taken to the sea by the hundreds, and were wreaking devastation in the West Indies. The London *Pilot* in March, 1813, startled the City and produced a stock market slump with an announcement from Lloyd's that five hundred British merchantmen had been captured by American privateers in seven months.

The sensational achievements of the Navy and the privateers quickly pumped up Madison's deflated political hopes. He was aided, too, by the courage of the Federalist elder statesman, Rufus King, in opposing Governor De Witt Clinton's presidential aspirations. The grounds of King's opposition and the manner of his statement were curiously reminiscent of Hamilton's attack on Burr in 1800. King warned Federalists everywhere that it would be better for the Federalists to be defeated with a candidate of their own party than to win with a dangerous Republican demagogue like Clinton, "a retail dealer in all varieties of political opinion." His implicit support of Madison may have decided the presidential contest, which was so close that a shift in twenty electoral votes would have given Clinton the presidency. There was even a suspicion that the popular vote, which was not tabulated, might have favored Clinton for, in the North, Federalist voters turned out in astonishing numbers, while the South and West were apathetic. The trend of national feeling showed itself in elections to the House of Representatives, where the Federalists doubled their numbers.

2. *Chaos*

Re-elected, Madison could breathe easier, but not much easier. Reports from Europe told of the calamity which had overtaken Napoleon in Russia, and predicted his early capitulation. England was filled with renewed confidence and battle lust, while at home morale was on the ebb. Gallatin reported that the Treasury was almost bankrupt, and that the war could not be continued without new taxes. Under these conditions, when in March 1813 an offer of mediation reached Madison from Czar Alexander of Russia

—who had his own reasons for fearing an uninhibited England—Madison seized upon it eagerly. Since Gallatin, besides being the ablest man in the administration, was anxious to escape from the Treasury crisis which he could plainly foresee, the President sent him to St. Petersburg to negotiate. England, however, by then had lost interest in the idea of an armistice. Plans for an invasion of the United States from the sea were already in the making, and the British Government was negotiating to obtain legal title to the Floridas from Spain, as a preliminary to physical possession.

Some comfort came to the President and the people from the Canadian border. The muddled War Department had been reorganized, better generals were at the front, creditable battles were won, and the British were driven from American soil. Commodore Perry's great sea fight on Lake Erie set the eagle to screaming with delight for a time. But underneath the glitter of military triumph was a dark hollow of bankruptcy. To meet the mounting expenses of the war, Madison at last persuaded Congress to grant new excise taxes—on sugar, salt, stamps, auctions, this, that, and the other—and the people paid them, if grudgingly. But it was not enough. Nothing was enough. The government's credit became so feeble that it was obliged to pay a 22 per cent premium to lenders, and even so had great difficulty in borrowing.

The essential fact was that New England—the only section of the country where trade continued to flourish—had acquired most of the nation's specie, and was not letting it go. From June 1811 to June 1814, the Massachusetts banks alone increased their holdings of hard money from $1,709,000 to $7,326,000. Seeking to stop the drain on western and southern banks, the President had recourse to a desperate expedient—an embargo on trade not only with other nations, but even between states, even in coastal traffic. In this way, too, he thought to punish "those who are most ready to sacrifice the interests of the country to their own"—meaning New Englanders. The result was one that he could hardly have failed to anticipate—a renewal of the threat of secession. This time the grim pro-British Federalist leaders went so far as to organize the notorious Hartford Convention in which to plan their strategy. Before the convention assembled, however, Madison realized that continuation of the embargo was about to destroy the union. Back to Congress he went in 1814 to ask for the repeal of the act which he had so strongly urged in 1813. To cover his defeat, he advanced a reason which convinced few: that as a result of Napoleon's defeat, Europe was once more an open market for American commerce, which ought to take advantage of "extensive changes favorable thereto." In reality, like Jefferson in 1808, he had come late to understand how much systematic preparation has to be made before established economic institutions and practices can safely be modified.

The plight of the South and West remained as discouraging as before. Commodity shortages appeared, prices rose, salt sold at five dollars a bushel, sugar at twenty-six cents a pound. Men began to doubt the future, to have a hard time remembering why they were fighting. A sense of futility spread like a plague. The perfervid patriots of 1812 grew silent. Curses against England became mere ritual. People could no longer be comforted by reports of minor military and naval successes. They were frightened. Then in the middle of 1814 the crisis came, touched off by the British raid on Washington, and the burning of the Capitol and Executive Mansion. Everywhere but in New England specie payments were suspended and banks closed. Congress and the Administration sought some way out of financial chaos, and found none.

3. Luck at Ghent

The only hope that Madison could see was in a report from Gallatin in St. Petersburg that, while England was unwilling to negotiate through Russia, she would consent to meet in Holland for direct talks with an American peace mission. The President's state of mind can be discerned in the speed with which he appointed and sent abroad a group of the country's best known men, including Henry Clay and John Quincy Adams, while Gallatin hurried from St. Petersburg to Ghent. There the Americans faced representatives of an England intoxicated with her European triumphs and the abdication of Napoleon. Rumors of an imminent invasion of the United States were on everyone's lips. Gallatin reported one such rumor to Madison—that the British intended to land twenty thousand men on the Atlantic coast, seize Washington and New York, and dictate the terms of America's surrender. Later, however, he sensed that such talk was only a cover for a very different project—the capture of New Orleans, the delta of the Mississippi, and the Floridas. A letter from Gallatin to Madison, dated August 21, 1814, and received in October 1814, warned of this intention. But the administration was then still disorganized by its flight from Washington, and no action was taken. When Andrew Jackson came to New Orleans that December, he found the city almost defenseless.

The negotiation of the treaty at Ghent was one of the luckier achievements of American statesmanship. It was lucky, to begin with, in the calm bearing and patience of Albert Gallatin. England's first proposal at Ghent caused Henry Clay to explode, and begin to pack for his return home. Together with other territorial concessions, the British demanded that the United States give up most of the land between the Ohio River and the Great Lakes to the Indians. Gallatin himself thought the negotiations in grave peril, but he sensed—as others in his party did not—that London had not necessarily spoken her last word, and he kept the negotiation alive. His intuition was sound: England was formally making good a promise given by Sir James Craig to the tribes to seek the return of their ancient lands, and had no intention of prolonging the war merely for the sake of her Indian allies. The proposition's main value, so far as the British were concerned, was merely to gain time while awaiting reports from their military commanders in Canada.

From Madison's standpoint, news of England's outrageous demand came at a fortunate moment. American morale on the home front was near the cracking point. Reading the notes which had been exchanged at Ghent, he sensed their psychological significance, and promptly released them to the press. The resulting wave of indignation that swept the country did more to unify the nation than any preceding event of the war. Even Federalists rose in patriotic wrath. State legislatures passed resolutions calling for a massive war effort. "Don't give up the soil!" became the slogan of the day. Parades in the cities whipped up popular enthusiasm. A spirit of renewed determination showed itself in subscriptions to government bonds and a large increase in the number of volunteers for military and civilian service. This change in attitude made it possible for the President to encourage Gallatin and his fellow commissioners to stand firm; and the British were told that either their offensive proposition must be withdrawn, or the war would go on.

The potato had turned out to be a little too hot, and the British dropped it with a thud. From this point, the only provision asked in behalf of the Indians was a promise of amnesty by the American government. The conference then got down to serious business. The next British position was that the treaty map be drawn to the doctrine of *uti possidetis*, actual possession of territory by military forces at the time of signature. Behind this proposal was the expectation that a Canadian force then invading the United States by way of Lake Champlain, and the British expedition aimed at New Orleans and already at sea, would both succeed. Again the Americans resisted, again the conference seemed about to founder, again, at the critical moment, unexpected news came to its rescue. Word was received that Canadian forces on Lake Champlain had been turned back by a small American squadron, under Commodore Thomas Macdonough, in a victory the enormous implications of which were out of all proportion to the small forces engaged. At Ghent, Gallatin and his colleagues for the first time felt a surge of confidence, as they insisted that the peace could be established only on the basis of *status quo ante bellum*.

England's first response was to refuse, for British troops had occupied the northern part of Maine, as well as a fort on the American side of the Niagara—and the New Orleans expedition still remained to be heard from. Now, however, the Americans were aided by influences of which they were

unaware. Lord Castlereagh was then in Vienna, negotiating for the surrender of France with Talleyrand, and finding that although the defeated
Napoleon was on Elba, the French were by no means in a submissive mood.
Anticipating a further campaign on the continent, Castlereagh counseled
the Prime Minister, Lord Liverpool, that England "be released from the
millstone of an American war." Similar advice came from England's foremost military authority, General Arthur Wellesley, who had just been made
Duke of Wellington for his services in Spain. Refusing a suggestion that he
take personal command of British forces in America, Wellington bluntly
told Liverpool: "I confess that I think you have no right, from the state of
the war, to demand any concession of territory from America . . . and you
only afford the Americans a popular and creditable ground . . . to avoid
to make peace."

And beyond the diplomatic and military reasons for a quick peace with
America were others strongly reminiscent of those which had pressed on
Shelburne in 1782. Shortages of grain had produced popular rioting in
several cities. Resentment of high taxes was threatening the hold of Lord
Liverpool and the Tory party on British property owners. Textile manufacturers were demanding early restoration of the American market, and of
American cotton imports. Shipowners wanted to put an end to the depredations of American privateers, which had caused insurance rates to double.
The Admiralty was concerned over the necessity of diverting squadrons
of the fleet from European stations in order to convoy merchant vessels to
the West Indies and South America. The totality of the advice reaching him
caused Liverpool to dismiss for the sake of peace even his hopes for the New
Orleans expedition. Word went to his representatives at Ghent to accept
the American stipulation on territory; and all at once, a treaty became
possible.

3. Anticipation and Reality

The peace which Gallatin and his fellow commissioners made at Ghent
was a boon to the United States, but it could not save Madison's prestige.
None of the issues which were supposed to have produced the war were
even mentioned in the treaty. Every protestation that he had made to justify
the war to the American people was revealed as meaningless. Impressment
had been his great reason for war. In the summer of 1812, nothing less than
complete British capitulation on the issue would serve for peace. By April
1813 doubts had already set in, and Madison wrote to Gallatin that in
return for British renunciation of the impressment policy, the United States
would agree to exclude all native Englishmen from American crews. June
1814 saw the President retreat still farther. With France beaten, was it worth
while, he asked his Cabinet, for America to continue the war in defense of

a theoretical right which England was not any longer likely to violate? Gone now was talk of national honor. He urged the Cabinet to agree to accept a treaty which would be silent on the subject of impressment; the secretaries bleakly concurred; and the commissioners at Ghent were so instructed.

Nor was anything said in the treaty about Orders in Council, blockades, or unlawful harassment of shipping. The tacit assumption was made that England would no longer need to avail herself of such practices, and there the matter was dropped.

The promises given to the American people of territorial gain had similarly evaporated. When the war began, Madison had told Jonathan Russell to advise the British Government to make peace on American terms before Canada was conquered, for American possession of Canada would be a later obstacle to peace. A year later, he modified this stand. Now he thought that England ought to surrender Canada because in the long run she would gain more from North American trade than from actual possession. This argument, which Franklin had advanced from a far better bargaining position in 1782, was highly artificial in 1813. By the time of the conference at Ghent, Madison was glad to see the old Canadian border restored. Even the expansionist drive to the south proved abortive. In the spring of 1813, Madison instructed Gallatin to insist on America's right to the Floridas in the treaty negotiation. Gallatin vigorously objected. The Florida policy, he wrote, represented only a sectional interest and had no moral or legal basis. He insisted that, far from pressing so weak a point, American troops be withdrawn from East Florida, and to this Madison had to consent.

4. "A Damned Bad Treaty"

The most unexpected clause in the document that emerged at Ghent was written into it at the request of the British Government and gladly accepted by Gallatin—a pledge by the two governments to co-operate in suppressing the African slave trade—one of the few times that a specific humanitarian purpose has been incorporated in a treaty of peace. From England's standpoint, however, more than humanitarian sentiment was involved. Not only were some of her shipowners protesting the unfairness of barring them from the immensely profitable slave trade to the benefit of Yankee rivals; most of her manufacturers and exporters, for whom the economic advantages of colonial slavery were fast dwindling, wanted to see the United States move in the same direction as themselves. Only the British textile industry, with its low-priced raw cotton imports from America, still stood to gain from slave labor. For the rest, there was obvious danger in having the United States continue to build up a huge supply of very low-cost labor, which would eventually enable her to undersell England in world markets. As for the Americans, even those among them who, like

Henry Clay, were not opposed to slavery, could safely agree to the pledge on the slave trade, which was too vague to be a burden to the government. Clay was aware, moreover, of the growing conviction among southern leaders that the Negro birth rate would in future provide ample supplies for the American slave markets without additional importations from Africa.

When Clay held up agreement on the treaty by insisting that England renounce in writing her tyrannical practices at sea, trouble flared in the American delegation. For some nerve-racking days the arguments of Gallatin and John Quincy Adams ("a foreigner and a Bostonian") left "the Western Star" unmoved and it was only after much bickering that he finally yielded. Adams made no secret of his belief that the Kentuckian's last-ditch bellicosity had been for the record, and was calculated with an eye on the voters back home. However this may have been, the fact remained that with Clay dissatisfied, and saying that it was "a damned bad treaty," the signatures of the commissioners gave no assurance that the Senate would ratify their work. But here the advocates of peace were once more helped by the unpredictable. Reports from New Orleans that Andrew Jackson's little army had beaten back England's invading force assuaged America's wounded pride. Men cheered, drank toasts to Jackson, jeered at England—and consented to the war's end. The need for a show of victory had been satisfied. The Senate's vote in approval of the treaty was unanimous.

The war, thirty years in the coming, was over within three. Some historians contend that it consummated America's independence from England, and that it advanced national unification. Others believe that it aggravated the division of northern and southern interests, and accelerated forces making for secession and civil war. All of these statements, doubtless, can be proved. In the broad and iridescent flow of human activity leading up to and away from a war, it is always possible to discern those "causes" and "consequences" which are most congenial to the seeker.

CONCLUSION

ON THE COMING OF WAR

On the Coming of War

1. The Question of "Inevitability"

It seems safe to say, on the basis of the historical evidence, that the War of 1812 was not inevitable—except perhaps in the Tolstoyan sense that everything that happens is inevitable because it happens. If, however, one assumes the reality of chance and of a degree of choice in human behavior, then it is difficult to find justification for the view, put forward by some historians, that the war was bound to occur sooner or later. Such assertions can be nothing but a display of hindsight prediction. There is no warrant whatever in the facts for the assumption that the War of 1812, or any other, could not have been avoided indefinitely. Very slight changes in the knot of fortuitous circumstance that linked England and America at the time would have left no more reason for fighting the war than existed in the many subsequent Anglo-American quarrels which were settled by peaceful negotiation.

The conviction that war is imminent and inevitable arises in some minds in almost every crisis, and often in supposedly informed circles. In 1794 the Governor General of Canada said in so many words that war was coming that year. In 1797 half of the American Senate was of the same mind. In 1808 James Madison did not see how war could any longer be avoided. Yet they were wrong. Repeated crisis does not necessarily lead to war any more than repeated clouds necessarily signify a storm. The fact that men in high places believe that war is at hand by no means makes it so. Henry Adams, in his *Education*, recounted how in 1863 his father, Charles Francis Adams, then minister to England, was so convinced that the peace between England and America had been shattered that he hotly informed Lord Russell, England's Foreign Secretary, "My Lord, this is war!" He had not allowed for the play of circumstances beyond his ken. Half a dozen times since the Treaty of Potsdam men in the higher circles of the American government have solemnly assured each other of war with Soviet Russia within a few months. In 1946, at the time of the Iran crisis, the late Admiral William Leahy, then Chief of Staff to President Truman, flatly stated to a group of government officials that he expected war "within a year." Similar opinions were expressed by others in 1947 (the Trieste crisis), in 1948 (the Berlin crisis) and in 1950 (the Korean crisis). Doubtless there were many in Moscow who held views of the same kind. But in each of those years the interlocking chances needed to translate the competition of the great powers from the terms of diplomacy to the terms of war were absent.

In part, the conviction that a given war is on its way arises from a deeper, and often hidden belief that war, as a phenomenon of human experience, will persist as long as the species does. By accepting the inevitability of war in the abstract, we condition ourselves to assume it in particular cases. And an astonishing number of people who do not regard themselves as mystics have resigned themselves to the notion that because there always has been war, there always must be war. For many, the alleged inevitability of war is almost a comforting thought, relieving the individual of responsibility, and seeming to justify those who have a powerful impulse to aggress. In an effort to find a "scientific" basis for this fatalistic belief, some statistical-minded historians have even compiled awesome charts showing the frequent incidence of war for thousands of years past. Is it not unreasonable, they suggest, to expect that a phenomenon so constant in human history should terminate abruptly in this century? But a statistician might with equal sense, or nonsense, make a chart showing the growth of the human species for the past million years or so, and ask whether it is likely that mankind will come abruptly to an end in our own lifetimes—as it might if there were to be a major nuclear war. One chart would be as plausible as the other.

Statistics of the past can tell us little of the future of war. As a primitive means used by human groups in an effort to escape from their societal predicaments, war's continuance can hardly fail to be dependent on the feeling of men about their own chances of survival, and on the alternatives to war that may be provided. One thing we know—that long established human institutions and practices have often been swept suddenly away by the winds of change. Under the pressure of new inventions and ideas, the inevitabilities of one age frequently become the antiquarian curiosities of the next. The human condition in its societal aspects, at least, can change with surprising speed. What Marquesan Islander in 1800 would have believed that his countrymen would no longer be eating human flesh in 1900? We do not say that because men have always died of cancer, so there must always be cancer; since man has always been earth-bound, so he must always be earth-bound; because half of humanity were once slaves, so there must always be slavery. In our thinking about medical research, the technology of travel, and the evolution of institutions we recognize that this age has points of difference from previous ages. We know that it has so immensely expanded man's horizons as to be certain to effect enormous changes in his outlook and behavior. More than ever before in their experience, men everywhere fear war, and for the first time a political mechanism has been established, however tentatively, to prevent it. That war is always possible,

and even probable, goes almost without saying; but given the unprecedented pressures for peaceful adaptation now operating on human societies,
to assume the inevitability of war reveals a predisposition of the mind
rather than a valid conclusion.

Unfortunately, this widely encountered predisposition to the doctrine of
inevitability actually tends to destroy peace, for it undermines the morale
of many a man whose task it is to try to prevent war. Whatever might be
creative and hopeful in the mind is stifled by premonition of doom imminent. Although a national leader may sincerely want to avoid war, if he
nourishes a conviction that sustained peace is impossible, he cannot be
zealous in its service. Men wearied by the long and demanding sessions of
crisis negotiation are often tempted to throw in the diplomatic sponge. "If
it must come, let it come" is a common thought which accompanies the
sinking of the heart among dispirited statesmen. Some even end by wel-
coming war as a way out of their diplomatic frustrations. Trudging behind
their armaments on the road to Armageddon, men are often so overawed
by the grinding movement of events toward war that they never look up
long enough to see where the road forks.

To be effective in negotiating for peace, a statesman has to believe that
it can be achieved and sustained—that if nations continue long enough to
postpone the resort to arms, sooner or later changing circumstance will
come to their aid, reducing the tensions between them. But this faith in
the possibility of a lasting peace is relatively rare. Many present-day statesmen were in their youth so steeped in outworn doctrines about war and
have so steadfastly avoided later enlightenment that they are psychologically
unfit for the tasks of peace diplomacy. To ask them, with Sam Johnson, to
clear their minds of cant would be to expect too much. In some, the belief
in war's inevitability has a religious foundation. More than one powerful
minister of state in our time has made it clear that he sees humanity caught
in a great contest between God and the devil, a contest which only war
can resolve. The devil, of course, is represented by the potential antagonist.
And what self-respecting angel would seriously bargain with him? It is an
awesome thought that national policy in our age may still be set by men
whose inner goal is the obliteration of the unbeliever.

There are yet others in positions to affect humanity's future who, by
their acceptance of doctrines of predestination, gravely limit their usefulness. Fatalism is always a short cut to war. To help their countries peacefully
adjust their established ways to a changed societal environment is not easy
for men who believe that humanity's choices are meaningless. Their world
outlook was satirized by the irreverent Anatole France when he said, "Before feet and rumps had been created, the concept of a kick in the rump
lay slumbering from all eternity in the womb of the Almighty." Some even

seem to think that the human race "deserves" a nuclear kick, and that in any event, if it is going to happen, it will happen.

Belief in war's inevitability can be arrived at by allegedly scientific, as well as by allegedly religious paths, but it remains equally devoid of foundation. It is a suggestive fact that the findings of social scientists on the ways of war have often fallen in conveniently with the political purposes of their governments. The theory that war is nature's method of "selecting" superior races was long a favorite among peoples whose governments had superior military power—as in England in the later Victorian era, and in the German Empire of Wilhelm II and Hitler's Third Reich. Houston Stewart Chamberlain and Alfred Rosenberg, among others, assiduously spread this doctrine, conveniently ignoring the fact that Darwin himself, before his death, sharply modified his earlier position on war as a factor in the progressive development of human societies. Even though Social Darwinism has today lost its credit among most men of science, it has not been cleaned out of the minds of some who sit at international conference tables. Having been taught to believe in their formative years that "the fittest" nations somehow survive in war, they secretly cling to the cliché, never stopping to ask themselves, the fittest for what?

With the decline of the aristocratic and breed-worshiping state, however, the fashion in inevitability doctrines has changed. Each great power has now evolved a political theory which "proves" that, when the inevitable war comes, it will only be defending itself against aggression. The belief has been instilled in the minds of many Americans that so long as nationalism, totalitarianism, and imperialism exist in the world, there will be war. Since Russia is nationalistic, totalitarian, and imperialistic, the inference is that any future war will be of her making. The Russians, on the other hand, have been assured since 1917 that only capitalistic imperialism, and its implicit contradictions, prevent the abolition of war. For orthodox Marxists it follows that the "guilt" for another war would lie squarely on America.

A more sophisticated rationale for the belief that war is inevitable falls back on Freud. Some contemporary prophets of doom hold, as he did at one time, that man is innately destructive beyond hope of self-discipline, that the members of a human society have only two choices—either to turn their destructiveness on each other, or to direct it against external groups whose interests conflict with their own. On this ground, war is taken to be inseparable from the future as from the past history of mankind. It has not yet been sufficiently recognized that Freudian, like Darwinian theory in this area, no longer carries much weight with the modern apostles of their sciences. As Franz Alexander concludes, in commenting on Freud's work in war psychology, "The mere fact that man has aggressive impulses does not permit us to postulate that war is unavoidable . . . The existence of an innate destructiveness for its own sake, which goes beyond the limits of self-preservation, has not been convincingly demonstrated." Freud himself, like Darwin, substantially changed his mind about the nature of the war phenomenon in his later years.

Whatever the source of the inevitability doctrine, it drains diplomacy of its vital juices. Its effects show most clearly when statesmen begin to rely on armament alone to sustain policy. The last refuge of the hopeless leader is the hoary saying of Vegetius, who in the fourth century A.D. wrote, "Let him who desires peace prepare for war." Some statesmen who repeat this may perhaps believe it, but if so, they have shut their eyes to the unmistakable fact that military preparedness, however necessary, has never been effective in preventing war for any considerable time. Even if a statesman regards himself as a sincere peace seeker, he is not likely to be very active or creative in pursuing his aim so long as he regards large armaments as virtuous.

One especially dangerous by-product of belief in the inevitability of war is the expectation that the war to come may be limited—that is, fought without the use of nuclear weapons. This prospect appears to give some persons of influence almost a sense of relief, comparable to the relief of a patient told by his doctor that he is not dying—he will merely be crippled for life. That a country reduced to desperation by so-called conventional arms would refrain from using nuclear missiles and bombs if it had them is something less than probable; but even on the best of assumptions, there is still little promise of salvation in the concept of limited war. If fought between great powers it could hardly fail to end in a welter of destruction, misery, and revolutionary change. When prominent men advise their governments not to repeat, in the next war, the mistakes of World War II, but this time to plan strategy so that the nation's political as well as military objectives will be achieved, the counsel has a fine Clausewitzian ring; its only defect is that the objectives for which the leaders of the nation might take the people into another great war would not be likely to have much meaning after the holocaust.

The hope of civilized man is obviously not in the limiting but in the preventing of war. That is why the need to audit the states of mind of the men who make the world's high diplomatic decisions has become acute. Nothing could be more irresponsible on the part of a contemporary government than to send confirmed Clausewitzians or inevitability-accepters to deal with international crisis.

As everyone knows, the will to negotiate is not very meaningful unless the spirit of compromise exists on both sides of the conference table. But the spirit of compromise is generated mainly by fear, and it is not to be mistaken that every great nation in the nuclear age is fearful of large-scale war. Patient and persistent efforts to work out viable compromises for peace probably have a better chance of success in our time than at any previous period of history—provided, of course, that the negotiators are backed by competent leaders in their home countries. Where demagogues are not effectively rebutted by responsible government leaders, and are allowed to set the popular standards by which statesmen are judged, the ground is cut from under the negotiators of peace. Without inspirational guidance to turn them from war, a people can hardly be blamed if it falls into the easy fashion (like Americans in the time of Madison) of praising the militants as the true patriots, and scoffing at the peace seekers.

Few nations realize in time their good fortune when they are represented in foreign affairs and led at home by men qualified for peacemaking—men, that is, who have courage, imagination, patience, tolerance, a sense of proportion, psychological insight, and power of persuasion, and who clearly grasp the distinction between compromise and surrender. It requires such men to risk their futures, as Franklin and Shelburne did, and to brave a storm of popular protest, as Washington and Jay did, until the shocks of diplomatic compromise can be absorbed by the public.

Are we then finally dependent on the hope that great leaders for peace will be found on both sides in the present world struggle? Perhaps the chance is not so remote as it first sounds. Crises of fear have often brought remarkable men to power under all forms of government. It is not inconceivable that another wave of large-minded statesmanship, responding to pressures in East and West alike, may rise in time to save humanity from ruin.

2. *The Moral Question*

In one respect, the statesmen of the period prior to the War of 1812 were in a better position to work for peace than those of our own decades: they were willing to forego moral judgments of other nations. Not that they were less religious than today's national leaders. On the contrary, most of them had simple and profound religious faiths from which they derived strength and comfort. They did not, however, wear moralistic blinders. In the words of Professor Butterfield, "It was perhaps one of the virtues of the older type of diplomacy that in time of war it did not allow itself to be entirely obsessed by the responsibility for violence . . . but recognized that the war itself was . . . partly due to a predicament." Men like Grenville and Jay concentrated on a search for viable diplomatic solutions where men like Dulles and Molotov made enormous efforts to exonerate their countries from all blame for the trouble they were in.

War tramples over man-made moral attitudes as if they were no more than the whims of a day. Who is right, who is wrong in war? Each belligerent asserts a moral claim, but what is it worth? Was Rome or Carthage morally right? Was England morally right in the Hundred Years' War, or France? Was Russia or Japan right in 1905? In the upshot, the winner's moral position usually looks better, but only because he is better able to advertise it. To enjoy the luxury of alleged moral supremacy, a nation must first achieve supremacy of power. Then it quickly manufactures a moral justification: imperial England in her heyday was only accepting "the white man's burden"; Germany under the triumphant Hitler was merely aiding nature to evolve a superior human breed. If Germany and Japan had won the Second World War, the peoples of the conquered Allies would soon have been brainwashed into guilt feelings for their "aggressions." For did not the United States and England try to keep the German and Japanese peoples in a reduced status? To measure accurately the comparative morality of nations in going to war requires finer judicial perceptions than propaganda generally permits.

Today it is increasingly recognized that the ultimate test of the morality of nations is their relation to the continued development of the human species. Where instinct revolts against a nation's behavior, as in the instance of the Nazi atrocities, it is because of pity for the victims, of a sense that the human spirit has been degraded, that the beast within threatens to resume his primordial mastery of mankind. But even when we are reasonably sure of our moral ground in condemning an outrage committed by a nation, we cannot escape the fact that in the modern world such acts are to some extent international in origin. It is often forgotten that Hitler was the product not only of Germany but of all western civilization at a time of despair.

War, as distinguished from deliberate bestiality, is essentially an amoral phenomenon. That is why great-power statesmen who strike moralistic attitudes and seek religious justifications as they stand on the brink of the abyss appear tragic or ridiculous to later generations. That such men are often sincerely dedicated to peace makes no difference, if their doings and sayings tend to bring on the wars which they profess to abhor. No man can be effective in the complex bargaining of peacetime if he is obsessed with the conviction of his moral superiority. Through the thick spectacles of moral judgment the competitor nation always shows the face of the devil. As revolutionary France in the 1790s was the devil for William Pitt, so revolutionary China in the 1950s was the devil for John Foster Dulles. Self-righteousness can only defeat realistic efforts to adjust differences. In a moralistic atmosphere, "right and wrong" replaces "true or false"; energy that might go into fact-finding is used up in indignation; policy becomes ominously rigid; and the chance of averting war steadily dwindles.

The Secretary-General of the United Nations, Dag Hammarskjöld, has warned that "we are on dangerous ground if we believe that any individual, any nation, or any ideology has a monopoly on rightness, liberty and human dignity." In spite of this admonition, some contemporary diplomats seem to feel that their main functions are to point the finger and pound the fist. Even in the United Nations itself, the moralistic view has forced itself into prominence, through the principle that a nation which takes the military initiative in war is necessarily an "aggressor." This would imply that the United States, in the War of 1812, was the aggressor, and so morally culpable—although she had repeatedly turned the other cheek to England's provocations for years preceding the war. To ignore the element of provocation in many acts of aggression is to run counter to all human experience. The Boston revolutionists who struck the first physical blow against a British tyranny which was systematically impoverishing the American colonies were aggressive, but they had ample provocation. To limit the definition of aggression to the actual use of weapons is to take away its meaning. If Nation A builds up armaments on the border of Nation B, and Nation B attacks to forestall their use against her, the provocation was certainly as aggressive in spirit as the military response. Even in cases of individual crime, it is often difficult to identify the real aggressor and assign guilt. In the tangle of international affairs, the moralistic concept of aggression in terms of merely physical violence is as insubstantial as spider silk. Until such time as there is an international military force capable of deterring any nation from a resort to arms, not much comfort is to be found in the assertion that the guilt for war rests on the striker of the first blow. It is only by seeking to reduce provocation before physical aggression takes place that statecraft can work effectively to avert war. If a military blow justifies international intervention, so do the provocations that incite it.

This is not to belittle the great contributions made by the UN in its investigatory, arbitrating, and economic functions. But its narrow doctrine of aggression, by putting emphasis on responsibility for the first overt attack, makes it easy for statesmen to indulge freely in military, economic, and propagandistic provocations short of war, without being called seriously to account. As for the effect on public opinion of this UN doctrine, it is simply stultifying. Nothing could be less likely than a UN debate in a diplomatic crisis to instruct mankind in the nature of the large societal forces which continually press us toward tragedy. Speech after speech by statesmen "on the world situation" turns out on analysis to be bald-faced national propaganda. The UN concept of aggression tends to make the problem seem to the peoples involved as simple as a morality play, with the good people on one side and the wicked on the other. And who would compromise with Belial?

These statements are not intended to deprecate the value of moral judgments. They do not lose sight of the fact that the evolving faculty of moral indignation is one of the hopes of mankind. But moral judgments can hardly be useful in situations the origins of which are not clearly comprehended. It is one thing to condemn, in moral terms, such manifestations of individual sadism and group cowardice as a lynching, or the torture of prisoners in a Buchenwald. Reversions to brutishness symbolize a threat to survival of mankind and their psychotic origins are unmistakable. Similarly, one may say with assurance that it is immoral in our time to glorify war, since such propaganda, which carries in it the seed of species-destruction, is the product of the egocentric power-lust. But the phenomenon of war—society's repeated effort to escape from its predicaments by mass violence—is on a very different level. The assignment of comparative responsibility for national aggression opens up so enormous a complex of provocation and counterprovocation, running far back into time, as to make moral judgment exceedingly hazardous.

The point, to paraphrase Bertrand Russell, is that moral considerations have no place in objective investigation of phenomena. They should appear only after truth has been determined. Then they serve a purpose by helping us shape a sound attitude toward the truth. But if we allow them to interfere with the process of discovering the truth, we invalidate reason and ethics together. The hope of peace is not strengthened, it is weakened, by the infusion of moral issues into international negotiation.

3. The Question of Cause

As the inevitability and morality fallacies operate to produce war, so does misunderstanding of the nature of the war phenomenon. The obscurity which still surrounds the way of the coming of war gives point to the remark of G. Lowes Dickinson that "the most important things are precisely the last to be known about, and it is exactly where it is most imperative to act that our ignorance is most complete." Before the timeless mystery of war, humanity has always bowed down unquestioning, like Juggernaut's worshipers. Men have dared to probe the structure of the universe and to expose the inwardness of religion, but the mind draws back when war is at issue, and we accept its onslaught as resignedly as we accept an earthquake or a hurricane. Even in our own age, knowing as we do the probable consequences to humanity of a war in which nuclear missiles are widely employed, we remain relatively apathetic in the face of the threat. With a kind of fascinated incredulity, the nations watch the relentless approach of war, resigned to the probability that at a certain moment to come masses of previously peaceable men will suddenly and eagerly set about the business of inflicting agonizing deaths on each other, driven by causes comprehended only remotely, if at all. To be sure, they will have the pat formulas of international politics to serve as reasons: The enemy leaves us no choice. The nation's honor is at stake. We must fight or starve. It is better to die in glory than live in slavery. We are only defending ourselves. We ask only for our rights. Defy the foul fiend! But these time-honored simplicities explain the nature of the catastrophe about as much as demonology explains a volcanic eruption. "Where ignorant armies clash by night," in Matthew Arnold's phrase, they need a scapegoat to bear the blame for their sufferings, and who better than the other side?

The many learned and compendious books about the causes of war written by philosophers, historians, and sociologists have had a singularly small impact on the public mind. It is easy to see why this is so. Bertrand Russell, Sigmund Freud, Charles Beard, Pitirim Sorokin, and Quincy Wright, to name a few, have contributed in this field. Their erudition is of course immense, their methods impeccable, their insights profound, but their findings are strangely elusive, slipping away from the mind like eels from the hand. A number of formidable symposia on the subject conducted by UNESCO and by various universities are even more frustrating. Most studies in the etiology of war give wry emphasis to Lecomte de Noüy's comment that "the more deeply man analyzes, the farther he gets away from the principal problem which he meant to solve." Every aspect of the subject has been analyzed and atomized, but the propulsive forces which produce the periodic holocausts of history remain as obscure as the background of an overexposed photograph. The investigators have not even created an organized body of animating ideas on which further studies might be based. It is worth noting that while there exists a solid science of criminology which describes the nature, origins, and methods of detection of individual violations of social rules, no equivalent science (which might perhaps be called "polemology") has emerged to deal comprehensively with the collective crime of war.

War is caused by—what? Nationalism is the cause, we have been told. So is economic competition for markets and raw materials; and despotic imperialism; also capitalistic imperialism. Books have been written to prove that war is the result of the pressure of population on the food supply; that it manifests the process of natural selection in which the "fittest" survive; that it expresses an instinct in man to kill and destroy; that it bespeaks a sadistic neurosis in human societies; that it grows out of herd susceptibility to hysteria. According to some historians, shortsighted national leaders bring war upon us by their egotism and their mistakes; according to others, munitions makers, international bankers, oil companies, and publishers manufacture wars to satisfy their greed; and there are still others to tell us that the same wars are produced by traditional national antagonisms, embodied in ossified educational methods. Marx said that war is the inevitable outcome of capitalistic class struggle, and Spengler that it is the inevitable concomitant of the growth and decline of empire, while Toynbee strongly suggests that it is the inevitable consequence of religious error. The familiar phrases have a fugitive, unreal sound, like the soughing of trees in a heavy wind.

Inadequate ideas about the causes of war in the minds of statesmen are today a major danger to humanity. For, believing that they know the "cause" of a threatened war, they may easily arrive at a feeling of total futility. For example, the rigid conviction of some American statesmen during the Cold War was that the Communist doctrines of Soviet Russia and Red China were the cause of the crisis. The inference was that if these countries would only reform, the threat of war would cease. Those overwhelmed by the ideological question completely overlooked the point made by Professor Butterfield when he said, "We did not have our present fears and panics on the subject of communism till Communism had come to be identified with the formidable European position of Russia as it has existed since 1945."

In the Communist camp, orthodox Marxists have clung with equal fervor to the theory that the cause of war is capitalistic exploitation. From this they concluded that peace would become possible only when the rest of the world had become socialistic. Publicists in many countries have taken the stand that excessive nationalism is the root of war, and that the only way by which the great powers can find peace is to subordinate themselves to international rule. Sociologists have advanced the theory that the pressure of increasing population on the world's resources is responsible for the urge to war, implying that only birth control and scientific methods of production together would put an end to the danger.

When rigid ideas of causation are held by men who are in a position to shape history, they can be infinitely harmful to peace diplomacy. For they subconsciously destroy hope of peace. If one really believes that peace can only be preserved by some enormous and altogether unlikely transformation of world conditions in the immediate future—such as submission of the great powers to a sovereign world government, or voluntary democratization of the Communist nations, or voluntary acceptance of socialism by the United States, or world-wide co-operation for birth control, or universal disarmament—then, regardless of the merits of these ideas, one cannot seriously expect to prevent another war in tomorrow's crisis. A psychological commitment by a statesman to a theoretical panacea does not promote peace; on the contrary, it acts as a dead weight on the mind and spirit, it makes for paralysis and frustration, it blocks the road for hopeful and creative possibilities of compromise.

Today the rulers of nations—all devotees of peace, if we accept their

word for it—take a gingerly approach toward the problem of war's causation. They tiptoe toward it like a person entering a sickroom. Theirs is the
uneasy spirit of physicians assigned to rid a troublesome patient of a
dread disease, but who cannot even decide on a diagnosis. In consequence,
they deal only with the superficial symptoms of the moment. Contemplating
a rash of armaments they may prescribe a conference: for an outbreak of
hostile propaganda, they recommend a rise in the military budget. The truth
is that the world of the space age is nearly as baffled by the war phenomenon
as the world of antiquity, which ascribed wars to the will of the gods.

Ideally, the question of causation should be answered by many careful
studies in the etiology of the war phenomenon, studies free from nationalistic bias, relating historical, sociological, economic, and psychological data,
and on which a general theory of causation could be firmly based. But it
will certainly be a long time before works of this type are forthcoming in
quantity, and the world cannot wait for the social sciences to catch up with
reality. In the crisis of today, men must depend in large measure for their
survival on the intuitive realizations of statesmen as to the causal process
leading to war, and its implications for their policies.

4. The Web of Causation

For thirty years, from 1782 to 1812, the United States and England faced
each other in hostile attitudes. During this prolonged period of tension
informed men frequently expected and predicted an actual war, and were
proved wrong. It is an arresting fact that the ominous predictions remained
unfulfilled when the danger appeared greatest. For it was then that extraordinary efforts were made by skilled diplomats to preserve peace; but when
the troubles between the two nations had begun to ease, and diplomacy
grew careless, rigid, and uncreative, the war came.

Some historians have asserted that the War of 1812 was essentially a contest for maritime power; some that it grew out of the American West's urge
toward territorial expansion; some that it was the consequence of slow communications; and some that it was "Mr. Madisons' war," or "Mr. Clay's
war." One writer on the subject has listed no less than a dozen causes of
the war, ranging from the land hunger of western farmers to a desire to
defend the national honor, and from American Anglophobia to the impressment controversy. Where there are so many explanations, nothing has been
explained. Static analysis of historical data can no more reveal the causes
of the war phenomenon than dissection of a suicide's body can reveal his
despair. The reasons which a nation's leaders advance for going to war are
usually extracted from the political context to serve their own purposes.
And those other reasons which historians subsequently uncover in the state
papers, letters, journalism, and speeches of the time seldom relate to the

larger forces which held the belligerent peoples in their grip. One could list fifty motives for a war, and call them causes, and still be no closer to an understanding of how the war came about.

Even so compressed a record as that in the preceding chapters of this book makes it clear that the War of 1812 arose out of a complex interplay of forces going far beyond the moods and motives of the year. The coming of the war can be understood only in terms of dynamic process—of the evolution of ever shifting pressures and events, operating on the minds of the involved societies and their leaders. Seen in long perspective, this causative process began to take definite shape when the treaty of 1783 between England and America acknowledged the political separation of the two countries. They then entered upon a period of peace in a competitive relationship. It became the function of their diplomacy, as it is always the function of diplomacy, to establish the terms of that competition, and to embody those terms in contractual agreements, or treaties. The terms agreed upon represented the best diplomatic judgment of the relative power of the two nations—power in the sense of energy available for use in compulsion or persuasion.

The negotiating statesmen knew, however, that national power is not a fixed, or even a predictable quantity for any considerable time. It comprises many variable elements, such as the size, composition, and health of the population, and its geographic situation; the quantities and types of armaments; the discipline, training, and morale of soldiers and civilians; the customs and traditions of the people, their unity, homogeneity, and devotion to national symbols and the personalities of leaders; their economic productivity, self-sustaining capacity, and state of technological development; the nation's communications and education; its wealth and its credit; its alliances and national traditions of friendship and enmity; its military commitments; the quality of its diplomacy and espionage as reflected in accurate information about other nations; the effectiveness of its ideological propaganda and its economic influence abroad; the readiness and ability of allied nations to lend financial and military aid; and the like.

A change in any one component of power could greatly affect the aggregate. After 1783, an important factor in the power of the United States relative to England derived from the Franco-American alliance. Once that collapsed, the balance of power shifted strongly to the British side. On the other hand, the more rapid rate of growth of the American population and its high productivity made for a long-range increase in the relative power of the United States. The problem of preserving peace, therefore, lay in the ability of the two nations to agree on successive modifications of their treaties—the terms of their competition—to accord with actual and mutually understood changes in their relative power. A realistic treaty made for peace; an obsolescent treaty for war.

Since there was no scientific way to measure or compare the shifting power aggregates of the two nations (any more than there is today) the judgments formed by statesmen had to be largely intuitive. Agreement could be reached only when responsible leaders on both sides arrived at similar realizations of their countries' total situations. Shelburne and Franklin sensed the Anglo-American power relationship in much the same way, and so were able to promote a viable treaty. Similarly, Jay and Grenville came to the same general conclusion as to the significance for American power of the French Revolution. Even Jefferson and Canning, despite their polar differences in political theory, were not far apart in their judgment of relative national power in 1807. To be sure, Jefferson miscalculated the time needed to enable the United States to influence British policy by economic measures, but his feeling for the total power relationship was such that he regarded an Anglo-American war as an evil to be avoided except in the last extremity. It was when two non-intuitive men assumed leadership at the same time in both countries—the narrow, stubborn Perceval and the over-intellectualized and uncertain Madison—that the diplomacy of the two nations became inadequate to preserve peace.

As changes took place in the power aggregates, they were immediately reflected in pressure on the established ways of the two countries. Thus, the rapid growth of America's population and fertile land area led early to the production of a large surplus of agricultural commodities. Given the incentive to export and the need for imports, and given the availability of lumber and iron for ships, of improved construction techniques and experienced sailors, it was not long before America possessed a merchant marine strongly competitive to that of England. Over the first two decades of her national existence, this development represented a significant increase in her coercive power. But England declined to recognize America's increased power by changing her established ways; and having been refused a reciprocal commercial treaty by England, the new American merchant marine found itself seriously restricted by established British "rules" of the sea, notably by the Rule of 1756, and the even more stringent Orders in Council. The controversy centering on those rules then became a major source of hostility and war threats.

Whenever a significant shift in the power aggregate of one nation took place, its result was a display of aggression, centering on the established ways. The collapse of the Franco-American alliance, by manifestly weakening America's power, impelled her to accept, in Jay's Treaty, restrictions which did violence to her institution of national sovereignty. The Louisiana Purchase generated an expansionist urge which gripped the American West and threatened the established boundaries of Canada. The rapid growth of the American population, by creating a large market for British cottons, and the invention of the cotton gin, by establishing America as England's best source for raw cotton, made England's textile industry highly vulnerable to punitive American trade policies, and put heavy pressure on British maritime laws and policies. In each case, changes in the American power aggregate led to a renewed controversy to determine whether one country's established policies and practices should be kept intact or should be modified to the benefit of the other country.

Since shifts in relative power took many forms and were frequent, one or more of the established ways of the two countries was almost continuously under pressure. This pressure generally expressed itself in diplomatic protest. Many of the protests carried an implied threat of war; and their effect was to give rise to successive waves of crisis. The specific forms of the crises varied greatly. As the precise shape of an ocean wave can be affected by the winds of the moments, so comparatively minor unpredictable events had much to do with the precise nature of the war threats which presented themselves to the statesmen of the two countries over the years. If four deserters from a British squadron had not enlisted on the *Chesapeake* in 1807, the *Leopard* would not have hunted her down, and the resulting crisis over impressment would not have occurred—although crisis due to some other chance event might well have replaced it. Similarly, chance events in many instances facilitated non-violent resolutions of crisis—as when an epidemic of yellow fever aided Washington in resisting pressure to go to war in 1793.

Shifts in the fundamentals of power—strain on the established ways—chances of the moment—on these three levels, the causative process which led to the war revealed itself over the years. It is hardly necessary to add that events on any one level were inextricably involved with events on the others. It is not fanciful to think of the war as having emerged from a long, vibrating web of causation. The thickest strands of the web, its framework, so to speak, were those formed by substantial changes in the relative power of the competitive societies, but the connecting filaments were no less important in producing the final result.

5. Every War a War of Rebellion

The thesis here is that the coming of the War of 1812 is best understood by putting aside the concept of "cause," in the familiar sense of motive, and recognizing a dynamic process of causation, which stems from changes in the power aggregates of the nations concerned. Perhaps another example within our own century may serve to illustrate this process more emphatically—the Russo-Japanese War of 1905. The pressures which brought about this war were fifty years in developing. Prior to 1854, when Commodore Perry compelled the Japanese to trade with the United States and introduced them to the industrial revolution, there was no trouble between Russia and Japan. Thereafter, Japan's birth rate soared and her population rapidly became urbanized, while her island resources remained sharply limited. Her internal strain grew as typical standards of living declined, but her total productivity and potential coercive power nevertheless increased with mechanization of factories. Pressed by ever increasing need for foodstuffs and other raw materials, she turned her eyes to the resources and markets of China, Manchuria, and Korea.

Meanwhile, the monied class of Russia had acquired economic interests in China, Manchuria, and Korea. Russia was not especially disturbed when Japan in the 1890s defeated the Chinese in a few one-sided battles and acquired extraterritorial rights such as the other great powers already held in China. But when Japanese traders sought to penetrate Manchuria and Korea the Russians blocked the way. Japan, with the aid of British and German arms manufacturers, then began to build a modern army and navy. For a time England supported Japanese diplomatic efforts to persuade Russia to share with Japan her commercial privileges in Manchuria and Korea, without war, and these attempts for a time showed some promise of success. The Russian Government, however, was then being harassed by strikes of workers in industrial centers, and by the restiveness of peasants on the great rural estates. Advisers close to the Czar felt that war with Japan would strengthen the government's hand in dealing with dissident elements at home. At the same time, faulty Russian military intelligence grossly underestimated Japan's chances of success in a war. In consequence, Russia refused to adjust her established ways to the changed reality of her situation vis-à-vis Japan. War followed, and Japan began the course of expansion which culminated at Pearl Harbor in 1941.

In 1905 there was a great deal of talk about Japanese aggression, but it is obvious that the word, with its moral implications, was actually irrelevant. The Russo-Japanese predicament grew largely out of an unforeseen rise in Japan's population and industrial productivity—changes for which no adequate provision could be made by international diplomacy. Seen from a sociological standpoint, the Japanese nation was rebelling against another nation's established ways—territorial demarcations which were stifling a Japan conscious of her increased potential power.

In a very real sense, every war is a war of rebellion—rebellion against frustration. Whenever a nation satisfied with its established ways refuses to modify those ways to accord with societal changes which operate to increase the potential power of a rising competitive nation, war threatens. While the causal process leading to World War I is very intricate, it is not unrealistic to conceive of it as *au fond* a rebellion by Germany, whose population, technology, and internal unity for decades past had been developing at an extraordinary rate, against the frustrating system of treaties, commercial agreements, and colonial claims established by England and France for their own benefit in the preceding century. England's and France's refusal to make substantial voluntary modifications of their established ways resulted in successive crises, the last of which was translated into war by the bullet fired at Sarajevo.

The fundamental relation between the threat of war and the large, impersonal shifts in societal power which generate that threat can be seen in the records of wars of every age and of every type—the wars of savage tribes, of city-states, of feudal lords, and of political and religious factions, as well as of nations and empires. What is known of the history of the American Indians strongly suggests that when the relative power of neighboring tribes remained fairly constant over a period of time, they respected each other's hunting grounds; but when a sharp change took place in the relationship—a decline in one tribe's food supply, or an unusual increase in its male population, or the rise of an exceptionally gifted military leader—the affected tribe found reason, such as "the wish of the Great Spirit," to challenge the established ways of its neighbors by war.

Europe's religious wars of the sixteenth century were similarly preceded by sharp increases in the power aggregates of Protestant factions. This shift in relative power resulted largely from Protestant predominance in trade at a time when an influx of gold from the New World was producing an abrupt expansion in the supply of money. When heavy pressure by Protestants on laws created for Catholic societies failed to bring voluntary concessions, crisis was quickly aggravated by religious differences to the point of explosion.

Nor is the process different, in principle, in civil wars. In the case of the American Civil War, it is easy to perceive that the comparatively large rise in the North's population and industrial productivity over the preceding fifty years put steadily increased pressure on the established institutions of the agrarian South. Refusal to adjust to the pressure led to prolonged crisis on which chance events played until the South's leaders decided to gamble on secession and war.

The societal predicament leading to war begins when two human groups (nations, parties, sects, tribes, or gangs) have established a relationship to each other. An unforeseen development (such as an increase in population, new discoveries or inventions, new ideas, new leadership, or energizing glandular stimulation due to religious frenzy or superstitious zeal) generates a sense of increased power in one or the other group and makes the old relationship appear no longer tolerable to it. The stimulated group thereupon demands a change in the relationship. Its demands threaten the established ways of the satisfied group and they resist. Frustration on the one side and fear of change on the other create feelings of mutual resentment and hostility. Whether or when violence results, and for how loi.g, is determined largely by the desire and ability of the group leaders to effect indicated adjustments of the established ways by persuasion and negotiation. Where there is a highly developed diplomatic tradition and where adequate means of communication exists, the effort to bring about change without violence may be sustained for a considerable time. During that time, new unforeseen events may reduce the drive to violence. But when emotion runs away with group policy, or when persuasion is ineffectual, war usually occurs —that is, lethal violence between opposed groups involving large numbers of people over a prolonged period.

6. At the Root of War

Men are usually less frightened by the terrors of war than by the threat of change in their established ways—the institutions, organizations, systems, traditions, taboos, customs, and practices which they associate with their survival. For those ways they will fight to the death; in this sense, it is correct to say that war, in which men die, manifests their instinctive urge to live. That the established ways for which they fight may not in fact be important to their well-being does not necessarily matter. Nor does it necessarily matter that the real beneficiaries of a challenged institution or practice may be only a small group in the population. If the citizen is made to feel that a change in the established ways would make life unbearable, whether it actually would or not, he will call for war, kill and be killed, rather than adjust himself to the unfamiliar.

At the root of war, nourishing his aggressive tendencies, lies man's passionate attachment to the past. His evolutionary experience has made him conservative, if less so than the other herd animals; and conservatism, as expressed in politics, has been his constant shield againt the wildly impulsive and the recklessly experimental. But conservatism petrified is the precursor of the war-doom. A nation gripped by the urge to preserve its established ways intact in defiance of changed world conditions is pointed toward disaster. The knot which Alexander cut with his sword at Gordium represented the pressures of an ever changing world on peoples who have been conditioned to resist change.

The common predicament of the statesman seeking peace is that he dare not, if he is to preserve his popularity, openly advocate the changing of established ways, even when he believes such changes to be necessary. In consequence, most peoples have no idea whatever of the real issues confronting them in a war crisis. They think they are for peace when actually their rigidity is preventing peace. Because they are "against war" or "against unjust war," they believe themselves to be right-thinking and moral, but they might as well be for or against volcanoes, for all the difference their pacifism makes.

If fact, many citizens who regard themselves as peace lovers are continuously, if unconsciously, pushing their countries toward war by their rigid insistence on preserving their established ways intact in the face of tremendous societal changes in the world. The experience of the American people in the 1920s is a case in point. For more than a decade, the nation, in all its words, strove for peace. It responded enthusiastically to the Kellogg-Briand pact "to outlaw war." The United States sponsored a disarmament conference, and voluntarily reduced its Navy as an example of good will and faith in enduring peace. But at the same time, the people voted into office an administration whose tariff and financial policies contributed strongly to the world-wide economic collapse of the 1930s, which in turn helped to produce the military recrudescence of Germany. Although American diplomacy was theoretically peaceful, it could not offset the war-generating character of the country's economic policy.

Nations agree, in principle, that war should be outlawed, but wherever the desire for peace challenges the established ways there is usually a large gap between word and deed. In principle, most peoples in the world today subscribe to the idea of the United Nations. Almost everyone is glad to see an international agency serve as arbitrator of other peoples' disputes. But this is a far cry from willingness to submit one's own country to a supra-national authority. Governments may in all sincerity pledge their nations to abstain from the unauthorized use of force and to bring their differences to a General Assembly or a World Court for settlement; but in the final test such pledges have meaning only if peoples can be brought to accept change for the sake of peace.

That the relatively contented peoples of the world will continue to be reluctant and slow to change their established ways is obvious enough. Men generally have not yet faced the implications of the facts that nature, in a state of constant flux, is constantly imposing new requirements on the human species, and that no nation is "an island, entire of it self." To pin the hope of peace on great and swift transformations in competitive societies would be, to say the least, optimistic. It is only in the ability of statesmen to find means of bringing about gradual and continuous readjustments that there lies any substantial chance of preventing war in our time.

The universal fear of nuclear war provides both some time and incentive for innovating in the field of peace diplomacy; and the potentialities of that field have hardly begun to be tapped. The initial need, there can be little doubt, is to create an atmosphere of discussion in which statesmen can talk of mutual and gradual readjustments for the sake of peace without becoming instantly suspect to their peoples.

Many ideas of this nature are already being explored. But it is not enough to try to draft agreed principles for internationally controlled reduction of armaments, and for cessation of the manufacture and testing of nuclear weapons. It is not enough even to obtain pledges against surprise attacks and the use of nuclear, chemical, and biological warfare, or to examine the possibility of creating an international police force. Such efforts, while obviously desirable, are only a beginning of the long-term diplomatic process required to preserve peace in our time. The chances of success for any one diplomatic conference held under mid-twentieth-century conditions are not large enough to justify reliance on them. The importance of peace talks at this stage perhaps lies less in their specific results than in the fact that they are held and continue, allowing time for the easing of tensions and the reinvigoration of statesmanship. For this reason, the high international conference needs to be multiplied, and not only in connection with armament.

If some of the subjects which might be discussed are touchy, that is all the more reason to let them be exposed to careful investigation. One such subject is the problem of removing nationalistic and imperialistic strings from aid to underdeveloped nations. Another is the revision of the UN Charter, both to increase its powers, and to improve the present method of voting in the General Assembly, which now disregards the size and productivity of its constituent nations. Studies might also be made looking toward a permanent international agency with powers to initiate renegotiation of existing treaties, the obsolescence of which may provide provocation for war.

There are also non-controversial areas in which preliminary moves might be taken for the gradual extension of international authority in the maintenance of peace, without challenging the traditional sovereignty of the powers. As Professor H. S. Commager has suggested, international universities might be created to increase understanding of mutual problems among competitive nations. Common international standards might be strongly promulgated for the teaching of history, with a view to the abatement of national prejudices. The psychological requirements for effective peace diplomacy could be studied on an international level, and put into the consciousness of heads of state as they select their nations' spokesmen for key assignments.

So long as the diplomatic effort is not allowed to dry up and crack from sheer saplessness, so long as there is a continuance of imaginative and patient negotiation, the chance of sustained peace will remain alive, and competent statesmen working together can file the jagged edges off their points of conflict. For there is no good reason to believe that war is inevitable. It is not a moral question. It is not caused by this or that condition or circumstance or person. The threat of war emerges from a long process of complex causation, the roots of which are fixed in man's difficulty in adapting to an ever changing environment. Recognition by contending statesmen of the universal human predicament is the foundation of the compromises out of which peace diplomacy is constructed. Much of the strength of America's great founders lay in their perception that the unpopular word "compromise" contains the life-sustaining word "promise." It is in the spread of this idea on a world scale that the hope of humanity rests.

Bibliography

Those familiar with the historical literature of the period covered in this book will recognize, as I do, my indebtedness to the historians and scholars who have over the years diligently mined the available source material. Especially I am conscious of having depended heavily for data, clues and insights on the splendid writings of Samuel Flagg Bemis and Henry Adams, and on Herbert Butterfield's deep-probing studies in the methods of historiography. I am grateful to Professor Butterfield for permission to quote from his *History and Human Relations*, and *The Whig Interpretation of History*. Claude Bowers, Gilbert Chinard, E. G. P. Fitzmaurice, E. W. Lyon, Bernard Mayo, Carl Van Doren, and A. P. Whitaker are among the other well-known historians and biographers whose work was of very great value to me, although of course they cannot be held responsible for the inferences that I have drawn.

This bibliography is conceived primarily as an acknowledgement of obligation, rather than as a guide to scholarship. While some manuscript sources were examined, I cannot claim to have added anything significant in the way of new factual material to the immense body of knowledge comprised by the works listed below. The main research effort here has been to correlate known data in such a way as to throw light on situations which, historically, have been somewhat obscure. It is always difficult to comprehend the actions of men, and especially of those who lived in the distant past, unless we know a good deal not only about their times, but also about the specific information available to them at their moments of decision. To estimate this information, world events need to be put in context, and realistic allowance has to be made for the intervals necessary for the transmission of news. Such correlations are more than ever essential if we are to put ourselves in the place of the statesmen who dominated the Atlantic nations in the age of the sailing vessel and the horse. My reconstructions of motives and states of mind have been based largely on what these men must have known, or could not have known, about events occurring at some distance away. If certain reconstructions have been somewhat speculative, so, I believe it is fair to say, are most historical interpretations of events long gone by.

The present bibliography is limited to works from which data were taken, or which opened up the road to other sources, or which helped to evoke a feeling for the period and its personalities. It omits many books which were consulted but found not specifically to the purpose. For convenience, the listed works have been organized in categories: Specialized Historical Studies; Historical Summaries; Biographies; Collected Works and Letters; Government Documents; Manuscript Collections. To these listings have been added an informal statement indicating works which especially aided the writing of each chapter of the present volume. A great many other books and articles, studies in the etiology of war and works of a general philosophical or sociological nature, which were read with one eye on the present volume, have not been included, since their value was as general intellectual conditioners rather than as source material.

In compiling the bibliography from my notes, I have repeatedly felt a sense of gratitude to a number of librarians whose co-operation has been extraordinarily helpful, over years of inquisitive reading. At the Library of Congress (especially in the Division of Manuscripts), the Harvard College Library, the New York Public Library (especially in the American History and Rare Book Rooms), the Library of the British Museum, and the Bibliothèque Nationale, I was given unstinted assistance by courteous men and women whose sincere dedication to their work and whose generous interest in mine made an unforgettable impression on me.

A.Z.C.

SPECIALIZED HISTORICAL STUDIES

Abernethy, T. P., *Western Lands and the American Revolution*, New York, 1937.

Adams, Ephraim D., *The Influence of Grenville on Pitt's Foreign Policy*, Washington, 1904.

Adams, Henry, "Count Edward de Crillon," *American Historical Review*, Vol. I, 1896.

Adams, Henry (ed.), *Documents Relating to New England Federalism* (1800–1815), Boston, 1877.

Adams, John Quincy, *The Life and Character of James Madison* (pamphlet), Boston, 1816.

Alexander, Franz, "The Psychiatric Aspects of War and Peace," *American Journal of Sociology*, Vol. 46, 1941.

Alvord, C. W., *The Mississippi Valley in British Politics*, Cleveland, 1917.
Lord Shelburne and the Founding of British-American Goodwill (The Raleigh Lecture in History, London, 1925).

Anderson, D. R., "The Insurgents of 1811," *American Historical Association Annual Report*, 1911.

Barbé-Marbois, *History of Louisiana*, Philadelphia, 1830.

Baring, Alexander, *An Inquiry into the Causes and Consequences of the Orders in Council*, London, 1808.

Barnes, Harry Elmer, *Some Reflections on the Possible Service of Analytical Psychology to History*, New York, 1921.

Beard, Charles A., *Economic Origins of Jeffersonian Democracy*, New York, 1915.

Bemis, Samuel Flagg, *Diplomacy of the American Revolution*, New York, 1935.
"The Rayneval Memorandum," *Proceedings of the American Antiquarian Society*, Vol. 47, 1937.
John Jay (in *American Secretaries of State*, Vol. I) New York, 1927.
Jay's Treaty, New York, 1923.
Pinckney's Treaty, New York, 1926.

Bernardo, C. J. and Bacon, E. H., *American Military Policy: Its Development since 1775*, Harrisburg, 1955.

Callender, James T., *History of the United States during 1796*, Philadelphia, 1797.

Caraman, "Les États-Unis il y a Quarante Ans," *Revue Contemporaine*, (August, 1852).

Chadwick, F. E. (Rear-Adm.), "Jefferson's Naval Policy," *Proceedings of the Massachusetts Historical Society*, Vol. 46.

Chinard, Gilbert, *The Correspondence of Jefferson and du Pont de Nemours*, Baltimore, 1931.

Clarke, Rev. Dr., *A Survey of the Strength and Commerce of Great Britain*, London, 1801.

Clauder, A. C., *American Commerce as Affected by the Wars of the French Revolution and Napoleon* (1793–1812), Philadelphia, 1932.

Cobbett, William, *History of the American Jacobins*, Philadelphia, 1796.
Porcupine's Works, London, 1801.
Letters to the Rt. Hon. Lord Hawkesbury and the Rt. Hon. Henry Addington, London, 1802.
Letters on the Late War between the United States and Great Britain, New York, 1815.

Corwin, E. S., *French Diplomacy and the American Alliance of 1778*, Princeton, 1916.

Cox, I. J., *The West Florida Controversy*, Baltimore, 1918.

Davenport, F. G., *European Treaties Bearing on the History of the United States and its Dependencies*, Washington, 1917–34.

Didier, L., "Le Citoyen Genêt," *Revue des questions historiques*, Vol. 93, 1912.

Dwight, Theodore, *History of the Hartford Convention*, New York, 1833.

Edler, Friedrich, *The Dutch Republic and the American Revolution*, New York, 1833.

Elliot, J. (ed.), *The Debates in the Several State Conventions on the Adoption of the Federal Constitution*, Philadelphia, 1891.

Elliott, C. B., "The Doctrine of the Continuous Voyage," *American Journal of International Law*, Vol. I.

Faÿ, B., *The Revolutionary Spirit in France and America*, New York, 1927.

Foster, Sir A. J. (Bart.), "Notes on the United States, *Quarterly Review*," (London) Vol. 68.

Gayer, A. D., *Growth and Fluctuations of the British Economy* (1790–1850), Oxford, 1953.

Goodman, W. H., "Origins of the War of 1812," *Mississippi Valley Historical Review*, Vol. 28, 1941.

Hacker, L. M., "Western Land Hunger and the War of 1812," *Mississippi Valley Historical Review*, Vol. 10, 1924.

Hanson, Alexander, *Reflections upon the late correspondence between Mr. Secretary Smith and Francis James Jackson*, Baltimore, 1810.

Hazen, C. D., *Contemporary American Opinion of the French Revolution*, Baltimore, 1897.

Heath, Phoebe Ann, *Napoleon I and Origins of the Anglo-American War of 1812*, Toulouse, 1929.

Heckscher, E. F., *The Continental System*, New York, 1922.

Holtman, R. B., *Napoleonic Propaganda*, Baton Rouge, 1950.

Irwin, R. W., *The Diplomatic Relations of the United States and the Barbary Powers, 1776–1916*, Chapel Hill, N.C., 1931.

Jacobs, James R., *The Beginning of the U. S. Army, 1783–1812*, Princeton, 1947.

James, James Alton, "French Diplomacy and American Politics," *American Historical Association, Annual Report*, 1911.
—— "French Opinion as a Factor in Preventing War between France and the United States (1795–1800)," *American Historical Review*, Vol. 30, 1924.

Jay, John, *The Peace Negotiations of 1782–83 as newly illustrated by confidential papers of Shelburne* (New York Historical Society, 1884).

Lambert, John, *Travels through Canada and the United States in 1806, 1807 and 1808*, London, 1814.

Lansdowne, W. P. 1st Marquess (Earl of Shelburne), *An Examination into the Principles, Conduct and Designs of the Minister*, London, 1783.

Lewis, H. T., "A Re-analysis of the Causes of the War of 1812," *Americana*, Vol. 6, 1911.

Lingelbach, W. F., "England and Neutral Trade," *Military Historian and Economist*," Vol. 2, 1917.

Lowell, John, *Mr. Madison's War*, Boston, 1812.

Lyon, E. W., "The Directory and the United States," *American Historical Review*, Vol. 43, 1938.
—— "The Franco-American Convention of 1800," *Journal of Modern History*, Vol. 12, 1938.
The Man Who Sold Louisiana, Norman, Okla., 1942.
Louisiana in French Diplomacy, Norman, Okla., 1934.

Maclay, Edgar S. (ed.), *Journal of William Maclay* (*Senator from Pennsylvania, 1789–1791*) New York, 1890.

Manning, W. R., "The Nootka Sound Controversy," *American Historical Association, Annual Report*, 1904.

Mirsky, Jeanette and Nevins, Allan, *The World of Eli Whitney*, New York, 1952.

Morison, Samuel Eliot, "The Henry-Crillon Affair of 1812," *Massachusetts Historical Society Proceedings*, Vol. 69, 1950.

O'Bryan, Dennis, *A Defence of the Right Hon. the Earl of Shelburne*, London, 1782.

Perkins, Bradford, *The First Rapprochement: England and the United States, 1795–1805*, Los Angeles, 1955.

Pitkin, T., *A Statistical View of the Commerce of America*, New York, 1817.

Pratt, Julius W., *Expansionists of 1812*, New York, 1925.

Rippy, J. F. and Debo A., *The Historical Background of the American Policy of Isolation* (*Smith College Studies in History*, Vol. 9), Northampton, 1924.

Russell, Nelson V., *The British Regime in Michigan and the old Northwest, 1761–96*, Northfield, Minn., 1939.

Sears, L. M., *Jefferson and the Embargo*, Durham, N.C., 1927.

Smith, Robert, *Address to the People of the United States*, Baltimore, 1811.

Stephen, James, *War in Disguise*, London, 1805.

Stoddard, T. L., *The French Revolution in Santo Domingo*, Boston, 1823.

Stourzh, Gerald, *Benjamin Franklin and American Foreign Policy*, Chicago, 1954.

Sumner, William H., *An Inquiry into the Importance of the Militia*, Boston, 1823.

Taine, Hippolyte, *The Ancient Régime* (tr. by John Durand), New York, 1876.

Talleyrand-Perigord, C. M. de, *Memoir concerning the commercial relations of the United States with England* (1797), London, 1814.

Tansill, C. C., *The United States and Santo Domingo* (1798–1873), Baltimore, 1938.

Taylor, G. R., "Agrarian Discontent in the Mississippi Valley Preceding the War of 1812," *Mississippi Valley Historical Review*, Vol. 10, 1924.

Tocqueville, Alexis de, *The Old Regime and the French Revolution* (tr. by Stuart Gilbert), New York, 1955.

Tucker, Josiah, *Four Letters (to Lord Shelburne) on Important National Subjects*, London, 1783.

Turner, F. J., *The Significance of Sections in American History*, New York, 1932.

Updyke, F. A., *Diplomacy of the War of 1812*, Baltimore, 1915.

Van Doren, Carl, *The Great Rehearsal*, New York, 1948.

Warren, Charles, *The Making of the Constitution*, New York, 1928.

Wead, Eunice, "British Public Opinion of the Peace with America, 1782," *American Historical Review*, Vol. 34, 1929.

Webster, A. W., *Western Preliminaries of the War of 1812*, St. Louis, 1926.

Whitaker, A. P., *The Mississippi Question*, New York, 1934.

White, E. B., *American Opinion in France*, New York, 1927.

Wood, George C., *Congressional Control of Foreign Relations during the American Revolution*, Allentown, Pa., 1919.

Worthington, Thomas, Mss. Diary, 1801–13 (in Library of Congress).

Zimmerman, J. F., *Impressment of American Seamen*, New York, 1925.

BROAD HISTORICAL SUMMARIES

Adams, Henry, *History of the United States during the Administrations of Jefferson and Madison*, New York, 1930.

Algernon, Cecil, *British Foreign Secretaries*, London, 1927.

Bailey, Thomas A., A *Diplomatic History of the American People*, New York, 1940.

Bemis, Samuel Flagg, A *Diplomatic History of the United States*, New York, 1936.

Bemis, Samuel Flagg (ed.), *American Secretaries of State*, New York, 1927.

Burt, A. L., *The United States, Great Britain, and British North America*, New Haven, 1940.

Channing, Edward, *History of the United States*, New York, 1929.

Cheyney, E. P., *Industrial and Social History of England*, London, 1901.

Cobbett, William (ed.), *Parliamentary History of England*, London, 1812–20.

Darling, A. B., *Our Rising Empire*, New Haven, 1940.

Doniol, Henri, *Histoire de la participation de la France à l'établissement des États-Unis d'Amerique*, Paris, 1886.

Echeverria, Durand, *Mirage in the West*, Princeton, 1957.

Gordy, J. P., *Political History of the United States*, New York, 1908.

Lecky, W. E. H., *History of England in the Eighteenth Century*, Vols. 5, 6, London, 1895.

Mahan, A. T. (Adm.), *Sea-Power in its Relations to the War of 1812*, New York, 1921.
The Influence of Sea-Power on the French Revolution, Boston, 1892.

Turberville, Arthur S., *The House of Lords in the Age of Reform*, London, 1958.

Ward, A. W. and Gooch, G. P. (eds.), *Cambridge History of Foreign Policy*, Cambridge, England, 1922.

BIOGRAPHIES

Adams, John Quincy, *The Life and Character of James Madison*, Boston, 1816.

Beveridge, Albert J., *Life of John Marshall*, Boston, 1916.

Bowers, Claude G., *Jefferson and Hamilton*, Boston, 1925.

Brant, Irving, *James Madison: The President, 1809–1812*, Indianapolis, 1956.

Brinton, Crane, *The Lives of Talleyrand*, New York, 1936.

Chinard, Gilbert, *Honest John Adams*, Boston, 1933.

Cleeves, Freeman, *Old Tippecanoe: William Henry Harrison and His Times*, New York, 1939.

Dodd, Anna B., *Talleyrand*, New York, 1927.

Fitzmaurice, Edward G. P., *Life of William, Earl of Shelburne (with extracts from correspondence)*, London, 1912.

Freeman, Douglas S., *George Washington*, New York, 1948–54.

Gay, Sidney H., *James Madison* ("American Statesmen Series"), Boston, 1885.

Godoy, Manuel de (Prince), *Memoirs*, London, 1836–38.

Hunt, Gaillard, *The Life of James Madison*, New York, 1902.

James, James Alton, *Oliver Pollock: The Life and Times of an Unknown Patriot*, New York, 1937.

Koch, Adrienne, *Jefferson and Madison: The Great Collaboration*, New York, 1950.

Las Cases, Emmanuel de, *Napoléon prisonnier*, Paris, 1896.

Lascelles, E. C. P., *Life of Charles James Fox*, Oxford, 1936.

Lodge, Henry Cabot, *Alexander Hamilton*, Boston, 1909.

Lodge, Henry Cabot (ed.), *Life and Letters of George Cabot*, Boston, 1878.

Loth, David, *Alexander Hamilton: Portrait of a Prodigy*, New York, 1936.

Loménie, Louis de, *Beaumarchais and his Times*, London, 1856.

Marshall, Dorothy, *The Rise of George Canning*, London, 1938.

Mayo, Bernard, *Henry Clay*, Boston, 1937.

Meng, John J., *The Comte de Vergennes*, Philadelphia, 1929.

Minnegerode, Meade, *Jefferson, Friend of France: the Career of Edmund Charles Genêt*, New York, 1928.

Monaghan, Frank, *John Jay*, New York, 1935.

Morgan, George, *The Life of James Monroe*, Boston, 1921.

Parks, J. H., *Felix Grundy*, Baton Rouge, 1940.

Pellew, George, *Life and Correspondence of the Rt. Hon. Henry Addington, Viscount of Sidmouth*, London, 1847.
John Jay, Boston, 1890.

Porter, K. W., *John Jacob Astor* (Harvard Studies in Business History), Cambridge, 1931.

Rose, J. H., *William Pitt and the Great War*, London, 1911.
William Pitt and National Revival, London, 1911.

Van Doren, Carl, *Benjamin Franklin*, New York, 1956.

Wirt, William, *Patrick Henry*, Hartford, 1854.

COLLECTED WORKS AND LETTERS

Adams, Charles Francis (ed.), *The Works of John Adams*, Boston, 1856.
Letters of John and Abigail Adams, Boston, 1876.

Adams, Henry (ed.), *Writings of Albert Gallatin*, Philadelphia, 1879.

Ames, S. (ed.), *Works of Fisher Ames*, Boston, 1854.

Cousins, Norman (ed.), *"In God We Trust"—The Religious Beliefs and Ideas of the American Founding Fathers*, New York, 1959.

Hamilton, S. F. (ed.), *Writings of James Monroe*, New York, 1878–1903.

Hunt, G. (ed.), *Writings of James Madison*, New York, 1900–1910.

Johnston, Harry P. (ed.), *Correspondence and Public Papers of John Jay*, New York, 1890–1893.

Lipscomb, A. A. and Bergh, A. E. (eds.), *Writings of Thomas Jefferson,* Washington, 1903–1905.

Lodge, Henry Cabot (ed.), *Works of Alexander Hamilton,* New York, 1904.

Padover, Saul K. (ed.), *The Complete Jefferson,* New York, 1943.

Smith, Charles G. (ed.), "Letters of Benjamin Vaughan," *Massachusetts Historical Society Proceedings,* June, 1903.

Smyth, A. H. (ed.), *Writings of Benjamin Franklin,* New York, 1907.

GOVERNMENT DOCUMENTS

Annals [of Congress], *Debates and Proceedings 1st to 13th Congresses* (1789–1814), Washington, 1834.

Cobbett-Hansard, *Parliamentary Debates,* London, 1805–1812.

Commager, Henry Steele (ed.), *Documents of American History,* New York, 1940.

Lowrie, W. and Clarke, H. (eds.), *American State Papers—Foreign Relations,* Washington, 1832.

Mayo, Bernard (ed.), *Instructions to the British Ministers to the United States, 1791–1812,* American Historical Association, Annual Report, 1936.

U. S. Department of State, *A Message of the President of the U.S. to Congress, Dec. 5, 1793,* Philadelphia, 1795.
Correspondence of U. S. Commissioners Pinckney, Marshall and Gerry (1777–79), Washington, 1800.

Wait, T. B. (ed.), *State Papers and Public Documents,* Boston, 1817.

Wharton, Francis (ed.), *Revolutionary Diplomatic Correspondence of the United States,* Washington, 1889.

MANUSCRIPT COLLECTIONS

Library of Congress, *Archives des Affaires Étrangères, Correspondence Politique, États-Unis,* Photostats.

New York Public Library (Bancroft Transcripts), *Archives Françaises: État-Unis.*

New York Public Library (Gordon Lester Ford Transcripts), British State Papers, Ministry to the United States.

Archives of the Foreign Office, London, British State Papers relating to France and the United States (1782–83).

Library of Congress, Diary of Thomas Worthington (1801–13).

Library of Congress, Letters and Documents of Sir Augustus J. Foster, Bart.

(A long list of newspapers of the period, examined at the British Museum and the Library of Congress, is omitted, since those of value to this book are mentioned by name in the text.)

SPECIAL ACKNOWLEDGEMENTS

The recapitulation below is limited to those few books or articles which, for each chapter, served to provide a springboard and a direction for the line of thought.

PART ONE: Chapter I, THE SHELBURNE WAY: The Fitzmaurice *Life of Lansdowne*, together with the Shelburne letters; Bemis's *Diplomacy of the American Revolution*; Van Doren's *Benjamin Franklin*; and Wharton's *Revolutionary Diplomatic Correspondence* proved especially valuable. Chapter II, ANXIETIES OF A PATRIOT: This chapter drew heavily on de Tocqueville's *The Old Regime and the French Revolution*; Bemis's *Diplomacy of the American Revolution*; on Meng's *The Comte de Vergennes*; on Doniol's *Histoire*; and on Monaghan's *John Jay*. Chapter III, THE RAYNEVAL AFFAIR: Bemis's "The Rayneval Memorandum" is the definitive source. Valuable insights were obtained from the Shelburne papers in the archives of the British Foreign Office, the Benjamin Vaughan letters, (C. C. Smith, ed.), Chinard's *Honest John Adams*, Van Doren's *Benjamin Franklin*, Abernethy's *Western Lands and the American Revolution*, and Edler's *The Dutch Republic and the American Revolution*. Chapter IV, PANDORA'S TREATY: Bemis's *Diplomacy of the American Revolution*; the *Cambridge History of British Foreign Policy*; and Channing's *History of the United States* contributed greatly; as did Eunice Wead's article on "British Public Opinion."

PART TWO: Chapter I, SECOND THOUGHTS OF A SECRETARY OF STATE: This chapter drew especially on Whitaker's *The Spanish-American Frontier*; on Chinard's *Honest John Adams*; on Bemis's *Pinckney's Treaty*, and his *John Jay* (in *American Secretaries of State*, Vol. 1). Volume 3 of Jay's *Correspondence and Public Papers* (H. P. Johnston, ed.) was continuously useful. Chapter II, AMERICA BECOMES CAPABLE OF WAR: Van Doren's *Great Rehearsal*; Charles Warren's *Making of the Constitution*; Elliott's *Debates in the State Conventions*, and Wood's *Congressional Control* opened up important avenues of thought. Chapter III, THE NOOTKA CRISIS: Clues to motivations in this affair were found in Manning's "Nootka Sound Controversy," Fitzmaurice's *Life of Lansdowne* and E. D. Adams's *Influence of Grenville*. Chapter IV, GRENVILLE VS. JEFFERSON: Bailey's *Diplomatic History of the American People*, Adams's *Influence of Grenville*, Bemis's *Jay's Treaty*, and Rose's biographical studies of Pitt were especially helpful.

PART THREE: Chapter I, PERSONA NON GRATA: This chapter drew on Hazen's *Contemporary American Opinion of the French Revolution*, Minnegerode's *Jefferson, Friend of France*, and Didier's "Le Citoyen Genêt"; and found useful indications in Channing's *History of the United States*, Vol. 4, and Thomas's *American Neutrality in 1793*. Chapter II, THE SUCCESSFUL MAN: Bowers's *Jefferson and Hamilton*, Lodge's *Life and Letters of George Cabot* and his *Alexander Hamilton*; Padover's *Jefferson*, and Bemis's *Jay's Treaty* strongly contributed to this chapter. Chapter III, "THIS DAMNED TREATY": Monaghan's *John Jay*; Bemis's *Jay's Treaty* and *Pinckney's Treaty*; Darling's *Our Rising Empire*; and Bailey's *Diplomatic History* were outstandingly useful. Chapter IV, X Y Z: This chapter drew on E. W. Lyon's article "The Directory and the United States," on Beveridge's *Life of John Marshall*, Henry Adams's *Life of Gallatin*. Chapter V, WITCH HUNT: Gilbert Chinard's *Honest John Adams*, Lyon's *Franco-American Convention of 1800* and B. Faÿ's *Revolutionary Spirit in France and America* were useful here, together with Gordy's *Political History*, Vol. I. Chapter VI, THE PENDULUM SWINGS: Valuable data and viewpoints were obtained from Lodge's *Alexander Hamilton*, Bowers's *Jefferson and Hamilton*, Chinard's *Thomas Jefferson*, Adams's *Life of Gallatin*, Padover's *Mind of Alexander Hamilton*; and Rose's *William Pitt and the Great War*. Chapter VII, A TIME FOR HOPE: Padover's *Complete Jefferson*, the studies of Henry Addington by Pellew and Bulwer-Lytton and Adams's *History*, Vol. I, were especially helpful.

PART FOUR: Chapter I, THE TRIGGERING OF WAR: Whitaker's *The Mississippi Question*, Lyon's *The Man Who Sold Louisiana* and *Louisiana in French Diplomacy*, and Tansill's *United States and Santo Domingo* were major sources of data, together with Henry Adams's *History of the United States*, Vols. 2 and 3. It should be noted that the affair of the Mississippi deposit baffled a long series of conscientious historians until Whitaker's scholarly work revealed Godoy's presumptive part in it, and made possible a reconstruction of the plot. Chapter II, THE HEADY WINE OF EMPIRE: I. J. Cox's *The West Florida Controversy*, A. C. Clauder's study, *American Commerce*, helped to condition this chapter which also drew strongly on Adams's *History*, Vols. 3 and 4. Chapter III, "WAR IN DISGUISE": James Stephen's book and Alexander Baring's reply, the Adams *History*, Vols. 3 and 4, and Bailey's invaluable *Diplomatic History* provided important foundation materials here. Chapter IV, PASSIVE RESISTANCE: E. F. Hecksher's study, *The Continental System* was instructive; and also Updyke's *Diplomacy of the War of 1812*, and Zimmerman's *Impressment of American Seamen*. Chapter V, "OGRABME": The *Cambridge History of Foreign Policy*, Adams's *History*, Vol. 4, Gordy's *Political History*, Sears's *Jefferson and the Embargo*, and Lambert's *Travels in Canada* provided the broad framework of fact for this chapter. Chapter VI, THE ERSKINE FIASCO: Significant parts of the Erskine correspondence with Canning quoted in the Adams *History*, Vol. 5 and C. C. Tansill's sketch of the career of Secretary of State Robert Smith, in *American Secretaries of State*, Vol. 31, (S. F. Bemis, ed.) were the sources of greatest value. Chapter VII, THE CADORE LETTER: P. A. Heath's *Napoleon I and the Origins of the Anglo-American War of 1812*, and Clauder's *American Commerce* provided a great deal of valuable detail, supplementing the thorough treatment in the Adams's *History*. Chapter VIII, VOICES OF THE FRONTIER: Sources of great value to this chapter included Mayo's *Henry Clay*; Pratt's *Expansionists of 1812*; Cleeves's *Old Tippecanoe*; Webster's *Western Preliminaries of the War of 1812*, and articles cited above by L. M. Hacker, G. R. Taylor, R. T. Anderson and H. T. Lewis. Chapter IX, SCRUPLE AND INHIBITION: Light on the attitudes of the American Congress came from E. B. White's *American Opinion of France*, from the chapters on Robert Smith and James Monroe in *American Secretaries of State* and from Gordy's *Political History*. Chapter X, THE CRILLON COMEDY: The chief sources for this chapter were Samuel Eliot Morison's article, "The Henry-Crillon Affair of 1812"; Henry Adams's article, "*Count Edward de Crillon*"; the Sérurier correspondence quoted in Adams's *History*, Vol. 6, and an article signed Caraman, in the *Revue Contemporaine* for August 1852. Chapter XI, THE BULLET OF CHANCE: Augustus Foster's manuscript *Letters and Diary* and British newspapers of the period provided useful supplements to Mayo's *Henry Clay*, the Adams *History*, and the *Cambridge History*. Chapter XII, "CHAFF BEFORE THE WIND": John Lowell's *Mr. Madison's War*, proved useful in conjunction with Adams's *History*, Vols. 5

and 6, and Mayo's *Henry Clay*. Chapter XIII, "GREATEST OF ALL THE LESSONS": This chapter drew on Bailey's *Diplomatic History*, Updyke's *Diplomacy of the War of 1812*, Dwight's *History of the Hartford Convention*, Mayo's *Henry Clay*, Adams's *Gallatin*, and the Adams *History*, Vols. 6 and 7.

Index